THE DEVELOPMENT OF
THE PROVINCIAL NEWSPAPER
1700–1760

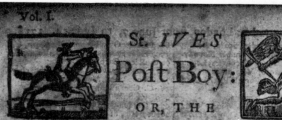

Vol. I.   Numb. 2.

St. *IVES*
Poſt Boy:
OR, THE
Loyal Packet.
BEING
A COLLECTION of the moſt MATERIAL
OCCURRENCES,

Foreign *and* Domeſtick.
Together with
An Account of Trade.

MONDAY, *June* 23, 1718.

To be Continued Weekly.

St. *IVES* in *Huntingdonſhire* :
Printed by R. RAIKES.   (*Price three Half-pence.*)

THE TITLE-PAGE OF THE *ST. IVES POST BOY* IN 1718.

Frontispiece

THE DEVELOPMENT OF
THE PROVINCIAL NEWSPAPER
1700–1760

BY

G. A. CRANFIELD

GREENWOOD PRESS, PUBLISHERS
WESTPORT, CONNECTICUT

Library of Congress Cataloging in Publication Data

Cranfield, Geoffrey Alan.
    The development of the provincial newspaper, 1700-
1760.

    Reprint of the ed. published by Clarendon Press,
Oxford.
    Bibliography: p.
    Includes index.
    1. Journalism, Provincial--Great Britain--History.
2. English newspapers--History.   I.   Title.
[PN5116.C7 1978]   072   77-16348
ISBN 0-313-20017-3

© Oxford University Press, 1962

Reprinted with the permission of Oxford University Press

Reprinted in 1978 by Greenwood Press, Inc.,
51 Riverside Avenue, Westport, CT. 06880

Printed in the United States of America

PREFACE

THE English provincial newspaper of the early eighteenth century has not hitherto been studied with any thoroughness. Certainly, it has not received the attention which it merits. The general attitude of historians has been to dismiss the country newspaper of this period as unimportant, as a mere parasite upon the London press whose news and views it faithfully reproduced, and no previous attempt has been made to study the provincial newspaper as a whole, describe its birth and growth, its printers and public, analyse its aims and content, and estimate its political, social and economic influence.

Small, badly-printed and primitive as these early newspapers may at first sight appear, they were a far more powerful and important force than is generally recognized. There was no country newspaper in existence in the year 1700; but by the end of 1760, no less than one hundred and thirty different newspapers had been started, together with a number of literary magazines and periodicals. The death-rate had been heavy: but by 1760 the local newspaper had established itself firmly as an essential part of country life. The main problems had been encountered and, to a considerable extent, overcome. The newspapers had successfully survived the various attempts of a hostile Authority to cripple their growth; circulation had risen steadily, until the more powerful papers could claim a weekly sale in the region of two thousand copies—and it was always accepted that a paper's influence was out of all proportion to the size of its actual sales, each copy being read by twenty or more people. At the same time, the immense difficulties of distribution had been solved by the organization of elaborate delivery-systems based upon agents and newsmen, enabling the newspapers to control amazingly extensive spheres of influence. Further developments depended largely upon factors outside the control of the printers.

The value of these old newspapers as sources for the history of the period has certainly been greatly underestimated. In their pages may be traced many of the changes which were then beginning to transform the face of England. There are few aspects indeed of eighteenth century life upon which these papers do not throw a vivid and often revealing light. What is still more important is the fact that, in many of these changes, the newspapers were themselves active forces. Their distribution systems helped to open up communications. Their advertisement columns stimulated economic progress. But their main significance lay in the social and political spheres. The country newspaper appealed mainly to a humble public. To many of its readers it represented not merely the only source of news but also the only reading matter of any sort available. To cater for the needs of such a public, the country newspaper rapidly assumed the task of educating its readers, and began to provide not only news but also what it called 'instruction and entertainment'. The 'entertainment' was often of a distinctly Rabelaisian character; but the 'instruction' was quite genuinely educational. And by stimulating the reading habit and supplementing the meagre education of the schools, the country newspapers played no small part in that growth of literacy which was so noticeable a feature of the period. At the same time, they were educating their readers politically. Far from voicing merely local and parochial sentiments, they largely ignored such issues, and instead reproduced the news and views of the leading London newspapers of the day. In this way, they educated their readers in the significant national issues, and helped to form a centralized, almost national, public opinion. Moreover, the views which they inculcated were mainly those of the Opposition newspapers in London. The later Radical Movement owed much of its widespread popularity to the years of instruction and preparation provided by the country newspapers.

This book is based essentially upon the newspapers themselves. A surprising number has survived, and, if complete and unbroken 'runs' are extremely rare, extensive collections are relatively common. These collections are, however, scattered throughout the country. The British Museum and the Bodleian Library contain only the nucleus of a national collection, and in most cases it is necessary to go to those provincial centres where local newspapers have been preserved. The wealth of material thus available, not to mention the expense involved, made it quite out of the question for the author to study every local collection in existence. Visits were made to Bristol, Cambridge, Derby, Liverpool, Manchester, Newcastle, Northampton, Nottingham, Oxford, Stamford, Worcester and York. These towns were carefully selected, not only because their holdings of local newspapers were particularly extensive, but also because they themselves either represented some significant trend of development during the eighteenth century, or had possessed some peculiar characteristic of their own in that period. York was a town with a very long historical past which, in the eighteenth century, was in a state of relative decline; Manchester was typical of the 'mushroom' towns of the period; Bristol, Newcastle and Liverpool were the rising seaports; Oxford and Cambridge the University towns with their own peculiar clerical background; Derby, Northampton and Nottingham were centres of growing industrial activity; and Stamford and Worcester were old county capitals, service centres of wide areas. To these local collections were added the more representative collections at the British Museum, Bodleian, London Press Club and the Cambridge University Library. These possess fine holdings of the papers of such towns as Canterbury, Exeter, Gloucester, Ipswich, Norwich and Reading. But no newspaper was entirely omitted from the survey, and in all some eighteen thousand copies of newspapers were examined.

The aim of this work is to trace the birth and early development of the provincial newspaper press. The year 1760 was selected as the *terminus ad quem* of the survey, for by that year the country newspaper was certainly firmly established. Moreover, in so far as any one year may be said to mark the end of an age, the year 1760 was the end of one epoch and the beginning of another. Not only was the whole domestic political situation transformed, but England was soon to be involved in the turmoil of the American and French Revolutions, while at the same time the economic revolution was advancing with greatly accelerated speed.

Wherever possible in this study, the newspapers have been allowed to speak for themselves, and direct quotations have been preferred to paraphrases.

In the course of his work, the author has met with nothing but the most generous assistance, particularly from the librarians of all those libraries which he visited. Others went to great pains to provide him with detailed lists of their holdings. Canon F. Harrison, the Chancellor of York Minster, and the managers and directors of the *Lincoln, Rutland and Stamford Mercury* and the *Yorkshire Herald* very kindly granted him special facilities. Mr. Ellic Howe, of the Worshipful Company of Stationers; the late Colonel W. S. Potter, D.S.O.; Mr. W. B. Morrell; Professor A. Aspinall; the late Dr. John Johnson; and Mr. D. F. Gallop all gave invaluable advice and assistance. The author owes a particular debt of gratitude to Dr. J. H. Plumb, a source of never-failing inspiration and constructive criticism; to the President and Fellows of Queens' College, Cambridge; and last, but certainly not least, to the Ministry of Education, whose grant under the Further Education and Training Scheme made this work possible. He would like also to express his sincere thanks to the staff of the Clarendon Press who, because of the fact that twelve thousand miles separated him from his typescript, were called upon to perform many tasks which would normally have been his sole responsibility, and who undertook these extra responsibilities most willingly and efficiently. To no one is he more indebted than to his wife, however: her patience and understanding from the time this work was first conceived to its final painful birth-pangs were worthy of a far better cause.

G. A. C.

Newcastle,
New South Wales.
July, 1959.

CONTENTS

LIST OF ILLUSTRATIONS

A NOTE ON EIGHTEENTH CENTURY DATES

EIGHTEENTH century English newspapers pose certain peculiar problems in the matter of dates. True to its traditional conservatism, England did not adopt the modern Gregorian calendar until 1752, long after the rest of Europe had done so. This delay meant that, by that year, England had fallen eleven days behind the Continent in its dates, the day which was called May 12th by the rest of Europe being only May 1st in England. From this resulted what, at first sight, appears to be the amazing ability of English newspapers in the first half of the eighteenth century to foretell the events of the future, for a newspaper published in England on May 1st will contain news items from the Continent dated May 9th or 10th. This somewhat extraordinary state of affairs lasted until 1752, when, by Act of Parliament, England adopted the 'New Style' calendar. The problem of the eleven days was solved by the simple process of ignoring them altogether, September 2nd 1752 Old Style being followed by September 14th 1752 New Style —to the great alarm and despondency of more conservative Englishmen, who were convinced that they had been robbed of eleven days of their lives by a wicked government.

The Act of 1752 also cleared up an even more confusing problem, that of the day on which a new year began. Under the Old Style, the year began officially not on January 1st but on Lady Day, March 25th. Thus, December 31st 1751 Old Style had been followed not by January 1st 1752 but by January 1st 1751, and the year 1752 did not begin until March 25th. Long before this time, however, many Englishmen, and many newspaper printers, had come to use the New Style system whereby the new year began on January 1st. Unfortunately, not all of them made it perfectly clear which system they were following. Some added the abbreviations 'O.S.' or 'N.S.' after their dates, but many did not; and it is therefore extremely easy for the modern reader to be a year out in his dates in the awkward period from January 1st to March 24th in any year before 1753. In order to avoid confusion, some printers made use of the very practical device of 'double dates', in the following form:

December 31st 1709

January 1st 1709/10 (that is, 1709 by the Old Style, but 1710 by
   the New)
March 24th 1709/10
March 25th 1710.

This system has been adopted throughout the present work. Dates
are given either as New Style, where the printers themselves had
adopted this form, or as 'double dates' in the case of those newspapers which had themselves made use of this device, or had clung
rigidly to the Old Style calendar.

CHAPTER ONE

THE BIRTH AND GROWTH OF THE PROVINCIAL NEWSPAPER

HARDLY had the printing press come into existence before its persecution began. The almost instinctive suspicion with which Authority first greeted its introduction into England hardened rapidly into an unconcealed and increasingly aggressive hostility as each new religious and political crisis confirmed its subversive potentialities. Henry VIII found in the printing press a useful weapon against the Bishop of Rome; but he was soon to find that he had allied himself to a force he could not easily control. From his time onwards, the story of the press is largely the story of the efforts of Authority to control it. All the resources of Church and State alike were thrown into this struggle, and for more than two hundred years the press was to enjoy only exceedingly brief and virtually accidental intervals of official liberty, separated by long periods of prohibition and repression.

For most of this time, journalism was a dangerous profession, followed only by desperate and hunted men, in whose lives the shadow of prison and the pillory loomed large. Nevertheless, each succeeding crisis revealed a press wielding ever greater power and influence. All Elizabeth's efforts to dam the flood of Jesuit and Puritan pamphlets which threatened the success of her religious settlement were doomed to failure; and the unusual bitterness which characterized the disputes of the early seventeenth century was in no small measure due to the sustained and venomous propaganda of the innumerable newsbooks and pamphlets which flourished despite all attempts to suppress them. Phoenix-like, the press seemed to emerge from the flames of persecution with renewed vitality and vigour. And the almost monotonous regularity with which repressive measures were promulgated was indicative not so much of the determination of Authority to control the press as of the comparative ineffectiveness of its efforts.

The long stream of Star Chamber decrees, Statutes, Parliamentary Ordinances and Royal Proclamations culminated in 1663 in the famous Printing Act of Charles II (13 and 14 Car. II, c. 33). This

was a definitive measure, embodying all the experience of these
long years of governmental endeavour. Because it laid down that all
writings were to be submitted to an official licenser prior to publication, the Act has come to be known as the Licensing Act. In fact,
however, it was intended to establish a system of control far more
comprehensive than a simple censorship, and it went on to subject
the whole printing trade to a series of restrictions so severe as to
make any expansion or development quite out of the question.
Printing was henceforward to be confined to London and to the two
University towns, and no man might lawfully set up a printing press
in any other part of the country. At the same time, the number of
Master Printers was to be limited to twenty, and, as a further safe-
guard, the number of actual presses and apprentices allowed to each
was rigidly controlled.

So long as these stringent regulations could be enforced, not only
would the total number of books and pamphlets published be extremely limited, but newspapers would be virtually non-existent.
The notorious Sir Roger L'Estrange was soon to be appointed
Surveyor of the Press, with the sole privilege of writing, printing and
publishing news, and for some years the whole country was officially
dependent for its printed news upon the meagre supply sanctioned
by him and his successors, and, after 1665, the official newspaper,
the *London Gazette*.

These restrictions were felt very differently in London and the
provinces. Anyone who lived in London had ready access to news.
The Court was there, and the Parliament. Already there were the
embryonic political clubs and a multitude of coffee-houses, where
citizens could meet to discuss business and exchange news and
gossip. No one, however humble, was ever likely to be starved of
news in a city which was so pre-eminently the capital, the centre
of the political, economic and social life of the kingdom.

The situation was different in the provinces. For the well-to-do,
several channels of information were available. They could take out
a subscription to the official *London Gazette*. That paper was to be,
for many years to come, the most authoritative and reliable. But
from the point of view of the news-hungry squire or clergyman, far
removed from the political centre, it left much to be desired. As
Samuel Pepys said, it was 'very pretty, full of newes, and no folly
in it'.[1] It was an official organ, and naturally contained no criticisms
of the government and very little political comment. As such, it
would hardly satisfy the appetites of those who wanted not merely

[1] Samuel Pepys, *Diary*, entry for 22 November 1665.

the news but also the 'inside story', who wanted to read about the cut-and-thrust of politics and to know what was really happening in the capital.

Such people turned to the news-letters, the letters of intelligence supplied by professional news-writers in London. These news-letters were written, not printed; and their out-moded method of production inevitably made them expensive. Henry Muddiman charged five pounds a year for his news-letter, and Ichabod Dawks thirty shillings a quarter. Such prices automatically restricted the news-letters to the wealthy few. On the comfortable assumption that wealth and political responsibility went together, Authority was always less concerned about the contents of the news-letters than it was about news in cheap printed form, and the news-letters were virtually exempt from the licensing system. They contained news and comment that no newspaper could print, and not surprisingly they became enormously popular—so popular, in fact, that their authors were forced to employ a veritable army of scribes to copy out the necessary number. The highly informal manner in which they collected their news, and the vitally important part they played in the life of the nation, have been vividly described by Macaulay:

'the newswriter rambled from coffee house to coffee house, collecting reports, squeezing himself into the Sessions House at the Old Bailey if there was an interesting trial, nay, perhaps, obtained permission to the gallery of Whitehall, and noticed how the King and Duke looked. In this way he gathered materials for the weekly epistles destined to enlighten some country town or some bench of rural magistrates. Such were the sources from which the inhabitants of the largest provincial towns, and the great body of the gentry and clergy, learned almost all that they knew of the history of their own times.' [2]

Indeed, these news-writers have scarcely received from historians the credit due to them, for they were for many years the main link between the capital and the ruling classes of the countryside.

The written news-letters and the *London Gazette*, undoubtedly the principal source of news in the country, could be supplemented by private correspondence. During the eighteenth century, people in London were expected to keep their friends in the country fully informed of events at the political centre.[3] Again, however, this

[2] Lord Macaulay, *The History of England* (1864), i. 185.
[3] Cf. *Carlisle Papers*, H.M.C. 11th Report. App., pt. vi, especially the letters from Lady Irwin, Colonel Howard and Sir Thomas Robinson; L. Dickins and M. Stanton, ed. *An Eighteenth Century Correspondence to Sanderson Miller of Radway* (1910), p. 100 et seq.; Lady M. Verney, ed. *Verney Letters of the Eighteenth Century* (1930), i. 224.

correspondence was confined to those who could afford the heavy postal charges involved, or to those few who possessed influential 'connexions' in London with the privilege of sending letters post-free, under frank.

The mass of the population could not afford such luxuries, even if it had been able to read; and, although no exact information is available for this period, it is certain that the level of illiteracy was extremely high. The ordinary country-folk had therefore to be content with the odd items of news they could pick up from the proclamations and public announcements of the bell-men and town-criers; the snatches of conversation overheard by the servants of local notables; the topical songs and rhymes of the ballad-mongers; and the pronouncements from the pulpit of clergymen who, then as now, often dealt quite as freely with the events of this world as of the world to come.

Such were the sources of information available in the late seventeenth century and apparently they sufficed. The people who really mattered formed a small and intensely intimate caste; news of any moment would circulate rapidly and easily amongst them, and, save in times of unusual excitement, there was little need for any more elaborate supply of news than was provided by the *Gazette*, the news-letters and private correspondence. Of course, the vast mass of the population lived on a starvation diet so far as news of the outside world was concerned. But it seems unlikely that, outside London, the lower classes took much interest in such matters. They were certainly not encouraged to do so. A knowledge of affairs of state was regarded as the prerogative of gentlemen, and any popular interest in such matters was dismissed as idle and foolish curiosity. Sir William Berkeley, Governor of Virginia, was simply voicing the sentiments of his class when, in 1671, he piously gave thanks to God that, in Virginia, 'we have not free schools nor printing; and I hope we shall not have these hundred years. For learning has brought disobedience and heresy and sects into the world; and printing has divulged them and libels against the government. God keep us from both.' [4]

For these reasons, the government's determination to prevent the extension of the art of printing into the provinces was achieved without much difficulty. Both legally and literally, printing was confined to London and the two University towns specified in the Printing Act. It is true that, in London, the anticipated results of this policy had quite failed to materialize. So politically-conscious

---

[4] Quoted F. L. Mott, *American Journalism* (New York, 1949), p. 6.

was the capital that a licensed press soon called into existence an
unlicensed rival, and the cautious official publications found themselves challenged by very outspoken and highly unofficial pamphlets
and news-sheets printed on 'moonshine' presses hidden away in the
teeming warrens of the City, and defying all attempts at discovery
and suppression. But if Authority was not finding it easy to control
the press in London, it had at least been able to isolate the problem.
An illicit press was out of the question in the country towns of this
period, when they were still little more than sprawling villages, in
which every man knew his neighbour's business. In any case there
does not appear to have been any great demand in the country for
cheap printed news. By and large, the countryside was satisfied with
the supply of news available to it.

Then, in 1679, the Printing Act expired, and was not immediately
renewed; and the London press proceeded to make the most of its
unexpected opportunity in the hectic days of the Popish Plot. These
years when the press was free were ugly years, when scurrilous news-
sheets deliberately aroused and exploited the passions of the dreaded
London mob; and a proclamation of 12 May 1680 protested with
some reason that

'of late many evil-minded persons have made it a common practice to
print and publish pamphlets of news without licence or authority, and
therein have vended to his Majesty's people all the idle and malicious
reports that they could collect or invent . . . the continuance whereof
would in a short time endanger the peace of the Kingdom.'[5]

Again, however, such activities were confined to the capital; and
when, in 1688, William of Orange landed at Torbay and marched
on Exeter, that city, the acknowledged capital of the south-west and
one of the largest and most important cities in the kingdom, was
unable to produce either a printer or a printing press to strike off his
manifesto. For obvious reasons the London printers would have
nothing to do with so dangerous an assignment—in which prudent
resolution they were encouraged by a proclamation by King James II
threatening with the direst penalties all who should circulate or even
read the Prince's declaration. And it was not until John White,
printer in far-off York, undertook the task that the manifesto could
be printed in England. For that act of boldness, the printer was rewarded by both the interested parties, for he was cast into prison
at Hull by the supporters of James, and granted the imposing title

[5] Quoted C. H. Timperley, *Encyclopaedia of Literary and Typographical
Anecdote* (1842), p. 560.

of 'their Majesties' Printer for the City of York, and the Five Northern Counties' by the grateful William and Mary.[6]

The Glorious Revolution produced no immediate improvement in the position of the press. Indeed, Freedom of the Press was hardly a cause likely to commend itself to these cautious revolutionaries with their bitter memories of the turbulent past. Some of them would be able to recall the part played by the press in the Civil Wars; and all of them had had first-hand experience of the Popish Plot crisis. That crisis had demonstrated with devastating conclusiveness the dangers inherent in an instrument of publicity and criticism which, by its very cheapness, was calculated to appeal to the public at large, that public which, ignorant, inarticulate and vote-less, found in rioting its only form of political expression. It had been an object-lesson in the folly of lifting the time-honoured restrictions upon the press, and seemed to have confirmed beyond any shadow of doubt the essential soundness of the traditional attitude of Authority. Against such a background, the men of 1688 not unnaturally preferred to tread once again the ancient ways. The Revolution Parliament omitted all reference to the press from its Bill of Rights, and, in 1692, renewed the Printing Act. Once again, the nation was to be dependent for its news upon the *London Gazette*, the handful of licensed papers and the news-letters.

Times were changing, however, and the arrangements which had sufficed in the past were no longer satisfactory. The political and economic conditions of the last decade of the seventeenth century made the traditional policy of censorship and repression increasingly futile. The great continental campaigns of William III against Louis XIV, the ever-imminent threat of invasion from France, and the doubts entertained by all but the most sanguine as to the permanency of the Revolution Settlement created a demand for news which was merely whetted by the meagre and grudging supply sanctioned by Authority. No one with a material stake in that Settlement could remain disinterested so long as its very future was menaced by the possibility of a French victory and a Stuart restoration. But the agitation was by no means confined to those propertied classes whose privileged position in state and society had been supposedly confirmed once and for all time by the Revolution. Few Englishmen, no matter how humble their station in life, could view with equanimity the prospect of a French victory and the consequent introduction into England of those three abominations which were so invariably associated in the popular imagination with the national

[6] R. Davies, *A Memoir of the York Press* (1868), p. 119.

enemy—rape, Popery and wooden shoes, the symbol of slavery. In fact, self-interest, patriotism, physical fear and religious enthusiasm combined to produce an atmosphere of sustained and highly emotional tension, reflected in the bitter political struggles of the period. In such an atmosphere, when news of any sort was at a premium, the government's efforts to suppress it were both unrealistic and hopeless. Finally, party politics proved the decisive factor; and it was the valiant but one-sided efforts of William III's Tory licenser to perform his duties at least so far as the Whig press was concerned that brought the whole question to the foreground of party politics. In 1695, a predominantly Whig House of Commons raised so many objections to the expiring Printing Act that it could not be immediately renewed. And in this negative and uninspiring way was the Freedom of the Press achieved: not as the result of any resounding statement of principle, but by the simple refusal of a House dominated by party politics to renew in its existing form the old Printing Act. The objections were directed not so much against the principle of that Act as against its details; and Authority, recognizing that the Act had largely failed in its purpose, had every intention of formulating more effective and less politically-objectionable measures.[7] But the session came to an end before a Select Committee had been able to come to any agreement, and the Printing Act quietly expired. And although succeeding sessions of Parliament were to witness frequent ministerial attempts to remedy this quite unexpected and undesired state of affairs, all the various proposals were defeated on party grounds.

Once the Printing Act had expired, it became legally possible to print and publish a newspaper without a licence; and, despite the apparently precarious nature of the new freedom, newspapers sprang up in the capital like mushrooms. The lapse of the Printing Act meant also the lapse of the former restrictions upon the printing trade generally. No longer was the number of Master Printers and their apprentices strictly limited. Every journeyman could now set up in business for himself; and every apprentice could hope, in time, to become a Master Printer. An eager, news-starved public was ready and waiting; and not unnaturally one of the first acts of many of the new Master Printers was to exploit this news-hunger by producing a newspaper, which required only a relatively small financial outlay, but which promised quick returns. For a time, the demand was sufficient to absorb the supply; but the trade soon began to show signs

---

[7] See L. Hanson, *The Government and the Press, 1695–1763* (Oxford, 1936), pp. 7–15, for an elaboration of this point.

of overcrowding. The steadily-growing competition within the capital, in fact, forced printers to seek their fortunes elsewhere. The whole kingdom beckoned, for printing was no longer confined to London, the two Universities and, since the accession of William III, York. And so began that migration of trained printers from London which was to continue for the next half-century and more. As early as April, 1695, one William Bonny—who, significantly enough, was reported to have suffered 'great Losses in Trade' in London [8]— petitioned the Common Council of Bristol for permission to estab- lish a printing-house in that city; in 1696, Thomas Jones arrived in Shrewsbury; and by 1700 Francis Burges had set up business in Norwich.

The arrival of such men did not lead immediately to the publica- tion of local newspapers. Indeed, conditions in the provinces did not seem to offer any great inducement to printers to embark upon such ventures. A newspaper was still a distinct novelty in the country; very few of the country-folk could read—and of those who could, many of the gentry, clergy and town merchants would continue to prefer the written news-letter, supplemented now, perhaps, by a subscription to one or more of the London newspapers; communi- cations were slow and primitive—an important consideration to printers who would be utterly dependent for their news upon a regular supply from London; and few country towns were as yet populous enough to support a local newspaper of their own. Above all, there seemed little likelihood that the newly-won Freedom of the Press would be of long duration. All the signs seemed to point in the opposite direction, for as early as November, 1695, a Bill to regulate the press passed its second reading in the House of Commons. On that occasion, it is true, the two Members for Bristol assured John Cary, a prominent citizen of that city, that his fears for the future of printing there were unfounded, since the purpose of the Bill was to sanction printing-presses in such large towns as Bristol, Exeter and York.[9] Nevertheless, the future of printing in the provinces could hardly be regarded as bright. Very naturally, the new printers confined their activities to general printing. From time to time they might issue broad-sheets to commemorate events of more than ordinary interest, but beyond that they did not go; and they were certainly not so foolhardy as to waste their time and money on so uncertain and probably unprofitable a venture as a regular newspaper. However, just as the removal of the previous restrictions

[8] John Dunton, *Life and Errors* (2nd. ed., 1818), i. 247.
[9] J. Latimer, *Annals of Bristol in the Eighteenth Century* (1893), p. 48.

upon the printing trade had made provincial newspapers legally possible, so the presence in country towns of trained printers made such newspapers technically and physically practicable. And, one by one, the various obstacles in the way of such a development were disappearing.

In reality, the prospects for a provincial newspaper press were not as black as they might, at first sight, appear—particularly when it became apparent that the new Freedom of the Press was likely to endure. The provincial reading public was small, but it was growing. Trade and commerce were expanding, and creating a steady and insistent demand for literate clerks and artisans—a demand reflected in the increasing attention now being paid to education. In the reign of Queen Anne, Charity Schools were founded by the hundred, not only in London but all over the kingdom, to educate the children of the poor in reading, writing and Christian obedience. At the same time, the Dissenters were busily engaged in establishing schools of their own. Literacy was no longer quite so rigidly confined to the favoured few, but was increasingly within reach of the children of the shopkeeper, the artisan, the small farmer and even the humblest labourer. In effect, a new reading public was coming into existence, and more and more people, even in remote villages, could read and write. Here was a potential market for a cheap local newspaper: for these people shared the appetite for news of their social superiors, although they did not possess the same means to gratify it, and as yet little printed matter other than the occasional chap-book came their way.

At a higher social level, conditions were also working in favour of a local newspaper. The gentry, clergy and more prosperous townsmen would be subscribing to London newspapers. But there had been an enormous expansion of the London newspaper press, and this had certain definite drawbacks for the country subscriber. In the capital, the urgent demand for news and the growth of the new reading public had acted as powerful stimulants upon the infant newspaper press, and induced in it a kind of hot-house growth. 'About 1695,' said the *British Mercury* later,

'the press was again set to work, and such a furious itch of novelty has ever since been the epidemical distemper, that it has proved fatal to many families, the meanest of shopkeepers and handicrafts spending whole days in coffee-houses to hear news and talk politics, whilst their wives and children wanted bread at home, and, their business being neglected, they were themselves thrust into gaols or forced to take sanctuary in the army. Hence sprang that inundation of *Postmen, Postboys,*

Evening Posts, Supplements, Daily Courants and *Protestant Post Boys*,
amounting to twenty-one every week, besides many more which have
not survived to this time, and besides the *Gazette*, which has the sanction of public authority.' [10]

In fact, the would-be country subscriber now had an embarrassingly
large choice of London newspapers. Unfortunately, to be certain of
reading all the latest news, it was really necessary to read all the
different newspapers. At that time, and for long afterwards, there
existed in the capital no reliable system of reporting. For their
'official' items, all the newspapers drew unblushingly upon the
London Gazette and its continental counterparts. But even here, as
Addison remarked, despite the fact that 'they all of them receive
the same advices from abroad, and very often in the same words . . .
their way of cooking it is so different, that there is no citizen, who
has an eye to the public good, that can leave the coffee-house with
peace of mind, before he has given every one of them a reading'.[11]
The discrepancies were even more marked in the rest of the news
items. Obviously, a newspaper could not thrive simply on the
accounts it could abstract from the *Gazette*. The public wanted
something more stimulating, both news and comment; it wanted the
more intimate and confidential reports of the type now known as
the 'inside story' and the 'human interest story'; and above all it
demanded the very latest news and rumours. For such items, the
newspaper printers had to rely upon highly unofficial and unreliable
private sources of information, upon tavern-rumour and coffee-
house gossip, hearsay and the eye-witness accounts of soldiers and
sailors returning from abroad. The reports derived from these
sources were almost invariably published without any attempt to
verify their accuracy. Sometimes, of course, they proved to be completely authentic, and the fortunate newspaper which had printed
them had achieved the eighteenth century equivalent of the 'scoop'.
More often, they proved to be either highly exaggerated or completely false. To make matters still more confused, it seems clear that
some newspaper printers were not above deliberately inventing exciting news items. This was certainly a common charge levied by
rival printers against one another. Naturally, as the number of different newspapers increased, so did the number of wildly contradictory reports and rumours multiply. This basic unreliability was to

[10] *British Mercury*, 2 August 1712.
[11] Addison, *Spectator*, no. 452, quoted W. B. Ewald, *The Newsmen of
Queen Anne* (Oxford, 1956), p. 15.

remain a feature of the newspaper press for many years to come;
and by 1730 it had become so notorious that a weekly paper, the
famous *Grub-Street Journal*, won considerable popularity by reprinting side by side each week the accounts of the same event taken
from the different newspapers, with humorous comments upon their
obvious discrepancies.

This meant that a subscription to a single London newspaper
might leave the countryman still very much in the dark. But the
heavy costs involved made a subscription to more than one a very
expensive luxury indeed, and as early as 1704 the *Evening Post*
could remark on

'the great Expence Gentlemen are put to in buying 6 or 7 Prints of a
Post-Day that bear the Title of Newspaper'.[12]

Each printer, of course, insisted that his newspaper, and his alone,
contained the truth and nothing but the truth: but there was really
very little to choose between the various papers, for no printer could
afford to ignore what reports and rumours came to his hands, however unfounded they might seem to be. To meet this problem, the
coffee-houses began to take in a large selection of newspapers for
the information of their customers. These coffee-houses offered
material comforts at a time when, particularly in the City itself,
housing conditions were generally poor: they provided pleasant
surroundings in which gentlemen could meet to transact business
and exchange news and gossip; but one of their greatest attractions
was undoubtedly the fact that they supplied newspapers. As Misson
observed, they were

'extreamly convenient. You have all Manner of News there: You have
a good Fire, which you may sit by as long as you wish: You have a
Dish of Coffee, you meet your Friends for the Transaction of Business,
and all for a Penny, if you don't care to spend more.'[13]

In the future, the coffee-houses and the newspaper were to develop
side by side; and their development in Cambridge has been admirably described by the very disapproving Roger North. In the seventeenth century, wrote North,

'coffee was not of such common use as afterwards, and coffee-houses
but young. At that time, and long afterwards, there was but one, kept
by one Kirk. The trade of news was also scarce got up; for they had

---

[12] *Evening Post*, 6 September 1704.
[13] *M. Misson's Memoirs and Observations in his Travels over England*,
trans. Ozell (1719), pp. 39–40, quoted Ewald, op. cit. p. 8.

only the public *Gazette* till Kirk got a written news-letter circulated by one Muddiman. But now the case is much altered, for it is become a fashion, after chapel, to repair to one or other of the coffee-houses, for there are divers, where hours are spent in talking, and less profitable reading of newspapers, of which swarms are continually supplied from London. And the scholars are so greedy after news, which is none of their business, that they neglect all for it; and it is become very rare for any of them to go directly to his chamber after prayers without doing his suit at the coffee-house, which is a vast loss of time.' [14]

Around the turn of the century, however, coffee-houses in provincial towns were few, and for most squires and clergymen a visit to such an establishment must have been a rare treat indeed. And not every visitor to so congenial and convivial an establishment would wish to spend his time wallowing in the great mass of London newspapers now available. Even by 1700, in fact, the complaint to be voiced later by the *Gentleman's Magazine* was already applicable: the London newspapers were 'so multiplied as to render it impossible, unless a Man makes it a Business, to consult them all'.[15]

The stage was being set for the appearance of the country newspaper. There existed a clear opportunity for some enterprising provincial printer to provide, in one cheap newspaper, the most important items contained in the various London newspapers of the previous week or so. A public was ready and waiting. The well-to-do might continue to subscribe to London newspapers: but these subscriptions were no longer altogether satisfactory, and such people might well supplement these subscriptions with a local and cheap paper which claimed to have selected the main items from all the different London papers. At the same time, a new reading public was steadily growing. There was no dearth of news, for the great continental campaigns promised an abundance of exciting copy. Finally, the last serious obstacle was removed when, towards the close of the seventeenth century, increasing attention was paid to the speed and punctuality of the postal services. Regular posts meant the regular arrival of news and newspapers from the capital, and encouraged the transition from the broad-sheet produced at irregular intervals to the true newspaper. Admittedly, the difficulties which remained were formidable enough. Circulation was likely to be small, the new reading public which was emerging was largely an unknown quantity, of uncertain tastes and means. The problem of distribution was likely to be serious. Nevertheless, the conditions

[14] Roger North, *Life of the Norths* (1741), p. 249.
[15] *Gentleman's Magazine*, preface to 1731 volume.

were such that, sooner or later, some enterprising country printer
would make the attempt.

Which provincial town may justly claim the honour of having
been the original birth-place of the provincial newspaper is a question which has aroused fierce controversy and even fiercer local
patriotism. Very few copies of the earliest provincial newspapers
have survived. The earliest extant copy is the issue of William
Bonny's *Bristol Post-Boy*, dated 12 August 1704, and numbered 91.
The date and number would suggest that the first issue of this paper
had appeared in November, 1702. Unfortunately, this method of
calculating back from the date and number of the first known issue,
taking a weekly paper to be the general rule, is open to serious
objections. In the first place, eighteenth century newspaper printers
were fantastically careless in the numeration of their papers, repeating numbers, omitting them and often starting on a new system
of numeration without any prior warning. Secondly, although the
weekly paper was the general rule, printers were sometimes encouraged by the exceptionally favourable conditions prevailing in
the first decade or so of the eighteenth century to publish their
papers more frequently, reverting to the weekly rule only when
news ran short. Such changes ruin any calculations based upon a
weekly rate of publication and an accurate system of numeration,
and for these reasons any dates arrived at by the process of calculating back from the date and number of the first known issue must be
regarded with suspicion. Unhappily, this is often the only method
available.

What evidence there is suggests that the first provincial newspaper was the *Norwich Post*, printed by Francis Burges. The earliest
known issue is dated 1 May 1708, and numbered 348—which implies
that the first issue appeared on 6 September 1701. How much faith
may be placed on the accuracy of such a calculation, involving as it
does a period of seven years, is, of course, open to doubt.[16] But this
paper's claim to be the first provincial newspaper is to some extent
corroborated by one of the rare contemporary allusions to country
newspapers, in a letter written in 1706 by Dr. Tanner, Rector of
Thorp Bishop's, Norwich, and later Bishop of St. Asaph's, to
Browne Willis, the famous antiquarian.[17] Dr. Tanner had apparently

---

[16] Its accuracy is confirmed by the ingenious cipher key incorporated in the
title. See A. D. E(uren), *The First Provincial Newspaper* (Norwich, 1924), p. 7.
[17] Dr. Thomas Tanner to Browne Willis, letter dated 1 August 1706, Browne
Willis MSS, Bodleian Library, vol. xcv., fol. 259.

made some study of the whole problem of the origins of the country newspaper, for he wrote that 'as far as I can judge, this Burges first began here the printing of news out of London; since I have seen also the Bristol *Postman*, and I am told they print also now a weekly paper at Exeter'. Admittedly, this statement could mean simply that Burges was the first printer *in Norwich* to publish a newspaper: but Dr. Tanner's subsequent references to Bristol and Exeter would surely suggest that he meant that the *Norwich Post* had been the first newspaper to be printed outside London. The Bristol newspaper referred to was obviously William Bonny's *Bristol Post-Boy*. The Exeter paper was presumably *Sam Farley's Exeter Post-Man*, of which only one issue, Number 556 of 10 August 1711, seems to have survived.[18] By this time, this paper was published weekly; and the date and number would, of course, imply that it had actually preceded the *Norwich Post*. But Dr. Tanner did not think so, and his opinion is confirmed from a somewhat unexpected source, an early American newspaper called the *Boston News Letter*, which first appeared in 1704, and, the following year, stated that 'we set the half-sheet at a more moderate price than it was set at Exeter in England, where they began to print much about the same time that we began here'.[19] It would seem, therefore, that the Exeter paper was first published in or about the year 1704, and that either its later numeration was inaccurate, or that, as is equally possible, at some time between 1704 and 1711 it had been published more frequently than once a week. Until further evidence becomes available, it would seem that the palm must go to the *Norwich Post*. It is true that the modern *Berrow's Worcester Journal* has claimed to be descended from a news-sheet published in the last decade of the seventeenth century.[20] But proof is lacking, and it is extremely unlikely that any provincial town had a regular newspaper, as distinct from a news-sheet or broad-sheet produced at irregular intervals, before the turn of the century. At least the Worcester newspaper, which can trace its direct descent back to the *Worcester Post-Man* of 1709, may rightly claim the honour of being the oldest surviving provincial newspaper in the country—and, indeed, after the *London Gazette*, the oldest surviving newspaper in England. On the existing evidence, we must say that the provincial newspaper was born in Norwich in the year 1701. But the question is by no means decided,

[18] In the Collection of Ephemera at the University Press, Oxford.
[19] *Boston News Letter*, 9 April 1705, quoted W. G. Bleyer, *Main Currents in the History of American Journalism* (Boston, 1927), p. 48.
[20] See I. Griffiths, *Berrow's Worcester Journal* (Worcester, 1942).

The Bristol Post-Boy,

Giving an Account of the most Material N E W S both

foreign and Domestick.

From **Saturday** August the 5th, to **Saturday** August the 12th, 1704.

Amsburg, July 24.

THE Capitulation desired by Count Merci for the surrender at Rain, of which he was Governor, at the time it was besieg'd by the Troops of the Allies, Commanded by Count Frite, is as follows, viz

1. That Count Merci, Brigadier General of the Armies of his Electoral Highness of Bavaria, and Governor of Rain, shall go out of his place with his Garison, comprehended therein the Militia on the 18th of this Month, with their Arms Drums beating, Coulours flying, all their Baggage and Ammunition for 30 Shots each, in order to be Conducted to their Army

2. That he may likewise carry away 6 peices of Cannon, with Ammunition for 10 Shots, and that the necessary Officers of Artilery be given him.

3. That 50 Waggons shall be furnish'd him for Transporting the Artillery, Baggage, &c. and 6 Covered Wagons that shall not be visited.

4. That the Sick and Wounded shall stay behind, with as many others as shall be thought necessary for assisting them, and that at the Charges of the City.

5. That the City shall remain in all its ancient Privileges.

6. That no Solldier shall be taken out of his Rank when the Garison marches out.

7. And that the Garison shall be Conducted with all safety, to the place desired.

The Capitulation granted by Count Firse, to the Garison of Rain, by orders of his Highness the Prince of Baden, and his Grace the Duke of Marlborough.

1. The Governor is permitted to march out of the place with Officers and Regular Troops, with the usal marks of Honour and Powder for 12 Shots each, but without Cannon, or any further Ammunition. As for the Militia, they shall be permitted to march out without Arms, on Condition they shall never take up Arms more against his Imperial Majesty, or his High Allies.

2. Some Waggons shall be allowed for transporting the Officers Baggage to the first Bavarian Fortress.

3. All the Electors Money and Gain of his Electoral Highness of Bavaria, as also the papers shall be faithfully delivered to his Imperial Majesty, Commissioners, and some Bavarian Commissioners, shall be left for that purpose in the place.

4. The Officers of the Bavarian Artillery shall remain likewise at Rain, till the Cannon, Ammunition &c. shall have been faithfully inventoried, and put into his Imperial Majesty's Hands.

5. The Troopers and Dragoons shall march out without Horses.

6. All Prisoners of War and Deserters shall be restored.

7. The Sick and the Wounded shall be permitted to stay in the Place at the Charges of his Electoral Highness of Bavaria.

8. The City of Rain shall be under protection of his Imperial Majesty, as well in relation to Eclesiastick, as civil Affairs.

9. Such Inhabitants as shall desire to march out with the Garison shall be permitted so to do.

10. A Convoy shall be allow'd to the Governor and Garison, to conduct them safe to their Camp.

Kingsale, July 28. On the 24th came into this Port the Providence of London, Burthen 50 Tuns, Francis Gerrard, Master from Flushing, bound for Dublin, She was taken by a French Caper of 10 Guns, the day after She left Flushing, and ransomed for 1400 Livres, She sailed from hence yesterday. Sixteen sail of Ships are arrived here from Cork, with 2 Colliers and a Ship of Bristol.

London Aug. 8. The Virginia Fleet are come safe into the Downs.

The Customs of the Virginia Fleet will be by Computation worth 50000 l. without reckoning the Draw Back.

The Queen Ann, Jacob and Tuscan Gallies are arrived safe in the River Thames from Leghorn, being richly laden; the latter of them took a French Privateer of 6 Guns, 4 Pateraroes, and 50 Men.

London, Aug. 8. The Troops for Portugal will forthwith imbark for Lisbonne, and we hear some of the Men of War which

were

1. THE EARLIEST EXTANT COPY OF A PROVINCIAL NEWSPAPER. THE TITLE-PAGE OF THE *BRISTOL POST-BOY* OF 12 AUGUST 1704.

for the claims of the *Norwich Post* depend very largely upon assumption and guess-work.

What is far more important, however, is the fact that, after a slow and understandably hesitant start, the provincial newspaper press began rapidly to expand. The times, as we have seen, were propitious, and the *Northampton Mercury*, during a later period when copy was neither so abundant nor so exciting, looked back with envy upon the eventful years of Queen Anne's reign:

> 'Good L—d! what silent Times are these!
> All's Peace at Home! abroad all Peace!
> Our State secure! Ch—h out of Danger!
> D—n it! 'twould make one burst with Anger.
> Not so when Glorious ANNA reign'd!
> New Things each Packet then contain'd.' [21]

Despite the comparative scarcity of news, however, the period of relative tranquillity which followed the reign of Anne was, in its own way, almost equally favourable to the growth and development of the newspaper press. In contrast to the stormy century which had preceded it, and to the turbulent and disturbed decades which were to follow, the age of the first two Georges was relatively placid. It was a time of growing prosperity, and, since the size of the population remained virtually the same, of a rising standard of living. Enclosures, industrialization and the immense growth of cities—all these terrible problems of the future, with their attendant social dislocation and unrest—were as yet little more than clouds upon the distant horizon. The early eighteenth century was, in fact, an age of relative content—and later generations were to look back upon it as a Golden Age. Politically, the age of the Whig Supremacy was certainly not the period of stagnation it has often been called. Nevertheless, there was nothing to arouse really violent passions. The age was not, of course, without its share of exciting events and controversial personalities. Such characters as Walpole, Lord Bolingbroke and the great Chatham, such events as the two Jacobite risings, the absorbing political struggle between Walpole and the so-called 'Patriots', not to mention the War of Jenkins's Ear and the culminating excitement of the Seven Years War, were quite sufficient in themselves to arouse and hold the popular interest. That interest, carefully exploited by the press, was undoubtedly intense: but there was nothing about it to justify any return to the repressive policies of the past, and although various ministries toyed wistfully with the idea of placing fresh controls upon the press, they could go no further

[21] *Northampton Mercury*, 8 August 1726.

than to impose the Stamp Acts which, although vexing, were certainly by no means crippling. By and large, it was a peaceful and tolerant period: and in this sort of atmosphere the press could become firmly established. Its future advances owed much to this period of consolidation.

Any account of the numerical growth and geographical distribution of the provincial newspaper press must inevitably be based upon somewhat inadequate evidence. In some cases, where no issues at all have survived, the very existence of a newspaper must be regarded as doubtful; and difficult as it is to date the first issue it may be even more difficult to determine when a newspaper expired. Few printers gave any publicity to the impending demise of their product, and in some cases we have nothing to go on apart from the date of the last-known issue. Occasionally, however unfeeling rivals would gleefully announce the sudden death of a competing paper; and sometimes their bitter attacks upon rival newspapers prove that a paper was still flourishing long after the date of the last-known issue. A further check is provided by the list which the *Gentleman's Magazine* printed each month showing the country towns from whose newspapers it had extracted some of its articles. Unfortunately, that list, although it shows the number of newspapers published in each town, does not give their titles: but it often adds to our knowledge of the length of life enjoyed by individual papers. By combining all these shreds of information, it is possible to give a reasonably accurate picture of the growth of the provincial newspaper press.

The provincial newspaper was born in 1701, with the publication of the *Norwich Post*. In the following year came William Bonny's *Bristol Post-Boy*; in 1704, *Sam Farley's Exeter Post-Man*; and, by 1705, the Shrewsbury paper, *A Collection of the most Material Newes*. These papers were the true pioneers; for when other printers began to enter the field, they preferred to try to challenge these already-established papers, and so take advantage of their preparatory labours, rather than break new ground elsewhere. Thus, towards the end of 1706, the original *Norwich Post* found itself challenged by two local rivals, the *Gazette*—which, under the eccentric Henry Cross-grove, was to have a long and somewhat turbulent career—and the *Norwich Post-Man*. In 1709, another newspaper, the *Exeter Post-Boy*, made its appearance in Exeter. And the same year saw the establishment of the country newspaper destined to outlive all its contemporaries, the *Worcester Post-Man*.

The first great peak was reached in 1710, a year of exceptional excitement, when the Whig ministry imprudently decided to impeach the Tory Dr. Sacheverell for his provocative sermon attacking the Revolution Settlement. From the Whig point of view, that impeachment was an abject failure: but the tremendous publicity which the elaborately stage-managed trial received succeeded in raising party passions to an unprecedented pitch—and no less than six country papers were started in this one year to capitalize upon the popular interest. These were the short-lived *Leverpoole Courant*, the *Newcastle Gazette*, *Stamford Post*, and two papers at Nottingham, the *Nottingham Post* and the *Nottingham Courant*. By the end of this year, thirteen papers had been established in nine different towns, and there seems to have been only one casualty, the Shrewsbury paper. This low death-rate suggests that the country newspaper satisfied a real need, at least in times of exceptional interest. The summary dismissal of the Whigs, the disgrace of their great war-leader, the Duke of Marlborough, and, with the advent to power of the Tories, the peace party, the growing rumours of a speedy and, in the eyes of many Englishmen, a dishonourable peace with France maintained the popular excitement at fever-pitch, and although in 1711 only one country newspaper, the great *Newcastle Courant*, was founded, no paper died. In the early months of 1712 there were still more than a dozen provincial papers in existence.

The year 1712 was, however, the point at which the press was to suffer its first serious set-back. The Tory ministry's efforts to conclude a peace treaty with the national enemy had been sorely embarrassed by the vociferous outcries of Whig pamphleteers; and in 1712 the ministry sought to muzzle such criticisms by means of a Stamp Act (10 Anne, c. 19)—the first of a long series of what were later to be known as the 'taxes on knowledge'. The Stamp Act was aimed primarily at the political pamphlet, which, in this Golden Age of pamphleteering, was still by far the most effective weapon of propaganda. All pamphlets were to pay a stamp duty of two shillings on every sheet in a single copy; a copy of every pamphlet was to be registered at the Stamp Office in London (or, in the case of pamphlets printed in the country, with the local distributor of stamps); and it was an offence to publish a pamphlet which did not bear the printer's name and address. The Act was thus a simple police measure. As regards what were called 'newspapers, or papers containing public news, intelligences or occurrences', a stamp duty was imposed of one half-penny on every copy printed on paper of half-sheet size, and one penny on every copy on paper 'larger than half a sheet and not exceeding one whole sheet'. This meant that all printers would have to pay a duty of either one half-penny or one penny on every copy of their newspaper that they sold—and not, as was the case with pamphlets, a duty levied only upon each edition.

The immediate effects of this Stamp Act upon the newspaper press were drastic in the extreme. A newspaper, and particularly a country newspaper, was still something of a novelty and certainly a luxury. Now, not only was the imminent peace with France to rob it of all the sensational war news upon which it had hitherto greatly depended, but also its price would have to be sharply increased. This double blow was generally expected to be fatal: as Addison put it, 'few of our weekly historians, who are men that above all others delight in war, will be able to subsist under the weight of a stamp duty in an approaching peace'.[22] In the case of the provincial newspapers, his gloomy forebodings seemed at first to have been amply justified. The Stamp Act came into force on 1 August 1712: and by the end of the same year no less than seven country newspapers appear to have expired.

If the immediate effects of the Stamp Act were violent, however, the long-term effects were almost negligible. It was not very long before ingenious minds perceived a loop-hole in the wording of the Act. It was described by the disapproving John Toland a few years later:

'it having been the design of the Parliament, that all News-papers shou'd pay a duty of one half-penny for each half-sheet, this end is manifestly defeated by printing of News-papers on a sheet and a half . . . whereby they become not lyable to be stampt, and so pay nothing. . . . Nor is the source of this mischief confin'd to London alone, since the News-papers printed at Norwich, Bristoll, and a great many other towns over the kingdom, are all without Stamps.'[23]

In fact, a mere technicality enabled the newspaper printers to evade most of the duty. Toland was mistaken when he said that they paid nothing: they did still pay a duty—but it was much lower than the Act had intended. According to the Stamp Act, if a newspaper were printed on a half-sheet of paper—that is to say, if it were a single-leaf newspaper—it had to pay one half-penny duty on every copy; if it were printed on a whole sheet—a four-page newspaper—it paid one penny. If, however, it should be printed on a sheet *and* a half, it became officially a pamphlet according to the definition in the Act. The distinction was important, for although pamphlets had to pay a duty of two shillings per sheet, that duty was paid only once for

[22] Addison, *Spectator,* 10 June 1712.
[23] John Toland, *Proposal for Regulating ye News-papers, circa* 1717, B.M. Add. MS. 4295, ff. 49, 50, reprinted in Hanson, op. cit. p. 136.

each edition printed. A newspaper of the half-sheet size (a single leaf) with a circulation of three hundred copies would have to pay twelve shillings and sixpence in duty; one of the whole-sheet type would pay twenty-five shillings; but a pamphlet of a sheet and a half paid only three shillings. The difference far outweighed any extra cost of paper and typesetting.

According to Toland, this 'contrivance' had been first hit upon by the *Daily Benefactor*, a very obscure London paper. But, he said, it was 'straight imitated by the *St. James's Evening Post*'—and that paper was for many years one of the principal sources from which the country printers took their news. Any device used by such an authority was sure to be both widely known and generally imitated. And very quickly all the country newspapers enlarged their size and became officially pamphlets. So general did this evasion of the Stamp Act become that by 1717 even the official *London Gazette* had fallen into line with the other newspapers.

The country newspapers had thus overcome their first serious setback, and soon the number of newspapers began to increase again, stimulated by such events as the popular interest in the terms of the Peace of Utrecht of 1713, and, above all, the growing uncertainty as to the national future. Anne had no direct heir, the nearest claimant to the English throne was the German Elector of Hanover; the whole future of the Protestant Succession seemed threatened, and a Stuart restoration by no means out of the question. In 1713, there were published *Sam Farley's Bristol Post-Man* and the *Stamford Mercury*; in 1714, one of the greatest of all provincial papers, the *Norwich Mercury*; and then, with the excitement of the Jacobite Fifteen with its aftermath of great trials and plots, new papers sprang up all over the country. It is unnecessary to give the names of all of them, but mention should be made of such notable papers as the *Kentish Post* and the Exeter *Post-Master*, both started in 1717, the *Leeds Mercury* (1718), *York Mercury* (1719), *Northampton Mercury* (1720), *Gloucester Journal* (1722) and the *Reading Mercury* (1723).

Saturation point appears to have been reached in 1723, when there were some twenty-four provincial newspapers in existence. By then the purely pioneering and experimental stage was over, and the country newspaper had proved its ability to flourish, at least in times of excitement and tension. Also, it had survived, although by somewhat dubious means, the first serious attempt on the part of Authority to cripple its growth. Now, however, it was called upon to face still sterner tests. The 1720's were relatively uneventful years—

and all previous experience suggested that the infant country newspaper press needed sensational copy if it were to flourish. And in
1725 Parliament effectively removed the loop-hole in the wording
of the Stamp Act which had enabled newspapers to evade the greater
part of the stamp duty.

The preamble to the Stamp Act of 1725 (11 Geo. I, c. 8) complained with some justice that

'the Authors or Printers of several Journals, Mercuries, and other News-
Papers do, with an Intent to defeat the aforesaid Payments, and in
Defraud of the Crown, so contrive as to print their said Journals, and
News-Papers, on One Sheet and Half-Sheet of Paper each, and by that
Means they neither pay the afore-said Duties of One Penny for each
Sheet, nor a Half-penny for the Half-Sheet, as by Law they ought to do,
but enter them as Pamphlets, and pay only Three Shillings for each
Impression, whereby his Majesty hath been much injur'd in his
Revenues.'

George I had no more tender spot. And the Act therefore laid down
that henceforward *every* sheet or half-sheet on which a newspaper
was printed was to bear its appropriate stamp—the rather attractive
red stamp which the very pro-government Andrew Brice of Exeter
was pleased to call 'the blushing Blood-coloured Mark of the whole-
some Severity lately stamp'd upon us'.[24]

The effects of this Stamp Act were serious. The extent of the
previous evasion of the duty is suggested by the fact that, once the
newspapers were prevented from posing as pamphlets, the income
from the pamphlet duty promptly fell from £300 per annum to a
mere £89 in 1728/9.[25] Now all the newspapers had to cut down their
size to a half-sheet, and increase their price: and such unpopular
changes, coupled as they were with a dearth of exciting news, produced their inevitable results. Before the year had ended, at least
four country newspapers seem to have disappeared. But just as
important as this immediate mortality was the fact that, for some
years to come, country printers were reluctant to launch new ventures. The effects of the Stamp Act of 1712 had been very temporary:
but those of the Act of 1725 were to be far more lasting. No new
paper appeared in 1726, only one in 1727—and it was not until 1732
that there was to be any real advance. From that year onwards, the
number of country newspapers began steadily to increase again.

[24] Quoted T. N. Brushfield, Andrew Brice and the early Exeter Newspaper
Press, *Transactions of the Devonshire Association,* xx. (1888), 181.
[25] A. Aspinall, 'Statistical Accounts of the London Newspapers during the
Eighteenth Century', *English Historical Review,* April, 1948, p. 203.

Domestic politics had become exciting, with the appearance on the political horizon of Walpole's famous Excise Scheme and the growing clamour of the Opposition. More important still, perhaps, the foreign situation became increasingly tense. Six new papers were begun in the year 1732 alone—including the *Derby Mercury, Howgrave's Stamford Mercury*, and, in Chester, *Adams's Weekly Courant*. Three more appeared in 1735, and four more in 1737, when war with Spain was imminent; and by the end of 1740 there were thirty-one provincial newspapers. By 1744, when France, the ancient enemy, had entered the war, the total had risen to thirty-six. And then came the crowning excitement of the Forty-Five, when the demand for news was such that the provincial press attained its highest peak for the whole period. By the end of the year 1745, there were no fewer than forty-one country papers; and in 1746 the total rose to forty-two.

Such a total could not be maintained indefinitely. Once the rebellion had been crushed in 1746, a general peace was obviously imminent, and there was clearly a great deal of truth in the observation later by *Berrow's Worcester Journal* that 'a very material Declension in the Sale of News-Papers in general is always the Consequence of a Termination of War'.[26] Only one new paper appeared in 1747, none at all in 1748, the year when the peace was actually signed, and one in 1749. And all the time newspapers were dying right and left. By 1753, in fact, the total number of country newspapers in existence had dropped to thirty-two. That figure rose to thirty-five in 1754, the year of the great General Election. And from then on it began to grow steadily again, with the obvious imminence of a war with France. By the end of 1756, when the Seven Years War had broken out officially—as distinct from the unofficial skirmishes which had for some time been a permanent feature of Anglo-French relations in India and North America— there were thirty-seven provincial newspapers in existence. But what might clearly have been a very great increase was arrested almost before it had begun when, in 1757, the government doubled the stamp duty (30 Geo. II, c. 19). The price of all newspapers had once again to be increased, and was obviously becoming dangerously high for a type of publication which addressed itself primarily to the humbler members of rural society. Even the triumphs of Chatham and the wonderful year of victories of 1759 could induce no significant expansion in the number of the country newspapers, and by the end of the year 1760 there were still only thirty-five.

[26] *Berrow's Worcester Journal*, 25 August 1763.

This may not seem an impressive total after nearly sixty years of growth: but bare figures rarely present an accurate picture. In all, since 1701, some one hundred and thirty provincial newspapers had been founded, together with a number of literary magazines and periodicals. Obviously, casualties had been heavy, but the rate of growth, if not spectacular, had been remarkably steady. After 1719, the number of country newspapers in existence in any one year had never fallen below twenty; after 1737, it had not dropped below thirty. Many newspapers had been established in this period which were to survive until the present century—the *Bath Journal, Bath Advertiser, Chester Courant, Coventry Mercury, Derby Mercury, Gloucester Journal, Ipswich Journal, Leeds Intelligencer, Leicester Journal, Sussex Weekly Advertiser, Newcastle Courant, Northampton Mercury, Norwich Mercury, Reading Mercury, Salisbury Journal, Stamford Mercury* and *Worcester Journal*. Others, although not so long-lived, were to play a significant part in the history of the early newspaper press. Among these might be mentioned such papers as the *Norwich Gazette, York Courant, Newcastle Journal,* and the various papers established in the south-west by Andrew Brice and the Farley family. Certainly, by 1760, the provincial newspaper was a firmly established local institution, and few towns of any importance lacked one.

It remains to discuss the geographical distribution of these early newspapers. It was no accident that the provincial newspaper was born in Norwich, for that city stood in a class by itself at the beginning of the eighteenth century. It had a population of some 29,000, a figure rivalled only by Bristol; and it was the metropolitan town of a thickly-populated and prosperous region. So favourable were the conditions here, in fact, that according to Dr. Tanner in 1706, 'the Norwich papers are the principal support of our poor printer here, by which, with the advertisements, he clears nearly 50s. every week, selling vast numbers to the country people'.[27] Such a profit was, at this time, enormous, and was not to be equalled again for many a year. And it is not surprising that other printers should have been attracted to the scene, so that by the end of 1706, at a time when, outside London, only Bristol, Exeter and Shrewsbury had seen a local newspaper, there were three published in Norwich. The only provincial city which could be compared with Norwich was Bristol, which was soon to forge ahead in size and wealth. And Bristol had its own newspaper in 1702. No other city approached these two in size, and few indeed had more than ten thousand inhabitants.

[27] Dr. Tanner to Browne Willis, 1 August 1706, op. cit.

Physical size was not, however, the only criterion by which the migrant printer judged a town. The printer was first and foremost a general printer, and for many years to come a newspaper was only one, and certainly not the most important, of his interests. What the printer sought was a market town which was the social centre for a wide area, or a sea-port or town whose commercial and industrial activity promised a steady income in the way of advertisements, trade bills and general announcements. Thus, Worcester and Shrewsbury were county capitals, possessing similar advantages to Exeter; Liverpool and Newcastle were rising sea-ports; Nottingham was another county capital, with the added advantage that it was also a growing centre of industry; and Stamford was most strategically situated upon the inter-section of the great post-road to the north and an important cross-road running from east to west, and so was the service centre of a very wide region.

As other towns began to produce newspapers, it will be found that they, too, possessed some particular attraction for the printer. Position on or near a post-road from London was, of course, an essential, and often some local improvement in the postal service would provide the final encouragement for a printer to make a start. In this way, the inauguration in 1740 of daily posts from London to Cambridge and to Bath led almost immediately to the appearance of newspapers in both towns for the first time, just as the extension of daily posts in 1755 to Middlewich, Warrington and Liverpool produced newspapers in all three within a year. In the case of Warrington, the presence of the great Dissenting Academy in that town probably had some influence upon the printer's decision, for it assured a literate public and a ready supply of private contributions in the way of letters and essays.

And yet some large and important towns were surprisingly late in acquiring a newspaper, lagging far behind much smaller and less significant places. In 1723, the printers of the *Reading Mercury* commented in their first issue on the fact that the success of newspaper printers at York, Bristol and Worcester had encouraged others 'to set up at far smaller Places, as Cirencester in Gloucestershire, St. Ives in Huntingdonshire, Gosport in Hampshire, and several other Places; which makes it to us a Wonder that Reading (a Place of far greater Note than any of the last nam'd) should be so long neglected by our Brother Typos'.[28] In fact, of the places mentioned, Cirencester had a newspaper, the *Cirencester Post*, in 1718,

[28] *Reading Mercury*, 8 July 1723.

and so had preceded the city of York by one year, while the tiny St. Ives had had a quite remarkable record, witnessing no less than three attempts to establish a local newspaper before 1720. Nor were these the only small towns to have their own newspapers. Maidstone had the *Maidstone Mercury*, in 1725, and the *Maidstone Journal*, in 1737; Whitehaven had its paper in 1736, Lewes in 1746, and Middlewich in 1756. In this last case even the printer apparently felt obliged to apologize for his temerity, explaining in extenuation that he had appointed 'numerous Correspondents in all the noted Towns in the neighbouring Counties, which will, I hope, in some Measure excuse for the smallness of the Town I reside in giving Birth to a Newspaper'.[29] But at the other end of the scale, Birmingham, which in 1700 had a population of about 15,000, had no newspaper until 1732, and no successful paper until 1741, when the *Birmingham Gazette* was established; Coventry had to wait until 1741, Leicester until 1753. Even the two University towns of Oxford and Cambridge had no local newspaper until 1746 and 1744 respectively. Despite the growth of trade and commerce, the sea-ports were also surprisingly slow in producing newspapers. Hull had its first newspaper in 1739; Portsmouth and Gosport had to be content with a local edition of the *Salisbury Journal*; Yarmouth in the first decade had a choice between local editions of two Norwich papers, but thereafter had to depend upon the newspapers of Norwich and Ipswich; and Falmouth, King's Lynn, Dover and Harwich had no paper at all during this period. Of course, many of these sea-ports were close to towns in which newspapers were firmly established: but the fear of competition had not deterred printers from starting their own ventures under similar conditions in other towns. Perhaps the most surprising case of all was that of Liverpool. That great sea-port had a newspaper as early as 1710; but after it failed in 1712, no printer seems to have attempted a local newspaper until 1756, when *Williamson's Liverpool Advertiser* appeared. And in his first issue, he remarked with some justice that

'it hath, a long Time, been a Matter of Surprise to many, that a Place so respectable in its Inhabitants, so advantageous in its Situation, and so important in its commercial Concerns, as Liverpool, shou'd be without those weekly and public Methods of conveying Intelligence which are to be met with in Towns of less considerable Note.'[30]

A vigorous newspaper is today commonly regarded as one of the

[29] *Schofield's Middlewich Journal*, 10 August 1756.
[30] *Williamson's Liverpool Advertiser*, 28 May 1756.

most accurate indices of a town's importance.[31] This was not so in the early eighteenth century. Until the very end of the period under discussion, the possession of a local newspaper provided no reliable indication of a town's size, wealth or significance. The all-important factor was the human one. A town might possess certain advantages which would encourage a printer to produce a local paper: but everything ultimately depended upon his decision. A country newspaper was always a hazardous undertaking. Its profits were small, the amount of time and energy it consumed were large; and it is not surprising that many printers remained content with their general printing business, combined with book-selling and the hundred-and-one side-lines with which an eighteenth century printer regularly supplemented his income. However, even while emphasizing the supreme importance of the human factor in determining where newspapers should be established, it is still possible to distinguish certain significant trends in the geographical distribution of the provincial newspapers.

Geographically, the cradle of the infant provincial press was the rural south and south-west, where, at least in the first half of the century, the bulk of the population still lived. As the century progressed, the population began slowly to move towards the north and midlands, which were already showing signs of that industrial expansion later to be dignified with the title of the 'Industrial Revolution'. This movement of population and this expansion were to be clearly reflected in the number of local newspapers established in this area.

For the purposes of comparison, a line drawn from the Severn to the Humber may be taken as the dividing-line between north and south. By the end of the year 1715, fifteen country newspapers had appeared to the south of that line, and eight to the north. The fifteen southern papers had, however, been produced by six towns only. Norwich alone had had five different papers, Bristol three, Exeter and Stamford two each, and Salisbury one, while at Yarmouth local editions of two Norwich papers had appeared. The eight northern papers had been produced by five towns. Newcastle had had two papers, Nottingham three and Shrewsbury, Worcester and Liverpool one each. The south retained its lead during the next period, from 1716 to the end of 1725, when it saw the publication of seventeen

[31] See R. E. Dickinson, *City, Region and Regionalism* (1947), pp. 211–12; M. J. Wise, 'Birmingham and its Trade Relations in the early Eighteenth Century', *University of Birmingham History Journal*, vol. ii, no. 1, 1949, pp. 72–73.

new papers. The north in this period produced only eight again. The provincial newspaper press was now beginning to expand, and many new towns now appeared on the list. In the south, Norwich produced yet another paper, and Exeter two; but otherwise all the towns were making their first appearance. They included Bury St. Edmunds, Canterbury, Cirencester, Gloucester, Ipswich, Maidstone, Northampton (with two papers), Plymouth, Reading, St. Ives (with three), and Taunton. It was a similar story in the north, where, apart from Newcastle, with one more paper, all the towns—Chester, Derby, Leeds, Ludlow, Manchester and York (with two)—were entering the field of newspaper production for the first time.

After 1725, the trend to the midlands and north began. Competition in the south was becoming increasingly fierce, and already towns in the north were beginning to show conspicuous signs of wealth and development. In fact, from 1726 to the end of 1740, while only ten new papers appeared in the south, twenty-two were founded in the north. The only new towns in the south were Colchester and Sherborne; otherwise, there had been no further geographical expansion, and what little activity there had been was confined to towns which had already produced a newspaper—to Cirencester, Exeter, Ipswich, Maidstone, Reading, Salisbury (two), and Stamford. In the north, however, there was a tremendous expansion. Naturally, some familiar names appear again as the scene of fresh printing activity. Manchester produced as many as four new papers in this period, and Newcastle two, while Chester, Derby and Nottingham were all represented again. But some significant new names appear for the first time, such as Birmingham, with two papers, Boston, Durham, Hereford, Hull, Kendal (two), Lincoln, Preston and Whitehaven, while one newspaper was printed in London for distribution in Shropshire.

In the final period, from 1741 to the end of 1760, the north retained its lead, with twenty-seven new papers as against twenty-three in the south. Its lead was actually rather greater than these figures suggest, for the south's total was largely due to a sudden outburst of activity in the south-west, where Bristol saw six new papers, and Bath four. Exeter had two more papers, and Northampton and Reading one each. Otherwise, there had been a further expansion in the south, with newspapers appearing for the first time in such towns as Cambridge, Eton, Gosport, Lewes, Oxford (three), Winchester and Yeovil. A similar expansion was noticeable in the north. There had been further activity in Hull, Leeds, Lincoln, Manchester (three new papers), Newcastle (three), Nottingham, Preston,

Worcester and York (two). But Liverpool, with two papers, re-appeared for the first time since 1712; and eight towns now produced a newspaper for the first time. And these included such growing centres of trade and industry as Coventry (two), Doncaster, Halifax, Leicester, Middlewich, Sheffield (also with two), Stratford and Warrington.

In all, newspapers appeared in fifty-five towns during the period, many towns producing far more than one. Bristol, for instance, witnessed no less than nine different attempts to establish a newspaper; Manchester had eight; Exeter, Newcastle and Norwich seven each; Nottingham five; and Bath, Derby and York four each. Throughout the period, however, the tendency was not only for the number of newspapers to increase steadily, but also for them to be produced in a steadily-growing number of different towns. And, as the period progressed, there was a clearly-defined movement away from the mainly agricultural south towards the hitherto remote and under-populated north, where the new towns and sea-ports were beginning to develop. The activity and obvious prosperity of these towns naturally attracted the printers: and in this period, the human factor was undoubtedly the decisive one.

CHAPTER TWO

THE CHARACTER AND PHYSICAL DEVELOPMENT OF THE PROVINCIAL NEWSPAPER

THE character of the provincial newspaper was determined by the conditions which had brought it into being. It was news of London and of the outside world as described in the London newspapers the public demanded: and this demand the country printer set out to satisfy. His aim was essentially to provide, for the price of one newspaper, usually published weekly, the main news items which had been contained in all the different London newspapers and news-letters of the preceding week. The *Protestant Mercury* of Exeter could therefore boast in 1715 that its news items were 'impartially collected, as Occasion offers, from the *Evening Post, Gazette, Votes, Flying Post, Weekly Pacquet, Dormer's Letter, Postscipt to the Post-Man,* &c. So that no other can claim to have a better Collection'.[1] Similar statements appeared in all the various country newspapers. Their aim was to provide 'a faithfull Abstract of all the Newspapers of Note', or, in rather more poetic phrasing, 'the Quintessence of ev'ry Print'.[2] The *Kentish Post* pointed out that its 'Collection of News taken as well from all the Newspapers printed at London as from Private Letters, &c. . . . will afford more News than any single Paper printed at London can possibly do';[3] and the *Newcastle General Magazine*, one of the early provincial periodicals, also emphasized its cheapness, reminding its readers that 'what they purchased for Six-Pence would have cost them Ten Times as much, had the Essays, &c. been bought separately'.[4]

The provincial newspaper was thus, in effect, a mere parasite

---

[1] *Protestant Mercury,* 7 October 1715.
[2] Respectively, *Exeter Mercury,* 14 September 1714, and *Brice's Weekly Journal,* 27 February 1730. Similar announcements appeared in the *Leverpoole Courant,* 18 July 1712; *Birmingham Journal,* 21 May 1733; *Harrop's Manchester Mercury,* 17 March 1752; *Berrow's Worcester Journal,* 8 November 1753.
[3] *Kentish Post,* 21 June 1746.
[4] *Newcastle General Magazine,* January 1747.

upon the London press. No country printer made any claims to originality: his appeal for popular support was based quite simply upon the completeness and impartiality of his 'collection' of news. In many cases, the name of the London paper from which each news item had been taken was given in brackets after the item; sometimes, particularly in the earlier years of the century, the news items were grouped together under the heading of the London paper from which they had been extracted. Whichever method was used, the printers made it clear that they accepted no responsibility for what they printed; and should a reader dare to complain of the inaccuracy of any of the reports, he was referred quite simply to the London paper from which the offending item had been taken. As the printers of the *Northampton Mercury* so disarmingly explained, 'we hope our candid Readers will not condemn our Mercury for the many Falsities that have of late been inserted therein, as we took them all out of the London Printed Papers, and those too the most creditable'.[5] This form of journalistic piracy was practised quite openly. It was, in fact, the custom of the land. And when, in 1747, some of the readers of the *Newcastle General Magazine* ventured to suggest that the printer's policy of taking essays out of the London magazines might be regarded as 'an Infringement upon the Property of our Brethren of London', they were very sharply reminded that 'the Proprietors of those Works take many of their Essays from the Weekly Papers, and that the Weekly Papers extract all their News Articles from the Evening Papers and Daily Papers'.[6] This was perfectly true. The monthly magazines 'borrowed' from the weekly papers, the weekly papers from the evening and daily papers. The last-named, of course, were not so fortunately placed: they took what they could from the *London Gazette* and its Continental counterparts, but otherwise they bore the weight of all the rest upon their somewhat reluctant shoulders.

In all their statements of their aims, none of the country newspapers made any mention of local news; they were local papers only in the sense that they were printed locally. This was natural enough. In the intimate little rural communities of this time, local news would be spread by word of mouth long before a weekly newspaper could put it into print, while local insularity ensured that what was news for one community would be of little or no interest to others.

The provincial newspaper was to retain this essential character throughout the period under review. From time to time, attempts

[5] *Northampton Mercury*, 13 March 1720/21.
[6] *Newcastle General Magazine*, January, 1747.

were made by the more enterprising printers to provide a genuine abstract of news instead of a mere 'collection' of often quite contradictory items; but such attempts were spasmodic and rarely lasted long. So primitive and uncertain were the methods of news-gathering employed by the London newspapers, in fact, that the country printers found it safer, and certainly infinitely easier, to concentrate upon presenting as large a 'collection' of items as possible, and to leave it to their readers to decide for themselves upon the relative merits of the different selections. The main advance, in fact, lay only in the use of more and more London newspapers. Often, the lists of the papers from which the country printers claimed to have taken their various items reached quite surprising lengths. In 1745, for example, the *Cambridge Journal*, which was by no means one of the greatest of the country papers, was boasting that its 'collection' was taken from the following sources:

'*Amsterdam, Utrecht, Hague, Leyden, Brussels, Paris* and *London Gazettes*; the *Paris-Ala-Main*; *London, General* and *St. James's Evening Posts*; *London Courant*; *Daily Advertiser*; *Daily Post*; *Daily Gazetteer*; *Universal Spectator*; *Old England Journal*; Dublin and Edinburgh News-papers; and *Wye's, Fox's* and other Written Letters; besides Private Intelligence.'[7]

Less exotic, but probably far more genuine, was the list which appeared in the *North Country Journal* in 1735. This paper was one of the many which continued to give the source of each separate news-item. And it therefore announced:

'This News Paper being collected from the following London Prints, etc. the Letters at the End of each Paragraph show from which the same is taken, viz.

GE	G. Evening	LE	Lon Evening
P	Post boy	SJE	St James' Ev.
Cr	Craftsman	DA	D. Advertiser
DG	D. Gazetteer	FJ	Fog's Journal
LP	London daily Post	WE	W. Even.
DJ	D. Journal	WL	Wye's Letter
US	Univer Spect	DP	Daily Post'[8]

The *Reading Journal* introduced refinements into this system, giving not only the sources but also the number of times each week the

---

[7] *Cambridge Journal*, 4 January 1744/45.
[8] *North Country Journal*, 8 November 1735. See also *Northampton Mercury*, 21 June 1756.

London paper in question was published. It insisted, however, that 'those Articles only are markt with the above abbreviations that are peculiar to each Paper, and not in any of the rest'.[9]

Throughout the period, the most regularly-used source of news was undoubtedly the *London Gazette*, whose official announcements and reports were almost invariably given the place of honour in the country newspapers, particularly in time of war. After the *Gazette* came the evening papers, such as the *Whitehall Evening Post* or the *St. James's Evening Post*—and, later in the period, the venomous *London Evening Post*. The weekly papers were used mainly as quarries for political essays or for literary and general articles, depending upon the taste of the printer and of his public.

But although extracts from the London papers provided by far the greater part of the contents, space was always found for items taken from the written news-letters. In these items, indeed, the country papers possessed their great advantage over their London rivals. Brief though the extracts might be, they provided the sort of intimate news which the country reader wanted: the snatches of Court gossip which the London papers were afraid to print, accounts of parliamentary debates which they were forbidden to print, and the vague hints at highly confidential information. In this way, the country printers sought to combine the cheapness of the printed newspaper with the exclusiveness of the news-letter: and the combination proved extremely popular.

The importance placed on the extracts from the news-letters is shown by the regularity with which they appeared. In the early years of the century, when the newspaper press was still in its infancy even in the capital, the country printers drew more heavily upon the news-letters for their news than they did upon the London printed papers. It is clear that a surprising number of these news-letters were in existence. A Nottingham paper, the *Weekly Courant*, regularly quoted from the letters of Fox, Miller, Roper, Dormer, Seddal, Seddon, Wye, Stanley, Jackson, Goodwin, Peck, Jones and Delpouch until about 1720; and the *Stamford Mercury* used Fox, Miller, Baker, Jones, Stanley and Delpouch. By the late 1720's, however, the expansion of the newspaper press had caused a noticeable decline in the number of news-letters, only three of which seem to have survived: Wye, Stanley and Fox. Weekly extracts from one or more of these news-letters continued to appear in almost every country newspaper, although by the 1730's Wye reigned virtually supreme. Few indeed were the provincial newspapers which did not regularly

[9] *Reading Journal*, 23 July 1744.

contain a section with the proud title, 'From *Wye's Letter*'. But not until the very end of the period did the long reign of the written news-letter come to an end. Long before this, however, its place of pre-eminence as the indispensable source of news for the well-to-do in the country had been taken by the newspapers. Not only were the printed papers cheaper, but they catered increasingly for individual tastes: there were political papers, literary papers, commercial, humorous, religious—even newspapers pure and simple. But in the pages of the country newspapers, the news-letter had certainly received a new lease of life, and it continued there to play a significant part in the political education of the new reading public growing up outside London.

If the character of the provincial newspaper was largely determined by the conditions which had brought it into being, its physical appearance and development were controlled by the printing methods then in use, and by the Stamp Acts. In no sense could printing in the eighteenth century be spectacular. The hand-press had changed little since the days of Caxton, and printing was still a very slow process involving considerable physical strength and much hard labour. The individual metal types had to be selected by hand and arranged in printers' 'sticks', made up into columns which were then inked by hand, and an impression taken from them on sheets of paper placed by hand under the press, which was then operated by hand.[10] Only two men could work at a press together; and their hourly production, at best, would be a 'token' of two hundred and fifty small-sized sheets, printed on one side of the paper only. And this was not a speed which could be maintained for long periods at a stretch.[11]

At first sight, it might not seem that the question of speed would be of any great significance in the printing of an eighteenth century country newspaper. The country paper was essentially a weekly newspaper. In the early years of the century, it is true, there were attempts to publish these newspapers twice, or even three times, a week. But this defeated one of the main attractions of the country newspaper—its cheapness. Many of its customers could not afford to buy more than one newspaper a week. Also, there was the problem of distribution. In the early days, not only was the circulation small, but it was largely confined to the immediate neighbourhood. Outside customers were expected to pick up their copies at the printing-office on market-day. As circulation grew, however, readers became more widely dispersed throughout the surrounding countryside. To

[10] Wickham Steed, *The Press* (1938), p. 119.
[11] A. S. Turberville, ed. *Johnson's England* (Oxford 1933), ii. 331.

reach these customers, the printers had to employ newsmen, who travelled around the countryside delivering the newspapers. As they had often to travel long distances, it might well be two or three days before they could return to their base. More frequent publication would naturally make this problem of distribution more complicated and, what was still worse from the printers' point of view, more expensive. Finally, a newspaper was only a minor and not the most lucrative part of a printer's activities; and as his general printing business expanded, so his press and types were needed for other work.

From about 1720, therefore, the weekly paper was the general rule; and it might well be thought that the technical problems were thereby reduced to a minimum. In fact, the limitations of the hand-press still determined the whole lay-out and composition of the provincial newspaper. In most towns, the post from London bearing the indispensable London papers arrived three times a week. Unfortunately, the country printer could not choose the day on which he would publish his paper: it had to be on the market-day, when the town would be thronged with people from the country, many of whom preferred to collect the newspaper then rather than wait for its delivery later by the newsmen. This meant that the printer might have a clear day between the arrival of the latest post from London and the publication of his own newspaper; equally, however, the post might well come in on the evening before publication day; or it might arrive in the small hours of the morning of that day—in which case he would have only a couple of hours in which to read through the London papers, decide which items to use, set up his type and go to press. The tendency throughout the period was for the printer to have less and less time between the arrival of the London post and publication; and with the spread of daily posts from the capital after 1740, most printers had only a few hours at most. Unfortunately, it was essential that the local paper should contain the main news items in the London newspapers brought in by that post: for if it did not, it laid itself open to the charge that it did not include the very latest news, and so could hardly compete either with the London newspapers themselves or with more enterprising local rivals.

Thus the limitations of the hand-press made it impossible for the printer to wait until he had the London papers of the whole week, sift and collate the various items contained in them, and present a true digest of the week's news. Instead, he had to print the news as it arrived, leaving a space for the later posts. Just as the printers of the early bi- and tri-weekly papers had printed each post as a separate newspaper, so throughout the period the printers of the weekly papers treated the contents of each post as a separate entity. Their newspapers were divided into three sections, headed 'Monday's Post', 'Wednesday's Post' and 'Saturday's Post', or according to the days on which the London post arrived in their particular town. Each 'Post' was printed off as it arrived, and in this way the last-minute printing was reduced to a minimum.

The main contents of the provincial newspaper were thus printed at leisure during the week, far more space being devoted to the earlier 'Posts', with their stale news, than to the last and most important. After the Stamp Act of 1712, for example, when the *Worcester Post-Man* became a six-page paper, its first four pages were filled with the news items brought by the first two posts—many of them being by then well over a week old; the news brought in by the last post was printed only on page five, for the last page was always left blank. If the news in that 'Post' proved unexpectedly important, a smaller type was used to ensure that it did not spill over on to page six; and if this smaller type proved not small enough, an almost minute type was used.[12] With the growing pressure of news and advertisements, the printer of this paper was eventually forced to give up his attempt to keep the last page clear: but the small type was used to ensure that the last 'Post' and the advertisements would be kept within the two pages allocated to them. And all the other country printers of this period adopted a similar system. In the case of *Farley's Bristol Newspaper*, typical of the four-page newspapers after 1725, the space was apportioned with almost mathematical precision. Pages one and two were given over to 'Monday's Post', page three to 'Thursday's Post' and page four contained 'Saturday's Post' and the advertisements. As the business of advertising developed, it soon became customary for the last page to be devoted purely to advertisements. Eventually, in the typical four-page country newspaper, page one would contain the first—and stalest—'Post', page two the second, page three the latest 'Post', together with advertisements, and page four advertisements alone.

In this way, the printers saved both time and trouble. Not only was the last-minute printing reduced to a minimum, but one whole side of the newspaper could be printed off in a single operation early in the week, when there was no great urgency. In the case of the *York Courant*, for example, the outside pages, containing the oldest news and the advertisements, were printed off on Friday;[13]

[12] e.g. *Worcester Post-Man*, 27 August 1714, 10 June 1715.
[13] e.g. *York Courant*, 1 June 1756.

page two, with the second 'Post', would be set up late on Saturday, or perhaps very early Monday morning; and page three, with the latest 'Post' and more advertisements, would be printed off as soon as the post-boy arrived, either late on Monday or first thing Tuesday morning, the day of publication. A similar technique was adopted by the *Northampton Mercury* and the *Reading Mercury*; and the *Kentish Post* achieved the same result, although its printer, an individualist to the last, printed the earlier 'Posts' on the two *inner* pages of his paper, together with the advertisements, and reserved the outside pages for his latest news.

The disadvantages of this method were obvious. Frequently a news item in one 'Post' was contradicted by a later 'Post' in the same paper. Often, too, the lion's share of the paper—taken up by the two earlier posts—consisted of trivialities, while an important item from the last post had to be squeezed into a couple of lines. The earliest extant copy of a country newspaper, the *Bristol Post-Boy* of 12 August 1704, is filled with odd items of no great significance: but in the last dozen lines of page two, in very small print, appears the famous dispatch written by the Duke of Marlborough to announce his victory at the Battle of Blenheim. The report reads:

'Whitehall, August 10. This Afternoon arrived an Express with a Letter from his Grace the Duke of Marlborough to my Lady Duchess written on Horseback with a Lead Pencil. A Copy whereof follows:

August 13 NS [14]

I have not Time to say any more than to beg of you to present my Humble Duty to the Queen, and to let her Majesty know, That Her Army has had a glorious Victory: Monsieur Tallara and two other Generals are in my Coach and I am following the rest. The Bearer, my Aid de Camp, Colonel Parkes, will give her Majesty an Account of what has passed: I shall do it in a Day or two by another more at lage [sic].

Marlborough'.

And that is all. There is no comment of any kind. It was, of course, quite impossible for the printer to know in advance whether or not the last post-boy would bring really important news. If he did, the space for the last 'Post' had already been allocated—and his news must therefore either be ruthlessly cut down, or included at the expense of some of the advertisements. In 1742, the printer of the *Bristol Oracle* admitted that ' 'tis impossible for us to know what Quantity of . . . News will be retailed out every Post', and he an-

[14] An illustration of the difficulties caused by the eighteenth century calendar.

nounced his intention of doing away with what he called 'the Vulgar Division of the News into Mondays, Thursdays and Saturdays Posts'.[15] But the division was too firmly based upon the printing methods of the time for this laudable intention to have any hope of success.

To make matters worse, the advertisements were steadily encroaching, and to estimate the space to be left for the final 'Post' and that to be allowed for advertisements often required the most delicate discernment. The tendency was for the latest news to be squeezed out. In the earlier years of the century, the printers were able to issue special supplements when the last post brought in news of exceptional interest. In 1712, when the Peace of Utrecht was being negotiated, the *Newcastle Courant* once appeared as an eight-page newspaper, twice its usual size; and in the following issue its printer announced the publication 'in a few Hours' of a supplement containing the demands of the States-General of the United Provinces, which, he declared, 'being very large, could not be compriz'd within this Paper'.[16] In 1717, the *Nottingham Mercury* once added an extra leaf.[17] But the Stamp Act of 1725 tended to discourage this, and when the government took vigorous action against the selling of unstamped newspapers in 1743 the practice almost came to an end. By section five of 16 George II, c. 26, all hawkers selling such papers could be committed by a Justice of the Peace to a House of Correction for a period of three months.[18] Although intended primarily for London, the measure was also effective in the provinces, and five of the news-hawkers of Andrew Hooke, the Bristol printer, were arrested for distributing 'two Letters publish'd in London without Stamps', and re-printed in Bristol, also without stamps, by that enterprising individual. Hooke protested violently against these arrests in his paper, and challenged the authorities to produce a single instance of a prosecution for printing without stamps what he called 'occasional Accounts of single Occurrences', as against regular newspapers.[19] There was some justification for his protests: but the risk of such prosecutions would deter most printers.

Few country printers went to the lengths of the *York Courant*. During the war with Spain in 1740, the printers of that paper wrote that

'in our paper designed for this Day We had left the usual Vacancy for

---

[15] *Bristol Oracle*, 17 April 1742.
[16] *Newcastle Courant*, 8 and 10 March 1711/12.
[17] *Nottingham Mercury*, 9 May 1717.
[18] See Wiles, *Serial Publication in England before 1750* (Cambridge 1957), p. 53.   [19] *Bristol Oracle*, 16 July 1743.

the last Post; but the *Gazette* which came in this Morning having brought the following Narrative of the glorious Success of the British Fleet under the gallant Admiral Vernon, We thought We could not give our Readers a greater Pleasure than by inserting the whole Account ... notwithstanding the extraordinary Expense of composing at least one Half of our Paper twice over.'[20]

In most cases, the last-minute news, however important, was ruthlessly hacked down, and sometimes the printers omitted it altogether, to give it at length the following week. During the South Sea Bubble crisis of 1721, when petitions urging the most savage penalties for the unfortunate directors of the South Sea Company were pouring in upon the government, the printers of the *Northampton Mercury* apologized for having left one out, explaining with disarming candour that the item had been omitted 'not through Neglect, but partly for Want of Room, and partly on Account of its coming with the Sunday Night's Post, which does not allow us the Time we can take with the two former'.[21] Such practices were, however, very promptly and properly denounced by rival printers, and the *Gloucester Journal* made much of the fact that it would 'contain (Weekly) all the 3 Posts regularly ... and not as some News Papers publish'd in this Country (an errant Cheat to the Publick) where the whole of the last Post is always left for the beginning of the next Week; so that the chiefest, greatest and most material Part of their News is a Week old before it comes out'.[22]

However treated, the last 'Post' ought to have been the most important section in the paper. This was generally appreciated, and printers were quick to sneer at rivals whose coverage of the late news had been over-hurried and too brief. As the printer of the *Bristol Advertiser* explained in 1745, 'as we generally give a pretty large Insertion of fresh News Saturday Mornings, and our Numbers exceeding greatly that of any other Paper publish'd here, it cannot consequently be publish'd with that Dispatch as those who put in but a small Part of fresh Occurrences'.[23]

Publication would be delayed until the last possible minute should the post-boy be late, as was often the case in the winter months. The winter of 1726–1727 was particularly severe in the south-west of England. On 16 December 1726 the Exeter paper, *Brice's Weekly Journal*, informed its readers that 'this Morning, about 8 o'Clock, came in the Post, wherefor having but a short Allow-

[20] *York Courant*, 18 March 1740.   [21] *Northampton Mercury*, 1 May 1721.
[22] *Gloucester Journal*, 16 April 1722.
[23] *Bristol Advertiser*, 31 August 1745.

ance of Time, we hope our brief Account will be accepted', and for some weeks afterwards Brice made a point of noting in his paper the time when the post had arrived, heading his last section '3 a.m. Mail from London', or 'about 5 o'Clock this Morning came in the Post',[24] so that his readers might be aware of the difficulties he was labouring under. During this same sharp winter, other papers in the south-west made similar statements and apologies. Usually the post-boy was merely delayed; but occasionally the trouble was more serious, and in December 1726 *Farley's Exeter Journal* remarked that

'the Western Post coming from Yeovil in Somersetshire being oblig'd to swim his Horse at a River . . . was unfortunately drown'd; but the Horse got safe to Shore with the Mail, which did not arrive here till Wednesday almost Noon. P.S. It being now 1 o'Clock, and the London Post not yet being arriv'd, we are obliged to publish without waiting any longer.'[25]

Certainly, the post-boys had a hazardous time. In the winter of 1747, the *Reading Journal* reported briefly that a post-boy had 'froze to Death',[26] and in 1749 the *Worcester Journal* had to inform its impatient customers that 'the Person employ'd to forward the Packet of News for the Use of this Paper, not being return'd, 'tis fear'd some Accident has befall'n him; and (after waiting several Hours for him) we are oblig'd to publish with the News that came Yesterday'.[27] Even more dangerous, perhaps, were the highwaymen. In 1755 the *Derby Mercury* announced that 'this Morning the Post came in without the Mail, and brought Advice that the Post Boy who rides betwixt Harborough and Leicester had been robbed of the same'[28] and similar notices appeared with distressing frequency.[29] And should the post-boys successfully survive all these perils, there was still no guarantee that they would bring the expected news—although it comes as something of an anti-climax to read the *Derby Mercury's* lament in 1747 that, because of an 'unlucky Mistake at the Post Office at Loughborough, the Post (who came in here about 8 o'Clock this Morning) brought the wrong Bag'.[30]

Any delay in publication meant that the newsmen had to be held back and their customers had to wait for their weekly newspaper.

[24] *Brice's Weekly Journal*, 3 March 1726/27, 30 December 1726.
[25] *Farley's Exeter Journal*, 9 December 1726.
[26] *Reading Journal*, 7 December 1747.
[27] *Worcester Journal*, 27 January 1748/49.
[28] *Derby Mercury*, 25 April 1755.
[29] e.g. *London Evening Post*, 19/21 September 1738; 5/8 April, 17/19 June 1740; 7/9 February 1744; 28 February/2 March 1754.
[30] *Derby Mercury*, 25 December 1747.

The great danger was, of course, that such customers, if disappointed too frequently, would turn to a rival newspaper. For this reason, the printer could not afford to wait too long before going to press. The problems posed by the late news were partly relieved later in the period when the more enterprising country printers sent special messengers to intercept the London post-boy some distance from town. However, the system of printing the weekly newspaper in separate sections, reserving a space for the last 'Post', was never abandoned during this period.

If the limitations of the hand-press largely determined the frequency of publication and the treatment of the news, the size and price of the provincial newspaper were decided by the various Stamp Acts. In the halcyon days before 1712 there were no artificial restrictions of any kind upon the printers, who were free to experiment, and to find by actual experience the size and price most suited both to their own needs and to those of their public. As men fresh from a London training, the pioneer country printers naturally took as their models the leading London newspapers of the day—the *London Gazette*, the *Post Man* and the *Post Boy*. The first provincial newspapers were therefore single-leaf papers, measuring some thirteen inches by eight inches, printed in double columns on both sides of the single leaf, and published once a week. Only the price varied, for the country printer still did not quite know how much he might reasonably charge. The *Bristol Post-Boy* cost either one penny or one halfpenny, according, presumably, to the financial circumstances of the customer—or his willingness to pay. The *Norwich Post* cost one penny. And *Sam Farley's Exeter Post-Man* seems to have cost as much as two-pence.

A single-leaf newspaper appearing only once a week was lenten fare indeed in those exciting days of great wars and intense domestic uncertainty, and the growing demand for news—plus the appearance of most unwelcome competition from other newspapers—soon stimulated developments. The evolution of the provincial newspaper in this highly formative period before the Stamp Acts is admirably illustrated by the story of the press in Norwich. The *Norwich Post* began life as a single-leaf newspaper, price one penny. In 1706, however, its reign was rudely challenged, first by the *Gazette*, a paper of similar size and price, and then by the *Norwich Post-Man*, whose price was 'one penny but one half-penny not refused'. The *Post* reacted to the challenge with commendable vigour, and appeared in a four-page form, double its original size, but retaining the old price. A bitter newspaper war then ensued, with the combatants displaying all the talent for invective which was to distinguish the country printers throughout this period. The *Gazette* might dismiss the *Post-Man* as 'a compleat Composition of Ignorance and Error';[31] but it apparently found the old *Post* a far harder nut to crack. And on 20 December 1707 the proprietor of the *Gazette*, one Sam Hasbart, made public the fact that he had entered into negotiations with Mrs. Burges, the widow of Francis. He had reminded her that the newspaper business in Norwich,

'as your Husband well experienced, is no more than what one Man can sufficiently perform; you yourself having given away half the Profit your Husband had by selling a Whole Sheet for a Penny; whereas your Husband never sold a Half Sheet for the less. So that 'tis plain, while there are Three of Us, no one can boast of the Gain that is now made.'

He therefore proposed that the two of them should join forces against the common rival: he suggested a partnership for seven years, and ended with the handsome offer that 'I will before we enter Partnership oblige myself in Bond under what Penalty you please, to lay down the Business wholly whenever you require it of me, you first paying Me or giving Security to pay Me for my Types, etc., and to provide Employ for my Man'. Mrs. Burges's reply to this proposal having been merely 'saucy', Hasbart proceeded to declare war. Not only would his paper double its size, but 'the Whole Sheet of News will be sold for a half-penny and Advertisements taken into the *Norwich Gazette* for nothing'. Later, Hasbart relieved his feelings in an open letter to Mrs. Burges in which he obviously chose his words with more regard to their force than to their politeness or grammatical accuracy:

'Mrs. Burges,
Had you saved your Dull Amanuensis the Trouble of scribbling that saucy Reply to my Proposals, you might possibly have been thought Mistress of some good Manners; but you have unmask'd yourself, and fum'd your obsolete News-paper with the Effluvia of a Dunghil, which always stinks when stirred. I admire, Madam, that you should claim a peculiar Propriety to Printing, and yet talk so very wide of the Matter: Your Husband bequeath it to you! How could that be? I am sure he had no Patent for it. Besides, Madam, you must know the Lords have declared for the Liberty of the Press; therefore it was not in your Husband's Power, neither is it in any other Person's, to lay Restrictions or Limitations on it; so that 'tis plain, you as Impudently as Ignorantly claim a Monopoly; but especially in this City, where you are (as was your Husband too) an utter Stranger, and myself a Towns-man. . . . As to your Insinuations about Perriwig-making, I positively averr it is

[31] *Norwich Gazette*, 5 January 1707, quoted A. D. E(uren), op. cit. p. 10.

wholy false; and you have thereby only informed the whole City what those of the best Rank in it knew before, that Lying is the Topick of your Ladiship's Qualifications. . . .' [32]

Having thus dealt with the *Post*, Hasbart turned his attention to the *Post-Man*, and in January 1708 produced the following lines:

'Hail mighty Fleckno, in whose thoughtless Brains
Nonsense exists, and Dullness Monarch reigns.
Thy Gen'rous Friend, in Verse, craves Leave to sing
Th'admir'd Strains, which from thy Dullness spring;
By that excited, he presumes to pay
Deferred Tribute to thy Pate of Clay:
With other Obligations he'll dispense
To give Thee due, thou Foe to common Sense.
Immortal Bombast, and Ne'er-dying Fustian,
Loudly proclaim You write the *Norwich Post-man*. . . .' [33]

Such cut-throat measures as the *Gazette* had taken could not long continue, however, and by 1710 it had to raise its price to one penny, clearly the economic price of a four-page newspaper. In this way, both the *Post* and the *Gazette* had evolved from a single-leaf newspaper to a four-page paper, price one penny. This more mature form had also developed, again under the stress of local competition, in Newcastle—although with the added refinement that both the *Newcastle Gazette* and the *Newcastle Courant* were published three times a week. The *Stamford Post* was also a four-page paper. Elsewhere, the single-leaf seems to have persisted, although the over-abundance of news and the threat of competition had encouraged the printers of Exeter, Bristol and Liverpool to publish twice a week. Frequent publication did in one respect simplify the printer's task, for the contents of each London post could be printed as a separate newspaper, greatly facilitating the task of selection and allocation of space. And perhaps the frequent publication of a single-leaf newspaper went a long way towards satisfying the demand for news. But the future lay with the weekly newspaper, nevertheless, and the four-page newspaper was the more flexible type. It provided more space for news and advertisements, and allowed the printer to experiment. Even before 1712, some of the more enterprising printers were including material that was not strictly news. The *Norwich Gazette* had a weekly section of general essays and articles; and the *Stamford Post* gave up half its space to what it called a 'Weekly

[32] Ibid. 10 January 1708, reproduced in *The Norwich Post: its Contemporaries and Successors* (Norwich, 1951), p. 10.
[33] Ibid. reproduced in the same, p. 11.

Miscellany' of extracts from the London papers and pamphlets 'and several other useful and diverting Subjects'. And it appealed to any readers able and willing either to 'instruct or divert the public' to submit their contributions'.[34] Such general sections were, of course, out of the question in the single-leaf newspaper. Most likely the provincial newspaper would have developed naturally into a four-page paper, published weekly, and costing only one penny. This, however, was prevented by the Stamp Act of 1712.

The intention of the government when it passed the Act was that single-leaf newspapers should pay a stamp duty of one halfpenny per copy, and that the four-page newspapers should pay one penny. The immediate reactions of the country newsapers to this drastic measure are unfortunately unknown, for very few copies have survived for this critical period. Evidently many papers expired almost at once. The rest presumably paid the duty—as the *Newcastle Courant* was doing at least until 1 September, one month after the Stamp Act had come into operation. But it was not long before the printers detected the loop-hole in the wording of the Act, and by the end of November 1712 the *Newcastle Courant* had become a 'pamphlet' of twelve very small pages; by January 1713 the *Worcester Post-Man* had achieved the same result, although its printer preferred six larger pages; and all the other papers followed suit. Officially, they were now pamphlets, and had to be registered at the Stamp Office. The *Worcester Post-Man* therefore informed the world that it was now 'register'd in the Stamp Office pursuant to Act of Parliament',[35] while the *Reading Mercury* was 'licens'd and enter'd at the Stamp Office'.[36]

The Stamp Act of 1712 thus introduced radical changes into the physical appearance of the provincial newspapers. From now on, newspapers fell into two clear groups: some consisted of twelve small pages, measuring about eight and a half inches by six, and looking more like pamphlets or small booklets than newspapers; the others contained six larger pages, measuring some twelve and a half inches by seven and a half. The price now was usually three-halfpence, although some papers, such as the *Nottingham Mercury* and the *Northampton Mercury* continued to charge a penny. The *Protestant Mercury* of Exeter gave its readers the choice, the printer announcing in 1716 that 'by Reason many Complaints have been made of the Badness of my Paper, which makes the Print appear

[34] *Stamford Post*, 17 April 1712, quoted S. Egar, *Fenland N & Q*, v. 1901, p. 47.   [35] *Worcester Post-Man*, 9 January 1712/13.
[36] *Reading Mercury*, 22 July 1723.

VOL. I.   Numb. I.

THE
Reading Mercury
OR
Weekly Entertainer.

Monday July 8, 1723.   (To be continued Weekly.)

READING.

Printed by W. PARKS, and D. KINNIER, next Door to the *Saracen's Head*, in *High-street* : Where all manner of Printing Business is handsomely done, as Books, Advertisements, Summons, Subpœnas, Funeral-Tickets, &c Shop-keepers Bills are done here after the best manner, with the Prints of their Signs, or other proper Ornaments. Also Gentlemen may have their Coats of Arms, or other Fancies curiously cut in Wood, or engrav'd in Mettal.

[Price of this Paper, Three-Half-Pence per Week.]

2. THE TITLE-PAGE OF THE *READING MERCURY* IN 1723.

the worse, and many Persons that buy my News being rather inclin'd to pay the Price for better, This is therefore to give Notice, that next Week I shall print a very fine Paper, Price Three Halfpence'.[37] And for some time afterwards, his price was stated to be 'Fine, $1\frac{1}{2}d.$, Coarse $1d.$'.

In contrast to the old days of the single-leaf newspapers, space was now abundant, often embarrassingly so. The printers were frequently hard put to it to find enough material with which to fill their pages. Often they devoted the whole of their front page to a highly elaborate title, lavishly embellished with wood-cuts, and including extended editorial announcements explaining to the ignorant the exact nature and purpose of a newspaper. The front page of the *Protestant Mercury*, to take a typical example, informed the public that the paper contained 'The most Remarkable Occurrences, impartially collected, as Occasion offers, from the *Evening-Post*, *Gazette*, *Votes*, *Flying-Post*, *Weekly Pacquet*, *Dormer's Letter*, *Postscipt* [sic] *to the Post-Man*, Etc. So that no other can pretend to have a better Collection'; it then went on to explain that the paper would be

'Publish'd every Tuesday and Friday. Price, seal'd for the Country, 10s. per Annum. And for the Convenience of those that will take the same but Once a Week, it is so order'd, that every Friday's Paper will contain three Posts, or the whole Week's News. Advertisements will be inserted at Reasonable Rates. This Paper circulates Forty Miles round, and several Hundreds dispers'd every Week.'[38]

Small cuts depicting figures of Mercury, post-boys and ships were used by almost every newspaper, balanced usually by cuts of the city arms. But some printers were more ambitious. The *Gloucester Journal's* front page was taken up with an elaborate wood-cut showing ships, winged Mercuries, clerks and writing-masters; the *Worcester Post* displayed a ship and a Fame on either side of a large seated figure of Britannia; and other papers sought to be equally attractive to the eye.

Then came the Stamp Act of 1725, and yet another radical change in outward appearances. Every newspaper was now printed on a sheet and a half of paper; and according to the Act, they would all be liable to a duty of three-halfpence on every copy. This meant, of course, a prohibitive increase in the price of a newspaper, and the printers of the *Northampton Mercury* pointed out that, 'were we to continue it in 3 Half-sheets, the Duty itself would amount to three

[37] *Protestant Mercury*, 4 May 1716.   [38] Ibid. 11 November 1715.

Half-pence a Piece, and consequently we could not vend it under Three Pence'.[39] Such a price was clearly out of the question. And with remarkable unanimity and speed, the printers adapted themselves to the new situation. All adopted the device described by the *Gloucester Journal*, reducing their size 'from a Sheet and a half of small Paper to one half Sheet of very large Paper, without omitting anything that it now contains'.[40] The Stamp Act had, in fact, omitted to give any official definition of the size of the sheet, and there was nothing to prevent the printers buying far larger sheets than they had used in the past, cutting them in half, and finishing up with paper which, although officially only a half-sheet, was in fact almost as large as their previous whole sheet. The printer of the *Worcester Journal* even promised his readers 'Paper of a prodigious large Size'.[41]

All the newspapers promptly appeared in the new form, each printed on a half-sheet of paper, which, folded once, produced a newspaper of four pages, measuring some fifteen and a half inches by twelve and a half. The only exception to the rule seems to have been the *Stamford Mercury*, which continued to favour eight small pages, and so still resembled a pamphlet rather than a newspaper. Otherwise, every newspaper had four pages. The general price was twopence and, as the printers of the *Northampton Mercury* were at pains to explain, they did not intend to

'imitate the Venders of many other Sorts of rated Goods, who for every 6*d.* impost advance a Shilling or more in the Price of their Commodity; but shall content ourselves to raise what the Act of Parliament requires to be the Duty on every Paper, and no more, appropriating nothing to ourselves but the Pleasure of adding this Mite to the publick Revenue'. [42]

It is interesting to note that this patriotic zeal did nothing to prevent the printers from publishing their newspapers for 26 April 1725 two days early, so avoiding paying the duty for the week in which the Act came into operation. The ostensible reason for this piece of sharp practice was, however, that it was 'for the Conveniency of such of our Readers who keep compleat Sets, or bind each yearly Volume'.[43] A few printers retained the old price of three-halfpence, and some still charged only one penny. But twopence seems to have been the economic price of a country newspaper after 1725, and

---

[39] *Northampton Mercury*, 5 April 1725.
[40] *Gloucester Journal*, 12 April 1725.
[41] *Weekly Worcester Journal*, 7 May, 1725.
[42] *Northampton Mercury*, 5 April 1725.   [43] Ibid. 19 April 1725.

any lower rate was usually the result of cut-throat local competition; in Norwich, for instance, both the *Norwich Gazette* and the *Norwich Mercury* cost only three-halfpence; in Manchester, the *Manchester Magazine* cost three-halfpence, while the rival *Lancashire Journal* at first charged only one penny; and when, in 1749, the *Bristol Weekly Intelligencer* was set up in the face of very powerful local opposition, it, too, charged only one penny.

The Stamp Act seems to have been accepted by the printers with remarkable equanimity. Andrew Brice, the Exeter printer, made one reference, phrased in his usual somewhat involved style, to the possible effects the increase in price would have upon his circulation:

'I hope, 't will be allowable for those who wear the shoe to have a Sense of its Pinching? Well! We must struggle with the Difficulty as well as we can. But I hope our Readers will not think it reasonable for us to bear the whole Burthen, nor leave us in the lurch for the sake of so small a trifle as one Half-penny per Week.' [44]

But there seem to have been no complaints, either from the printers or their readers, at the diminution in the size of the newspapers. In some ways, in fact, the reduction in size must have come as a relief to the printers. The Stamp Act was passed in what was certainly a dead season so far as news was concerned, and many of the printers were having difficulty filling their pages. And even from the readers' point of view, four well-filled pages were probably preferable to twelve small pages of undigested news items, trivialities and sheer padding. As the printer of the *Worcester Journal* remarked, its four pages now contained 'as much News as some are desirous of reading'.[45]

Pressure upon space soon began to increase, however. Even before the end of 1725, *Brice's Weekly Journal* and the *Gloucester Journal* had already introduced three columns to the page—in which innovation they preceded many of the great London papers. Advertisements were all the time growing in numbers and importance, and the printers had to utilize every inch of space. Rather regrettably, the decorative titles were among the first casualties in this economy-drive. As soon as the Stamp Act was passed, *Brice's Weekly Journal* and its rival, *Farley's Exeter Journal*, introduced a plain heading, and their example was followed by most of the other country papers. This did not improve the appearance of the newspapers, and the London printer Mist commented with some truth that 'while I look upon myself in this new Dress, the Gracefulness of my Figure seems

[44] *Post-Master*, 23 April 1725.   [45] *Worcester Journal*, 7 May 1725.

to suffer some Diminution from the Change. Methinks I look like some veteran Soldier, who, by Misfortunes of War, has lost a Leg or an Arm.' [46] As the printer of the *Derby Mercury* pointed out, however, the disappearance of the large wood-cut depicting a view of Derby which had hitherto embellished his title-page meant that extra space was available for news articles.[47] Occasionally, the decorative titles persisted, particularly in new papers trying to attract public attention. But after 1740 the plain title was the rule.

By the late 1730's, however, the printers were very obviously pressed for space. Advertisements regularly occupied a whole page, and, with the war with Spain in 1739, news was plentiful and exciting. The increased problems of distribution, not to mention the stamp duty, had made more frequent publication almost impossible —and after 1725 only two country papers were published more than once a week. These were the bi-weekly *Kentish Post* and the *Eton Journal*, begun in 1745. The *Kentish Post*—which remained a bi-weekly paper throughout the period—seems to have had a very restricted circulation, and did not go far afield; the *Eton Journal* was a new paper, founded with the deliberate intention of exploiting the popular interest in the Forty-Five—and once the excitement of that episode was over, the paper very quickly announced that 'this Paper was first published on the breaking out of the Rebellion in the North, and for the most ready Intelligence, published twice a Week: But in the present Happy Situation of Public Affairs, by the late Happy Defeat of the Rebels, it may be sufficient to print a Weekly Journal only'.[48] No printer dared to increase the size of his newspaper above the half-sheet, and so incur a stamp duty of one penny a copy. Instead, as before, the printers took advantage of the loop-hole in the wording of the Act. As early as 1731, the notorious Edmund Curll had noticed this avenue of escape, and had written to the Treasury proposing that Parliament should limit the size of the paper on which newspapers could be printed and the number of lines which could be used for newspaper advertisements, which were also taxed.[49] But the Treasury had done nothing about it, and the size of the newspaper page grew steadily. By about 1730, the average page was about eighteen inches by twelve; and by 1757 it had reached some twenty-two inches by sixteen and a half. At the same time, the size of the type had steadily diminished; and in 1740

[46] *Mist's Weekly Journal*, 1 May, 1725.
[47] *Derby Mercury*, 11 November 1736.
[48] *Windsor and Eton Journal*, 27 January 1746.
[49] *Calendar of Treasury Books and Papers, 1731–34*, p. 65. See also Wiles, op. cit. p. 33.

the printers of the *Derby Mercury* announced with some pride that 'we have considerably enlarged the Paper both in Length and Breadth, by which, in the Length alone, we have gain'd 64 Lines, which added to the smallness of our Character, contains as much as any neighbouring Paper'.[50]

In 1757, yet another Stamp Act (30 Geo. II, c. 19) imposed a duty of one penny on all newspapers, whether printed on a whole sheet or half a sheet. The price of most had to be raised to two-pence halfpenny, but this increase in price was obviously felt to make the cost of a country newspaper dangerously high. In contrast to the earlier Stamp Acts, this one was greeted with storms of protest and abuse. Otherwise, however, the Stamp Act of 1757 did little to change the physical appearance of the country newspapers. The printers carried on much as before, gradually increasing the size of their pages and diminishing that of their print. At times, indeed, the latter became so small that readers of the *Newcastle Journal* protested vigorously at 'the Injury thereby done to the Sight, and of the Difficulty they find in reading so minute a Character'.[51] By 1760, the provincial newspaper had reached what was to be its final form for some years to come. It was a weekly newspaper, costing two-pence halfpenny, and consisting of four pages (one half-sheet, folded once). The only exceptions were the *Kentish Post*, still published twice a week, and a new paper, the *Exeter Chronicle*, which first appeared in 1760, and resembled the papers of the 1712–1725 period in that it consisted of eight small pages.

The period had been one of considerable change and development, as the various restrictions imposed by the different Stamp Acts were met and overcome. In appearance and content the newspaper of 1760 was very different from its puny ancestor of 1701. It remained essentially a parasite upon the London press, but the actual selection of the items and the emphasis placed upon them depended absolutely upon the individual printers—and it was surprising what could be achieved in this way.

[50] *Derby Mercury*, 19 June 1740.
[51] *Newcastle Journal*, 8 September 1739.

CHAPTER THREE

THE PRINTERS

THE true hero of the story of the early provincial newspaper is that unassuming and apparently unheroic character, the country printer. The provincial press had its outstanding personalities; it even had its martyrs; but for the most part it was conducted by ordinary men and women who had no great claims to fame, and whose lives were spent in the patient but seldom glorious struggle to make a living. Such people did not consciously write for posterity; and consequently, we often know disappointingly little about them. Nevertheless, any study of the provincial newspaper must be largely concerned with its printers.

In the early years of the eighteenth century, the publication of a country newspaper depended upon the presence in a particular town of a trained printer from London—one who, moreover, was prepared to risk the financial loss always threatening such a venture. This dependence upon the capital diminished in time, and a new generation of printers made its appearance, a generation which had received its professional training at the hands of practising country printers; but the Register of Apprentices of the London Stationers' Company reveals that the migration of printers from London to the provinces continued steadily throughout the period, and that in all more than fifty of the provincial printers had received their training in London.

The London records throw invaluable light upon the social background and financial circumstances of the printers concerned. When a boy was entered as an apprentice, his father's profession, and the amount of the premium paid, if any, were always carefully noted. A study of these apprenticeship records reveals that the printers came from almost every walk of life. At the top of the social scale came Robert Walker and T. Norris, the printer of the *Ipswich Weekly Mercury*. Both were entered as the sons of 'gentlemen'. Stephen Bryan and Hervey Berrow, the successive printers of the Worcester newspaper, were both sons of clerks; Robert Raikes of the *Northampton Mercury* and the *Gloucester Journal*—two of the greatest of all provincial newspapers—was the son of a vicar; and Henry Cross-grove, the eccentric printer of the *Norwich Gazette*, had a merchant as father. Surprisingly few of the future newspaper printers were sons of booksellers or stationers. They were entered as the sons of 'poulters', grocers, barber surgeons and leather-sellers. One, Joseph Saywell, printer of the early *Newcastle Gazette*, was the son of a blacksmith; and David Henry, printer of the *Reading Journal* and successor to Edward Cave in the great *Gentleman's Magazine*, was the son of a gardener, as also was Jos. Bliss, the early Exeter printer. A few of the future country printers were clearly boys from fairly well-to-do families. The father of Caesar Ward, who was to achieve considerable fame both as printer of the *York Courant* and as a London printer and publisher, was able to afford the extremely high premium of £90 to ensure the best possible training; Joseph Pote, the well-known Eton bookseller and printer, paid a premium of £31 10s.; Thomas James, Walker's partner in the *Cambridge Journal*, paid £30; T. Warren of Birmingham £25 and W. Lee of the *Sussex Advertiser* £20. No other country printer paid more than £10, however, and the great majority paid no premium at all.

Once established in the provinces, the printers took apprentices in their turn. Many of the country newspapers passed from father to son, and the sons naturally received their training from their own fathers. But often apprentices came from outside the family. Andrew Brice, the son of an Exeter shoemaker, and originally intended for the Church, was apprenticed to Jos. Bliss; Sam Creswell, son of a Nottingham baker, went to John Collyer, printer of the *Nottingham Post* and later the *Nottingham Mercury*; John Newbery, son of a Berkshire farmer, went to William Ayres of Reading; Robert Moon to Thomas Gent of York, paying a premium of 20 guineas,[1] and so on. But the London men always tended to emphasize what they clearly regarded as their superior qualifications. The *Sherborne Mercury's* title-page always stressed the fact that its various printers had come from London; and when, in 1748, the *Worcester Journal* changed hands, its readers were informed that 'Mr. Bryan having declin'd the printing this Paper, it is now undertaken by H. Berrow (who serv'd a regular Apprenticeship in London)',[2] a piece of information that was later incorporated in the title. The reasons for this constant emphasis become understandable when we consider the slender qualifications possessed by some of the other provincial printers. It is clear that many of them had had no professional training whatsoever. Some were booksellers, and so had at least some

---

[1] J. H. Spencer, 'Preston's Early Newspapers,' *Preston Herald*, 18 August 1950. [2] *Worcester Journal*, 14 April 1748.

connexion with the trade—although, as Henry Cross-grove pointed out, with particular reference to William Creighton, printer of the rival *Ipswich Journal*, 'not every Person who reads a News Paper is a proper Judge of it, any more than such Printers themselves who are only Country Booksellers'.[3] But others seem to have had very little to do with the printing trade before they actually set up as printers themselves. According to Mrs. Burges, Sam Hasbart, the proprietor of the *Norwich Gazette*, was by trade a perriwig maker, though he denied it.[4] Francis Howgrave, printer of *Howgrave's Stamford Mercury* from 1732 onwards, was originally admitted to the freedom of Stamford as an apothecary;[5] Robert Williamson, of *Liverpool Advertiser* fame, was a broker and auctioneer; Isaac Thompson of Newcastle a land-agent and surveyor; John Berry, printer of the *Lancashire Journal*, was a watchmaker, and later became a grocer, and E. Ward, who printed the *Bristol Mercury*, was at various times accused by his rivals of being a maltster, distiller, vintner and haberdasher—anything, in fact, but a printer.[6] The professional pride of the qualified printers was naturally shocked at such irregularities: and on one occasion, *Berrow's Worcester Journal* launched out into a savage attack upon a rival, 'a Person who has not the least Right to exercise the Art of Printing, he having serv'd no Apprenticeship at all thereto, nor hath otherwise had an Opportunity of acquainting himself with the Nature thereof'.[7] In all fairness, however, it must be admitted that there was very little difference between the newspapers printed by the fully qualified men and those of their completely untrained rivals.

The techniques of printing were the least of the problems with which the printer was confronted. The illiteracy of his public, the difficulties of distribution, finance—these were the problems which demanded enterprise and considerable organizing ability. And, not surprisingly, a number of the country printers of this period achieved a more-than-local fame. In some cases, the earlier migration of printers from the capital into the provinces was actually reversed, as successful country printers found their little world too small for their ambitions, and decided to try their fortunes in London. In this way, some of the most outstanding figures in the London and national literary and publishing world were men who had been, or still were, intimately connected with the provincial newspaper press. Edward

[3] *Norwich Gazette*, 24 December 1743.
[4] See *Norwich Gazette*, 10 January 1708.
[5] Justin Simpson, *N & Q* 8s–vii–271.
[6] *F. Farley's Bristol Journal*, 2 June 1744, and *Felix Farley's Bristol Journal*, 11 January 1756.   [7] *Berrow's Worcester Journal*, 8 November 1753.

Cave, famous as the founder of the *Gentleman's Magazine*, began his career as printer of an early Norwich paper, probably the *Norwich Courant* of 1714.[8] His successor on the *Gentleman's Magazine* was David Henry, who had previously printed the *Reading Journal*. John Newbery, who dominated the London publishing world for many years, and is best remembered, perhaps, for his famous children's books, was also from Reading. He served his apprenticeship there, and for some years conducted the great *Reading Mercury*. And even after his departure for the capital, he retained an interest in that paper. Benjamin Collins, the printer of the *Salisbury Journal*, printed the first edition of Goldsmith's *Vicar of Wakefield*; and he, with Robert Goadby, the newspaper printer of Yeovil and Sherborne, managed successfully to break into the closed ring which then controlled the London publishing world. Caesar Ward and R. Chandler printed the *York Courant*, one of the most powerful of all the country papers of this period; but they were also well-known in London, and won great fame with their publication in 1741 of the ambitious *History and Proceedings of the House of Commons*, in twelve volumes. On the purely literary side, some famous writers were closely connected with the provincial press. Dr. Samuel Johnson wrote in his youth for a Birmingham paper [9]—probably Warren's *Birmingham Journal* of about 1732–1734; Dr. Byrom contributed the Tory arguments in the *Chester Courant's* violent political and religious controversy with the Whiggish *Manchester Magazine* after the Forty-Five;[10] and Laurence Sterne edited the *York Gazetteer* in 1741 in that paper's intensive election campaign against the *York Courant*.[11]

One of the most interesting figures was Robert Walker, in whose career may be glimpsed many of the leading characteristics of the 'press barons' of the future. Walker was one of the first London printers to recognize the existence—not to mention the commercial possibilities—of the new reading public, and to set out to cater for its needs. He was a prolific publisher of cheap newspapers costing a penny, a halfpenny, or even as little as a farthing. This he achieved by the simple process of ignoring the Stamp Act—for which initiative he was arrested in 1741, and, according to the report in the *Northampton Mercury*, charged with having defrauded the revenue of 'some Thousands of Pounds' due on the stamps and advertise-

[8] *The Norwich Post: its Contemporaries and Successors*, p. 11.
[9] H. R. Plomer, *Dictionary of Printers*, ii. 257.
[10] J. Harland, *Manchester Collecteana* (Chetham Society, 1867), ii. 106.
[11] L. Curtis, *Politicks of Lawrence Sterne* (Oxford, 1929), p. xi.

ment duty unpaid on 'Penny Journals, Half-penny Posts, and
Farthing Posts'.[12] Walker was not, however, the type of man to
allow this sort of report to go unchallenged. And in an 'Advertisement' which he had inserted very prominently in the *Lancashire
Journal*, in which he owned an interest, he inveighed furiously
against what he called a 'Scandalous Paragraph' which had appeared in several newspapers, to the effect that an order had been
issued 'against the Body and Goods of one Walker (which has been
supposed to mean Mr. Walker, in Fleet Street) for some thousand
Pounds . . . for printing and publishing News upon Paper not stampt;
and that the said Mr. Walker prints a Farthing Post'. Actually, he
insisted, at the examination 'it did not appear that he was indebted
to His Majesty 30 1'. He had never been concerned in a 'Farthing
Post'. Moreover, he 'now does, and for a considerable Time hath,
paid between 10 and 12 Pounds a Week Duty for stamping Paper'.[13]

Apart from his efforts to provide the new reading public with
cheap newspapers, Walker was a pioneer in the attempt to spread
knowledge in a form that was not only easy to read but was within
the reach of the pockets of the humbler members of society. He
achieved this end by publishing books in cheap weekly instalments,
and, according to the historian of serial publication in the eighteenth
century, to Walker must go the credit of printing and publishing
more books in fascicules than any other proprietor before 1750.[14]
Many of his books were no doubt pot-boilers, works of topical and
ephemeral interest, such as his *Just, Genuine and Impartial History
of the miscarriage of the British fleet in the Mediterranean in 1744*,
for which Admirals Matthews and Lestock were court-martialled.
That was published in eight weekly parts, each containing thirty-two
pages and costing three-pence.[15] Of a similar type were his *Female
Soldier*, describing the exploits of the famous Hannah Snell, who
enlisted in the army as a man; and, in 1755, his *History of the Earthquakes*, published just after the great earthquake which destroyed
Lisbon. But other books were of more enduring interest, and included an edition of *Paradise Lost* in sixteen three-penny numbers
—a piece of sharp practice in which Walker successfully defied both
the proprietor of that work and the law of copyright [16]—and his
edition of Foxe's *Book of Martyrs*, published during the heat of the
Forty-Five in forty numbers at six-pence each. His most famous

---

[12] *Northampton Mercury*, 2 March 1740/41.
[13] *Lancashire Journal*, 9 March 1740/41.
[14] R. M. Wiles, op. cit. p. 70.
[15] *Cambridge Journal*, 25 May 1745.
[16] R. M. Wiles, op. cit. p. 159.

work was, perhaps, his *History of the Holy Bible,* by Laurence Clarke, which became a best-seller. Such enterprises were imitated by other printers, and the country was flooded with these serial publications from about 1732 onwards. No doubt such works encouraged the spread of literacy, by making available to the poorer classes books which would otherwise have been far too expensive for them to buy. A letter in the *Grub-Street Journal* expressed the resentment which such activities could inspire:

'amongst several Monstrosities, I take notice of that strange Madness of publishing Books by piecemeal, at six or twelve Pennyworth a Week. . . . You can have Bayle's Dictionary and Rapin's History from two Places. . . . The Bible can't escape. I bought the other Day, three Pennyworth of the Gospel, made easy and familiar to Porters, Carmen, and Chimney-Sweepers . . . Well, what an Age of Wit and Learning have I the happiness to live in! In which so many Persons in the lowest Stations of Life, are more intent upon cultivating their Minds, than upon feeding and cloathing their Bodies. You shall see a Fellow spend Sixpence upon a Number of Rapin, or Three-pence upon a Bit of St Matthew's Gospel, when perhaps his Wife and Children want a Bit of Bread, and himself a Pair of Breeches. I used to think that nineteen in twenty of the Species were designed by Nature for Trade and Manufactures; and that to take them off to read Books, was the Way to do them Harm, to make them, not wiser or better, but impertinent, troublesome, and factious.' [17]

Walker still found time to pursue his political interests as well, and as a result was frequently brought into conflict with the authorities. He was taken up in 1728 for having in his possession a manuscript copy of Mist's notorious 'Persian Letter', a vicious libel upon Sir Robert Walpole; the following year he was once more in trouble, this time for printing a pamphlet obnoxious to the government; and again in 1732, for a similar offence.[18]

Robert Walker had a very keen and business-like appreciation of the possibilities of the provincial newspaper, particularly as a medium for advertising his numerous books and pamphlets, and he soon decided to print such newspapers himself. But his first ventures in this field were unusual in that they were printed in his London office for systematic distribution in selected country areas. Such a method of producing a country paper was practicable in this period, and it was to become quite general in the next century, when a distinguished publisher maintained that

[17] *Grub-Street Journal,* 19 September 1734.
[18] See *Northampton Mercury,* 7 October 1728 and 22 September 1729; and *Norwich Gazette,* 2 December 1732.

'it was better and more congenial employment to edit provincial newspapers in London, which, absurd as it may seem at first sight, is just as
effective . . . as if the writer resided at the place of publication; for the
political intelligence had to come down from town to be handled in the
country, and it was quite as easy and expeditious to have the news and
the commentaries sent down together.' [19]

But Robert Walker had anticipated this development as early as
the 1730's, when, in his London printing office, he had printed the
Shropshire Journal with the History of the Holy Bible, from 1737 to
1739; the *Warwick and Staffordshire Journal with the Exposition of
the Common Prayer*, from 1737 to 1741; the *Lancashire Journal with
the History of the Holy Bible*, in 1738; and, in the same year, the
Derbyshire Journal with the History of the Holy Bible. It is possible that the *Northamptonshire Journal with the History of the Old
and New Testaments* of 1741 represents yet another of Walker's
enterprises. Unfortunately, the imprint of the only surviving copy,
that of 19 March 1741, is missing. But the title, and the fact that the
newspaper had as a supplement one of Walker's religious publications which had already been issued to readers of his London paper,
the *London and Country Journal*,[20] suggest very strongly that Walker
was concerned in this paper as well. All these publications were
genuine newspapers, although the main emphasis was upon the
accompanying supplement. In the case of the *Derbyshire Journal*,
for instance, the news was confined to the two outer leaves only, and
the *History* occupied the remaining fourteen pages. All these enterprises may represent an ingenious scheme to promote the sale of his
religious *Histories* by giving away with each instalment a weekly
newspaper. Equally, it may be significant that the only extant copy
of the *Derbyshire Journal* is unstamped.[21] Although the *History*
would be subject to no tax, the half-sheet containing the news should
undoubtedly have borne the halfpenny stamp—and these newspapers
and their supplements may well represent another attempt on
Walker's part to avoid paying the stamp duty.

Most of these newspapers were failures, and soon disappeared.
Possibly they were purely experimental, exploratory moves to in-
vestigate the possibilities of the areas in which they were distributed.
If this initial reconnaissance suggested that there was no great demand for a newspaper locally, then the venture was abandoned—
without a fraction of the loss which would have been involved in
setting up a printing-office to print the paper on the spot. But if the

[19] Jerden, *Autobiography*, l. 110, quoted H. R. Fox Bourne, *English Newspapers* (1887), p. 383.   [20] R. M. Wiles, op. cit. p. 68.
[21] That of 31 May 1738, in the Derby Reference Library.

initial survey seemed promising, Walker was prepared not merely to continue the experiment, but to continue it along more orthodox lines, in partnership with a printer on the spot. Thus, he began printing, in London, his *Lancashire Journal* in 1738; but within two months, the paper was being printed at Manchester by John Berry. Although Walker's name no longer appeared on the imprint, his connexion with the paper remained close, and Berry advertised all Walker's publications very extensively. A similar development took place at Birmingham. In 1737, Walker began, in London, his *Warwick and Staffordshire Journal*, aimed at the Birmingham region, which at this time possessed no local newspaper of its own. The paper was apparently so successful that in 1741 Walker himself opened a printing-office in Birmingham, and remained in business there until 1743, when he was bought out by Thomas Aris, printer of the newly-established *Birmingham Gazette*.

This transaction left Walker free to turn his attentions elsewhere, and he fixed on two towns obviously ripe for a local newspaper—Cambridge and Oxford. Surprisingly, neither had yet seen a local paper, although both were market towns and county capitals, both lay on the post-road from London, and in both the presence of a University guaranteed not only a reading public but also a regular supply of private contributions in the way of essays and letters. So promising were both towns, in fact, that Walker dispensed with his usual preliminary reconnaissance, and immediately established printing-offices in partnership with a man on the spot. In 1744 he began, with Thomas James, the *Cambridge Flying Weekly Journal*; and in 1746, with William Jackson, the *Oxford Flying Weekly Journal*. In both cases, Walker's name appeared on the imprint; but he was a sleeping partner, for he seems to have remained in London throughout. However, his various business enterprises were extensively advertised in the two papers, and his influence was clearly visible in the inducements offered to would-be customers. The *Cambridge Flying Weekly Journal* gave away weekly his *Life and Reign of her late Majesty Queen Anne*, an ambitious work consisting of no less than eighty-eight numbers, together with six cuts—'Six Heads in Octavo' —depicting Queen Anne, Marlborough, Ormond, Eugene, the Emperor Charles VI and Philip V of Spain; fourteen large quarto 'Battle Pieces'; and two maps.[22] When this epic was concluded, readers received free numbers each week of Jacob Hooper's *History of the Rebellion and Civil Wars in the Reign of King Charles I*.[23] Oxford readers were similarly well catered for, although their fare

[22] *Cambridge Journal*, 8 June 1745.   [23] Wiles, op. cit. p. 351.

was somewhat lighter. With their weekly newspaper, they received
instalments of such works as Midon's *History of the Surprizing Rise
and Sudden Fall of Masaniello, the Fisherman of Naples*; J. Nalson's
Trial of King Charles the First; Henry Fielding's *The Mock Doctor:
or, The Dumb Lady Cur'd*; and George Lilo's *The London Merchant*.[24]

Even this does not exhaust the list of Walker's interests in the
provinces, for from 1739 to 1743 he published a special edition of
his paper, the *London and Country Journal*, for distribution in the
country. The London edition was published on Tuesday, and the
country edition on Thursday. Both, for nearly three years, had as
supplements *The History of the Old and New Testaments*.[25]

No other individual played quite so outstanding a part in the early
history of the provincial newspaper press. Many were, however, concerned in more than one country newspaper, so that the same names
tend frequently to crop up—the more so as the provincial newspaper was so often a family affair, with sons succeeding their fathers,
and widows carrying on after the death of their husbands. Robert
Raikes and William Dicey each attempted to establish a newspaper
in the tiny town of St. Ives in Huntingdonshire; they then joined
forces to launch what was to be one of the greatest of all provincial
newspapers, the *Northampton Mercury*, in 1720; and, not content
with this, in 1722 they proceeded to found another of the great
papers, the *Gloucester Journal*. Both founded what were virtual
printing dynasties, with the Raikes family taking over the Gloucester
paper, while the Diceys remained at Northampton. In Manchester,
Roger Adams began his *Manchester Weekly Journal* about 1719;
that paper was hardly a success, and died about 1726; but in 1732
the same printer finally succeeded with the great *Adams's Weekly
Courant* in Chester. Roger Adams himself died in 1741; but his paper
was continued by his widow, while a son, Orion Adams, began his
own paper in Manchester in 1752. In Norwich, the Chase family
controlled the *Norwich Mercury* from 1714 onwards; in Nottingham, the Ayscoughs were pre-eminent; and there were many others.

Perhaps none made so great a contribution as the Farley clan.
The story of the newspaper in the south-west—if not of the provincial press as a whole—could be written around the names of the
various members of this family, which was responsible for papers
in Exeter, Bristol, Salisbury and Bath. Not only did practically every
member at some time or another print his—or her—own paper
(often in opposition to the papers printed by other members), but

[24] Wiles, op. cit. pp. 72–73, 351–2.   [25] Ibid. p. 68.

most of them had very strong political views which they did not hesitate to voice. So provoking were these views, that printers of the opposite political persuasion were encouraged to set up in opposition, so that the press in the south-west was precociously political at a time when most country printers sought to avoid the tendentious. Certainly, too, the Farleys played a significant part in the wider struggle for the freedom of the press, a cause to which they contributed one of its earliest martyrs.

Little is known about the individual members of the family, partly because the Farleys showed so little originality in the choice of christian names—a defect which must be heartily deplored by all students of the provincial press. So the name 'Sam Farley' appears upon the imprints of various Farley newspapers, and it is difficult to disentangle the Samuels and decide how many different individuals actually bore the name.

Sam Farley first appears in Exeter in 1698 as the printer of a sermon. Thereafter, his name appears regularly on the imprint of papers printed, sometimes simultaneously, in places as far apart as Exeter, Salisbury and Bristol, until 1741. *Sam Farley's Exeter Post-Man* was printed in Exeter from about 1704 to 1714; in 1713 there appeared *Sam Farley's Bristol Post-Man*, which, under various titles, was to be one of the most enduring of all the provincial papers established during this period; and in 1715 there appeared *Sam Farley's Salisbury Post-Man*, an over-ambitious venture which does not seem to have lasted for more than a year or so.

Another Samuel was born in 1699, presumably 'Sam the Younger', attacked in the 1720's by Andrew Brice for his share in the printing of yet another Farley newspaper, *Farley's Exeter Journal*.[26] That paper was begun by the older Sam in 1723, and was handed over to another son, Edward—known to Brice as 'Farley the Third'[27]—in 1725. Edward Farley continued this paper until 1728, when he died in gaol. The picture so far is reasonably clear—at least so far as the city of Exeter is concerned. But all this time another newspaper, *Sam Farley's Bristol Post-Man*, was being published in Bristol: and it is by no means clear who was conducting this particular venture. We are told that two sons, Felix and Samuel, joined their father in that city in 1718[28]; and that Felix was printing on his own account at Bristol and Bath between 1734 and 1739, and at Exeter—where he revived *Farley's Exeter Journal*—in 1741, in which year his brother

---

[26] *Brice's Weekly Journal*, 17 June 1726.   [27] Ibid. 26 April 1728.
[28] W. George, 'The Oldest Bristol Newspaper', *Bristol Times and Mirror*, 4 August 1884.

Samuel had also set up a business at Bath.[29] What is not clear is whether the Sam Farley who was printing at Exeter and Salisbury was the same as the Sam Farley at Bristol—or whether there were two Sam Farleys, presumably father and son. That Edward Farley and 'Sam the Younger' who were printing at Exeter in the 1720's were brothers is known. So, too, were the Felix and Sam who were active in Bristol and Bath in the 1730's. But whether there were two sets of brothers, born of different fathers, or whether Edward, 'Samuel the Younger' and Felix were all sons of one original Sam Farley is by no means certain.

If we assume that one man could not conduct newspapers in two places at once, then the Sam Farley whose name appeared on the imprint of the Exeter and Salisbury newspapers was not the printer of *Sam Farley's Bristol Post-Man*. In the case of the papers published at Exeter and Salisbury, the question of simultaneous printing did not arise, for in 1714 Sam Farley seems to have come to some sort of arrangement with a fellow Exeter printer, Philip Bishop. The title of the paper was changed from *Sam Farley's Exeter Post-Man* to the *Exeter Mercury*, with Bishop's name on the imprint; and in the issue of 30 September 1715 Sam Farley informed readers that 'I am come to an agreement with Mr. Bishop (to save double Charges) that he shall always print the News; and you shall be as duly serv'd with this as hitherto with mine'. In this way, Sam Farley was free to move to Salisbury; and when that venture collapsed, he returned again to Exeter and, in 1723, started *Farley's Exeter Journal*, helped by his sons, Edward and Samuel. And all the time, according to this theory, the other Sam Farley was printing his *Post-Man* at Bristol, producing, meanwhile, two sons of his own.

This is the more plausible interpretation, although a case for the other theory, that there was only one original Sam Farley, who had three sons, Felix, Edward and Samuel II, can be made out. Of these, Felix must have been the eldest, for Brice called Edward 'Farley the Third', and the fact that *Farley's Exeter Journal* was given in 1723 to Edward and not to his brother Samuel suggests that Edward was the senior of the two. According to this theory, Sam Farley I must have been encouraged by his early success at Exeter to start another paper in Bristol. The Exeter paper could be left in the charge of his sons, for Edward was old enough to have a son printing on his own account in 1735.[30] Having successfully established his Bristol paper, Sam for some reason decided to move his press from Exeter to Salis-

[29] Information kindly supplied by Mr. D. F. Gallop, author of an M.A. thesis in the University of Reading.   [30] T. N. Brushfield, op. cit. p. 180.

bury. Later, he established *Farley's Exeter Journal*, handing it over
in 1725 to his son, Edward, assisted by his brother Samuel II, before
returning himself to Bristol to conduct the more important paper
there with the help of his other son, Felix. After the sudden collapse
of the Exeter paper in 1728 and the death of Edward, Samuel II returned to Bristol to join his father and brother. But the reunion was
to be short lived, and it was not long before Felix left to seek his
fortune elsewhere, leaving his father and brother in Bristol.

Such an interpretation is, of course, based upon pure assumption
—although the frequent separations it involves would not have been
unlikely in a family which was not remarkable for its feelings of
brotherly love. Fortunately, however, the picture now becomes
clearer. By 1741, the older Samuel Farley seems to have disappeared
from the scene. Felix, as the older son, abandoned his paper in
Exeter, and returned to Bristol to take over the family newspaper.
Almost simultaneously, his brother Samuel II departed for Bath.
Felix Farley had very definite ideas about the most profitable ways
of running a newspaper, for he proceeded to issue what were
ostensibly two distinct newspapers in place of the original paper,
then known as *Sam Farley's Bristol Newspaper*. The new papers
were called *Farley's Bristol Journal* and *Farley's Bristol Advertiser*.
They were numbered separately, published on alternate weeks, and
we can only assume that this was an ingenious attempt to evade the
stamp duty, on the theory that a fortnightly publication was not a
newspaper in the strict meaning of the Act. Whatever the reason,
Felix continued until January, 1748, when he was rejoined by his
brother Samuel. For a few weeks, the brothers evidently toyed with
the idea of continuing the dual system, with Felix publishing *F.
Farley's Bristol Advertiser*, and Samuel producing *S. Farley's Bristol
Journal*, each paper appearing once a fortnight. By 30 January 1748,
however, the two had decided to abandon this compromise, and had
joined forces to print the *Bristol Journal* along more orthodox lines.
But the partnership was not a happy one, and in 1752 the brothers
quarrelled violently, and separated once again. Rather surprisingly,
Samuel retained the *Bristol Journal* and the original printing-office,
and it was Felix who moved to a new printing-office, where he immediately produced a paper of his own, *Felix Farley's Bristol
Journal*, in opposition to his brother's paper.

Both brothers died in 1753—and both continued their quarrel
beyond the grave. In his will, Felix left only one guinea to his brother,
as a token of the fact that he was 'in peace, in love and charity with
him'. He added, however, that he prayed God 'that his eyes may be

opened that he may see the injury that he has done me and my poor
family, and that He would soften his heart and conscience to end
the partnership affair with justice, honour and integrity'. Not to be
outdone, Samuel replied with a bequest of one shilling to his widowed
sister-in-law, and one shilling to each of her children.[31] The war was
now waged by the Farley women-folk. Elizabeth Farley, the widow
of Felix, carried on his newspaper in opposition to Sarah, Samuel's
niece and daughter of Edward Farley, who had been left Samuel's
printing business on condition that she remained a Quaker and that,
should she re-marry, 'she do take a husband who professes to be a
Quaker'. This religious difference may well have been one of the
main causes of bitterness between the brothers, for Felix was a
follower of the Wesleys, and in his will had left one guinea each to
'John and Charles Wesley, my honoured and much-esteemed friends
and pastors'.

The Farley family was thus responsible for a very considerable
number of newspapers during this period. At Exeter, various members of the family printed *Sam Farley's Exeter Post-Man* from 1704
to 1714; *Farley's Exeter Journal*, 1723 to 1728; and a revival of the
same paper in 1741. In Bristol, they were responsible for *Sam
Farley's Bristol Post-Man*, which, under various changes of title,
flourished from 1713 until the beginning of the next century, and
also, from 1752 onwards, for *Felix Farley's Bristol Journal*. In Salisbury, they published the short-lived *Salisbury Post-Man* of 1715–
1716. And finally, yet another Sam Farley published *Farley's Bath
Journal* in 1756.

But the Farley family is important for other reasons. Politically,
the family sympathies lay with the Tories—if not the Jacobites. In
Exeter, they were soon in a state of open war with Andrew Brice,
who was decidedly Whiggish: and, indeed, in starting a newspaper
Brice was primarily concerned with 'obviating the scandalous Insinuations spread perpetually by Presses in this City, disaffected to
our happy Constitution'.[32] The ensuing political paper-war in Exeter
was to end only with the death in gaol of Edward Farley during his
prosecution for having rashly reprinted, in 1728, the notorious
'Persian Letter' from *Mist's Weekly Journal*. He was, in fact, the
second martyr of the provincial press, the first being Philip Bishop
—who, significantly enough, had been the close associate and partner
of Edward's father, Sam Farley. Sam himself was to come into con-

[31] For the wills, see *Bristol Times and Mirror*, 15. 22 April 1911.
[32] Andrew Brice, 'The Author's Case', at the end of his poem, *Freedom*,
1730, quoted Brushfield, op. cit. p. 165.

flict with Authority in 1731, when he reprinted in his Bristol paper a most irresponsible letter taken from the *Craftsman* which virtually betrayed England's foreign policy to her Continental rivals. Another member of the family, one Mark Farley, was sentenced to one year's imprisonment in Exeter in 1754 for printing a seditious song on the anniversary of the Pretender's birthday.[33] And, finally, Felix was in trouble in 1756, when he publicly charged the Whigs with gross corruption in a local election at Bristol.

No other family played quite so prominent a role in the development of the early provincial newspaper press. But a glance at the individual printers quickly reveals that many of them were very far removed from the type so harshly criticized by a writer in the next century, who maintained that 'the provincial journalist of that day was in fact not much above a mechanic—a mere printer—and intellect had as little as possible to do with it'.[34] The selection and the emphasis given to the various items of news were the printer's alone, and it is surprising how often his personality and idiosyncrasies obtrude through what is, on the surface, a mere collection of borrowed items. Andrew Brice of Exeter, for instance, who also left some account of his eventful life in a poem entitled 'Freedom', began as a shoe-maker's son, was brought up in the expectation of becoming a Dissenting minister, receiving 'an Education not common to all of our Profession. . . . Nor will it be unfair,' he added, 'however unprofitable to premise, that the Argument how much both by Principle and Natural Genius I appear'd form'd to serve my Generation in the Capacity of a Printer'.[35] In 1715, he was apprenticed to Jos. Bliss, the Exeter printer. Characteristically, he married before the expiration of his service, and ran away from his master to set up in business for himself. His first publication, if the indignant Bliss is to be believed, was 'a shameful obscene bawdy Ballad which deserve[s] to be burnt'.[36] As a journalist, Brice had a stormy career. Although a firm supporter of the Whig ministry, he was hauled before the bar of the House of Commons in 1718, and charged with breach of privilege in that he had published accounts of its debates. Next, he plunged wholeheartedly into a private war with the Farleys, and, in the middle of that, brought disaster upon himself from quite another quarter. Caution was obviously never his characteristic virtue, and his talent for invective was never better displayed than in 1727,

[33] A. Jenkins, *History of Exeter* (1866), p. 207.
[34] *New Monthly Magazine*, vol. xlviii. (1836), 137, quoted F. K. Hunt, *The Fourth Estate* (1850), i. 279.   [35] Quoted Brushfield, op. cit. p. 165.
[36] *Protestant Mercury*, 22 March 1717.

when his sympathies were aroused over the vile treatment meted out
to the unfortunate wretches imprisoned for debt in the local gaol.
He launched a blistering attack upon the officer responsible for
what Brice termed this 'Revenge, Savageness and Cruelty, and a
long Et Caetera of abhorr'd Things'.[37] For these well-intentioned
but undoubtedly libellous remarks he was duly prosecuted, and given
the choice, as he himself explained,

'of paying that other Honourable Man my gentle Adversary above one
Hundred Pounds, go to Gaol, or retire from and guard against the
horrid Catchpole's rapacious Clutches. The first none who can't instruct
me honestly to get the Sum (for like Brutus I can raise no Money by
vile Means) will I presume advise me to comply with; the 2nd., I've a
natural Antipathy against; and therefore the latter how much soever
it rub against the Grain I'm forced to submit to.'[38]

At this point, Brice seems to have retired from public life, leaving
his house only on Sundays, when debtors could not be arrested. Part
of this enforced leisure he spent composing his poem 'Freedom'—
which was 'written in time of Recess from the Claws of Bailiffs and
devouring bloody Fangs of Gaolers'—and eventually he succeeded
in raising enough money to compound with his creditors. Despite
such activities, he still found time to take a very active interest in
the local theatre, and he also published a *Grand Gazeteer* in forty-
four parts, at one shilling each.[39]

Another outstanding individual who deserves mention was Henry
Cross-grove, the Norwich printer, and a man of decidedly eccentric
habits. Cross-grove was first and foremost an ardent Jacobite; and,
despite the fact that Norwich was a Whig stronghold, he made no
attempt to disguise the fact. In a letter to a friend he wrote:

'I am an utter Enemy to Changes and have found, by History and Experience both, that poor England has never gain'd by the barter. . . .
Passive Obedience and Non Resistance is what I contend for, as a shin-
ing doctrine of our Church; and happy had it been for Britain if her
members had practised as well as preached that doctrine. . . . But I have
been too forward in expressing my approbation of Monarchy and
Episcopacy . . . 'tis but treading in my father's footsteps, who lost his
life at that fatal (I mean happy) Revolution.'[40]

Such views were dangerous enough in a private letter; when expressed, or even implied, in a public newspaper, they were almost

---

[37] *Brice's Weekly Journal*, 20 October 1727.   [38] Ibid. 27 February 1730.
[39] The foregoing account is based upon Brushfield, op. cit.
[40] Letter to Strype, dated 15 August 1715, quoted J. B. Williams, 'Henry
Cross-grove, Jacobite, Journalist and Printer', *Library*, 1914, p. 206.

suicidal; and it is not surprising that Cross-grove's life was punc-tuated by a series of prosecutions, from which, however, he emerged unrepentant and quite unchanged.

Such men as Brice and Cross-grove were, perhaps, exceptional: but many of the provincial printers of this time were clearly men of outstanding ability and enterprise. Their problems were consider-able, but it was in this period that some of the greatest country news-papers of today were first established. Many of the papers set up by these printers became famous, not only locally but in London, where the great newspapers did not hesitate to return the compliment paid to them by their country cousins by in turn filching any articles of interest from their pages. As early as 1732 the *London Evening Post* thought it important enough to announce the death in Stamford of

'Mr. William Thompson, one of the Aldermen of this Town, who in the Year 1708 set up a Printing House and Bookseller's Shop, by which and other large Dealings, he has been able to leave his Widow a hand-some Annuity; after whose Death it descends to a Nephew. The Widow has dispos'd of all Effects in Trade to Cluer Dicey, eldest Son of Mr. William Dicey of Northampton, who has, by his indefatigable Care and Industry, raised within a few Years, against strenuous Opposers, two of the most popular Country News-Papers, viz. the Northampton and Gloucester Mercuries, both remarkable for their Impartial and disinterested Collection of Intelligence.' [41]

Quite apart from their fame as newspaper printers, not a few country printers became local figures of importance. John White, printer of the *York Courant*, became Sheriff of York in 1734; John Gregory was elected mayor of Leicester in 1781; and Robert Raikes became a highly respected citizen of Gloucester, while his son, who took over the *Gloucester Journal* after him, achieved national fame as one of the founders of the Sunday Schools Movement.

Naturally enough, most of the country printers made their mark in the field of literature. Thomas Gent, the printer of the *York Mer-cury*, was the author of several books on local history; Andrew Hooke, another eccentric, ran a newspaper and a coffee-house, still finding time to conduct a 'General Intelligence' office, to give lessons in geography [42] and write a history of Bristol; also, he played a very prominent part in the planning and designing of the Bristol Ex-change, for which public service he was granted annuities by both the Common Council of that city and the Society of Merchant Ven-

[41] *London Evening Post*, 27/30 May 1732.
[42] *Bristol Oracle*, 16 October 1742.

turers.[43] Another printer, John Collyer of Nottingham, was made a burgess of the corporation for his 'good services in collecting the antiquities of the Town'.[44]

Enough has been said to show that many of the provincial printers of the eighteenth century were very far indeed from being 'mere mechanics'. The very character of the country newspaper imposed limitations upon them, but there remained considerable scope for the expression of the printer's personality, and many were by no means content to remain anonymous. Their personal prejudices and opinions were always liable to explode, suddenly, vigorously—and sometimes disastrously.

[43] *Bristol Common Council Proceedings,* 19 August 1749; *Records of the Society of Merchant Venturers,* 16 October 1749.
[44] *Records of the Borough of Nottingham,* 16 September 1714.

CHAPTER FOUR

BLOOD AND SEX:
THE CONTENT OF THE NEWSPAPER

THE provincial newspaper of the early eighteenth century may seem to bear little resemblance to the popular newspaper of today. But the differences are mainly superficial: for, however much the newspaper has changed in physical appearance, the tastes of its readers have scarcely altered at all. Then, as now, blood and sex reigned supreme in the pages of the popular press. The blood was preferably foreign blood, poured out in rivers in fruitless battles against the might of English arms. But any blood would serve: and when the readers were unable to gorge themselves upon vivid and gory descriptions of mass slaughter, they turned happily enough to equally vivid and gory accounts of the murder of a poor house-maid by her jealous lover. The same attitude was taken over that other object of perennial interest, sex. Country readers clearly preferred to be regaled with descriptions of the sinful doings of High Society, which they read with a curious mixture of fascinated interest and disgust. But they were quite prepared to relish stories of low life too —and the lower the better.

War was the major attraction. So long as a war was in progress, the newspapers were crammed with items about battles, sieges and grand strategy. Anything else was treated with scant respect, and domestic affairs in particular were almost completely ignored. On one occasion in 1739, the printers of the *Reading Mercury* obviously felt obliged to apologize because, 'as no Mail is arriv'd by this Post, either from Holland, Flanders, or France, we must content ourselves with giving an Account of our Domestic Occurrences'.[1] In fact, wars were reported with a wealth of detail which drove all other topics from the newspapers. British victories were described at inordinate length, considering the size of the newspapers, whole issues of the *London Gazette* being reproduced to the exclusion not only of the domestic news but even of the profit-bringing advertisements. The account of the Battle of Dettingen of 1743 took up so much

---

[1] *Reading Mercury*, 16 July 1744.

space in the *Derby Mercury* and the *Manchester Magazine*, to mention only two papers, that only one column was left for everything else;[2] the capture of the Island of Guadeloupe in 1759 occupied three pages of the *Derby Mercury*;[3] and the siege of Quebec took up three pages of one issue of the *Manchester Magazine* in the same year.[4] But it was not only the major battles that were reported in such exhausting detail: all the various sieges, campaigns and manoeuvres were followed with the same eager interest. Eyewitness accounts of battles were sure of a place of honour. On one occasion in 1747 the *Norwich Gazette* reprinted such a description by a Swiss officer, who began with the striking understatement: 'Excuse the Disorder of my Letter; a Man that writes from the Midst of a Field of Battle, cover'd with between 3 and 4,000 dead or dying Wretches, may claim some excuse for Want of Elegancy of Stile and Expression.'[5] Quite apart from such gory descriptions, however, all the various diplomatic exchanges and negotiations were faithfully reproduced.

Such an interest was perhaps natural in wars in which England was herself concerned. Not only did wars satisfy the popular craving for blood and excitement: they also appealed to that patriotic sentiment which found expression in the hero-worship of the Earl of Chatham. But the same interest was taken in wars in which England had no part. During the final months of 1733, for instance, when the already highly complicated European political situation was rapidly becoming even more complicated, the *Northampton Mercury* was almost full of the diplomatic notes passed between the King of France, the Emperor, the Primate of Poland and the various other dignitaries.[6] As soon as war was declared, the paper flung itself wholeheartedly into long accounts of the battles and sieges; and only with the publication of the final peace terms was the subject reluctantly allowed to drop.

It is not surprising, therefore, that a major war always encouraged printers to begin new papers. Similarly, of course, the absence of a good war acted as a distinct deterrent: and in that year of peace, 1752, the printer of *Harrop's Manchester Mercury* admitted in his first issue that 'in a Time of general Peace, a great Dearth of foreign Advices may be urged as a Discouragement to my Undertaking at

[2] *Derby Mercury*, 5 July 1743; *Manchester Magazine*, 28 June 1743.
[3] *Derby Mercury*, 28 June 1759. [4] *Manchester Magazine*, 23 October 1759.
[5] *Norwich Gazette*, 8 August 1747.
[6] *Northampton Mercury*, 15.22.29 October, 19.26 November, 3.31 December 1733.

this Juncture'.[7] Certainly, it was a bold man who began a newspaper without that guarantee both of intense public interest and of an abundance of exciting copy which a war provided. As the printer of *Berrow's Worcester Journal* so plaintively explained in 1763, when the Seven Years' War had at last come to an end, 'a very material Declension in the Sale of News Papers in general is always the Consequence of a Termination of War'.[8]

In time of peace, 'Foreign Advices' usually held pride of place at the beginning of each 'Post'—despite the protests of the *Grub-Street Journal* at what it called 'the great Impropriety to begin with foreign News and end with domestick . . . like travelling into foreign Countries before we have taken a Survey of our own'.[9] The modern reader may be puzzled by the preponderance of foreign items in any country newspaper of this period. But it has to be remembered that life in England—and particularly rural England—in the eighteenth century was comparatively dull and uneventful. The Church was no longer in danger; and, after 1715, the Protestant Succession seemed reasonably secure. The average reader of a country newspaper craved novelty and excitement as an escape from the dull routine of a hard-working life. That excitement and novelty he found in the foreign news. A war could usually be unearthed in some part of the globe, but even without wars the foreign news was usually more exciting than domestic affairs—or, rather, the domestic affairs the printers thought it safe to print. Domestic occurrences in England offered nothing as romantic and thrilling as the escape of King Stanislaus from Danzig in 1734—an escape which, under the title 'Letters from King Stanislaus', appeared in several provincial newspapers.[10] Church affairs at home were quiet and uneventful: but what memories of the recent and more hectic past were conjured up by the lurid descriptions of the Catholic persecution of the Protestants at Thorn in 1724! Those descriptions averaged a page of the *Northampton Mercury* for more than three months,[11] while the final speech of the Jesuit Advocate actually took up nine and a half pages of one issue of the twelve-page *York Mercury*.[12] No domestic news could compare with the great Lisbon earthquake of 1755;[13]

[7] *Harrop's Manchester Mercury*, 3 March 1752.
[8] *Berrow's Worcester Journal*, 25 August 1763.
[9] *Grub-Street Journal*, 5 July 1733.
[10] *Derby Mercury*, 14.21 November 1734; *Newcastle Courant*, 23 November 1734.
[11] *Northampton Mercury*, 21 December 1724 to 29 March 1725.
[12] *York Mercury*, 22 March 1725.
[13] Cf. *Norwich Mercury*, 6 December 1750.

nor with the sea-monster reported in the Paris papers in 1721, faithfully reproduced by the printers of the *Northampton Mercury* in a
wood-cut, and with the comment

'on Sunday night last we had the following Account from Paris in the
Evening Post, which we deferred then, by Reason the small Space of
Time we had on our Hands would not permit us so fully to oblige our
curious Readers, as we shall now endeavour.
Paris, April 7.
The Publick here has been entertain'd with a strange Account of a
Sea-Monster, who was seen on the 18th. of August 1720, in the Gulf of
South America, call'd Bonaventura. He had a Head like a Spaniel, with
an indifferent wide Mouth, broad flat Teeth, fiery Eyes, like those of an
enrag'd Person; lank Hair, a large flat Nose, Hands, Arms, Shoulders,
and all Motions like those of a Man; a brown Skin, full Breasts like
those of a Nurse; in what distinguishes the 2 Sexes resembling a Horse;
About 8 Foot in Height as near as could be guessed by the eye. He was
from 10 in the Forenoon till 12 within Arm's Length of a French Ship.
The Captain order'd his Men to endeavour to strike him with a Harp-
ing Iron; but he escap'd by diving twice under Water; then drew near
to the Ship again, and raising himself so high above the Water, that his
Knees were seen so far forgot the Respect due to his Tarpaulin Spectators, as to do what for Decency Sake the Author of the Relation has
left unexpress'd, and then disappear'd quite. . . .' [14]

Such an item might well make the front-page today. But in the
eighteenth century, even when the foreign mails failed to bring such
unusual items, the foreign news continued to take precedence both
in position and in the amount of space allocated to it. Wherever
possible, the emphasis was upon the exotic or the romantic, and the
printers would find room for articles and letters which, although of
topical interest, could scarcely be classified as strictly news. Thus,
the life of Khouli Khan was given at some length in both the *Worcester Journal* and the *Newcastle Journal* in 1747;[15] for six months, the
Bristol Oracle devoted a page of every issue to an account of the
people, customs, religion and government of Russia;[16] and other
newspapers included similar articles on such subjects as 'A Gentleman's Travels through Portugal, Spain and Galicia'; descriptions of
the port of Algiers and of Carolina; 'The Winter in Lapland'; and
so on.[17] These must have made fascinating reading for those who
had never ventured outside their immediate neighbourhood; and

[14] *Northampton Mercury*, 17 April 1721.
[15] *Worcester Journal*, 9.16 October 1747; *Newcastle Journal*, 10.17 October
1747.   [16] *Bristol Oracle*, 26 June to 11 December 1742.
[17] Respectively, *Bristol Journal*, 2 and 30 September, 7 October 1749; ibid.
10 February, 10 March 1749/50; *Ipswich Journal*, 9 February 1740.

3. A SEA MONSTER. ILLUSTRATION OF A NEWS-ITEM IN THE
NORTHAMPTON MERCURY OF 17 APRIL 1721.

they also had a very definite educational value, quite apart from their helping to draw people out of their old insularity and parochialism into an interest in the outside world.

Many foreign items, however, possessed none of this romantic appeal. A surprising amount of space was devoted to accounts of foreign politics and high diplomacy, and it is these excessively long and detailed descriptions which usually puzzle the modern reader, who finds it difficult to understand how the average eighteenth century newspaper reader can ever have been really interested in such matters. Many of the intrigues and negotiations so painstakingly described have long since vanished from the pages of the history books. Yet, of course, at the time they took place they were important; and they were certainly popular with the newspaper readers. After what, to the modern reader, seems to be a particularly tedious report of a long and technical quarrel between the King of France and his Parlement in 1732, the printer of the *Derby Mercury* received a letter to the effect that 'your News Paper gains much Credit in our Parts; we are particularly much obliged to you for the important Articles about the late Differences betwixt the King and the Parliament of France . . . several other important Articles which have scarce been mentioned in any of our Country Papers'.[18] And on another occasion, after the *Newcastle Courant* had adopted the practice of beginning each issue with a political or general essay, a reader wrote in approving the scheme, but insisting that such items must 'by no means . . . jostle the Emperor and his Dominions out of your Paper'.[19] In fact, these foreign items were highly regarded. The printers of the *Cambridge Journal* once had to insist upon the inclusion of an article of domestic interest, with the comment that 'the following authentick Piece must have a Place in our Paper, however disagreeable it may be to such as think of little else but foreign Interest'.[20] However unimportant and obscure many of these items may seem, therefore, they were of interest for the people of the time and served an educational purpose. As Dr. Johnson remarked, 'almost every large town has its weekly historian, who regularly circulates his periodical intelligence, and fills the villages of his district with conjectures on the events of the war, and with debates on the true interests of Europe'.[21] Before the advent of the provincial newspaper, those debates and conjectures would have been primarily

[18] *Derby Mercury*, 27 July 1732.
[19] *Newcastle Courant*, 3 March 1732/33.
[20] *Cambridge Journal*, 9 May 1752.
[21] Dr. Johnson, *Idler*, no. 30, 11 November 1758.

concerned with the weather, the condition of the crops, or the latest
piece of local scandal.

There was, however, another, and perhaps more powerful reason
for the obvious emphasis upon foreign news. A glance at the domestic
items in the newspapers of the eighteenth century shows why the
printers dreaded a period of peace, and why they filled their pages
as far as possible with foreign advices. The domestic news was far
more tedious. The London papers, on which the country printers
depended, were too close to Westminster and the Court; they were
prohibited from reporting the debates of Parliament, the government
tended always to be highly sensitive towards criticism of any kind,
and frank comment upon politics and politicians was always liable
to be regarded as seditious. But there were no such severe limitations
upon the reporting of foreign politics. In 1718, it is true, the *Worcester Post-Man* informed its readers that, 'the Muscovite Resident
having complain'd of Mr. Mist, the Printer, for having inserted the
following reflecting Words, viz. that the Czar had been safely deliver'd of a Son, Messengers are now in quest of him';[22] but such
mishaps were extremely rare, and printers generally enjoyed a freedom in their reporting of foreign politics unknown in the domestic
sphere. Undoubtedly, some of the London political papers were
prepared to take the risk, and were outspoken to the point of rash-
ness. But their printers were literally risking their necks, and all too
often their choicest pieces had to be so disguised as to be almost
unintelligible. The *London Evening Post* was to become notorious
for its inclusion of such mysterious and provocative paragraphs as
the following, which appeared in the *Northampton Mercury* in 1749:
'we are inform'd that a certain *Foreign* . . . who makes a very
splendid Figure amongst us, has already learn'd to pursue the old
English Maxim of *ploughing with the favourite Heifer*, which he
thoroughly understands in the *metaphorical Sense*; and that a certain *Naturaliz'd* C-n-ss [Countess], in Conformity to this Maxim,
was lately *entertain'd* by him with great *Splendour* and *Expense*'.[23]
Such insinuations can only have been intelligible to readers who were
on the inside, or who had access to other sources of information.

Not only was the government itself sensitive to criticism, but
private individuals also: frequent prosecutions of erring journalists
served to remind their colleagues that it was wiser to omit the
more interesting and intimate activities of High Society. By and
large, therefore, the London newspapers tended to confine their

---

[22] *Worcester Post-Man*, 19 September 1718.
[23] *Northampton Mercury*, 23 October 1749.

reports to the more trivial happenings in the capital, and to the lives
and deeds of less exalted, and therefore less dangerous, personalities. And for this reason, as Eustace Budgell explained, the domestic
items in the newspapers were very largely limited to

'Robberies, bloody Murders, Accounts of Draymen's Carts that have
run over People, with the Adventures of Post-Boys, Tide Waiters, and
Messengers, etc. The Promotions, Deaths and Marriages of the Nobility,
Gentry and Clergy, and of the Days when some of the Royal Family
go to the Play House, or take the Air. . . .' [24]

Daniel Defoe agreed:

'this Article call'd Home News is a new Common Hunt, tho' upon a
cold scent after Casualties; the Miseries of Mankind are the chief
Materials, such as Death and Marriage in the first Class; the Disasters of
Families, such as Robberies and Bankrupts, that's the second Class; the
Jail Deliveries, either to or from the Gallows, that's the third Class. If
indeed a flaming Rogue come upon the Stage, such as a Sheppard, a
Gow, a Jonathan Wild, or a Blueskin, they are great Helps to us, and
we work them, and work them till we make Skeletons of the very Story,
and the Names grow as rusty as the Chains they are hang'd in.' [25]

And in fact, the domestic news which the printers felt it safe to print
did consist very largely of such items. More important issues were
ignored—and Defoe complained with some justice that 'we read
more of our own affairs in the Dutch papers than in any of our
own'. [26]

Then, as now, the chief emphasis was placed upon crime, especially crime of a sexual nature, which, if it caught the popular imagination, was afforded ample space. The famous legitimacy case
between the Earl of Anglesea and a claimant to his title provided
the *Stamford Mercury* and the *Bristol Oracle* with the greater part
of their domestic news for over six months in 1744. [27] It was a case
which, involving persons in a high station in life, and revolving
round the eternally fascinating subjects of sex and adultery, would
have satisfied the most exacting Sunday newspaper of today. Another great eighteenth century case was the trial in 1752 of the pretty
and youthful Miss Blandy for the murder, at the instigation of her
fortune-hunting lover, of her uncle—a plot which might have come
straight from a cheap novelette. That trial took up a whole page of
the *Cambridge Journal* for a month, crowding out even the adver-

[24] *The Bee*, vol. i. (1737), 242.
[25] *Applebee's Original Weekly Journal*, 21 August 1725.   [26] Ibid.
[27] *Stamford Mercury*, 24 January to 18 September 1744; *Bristol Oracle*, 10
March to 30 June 1744.

tisements in the process.[28] The most sensational case was the mysterious affair of Elizabeth Canning in 1753. Canning, an eighteen year old maid-servant, disappeared for nearly a month; she returned in a state of collapse, and claimed to have been kidnapped by Mary Squires, an old gypsy, and 'Mother' Wells, the owner of a brothel. At the trial, these two were condemned to death, although both produced a strong alibi. Nevertheless, an investigation revealed so many discrepancies and contradictions in the evidence that eventually Canning herself was tried for perjury. The case aroused enormous public interest, and the nation itself was divided over the question whether the girl was truthful and innocent—or whether she was lying and guilty.[29] This interest was most skilfully exploited by the newspaper press all over the kingdom, and every country paper plunged wholeheartedly into the controversy, which raged until the remarkable political campaign against the so-called 'Jew Bill' in 1753 finally interrupted it.

Even when such eminently front-page cases were lacking, crime remained an essential ingredient of the eighteenth century newspaper. Highwaymen, thieves, murderers and pick-pockets throng the pages. In 1720, the *Northampton Mercury* devoted two pages or more every week to a series entitled 'the Ordinary of Newgate's Account of the Behaviour, Confessions and last Dying Words of the Malefactors that were executed at Tyburn on Monday, the 27th of June 1720'.[30] A few years later, the *York Journal* was giving weekly instalments of the 'Life and Actions of John Sheppard'.[31] And, in 1732, the printer of the *Derby Mercury*, in search of items to amuse his readers, hit on the idea of printing each week 'the most remarkable Tryals at the Old Bailey'—which, he considered, 'must be entertaining'.[32] Past history was often ransacked in search of particularly juicy crimes. Typical was the account in *Felix Farley's Bristol Journal* in 1752 of 'the Tryal of Mervin Lord Audly, for a Rape and Sodomy . . . 1631'.[33]

'Dying speeches' were always popular, and were often reproduced in full, together with descriptions of the actual executions. These descriptions regularly contained details which were, to say the least, macabre. Once, the *Norwich Gazette's* account of the execution of

[28] *Cambridge Journal*, 14 March to 18 April 1752.
[29] See Lord Russell of Liverpool, *Though the Heavens Fall* (1956), pp. 14–21.
[30] *Northampton Mercury*, 11 July, 8.15 August, 31 October, 14 November 1720.   [31] *York Journal*, 23 November 1724, 'to be continued'.
[32] *Derby Mercury*, 23 March 1732.
[33] *Felix Farley's Bristol Journal*, 16 September 1752.

a certain malefactor concluded with the comment that 'as he hung very low, he could not easily be seen, which was a Disappointment to perhaps 20,000 Spectators',[34] while the *Cambridge Journal* informed its readers that a condemned man's behaviour 'was very agreeable to his Circumstances. What is very remarkable, he was full 10 Minutes in visible Agitation after being turned off, which is 4 times more than is ordinary in like Cases.' [35]

The rest of the 'Domestic Occurrences' consisted in the main of a weirdly assorted collection of trivialities. Many of these were of the type known today as the 'human interest story'. The reported birth to a woman in Guildford, one Mary Toft, of nine 'perfect Rabbits' in 1726 aroused intense interest, and was given prominence in every newspaper in the country.[36] The story was still remembered in 1728, when the *Gloucester Journal* included the following item: 'from Galicia in Spain we are told a Story of a Woman that in the space of ten Weeks was deliver'd of 6 Boys and a Girl but not one Rabbit among them'.[37] Monstrous births were always certain of a place. In 1731, the *Northampton Mercury* contained a report of an Irish woman who had carried a child for seven years, and finally delivered it out of her navel.[38] In 1752, the *Cambridge Journal* devoted thirty-two lines to a detailed description of the birth at Monmouth of a girl with no arms or thighs, whose feet were turned backwards.[39] And on another occasion, the *Northampton Mercury* once again gave some considerable space to an account of a girl of only four and a half years of age, 'yet 4 Feet high, Neck, Breast, all the other Members like those of a Maiden of 20 Years, and ripe for Marriage'.[40]

Sentimental and inconsequential little items were very common indeed. Quite typical was the pathetic little story which appeared in the *Norwich Gazette* of the finding of two small children who had been missing for several days in the middle of winter: 'they lay side by side, one already perished, the other on the point of perishing, who yet retained just Life enough to caution the Gentleman against waking his Brother, who, he innocently said, had slept since Yesterday Morning'.[41] And on another occasion, the *Ipswich Gazette* re-

[34] *Norwich Gazette*, 1 October 1748.
[35] *Cambridge Journal*, 16 December 1752.
[36] Cf. *Farley's Exeter Journal*, 25 November 1726; *Brice's Weekly Journal*, 16 September, 16 December 1726; *Northampton Mercury*, 19 December 1726, &c.   [37] *Gloucester Journal*, 4 June 1728.
[38] *Northampton Mercury*, 11 October 1731.
[39] *Cambridge Journal*, 22 February 1752.
[40] *Northampton Mercury*, 30 September 1728.
[41] *Norwich Gazette*, 28 November 1749.

printed a letter written by a girl to her sweetheart, with the comment, 'I could not help comparing her Sentiments with those of Ovid's Heroines'. The letter read:

'Lovin Der Charls,
   This, with mi kind lov to you, is to tel you, after al owr sport, son i am lik to pay fort; for i am with Child, and where of mi sister Nan knos it, and cals me hore and bich. . . .'[42]

A Rabelaisian note was never long absent, however. The *Cambridge Journal* saw fit to include among its 'news' items the report that 'one Day last Week, a pretty lusty Gentlewoman going to a Necessary House at the Bottom of her Garden at Clapton, the Boards gave way, and she fell up to her Chin in the Soil'.[43] Only after some hours, and repeated cries of 'Murder!' had the poor woman been rescued. On another occasion, the *Bristol Oracle* reported that

'last Friday an honest Farmer, within a Mile of Shrewsbury, finding a young neighbouring Squire in too close Conjunction with his Wife, took Care to send him Home disabled from doing him the like kind Office for the Future; but 'tis hoped that with a little Instruction he may be qualified for a good Treble for the Opera'.[44]

This sort of note was always liable to crop up, often in the most unexpected places. In 1732, the *Kentish Post* in the middle of an account of the war between Spain and the Moors, mentioned that a Spanish General had captured two of the ladies of the Bey's harem. He had chivalrously insisted on returning them to their master—to the obvious surprise not only of the printer but the ladies themselves, who, said the paper, were greatly disappointed, being 'oblig'd to return to the Circumcision without any Trial of the Prepuce'.[45] Unfortunately, most of these stories cannot be quoted in these politer times. Their general tone is admirably indicated by the advertisement which appeared in the Nottingham *Weekly Courant* of 26 November 1717:

[42] *Ipswich Gazette*, 12 June 1736.
[43] *Cambridge Journal*, 27 August 1748. [44] *Bristol Oracle*, 29 August 1747.
[45] *Kentish Post*, 16 August 1732. See also the *Stamford Mercury*, 22.29 December 1720; *Ipswich Journal*, 3 December 1720, 15 July 1721, 23 February 1740; *Derby Mercury*, 17 May 1733; *St. Ives Post-Boy*, 25 August 1718; *Northampton Mercury*, 11 January 1730/31, 11 April 1736/37; *Norwich Mercury*, 6 April 1751, 27 June 1752; *Union Journal*, 5 February 1760, &c.

'any able young Man, strong in the Back, and endow'd with a good Carnal Weapon, with all the Appurtenances thereunto belonging in good Repair, may have Half a Crown per Night, a Pair of clean Sheets, and other Necessaries, to perform Nocturnal Services on one Sarah Y-tes, whose Husband having for these 9 Months past lost the Use of his Peace-Maker, the unhappy Woman is thereby driven to the last Extremity'.

In this way, blood, sex and sentimentality largely filled the 'Domestic Occurrences' of the provincial newspaper. Popular as these tales of the gallows and the tap-room stories were, however, a newspaper could not exist indefinitely upon such materials. Even crime can pall, and the printer of the *Derby Mercury* was forced to abandon his series of 'Remarkable Tryals' after readers' protests about the amount of space it was taking up.[46] As one such trial had dragged on through more than six pages of the newspaper in one month, we can only sympathize with the readers. Unfortunately, there was little to take the place of such items, and the rest of the domestic news consisted of a collection of extremely brief reports of births, deaths, marriages, preferments and so on. In time of peace, the printers must often have been quite desperate for copy.

Only once in a lifetime did anything so exciting happen in the domestic sphere as the Forty-Five—and that occurred very opportunely for the newspaper printer. The war in Europe had been approaching stalemate, the rumours of an approaching accommodation daily growing stronger. But then came the Forty-Five, which aroused the country to a state of emotional tension which more than made up for the lack of foreign news.

Quite apart from its intrinsic interest, the reporting of the rebellion excellently illustrates how the country newspapers covered an event of more than usual importance. Of course, the newspapers printed in such towns as Newcastle, Manchester and Derby had a personal knowledge of the rebel army, for which reason they were in great demand throughout the rest of the country. Most papers lacked this intimate knowledge, and it is interesting to see just how much they knew of what was taking place. The *Cambridge Journal* may, perhaps, be taken as a typical example.

The first news appeared in the *Cambridge Journal's* issue of 3 August, in a paragraph taken from the *Amsterdam* and *Hague Gazettes.* According to this report, 'the Young Pretender set Sail from Nantes the 15th. Instant with a Man of War of 60 Guns and a Frigate of 30 Guns, in Order to land in Scotland. . . . We don't doubt

[46] *Derby Mercury*, 4 May 1732.

but this Affair will make a great Noise abroad, but Men of Sense think the Pretender will only lose his Labour, if nothing worse comes of it.' There were no further details, and no comment. In the following issue, apart from a brief report that the Lords of the Regency had issued a proclamation offering a reward of £30,000 to anyone who should secure the person of the 'eldest Son of the Pretender', nothing further was added. Nor for yet another week was there any confirmation of the rumours, and there was clearly a great deal of uncertainty and doubt. According to a news item in one of the earlier 'Posts' in the *Journal* of 17 August, 'Affairs in the North remain as dark and perplexed as ever'; but a later post declared that the Pretender's eldest son had certainly landed at Mull with three hundred men. Even so, a serious invasion was regarded as out of the question, and a letter from Edinburgh informed readers that 'People here are so sensible of the Folly of any Scheme to invade England with such a pitiful Force as he carries along with him, that it is made a mere Jest.' A week later, a paragraph from the *Hague Gazette* reported that many people still looked upon the threat as 'Chimerical'. In fact, there was such confusion that very little space was devoted to 'Scotch Affairs'. In the issue of 31 August, for example, the whole emphasis was once again upon foreign news, with nearly a whole page on a Prussian manifesto to the Court of Dresden, and the revolt was not even mentioned until the last 'Post'.

Obviously, there was no trace of panic in the pages of the *Journal*. By now it was certain that the Young Pretender had indeed landed —and that he had won some local successes. But the *Journal's* attitude was summed up in its comment: 'and supposing it is true, they may be compared to the Street-Robbers last Winter, who went on unpunished till the Magistracy exerted themselves and broke their Knot, by tying a much stronger for them at Tyburn'.[47] This attitude was typical of many of the country newspapers, and the country as a whole was being lulled into a dangerous confidence. At worst, the rebellion was looked upon as a rather unusual type of riot, too far away to be of any great significance. The usual epithets for it were 'a mere Jest', or 'a very Don Quixote Enterprise',[48] and as late as 7 September the *Journal* was optimistically informing its readers that ' 'tis said the Highlanders, despairing of Success, have offer'd to lay down their arms'.

Despite the ridicule and disparagement, however, the affair was clearly no holiday excursion of a hare-brained youth, and Scottish affairs had to be taken seriously. The *Journal* began to fill its columns

[47] *Cambridge Journal*, 31 August 1745.   [48] Ibid. 7 September 1745.

with accounts of Loyal Addresses and Loyal Associations. With the issue of 28 September and the news of the defeat of General Cope at Preston, a turning-point was reached. For the first time, Cambridge seems to have realized the danger, and the *Journal* wrote

'the Rebellion in the North growing every Day more formidable, and the Well-being of this Nation depending intirely on the Zeal and Loyalty of his Majesty's Subjects; the Nobility and Gentry, Clergy, Freeholders and Inhabitants of the County of Huntingdon are earnestly desir'd to meet at the George Inn . . . to consult together and enter into proper Measures for the Service and Defence of King George and his Royal Family; and to manifest their Regard for the Protestant Religion and the Preservation of our Laws and Liberties'.

No mention had yet been made of the growing panic in the capital, the supine incompetence of the authorities in Scotland, or the general feebleness of the resistance so far offered to the rebels. The *Journal's* pages were now filled with the propagandist letters of various correspondents. One 'True Briton' combined a strong dislike of Catholicism with an equally strong regard for the sanctity of property, while 'Artifex' stressed at length the disastrous consequences a Popish victory would have upon England's trade and commerce.[49] Both appealed primarily to the self-interest of their readers. At the same time, the newspaper was working up the atrocity story. On 9 November it carried an item describing how a certain Scottish lady had visited the Young Pretender's camp:

'she set forward with a Coach and Six, but just as she was within a few Miles of the Camp, she was met by a Party of the Rebels, who readily show'd their Highland Civility. For this Purpose, they tied the Coachman Neck and Heels, and then seiz'd upon the Lady, pull'd her out of the Coach, and robb'd, ravish'd and abus'd her, in a Manner too shocking to relate.'

The report concluded that the lady had been 'highly disgusted' at such treatment. According to another report, the Pretender 'begins to throw off the Mask, and Popery displays itself in all Shapes of Barbarity and Cruelty',[50] while further details of rapes called forth the indignant demand: 'what does this wicked Crew deserve? How can these plundering Banditti be sufficiently punished?'[51] And on 19 October, the *Journal's* patriotism excelled itself, the slogans

'NO PRETENDER   NO SLAVERY   NO POPERY'

[49] Ibid. 2 November 1745.   [50] Ibid. 9 November 1745.
[51] Ibid. 30 November 1745.

being inscribed in heavy black capitals up and down the right- and left-hand margins of the front page, while across the foot of the page appeared

'NO FRENCH INFLUENCE   NO ARBITRARY POWER   NO WOODEN SHOES'.

Meanwhile, the *Journal* had also begun a series of practical hints for amateur soldiers. The Highland method of fighting had been described, with information on how to counter a broad-sword attack,[52] and a correspondent calling himself 'Citizen' had given no doubt useful advice on the correct way of using a bayonet against a buckler.[53] Events in the north were now being watched with great interest, although there was still uncertainty about where exactly the rebels were, and what they were doing. Rumours of their intended route were frequent and contradictory. The general mood of the reports was still confident—although the patriotic slogans were perhaps prudently dropped as the rebel forces advanced into England.

The danger passed with almost startling suddenness. Before many of the readers of the *Journal* can have realized how deeply into England the Pretender had penetrated, the retreat had begun. The decision to turn back, hinted at in the issue of 7 December, was not confirmed until 21 December—and the intervening issue reported a panic at near-by Stamford at a rumour that the rebels were approaching. Then, with the lifting of the tension, a humorous note appeared for the first time for some weeks, in the form of a mock advertisement: 'Escap'd from his Keepers at Rome, about 4 Months ago, A tall young Man about 25 Years of Age, very near-sighted and dis-order'd in his Senses, of Scottish Extraction, whose Father was Son (by Adoption) of Mr. James Stuart, who kept the Crown near St. James's in London, suppos'd to be gone towards Scotland. . . .'[54]

What is most striking about the reports in the *Cambridge Journal* is their extreme uncertainty. Clearly, the country as a whole knew very little about what was happening in the north. Estimates of the Young Pretender's strength varied greatly—although it was always emphasized that the rebels were 'such a Raggamuffin Crew as never were seen'.[55] Reports of the route taken by the Highlanders were even more contradictory. Undoubtedly, the *Journal* encouraged a sense of false security in its readers. Throughout, its reports insisted upon the extreme loyalty and zeal of the country as a whole, and of the north in particular, and its readers must have been surprised to

---

[52] *Cambridge Journal*, 26 October 1745.   [53] Ibid. 16 November 1745.
[54] Ibid. 21 December 1745.   [55] Ibid. 14 December 1745.

hear of the Prince's steady advance despite all this. Neither the printers of the *Journal* nor the local civil authorities took the rebellion seriously—until, perhaps, the very last moment.

Other printers and other civic authorities showed a keener appreciation of the danger, and made every endeavour to obtain accurate information about what was happening in the north. The *Stamford Mercury* on 14 November informed its readers that, 'having fix'd a Correspondence at Newcastle, we hope during the Commotions in the North to be able to furnish our Readers with some Particulars from thence, earlier than can be publish'd in any other Paper', and thenceforward it regularly included a letter from this special correspondent. The *Northampton Mercury* wrote that 'all these Letters agree that the intended Commotions in these Parts will be prevented or, at least, very speedily quashed in the Bud'.[56] But on 9 December it reported that the town was 'terribly alarmed at the Apprehension of a Visit from the Rebels. . . . In Order to prevent a too sudden Surprise, the Mayor and Gentlemen of this Place sent Expresses twice every Day last Week to Leicester, Derby and Nottingham, to bring Intelligence of the Proceedings of the Rebels.' These special reports were printed in the *Mercury*. At Bristol, a similar express service was organized, and on one occasion *F. Farley's Bristol Journal* announced that 'the following is what arriv'd here Express to the Committee of the Association at the Exchange Tavern, who have appointed an Express to arrive here every Day from the North for the Satisfaction of the City in general, and other neighbouring Places'.[57]

Some newspapers, of course, had a personal knowledge of the rebels. Throughout the Forty-Five, the *Newcastle Journal* was the generally accepted authority, widely quoted both by the London and the other country papers. This success so went to the head of the printer that, after the Battle of Culloden, he issued a special eight-page edition, with the statement that 'the present Conjunction of Affairs both at home and abroad, but more especially the first, having occasioned a very uncommon Demand for News Papers, and particularly for this Journal, we are extremely desirous to return the Obligation in the best Manner we can, by presenting our Customers with the most full Account of Things and finding both those in the *London Gazette* and from Edinburgh to be very long, we have taken the extraordinary Trouble upon us to extend our Journal

[56] *Northampton Mercury*, 2 September 1745.
[57] *F. Farley's Bristol Journal*, 7 December 1745. See similar item in the *Bristol Oracle* of the same date.

from the size of a News Paper into that of a Pamphlet of 2 Sheets. . . .' [58] The *Manchester Magazine* quoted the *Newcastle Journal*, and also such Scottish papers as the *Glasgow Courant*, *Caledonian Mercury* and *Edinburgh Evening Courant*. It displayed no fear, and was full of patriotic zeal and religious propaganda. Evidently, the printer had no suspicion of the route the rebels were to take when they invaded England. Then, suddenly, the newspaper did not appear. And its issue of 17 December stated that

'as we have not publish'd any News for a Fortnight past, it was our Intention to have given our Readers an Account of the Proceedings of the Rebels from their first coming to Town to this Time, but for Want of Room we are obliged to defer it till next Week. In general it may with Truth be affirm'd, that such a Parcel of shabby, lousy, shitten Scoundrels were never seen in England before.'

The following week's paper was largely taken up with 'an Account of the Rebels from their first coming to Manchester to the last Time they left it'. The printer had clearly had a great scare; and a few weeks later he was still referring to 'those Shabby, Scabby, Scratchy, lowsy, shitten Rebels'. [59]

Another paper which had temporarily to cease publication was the *Derby Mercury*. Again, the paper showed no fear and certainly no knowledge of the approaching danger. Its issue of 29 November reported that the rebels were expected in Manchester—but it also announced the steady advance of the royal army under the Duke of Cumberland. The next issue did not appear until 13 December, when the printer remarked that 'the Reason of our not publishing this Paper last Week as usual is too well known to all our Readers to need any Apology from us'. He proceeded to give 'a General Account of the Conduct and Proceedings of the Rebels during their Stay at Derby'—which was extremely hostile. As in the case of the *Cambridge Journal*, the retreat of the rebels gave the printer new courage, and he included a humorous advertisement, taken from the *General Evening Post*: 'run away from their Master at Rome . . . two young Lurchers . . . taken Abroad for King Charles the Second's Breed, but a Bitch from Italy unfortunately broke the Strain in 88 by admitting into the Kennel a base Mongrel of another Litter'. So popular was this eye-witness account of the rebels that a few weeks later it was printed separately 'on a large Sheet of Paper on one Side only'. [60]

[58] *Newcastle Journal*, 3 May 1746.
[59] *Manchester Magazine*, 14 January 1745/46.
[60] *Derby Mercury*, 17 January 1745/46.

With the sudden collapse of the Forty-Five, most printers were once again reduced to filling their domestic section with trivialities. One might think that, when hard pressed for interesting domestic items, the printers would have turned to local news. But there was little demand for such news, and indeed it might be resented, both by the readers to whom so much of it would be already familiar and by those people who were most likely to make it. It is clear that the local gentry and clergy did not care to have their personal affairs publicized in the pages of the local newspapers, and their reluctance is understandable. A country newspaper did not possess even the resources for collecting news of the London papers —and the unreliability of the latter was notorious. Even the task of printing lists of local deaths during a local smallpox epidemic in 1735 proved too much for the printer of the *Ipswich Journal*, who complained of the 'considerable Trouble and Expense' involved, and quickly announced his intention of abandoning the project altogether.[61] The day of the professional reporter was still far distant, and the country printer had therefore to rely either upon his own knowledge of local affairs—which would probably be extensive—or upon private information. One of the earliest full-scale reports of a local event was thus a two-column description in *Brice's Weekly Journal* of the visit to Exeter in 1726 of the Lord Chancellor. The work of the printer himself, it stated that the laudatory poem which concluded the report had not been 'compos'd for the Press till 4 a'Clock this Morning'.[62] Two years later, the same printer published an account of a personal interview with a condemned man in the local gaol.[63]

Usually, however, the printer had to rely upon private information; and appeals for such information were frequent. Again, it was news of the outside world that was wanted, not local news. In 1712, the *Newcastle Courant* realized that ships entering the port might well bring news which had not yet appeared in any of the London newspapers. And it announced that

'whereas many Persons living in or near Newcastle upon Tyne receive Letters from their friends or Relations giving an Account of the Arrival of Ships in divers Ports (and sometimes of other Occurrences that happen in their Voyage), the Knowledge whereof would be very acceptable to others, who may have Concerns in the same Ships; the Printer therefore of this Courant gives Notice that if any of his Acquaintances,

---

[61] *Ipswich Journal*, 6 September 1735.
[62] *Brice's Weekly Journal*, 26 August 1726.   [63] Ibid. 26 April 1728.

or others, will be pleas'd to communicate such Intelligences, or a Copy of it, to him, so that it may be inserted in this Paper for the Benefit of the Publick, They may be sure of a Reception and Acknowledgement of their Favours, with a suitable Return and Gratification for it.'[64]

No other printer during the period made any mention of payment for such information, although all the printers constantly appealed for such items of news.[65]

Occasionally these appeals bore fruit. Perhaps one of the biggest 'scoops' made by a provincial newspaper was that of the *Worcester Post-Man* during the excitement of the Jacobite Fifteen, when the paper reported that letters had been received by some local residents 'from their Friends towards Lancashire, of an entire Victory obtain'd by the King's Troops over the Rebels at Preston . . . the Particulars of which Action you may expect at large in our next, by Way of London'.[66] In this way, the printer had news of the battle of Preston a week before it reached him through the usual channel of the London newspapers. Again, in 1728, *Farley's Bristol Newspaper* received advance information of the arrival in England of the disgraced Duke of Ripperda from Spain. The news came from a passenger on 'a Vessel arriv'd at one Key from Ireland, who last Tuesday landed a grave Spanish Gentleman, with a young Lady and one Officer, at Comb-Martin in Devonshire. . . . He is suppos'd to be the Duke de Reiperda'.[67] Such 'scoops' were, however, rare, although printers did supplement the accounts they took from the London newspapers with private letters. During the War of Jenkins's Ear, the printer of the *Newcastle Journal*, Isaac Thompson, proudly reprinted a letter sent to him from a member of the British fleet which had taken Carthagena. The letter read: 'To Mr. T. Dear Sir, Being desirous of attending my Duty in the present Expedition against Carthagena, I have, according to Promise, sent you an Account by way of Journal, mentioning every Proceeding worthy of Observation; and also a rough Draft of the City, its Harbour, and Forts.' [68] The account and the plan took up the whole of the front page of the *Journal*. Later, another private correspondent, one William Richardson, sent accounts of the war in the West Indies.[69]

Such private resources of information were never so reliable in the

[64] *Newcastle Courant*, 12 January 1711/12.
[65] e.g. *Northampton Mercury*, 28 August 1721; *Derby Mercury*, 23 March 1732; *Reading Mercury*, 13 February 1743, &c.
[66] *Worcester Post-Man*, 18 November 1715.
[67] *Farley's Bristol Newspaper*, 5 October 1728.
[68] *Newcastle Journal*, 30 May 1741.
[69] Ibid. 21 June 1740, 18 April 1741. See also the same, 24 January 1741.

matter of local intelligence. The Bristol printer could only report the speech made by a local notable 'as near as can be recollected by a By-Stander who heard it';[70] a riot in Manchester in 1750 over the public whipping of some women received only the barest mention in the relevant issue of the local paper, the *Manchester Magazine*—which, the following week, was still apologizing for its continued inability 'to give an Account of the unhappy Affair that happen'd here last Week, sufficiently exact and circumstantial'.[71] The same paper had, on 3 June 1746, promised to give a full report of an anti-Popery riot in near-by Liverpool; but that report did not materialize for over a month, when the printer had to admit that 'if a more particular Account . . . could have been procur'd, our Readers should have had it sooner'.[72]

The reporting of local affairs was therefore unsatisfactory, partly because the paper possessed no facilities for reporting such news and partly because it was dangerous, particularly when matters of a controversial nature, or important local personalities, were concerned. In 1720, the *Worcester Post-Man* included an account of a local ceremony attended by 'the two Letchmeres'. The two gentlemen referred to without even the usual courtesy titles happened to be two of the leading Whigs in England—and in view of the notorious Tory sympathies of the printer, Stephen Bryan, it is unlikely that the omission of their titles was accidental. But the next issue of the paper carried a prompt, though hardly repentant, apology: 'we should also have been more particular in branching out the respective Titles . . . but as it was not done out of Disrepect, but thro' Inadvertency, so it's Matter of Amazement to find so great Umbrage should possibly be taken for so small a Fault'.[73] But not all the victims of such reports were satisfied with an apology. Andrew Brice's exposure of the cruelties inflicted upon prisoners for debt in Exeter gaols brought down a large fine upon his head;[74] Grace White and Charles Bourne, printers of York, were fined £80 for libel;[75] Alexander Staples, one-time printer of the *York Courant*, was reported by Thomas Gent to have been 'quite broken up by Dr. Burton';[76] and it has been suggested that the removal of Robert Raikes and William Dicey from the tiny town of St. Ives to Northampton was occasioned not so much by their businesslike appreciation of the superior attractions of the latter town as by the fact that

[70] *Felix Farley's Bristol Journal*, 6 April 1754.
[71] *Manchester Magazine*, 18 September 1750.
[72] Ibid. 8 July 1746.   [73] *Worcester Post-Man*, 15 January 1719/20.
[74] Described in full in Brushfield, op. cit. pp. 184–8.
[75] R. Davies, op. cit. p. 313.   [76] Gent, *Life*, p. 191.

the two printers had incurred the displeasure of a St. Ives notable, and had been heavily fined.[77]

Legal proceedings could be disastrous to the printers, whose financial margin of safety was never large. Their caution, especially with regard to private information, is not surprising. The printer of the *Norwich Mercury* rejected a letter from a reader on the grounds that 'tho' it appears very well intended . . . [it] is by no Means proper for us to print, as the Author has thrown out some Reflections which might be construed a Libel'.[78] Similarly, the *York Courant* refused to print a letter 'reflecting very unjustly on the Character of a Gentleman on the Commission of Peace in the Neighbourhood'.[79] Such rejections were common, but even so the printers often failed to see the implications of letters which they did accept for publication. Quite as common as appeals for private contributions were apologies for having printed such effusions, either because they were libellous, or because they were completely inaccurate. In 1725, the printers of the *Gloucester Journal* thought it advisable to issue an extended statement of their policy regarding their choice of news items:

'we are inform'd by several of the Distributors of this Paper that some of our Readers are very much displeas'd with our inserting (in our Weekly Papers) Home News which sometimes seems too surprising to be credited, or have any Shew of Veracity in it. . . .

As to the Domestic Occurrences we meet with in the London Prints, we take what care we can, to collect nothing from them but what seems creditable, and is generally confirm'd; But as to what is transmitted to us by private Hands, we can only make this Apology, That as a Newspaper is generally like a Coffee House, wherein every one expects to have his Intelligence taken notice of; for which Reason (in Condescention to our Correspondents) we generally have a favourable Opinion of what is so transmitted to us, believing that any one that sends us any Thing, is desirous it should be communicated to the Public; by which Means we are sometimes liable to be impos'd upon, notwithstanding we endeavour to publish Nothing but what is genuine.'[80]

Far more dangerous than mere inaccuracy was, of course, the threat of libel actions. Most printers soon insisted that all private letters should be signed. As the *Original York Mercury* explained,

'we must desire of those Gentlemen who send anything to be inserted for the Future, if they expect to be oblig'd, that they would be pleas'd to give Notice who they are, that in Case (as alas! it often falls out) the

---

[77] H. E. Norris, *N & Q* 11s–ii–481. [78] *Norwich Mercury*, 25 January 1752.
[79] *York Courant*, 5 February 1740.
[80] *Gloucester Journal*, 25 January 1725.

poor Printer of this Journal should be attack'd either by Lilliputians or those of a larger Stature, he may not want a fit Champion.'[81]

The *Norwich Mercury* curtly announced that 'the Letter from Wiveton with an Advertisement was received. The Writer of it tho' he makes free with other Persons' Names, has forgot to subscribe his own. If he does not already know, he is desired to observe, That the Printer of this Paper pays no Regard to Anonymous Letters.'[82] Most printers adopted a similar policy. As the *Reading Mercury* explained,

'we have receiv'd two Letters, which we are desir'd to give place to in this Mercury. But as they contain Personal Reflections (one of them on a young Lady, the other on a Gentleman) we desire to be excus'd for not publishing them since it is our Resolution never to give Encouragement to Things of that Nature. If the ingenious Wits of this Country are inclin'd to write Satyrically, let it not be Personal, but General Satyr; whereby the Vices of the age are expos'd, without taking away the dear Reputation of any particular Person. Such we shall be proud to make room for.'[83]

It was, moreover, quite likely that people who objected to the publicity they had received in the local newspaper might take the law into their own hands. There was hard social reality behind Andrew Brice's refusal to print a detailed account of four local criminals who had been sentenced to death, until 'we see 'em safe truss'd up . . . lest the Regina Rerum procure a Reprieve, and their Reprieve bring on our own Execution, as we are inform'd the famous unhang'd Gentleman threatens to attempt'.[84]

Quite apart from such considerations, the printer had every inducement to be cautious in his attitude towards local affairs. It was the aim of the provincial newspaper to be the county paper, and to make as few enemies as possible. The most innocuous paragraph might give offence—and the York printer even went to the lengths of deleting the names mentioned in a most lyrical love poem sent in to him, informing the proud poet that he 'must excuse my not mentioning Names, tho' even in Matter of Praise'.[85]

The reporting of local controversies was popular, and may well

[81] *Original York Mercury*, 12 November 1728.
[82] *Norwich Mercury*, 10 June 1758. See also the same, 15 February 1752; *Bristol Oracle*, 6 August 1748.
[83] *Reading Mercury*, 29 July 1723. See also *Northampton Mercury*, 16 April 1759; *Berrow's Worcester Journal*, 4 December 1755; *Kentish Post*, 27 May 1738; *Cambridge Journal*, 28 July 1748; *Jackson's Oxford Journal*, 19 May 1753; *Bristol Oracle*, 6 August 1748, etc.
[84] *Brice's Weekly Journal*, 12 April 1728.
[85] *Original York Mercury*, 2 January 1728.

have stimulated circulation. But disputes involving powerful local interests were either ignored or treated with suffocating tact. The printer of the *Derby Post-Man* rashly published the vitriolic letters of a Dr. Hutchinson, who was quarrelling with the Mayor and Corporation over the raising of funds to rebuild a local church. During that dispute, the printer had to apologize for the non-appearance of his paper one week, and hinted darkly at what he called 'black attempts' to injure him.[86] In most cases, however, prudence triumphed. The *Cambridge Journal* barely mentioned the uproar over the new University regulations proposed by the Chancellor of the Unversity, the Duke of Newcastle, in 1750;[87] and it relegated a highly technical discussion over the merits and demerits of a proposal to rebuild the Denver Sluice in the Fens to the advertisement columns. If the protagonists were prepared to pay to have their letters printed, the *Journal* obliged them: but the printer himself took care to keep out of the controversy. His decision was perhaps a wise one, for in 1747 the Cambridge Corporation petitioned against the proposal,[88] and no country paper could afford to risk making an enemy of so powerful a local body.

One of the few papers to throw itself into a local dispute with any enthusiasm was the *Norwich Mercury*. This was between the supporters of the Established Church—whose part the *Mercury* took—and the Methodists, and it consumed a surprising amount of space in that newspaper during 1750 and 1751. There was no mistaking where the printer's sympathies lay. Indeed, most unusually, the paper's policy was clearly stated: it was 'The Discovery of Truth—The Support of the Established Church—and the Defence of the True Religion'.[89] Apart from anything else, the notorious poverty of the Methodists made it unlikely that the newspaper would lose much custom by attacking them. Letters from the Methodists were occasionally printed, it is true: but, on one of the few occasions when that happened, the letter was printed in the vilest possible spelling and grammar, with a note stating that it was 'printed Word for Word according to the Copy'.[90] The opponents of Methodism

----

[86] *Derby Post-Man*, 13 July 1727. The incident is described in A. Wallis, 'A Sketch of the Early History of the Printing Press in Derbyshire', *Journal of the Derbyshire Archaeological and Natural History Society*, iii. (1881), p. 144.
[87] Described in D. Winstanley, *The University of Cambridge in the Eighteenth Century* (Cambridge, 1922), p. 199.
[88] C. H. Cooper, *Annals of Cambridge* (Cambridge, 1848), iv. 250; *Cambridge Journal*, 31 October, 7.28 November, 5.19.26 December 1747, 9 January 1748, 17 February, 17 November 1750.
[89] *Norwich Mercury*, 7 March 1752.   [90] Ibid. 4 April 1752.

descended to the lowest depths in their attacks. Their main target was James Wheatley, the local Methodist preacher. On 2 May 1752, it was reported that a 'cheating Twisterer' had been found out, cheating the Fillers of three-pence in every gross of yarn. He was, the paper added, 'a follower of W—y'. Later, one Elizabeth Inggett denied rumours that she had been scandalously involved with the preacher.[91] In 1754, Mary Mason was publicly accusing Wheatley of having 'deceiv'd and ruin'd' her,[92] while T. Paul maintained that Wheatley had confessed in his hearing to having committed indencies with a Miss Towler.[93] Other correspondents joined gleefully in this vicious attack, which culminated in an advertisement printed on 31 August 1754 in which a whole series of witnesses affirmed that they had seen the preacher indulging in indecent behaviour with one 'R—— P——'. No opportunity was missed to smear the Methodists, and the whole campaign was evidently of absorbing interest to the majority of the *Mercury's* readers—although one correspondent did reprove the printer for wasting so much space upon it, and remarked tersely that 'a News Paper is what we expect of you; not a dull Repetition every Week of such old Nonsense'.[94]

Few other local controversies offered such opportunities in the way of scandal. In 1749, the *Newcastle Journal* printed several letters concerning the bad state of the local roads. One John Brown, who was apparently responsible for their up-keep, replied spiritedly to the criticism, explaining the difficulties he had to work under, and laying the blame squarely upon the idleness and indifference of the local people. But the printers cut short the whole discussion:

'the Dispute about the Westmoreland Roads is like to go off into Flights of Wit and Criticism; which we shall not discourage, provided our Authors can prove themselves to have got the right Knack of tickling their Readers: But as the Entertainment of the Publick is ever in our View, if we find these choice Spirits fail of answering that End, they must pardon us that we close the Games'.[95]

Evidently, the correspondents failed to 'tickle' the public, for no further letters were published.

From time to time, therefore, local controversies were publicized. But the more fundamental issues of the day were studiously ignored. Few papers even mentioned the subject of enclosures: and only the

[91] Ibid. 10 February 1753.
[92] Ibid. 6 July 1754. See also the same, 13 July 1754.
[93] Ibid. 27 July 1754.   [94] Ibid. 9 May 1752.
[95] *Newcastle Journal*, 15 April 1749. The letters appeared in the issues of 14 January, 18.25 February, 18 March 1749.

Northampton Mercury seems to have been bold enough to flaunt powerful local interests in a letter attacking 'the growing Evil of these wicked Times, which is the visible Oppression of our English Yeomanry and Cottagers by our modern Inclosures and other ungodly Ways of racking and distressing poor Tenants'.[96] Later, the *Mercury* returned to the subject of 'the multitude of our modern Inclosures, or the Frequency of that ignoble and self-interested Practice of taking in and discommoning publick Fields'.[97] Both letters appeared in 1726, and certainly their writer showed considerable foresight. But the printer, not content merely to print such letters, went so far as to draw the public's attention to local Enclosure Bills which were to come before Parliament.[98] Other printers did not follow his example. No provincial newspaper adopted a positive attitude towards the exceedingly harsh Game Laws of the period; and little or nothing was ever said about the vicious system of the Laws of Settlement, or about the local administration of justice.

Such questions were, of course, highly controversial. Moreover, any sympathy towards the 'victims' would be only too likely to antagonize local interests which no struggling country printer could afford to offend. In other matters, however, a sympathy for the poor was very noticeable. Typical was the letter in the *Northampton Mercury*:

'the idle Man of Fortune and Dress is preferr'd to the more useful Members of Society, to the poor Man . . . I never see Lace and Embroidery upon the Back of a Beau but my Thoughts descend to the poor Fingers that have wrought it. . . . What would avail our large Estates and great Tracts of Land without their Labours?'[99]

Such sentiments were common and sometimes the printers showed their sympathy in a more practical way. The Norwich papers allowed space impartially in the 1750's to the master wool-combers and tailors, and to their journeymen who were seeking to combine to improve their conditions. The dispute really began in 1752, when the *Norwich Mercury* printed a resolution of the master wool-combers to the effect that 'all Combinations amongst the Journeymen are not only contrary to Law but are great Infringements of our legal Rights and destructive of our natural Liberties'.[1] Thereafter, letters poured in to the *Mercury*, which published at length 'the Articles of the

[96] *Northampton Mercury*, 22 August 1726.   [97] Ibid. 17 October 1726.
[98] Ibid. 22 March 1741/42, 6 April 1752.
[99] Ibid. 22 January 1738/39.
[1] *Norwich Mercury*, 18 July 1752.

Norwich Society for the Support of its Members when destitute of Work', in answer to 'false and scandalous Reports'.[2] Later, it printed 'an Account of the Disbursements made by the various Societies of Journeymen Worsted Weavers'—an account which called forth a highly lyrical poem from another reader:

> 'With Admiration I was pleas'd to see
> Thousands that in Unity agree'.[3]

And this was followed by an advertisement of a pamphlet—'Price only Two-pence, that the poorest Manufacturer in Great Britain may be enabled to purchase it'—attacking 'the slavish Principles advanc'd . . . in advising the Parliament to take away from the Manufacturers . . . a Privilege allow'd to all Mankind, even under the most arbitrary Governments, viz. that of uniting into Clubs and Societies'.[4] Undoubtedly, so far as the local paper was concerned, the journeymen had the best of the argument. Indeed, a correspondent in the *Mercury* commented that 'a great Many People are surpris'd to think, that the Master-Taylors never attempted to vindicate their Cause to the Publick'; and he went on to explain that 'they have taken a more cunning Method, being resolved to advertise in the *London Gazette, the Ipswich Journal*, etc.'.[5] The master-tailors had, apparently, decided that their cause was lost so far as Norwich was concerned, and had advertised in outside papers for workmen who were ignorant of the dispute.

Similarly, the *Post-Master* of Exeter printed a long statement from the weavers and combers of Cullompton in 1724. This explained and justified their attitude in a dispute over the payment of truck wages—which had recently resulted in a serious riot. The weavers emphasized the 'extream Poverty the working Party is reduced to . . . what Damage there was done we are heartily sorry for, and do heartily wish that there was a better Understanding between the Workers and Masters of all Parishes; and that they would no longer Bite and Devour one another'.[6] However, Brice's own unfortunate experience following his well-meaning efforts to champion the cause of the local debtors served to warn the printers generally of the dangers of any crusade on behalf of the poor and oppressed, and disputes likely to arouse local passions were usually carefully avoided. The attitude of the printers was summed up by the *North-*

---

[2] Ibid. 25 March 1749.
[3] Ibid. 16 September and 14 October 1749 respectively.
[4] Ibid. 27 January 1750.   [5] Ibid. 23 June 1753.
[6] *Post-Master*, 10 July 1724.

ampton Mercury: 'publick Reflections may bring an Odium upon
the Paper, the Business of which is to amuse rather than reform'.[7]
And although some of the printers plunged wholeheartedly into
local political squabbles, few showed any great zeal for social and
economic problems.

Of course, such questions could not be altogether ignored. But the
printers preferred to discuss them on the general and abstract plane,
without reference to local details. Indeed, about the only local issue
to be discussed at length was the uncontroversial one of the establishment of County Hospitals. Papers in the areas affected by this
movement gave the project much publicity; and the obvious enthusiasm makes it easier to understand how these hospitals could
be so effective in lowering the death-rate through the country. In
1750, for example, the *Norwich Mercury* printed a letter which, after
remarking that 'as an Hospital for Sick and Lame Poor is much
wanted in the County of Norfolk . . . and as it is possible Establish-
ments of that Kind may only want to be better known in order to
their becoming more general', proceeded to give a lengthy extract
from 'Dr. Clarke's View of the peculiar Advantages of a County
Hospital'. This pointed out that a public hospital was the only certain way in which the poor might be treated; it was cheaper than
relieving the poor in their own homes; and, finally, it was calculated
to spread 'a Spirit of Religion and Virtue amongst the Common
People'.[8] But other papers were quite as enthusiastic. Scarcely an
issue of the *Northampton Mercury* from 1743 onwards failed to refer
to the local hospital, and such papers as the *Manchester Magazine,
Harrop's Manchester Mercury, York Courant* and the *Newcastle
Journal* often devoted a whole page to the subject.[9]

Although attention to local issues increased during the period, the
local section of the country newspapers remained both meagre and
disappointing. Outside the advertisement pages, there were few references to advances in such matters as industrial techniques or agricultural methods. The printer of the *Union Journal* of Halifax was
clearly amazed at his own audacity in describing a local invention
for ventilating mines, and pleaded in justification that 'whatever may
be of publick Benefit, it is hop'd, may be publish'd without Offence'.[10]

[7] *Northampton Mercury*, 23 January 1720/21.
[8] *Norwich Mercury*, 24 November, 1 December 1750.
[9] *Northampton Mercury*, 15.22.29 August, 5.12.26 September, 5 December
1743, etc.; *Harrop's Manchester Mercury*, 14 April, 6.13 July 1753, 12 August
1755, etc.; *Manchester Magazine*, 16 April 1754, 27 April, 11 May 1756;
Newcastle Journal, 16.23 March 1751, 27 January, 3.10 February 1753; *York
Courant*, 29 August 1749, etc.   [10] *Union Journal*, 10 July 1759.

The *Norwich Mercury* on one occasion explained how, by 'varying frequently the Culture . . . a Tract of Land formerly esteemed poor and barren became one of the most fruitful', and on another printed a letter urging the planting of turnips,[11] while the *Kentish Post* told how 'good Manure improves an Estate 700 1. to 1500 1.'.[12] But reports of such major developments in agriculture as the rotation of crops, improved techniques of farming and breeding, enclosures, and all those other advances which history textbooks dignify with the proud title of 'The Agrarian Revolution', are not to be found. Nor would one guess, from reading these newspapers, that anything in the nature of an 'Industrial Revolution' was taking place.

The local section of a country newspaper was brief and extremely uninteresting. It was confined for the most part to births and deaths, horse races, local celebrations of royal birthdays, and, above all, crimes and accidents. And even here, the printer was rarely able to resist the temptation to capitalize upon the popular interest in some crime of a particularly revolting or enormous nature by printing it off separately as a broad-sheet—to which the readers of the news-paper were quite brazenly referred. In this way, the printer of the *Derby Mercury* simply stated of a local crime that 'a particular Account of the said Murder being printed by the Printer of this Paper, we refer our Readers thereto'.[13] Only very rarely did a news-paper find anything as exciting to report as the dragon described in 1715 by the *Worcester Post-Man*. This dragon had apparently caused a considerable amount of damage locally, and was, according to the paper, 'of a vast Magnitude, having Wings, four Legs, a long Tail, large Scales of a brightish Hue'.[14]

Nevertheless, it seems that the public was satisfied. A glance at some of the diaries of the time suggests that on the whole the readers were content with the assortment of odds and ends which then went under the heading of domestic and local news. John Hobson of Yorkshire and Benjamin Rogers were both ardent students of the London Bills of Mortality,[15] and Rogers spent a considerable

[11] *Norwich Mercury*, 1 December 1753, 19 October 1754.
[12] *Kentish Post*, 15 February 1755.
[13] *Derby Mercury*, 18 January 1732/33. Similar in *Norwich Mercury*, 1 September 1750; *Northampton Mercury*, 5.19 March 1721/22; *Cambridge Journal*, 6 April 1748, 28 October 1749; *Farley's Bristol Newspaper*, 8 April 1727, etc.   [14] *Worcester Post-Man*, 26 August 1715.
[15] 'Journal of John Hobson', *Yorkshire Diaries* (Surtees Society Publications, lxv, 1875), entries for 27 January 1725/26, 13 November 1729, 7.14 February 1730; *Diary of Benjamin Rogers, Rector of Carlton, 1720–71*, ed. C. D. Linnell, Publications of the Bedfordshire Historical Record Society, xxx, 1950, entries for 24 November and 29 December 1729.

amount of time copying out from the *Northampton Mercury* its
various cures for the 'Bite of a Mad Dog' and other afflictions.[16]
Hobson must in many ways have been the ideal newspaper reader
of his day, for he was most keenly interested in all oddities, and
regularly noted down in his diary examples of longevity, unusual
stars, the appearance of the Aurora Borealis, tombstone inscrip-
tions, and such curiosities as the birth of a calf with six legs.[17]
Rogers showed a similar interest in tombstones; [18] but, unlike
Thomas Turner, whose only comments on contemporary affairs
were limited to occasional references to the course of the Seven
Years War,[19] he confined his remarks on foreign events to the
single, though somewhat bloodthirsty, note that 'the Grand Seigneur
was depos'd and imprison'd, the vizier and Reis Effendi [or Secretary of State] were strangl'd and cut in pieces and so cast to the
Dogs'.[20] The public called the tune, as the printer of the *Lancashire
Journal* ruefully remarked on one occasion: 'tho' all Intelligence of
Importance lies in a little Compass, and flying Reports, political
Conjectures, and Accounts of trivial and common Occurrences fill
up the largest Part of the Publick Papers; yet in collecting from
these, an Omission of any Paragraph, tho' ever so insignificant, is
censur'd by several Persons'.[21]

Even so, a paper could hardly flourish indefinitely upon such
'trivial and common Occurrences': and it is hardly surprising that,
when really 'front page' news was lacking, the printers had to look
elsewhere for material.

[16] *Diary of B. Rogers*, pp. 60, 62, 71, 95.
[17] *Journal of John Hobson*, 24 August 1726, 10 March 1732/33, 1 December 1732, 8 October 1726, 10 October 1730, 5 November 1734, 20 May 1730
respectively.   [18] *Diary of B. Rogers*, 15 September 1732.
[19] *Diary of Thomas Turner of East Hoathley, 1754–65*, ed. F. M. Turner
(1925), 18 July 1756, 22 June 1757.
[20] *Diary of B. Rogers*, 10 October 1750.
[21] *Lancashire Journal*, 1 October 1739.

CHAPTER FIVE

'INTELLIGENCE, INSTRUCTION AND ENTERTAINMENT'

DURING this period, the provincial newspaper developed from the single-leaf news-sheet, with the briefest of items about the continental campaigns and the war at sea, into the mature newspaper described by Dr. Johnson:

'their cheapness brings them into universal use; their variety adapts them to everyone's taste: the scholar instructs himself with advice from the literary world; the soldier makes a campaign in safety, and censures the conduct of generals without fear of being punished for mutiny; the politician, inspired by the fumes of the coffee-pot, unravels the knotty intrigues of ministers; the industrious merchant observes the course of trade and navigation; and the honest shopkeeper nods over the account of a robbery and the price of corn until his pipe is out'.[1]

This universal appeal was achieved only slowly and painfully. It was never the conscious goal of the printers, but rather the fortuitous result of a combination of external factors. Wars, the Stamp Acts, developing popular taste, the growth of trade and industry, and the personal idiosyncracies of the printers—all played their part.

Of all the factors which influenced the development of the mature newspaper, war was undoubtedly the most significant. But so long as a war was in progress, there was no incentive for the printer to attempt to enlarge the scope and variety of his appeal, and his newspaper showed no signs of rising above the concept of a news-sheet pure and simple. In times of peace the printers were forced, however reluctantly, to provide something more than a mere news-summary and to cater for less predictable tastes. Reading was no longer quite so confined to the few, and a newspaper had to consider not only the gentry, clergy and town merchants, but also the farmers and shopkeepers, artisans and labourers. Without a war it was no easy matter to command the attention of so diverse a readership week after week.

The London printers were faced with the same sort of problem, although of course on a far larger scale. They sought to solve the

[1] Dr. Johnson, *Gentleman's Magazine*, preface to 1740.

difficulty by specialization, and as early as 1710 there were published in the capital not only news-sheets proper, but also political papers, literary periodicals and papers which concentrated upon commercial advices. Such a solution was out of the question for the country printer. His public, though quite as heterogeneous, was much too small for him to be able deliberately to restrict his appeal in this way. He had to cater for every taste: and in his newspaper, news items jostled with commercial advices, literary essays and poems with political diatribes, while underneath the whole there lurked a strong element of the 'yellow press'—the appeal, by means of deliberate sensationalism and suggestiveness, to those customers who were literate but uneducated.

Such variety was achieved only slowly, and often against the wishes of the printers concerned. Until 1712, the essential problem did not exist. But then came the Stamp Act, and, at almost the same time, the Treaty of Utrecht. Space was embarrassingly abundant, just at the moment when the supply of war news had been cut off. The harassed printer could not simply multiply the collection of trivialities which went under the name of domestic news, and the foreign news was unlikely to be very exciting or plentiful now that peace had been signed. He had, therefore, to enlarge the scope of his paper, if he were to survive this double blow.

Even before the passing of the Stamp Act, some of the printers who had already adopted a four-page form had experimented with a general section devoted to essays and correspondence. Among these were the printers of the *Norwich Gazette* and the *Stamford Post*. Such innovations were probably ahead of their time. The reading public outside London was hardly as yet capable of appreciating so refined a diet; and the few country readers with literary inclinations would almost certainly be subscribing to the fashionable London periodicals—as the Gentlemen's Society of Spalding, one of the earliest of all provincial societies of dilettantes, was subscribing in 1709 to the *Tatler*, and in 1711 to the *Spectator*.[2] Obviously, at this early stage, no country paper could hope to compete with such august rivals, and there was no general movement after 1712 to imitate these early literary ventures. Instead, the printers continued to emphasize a purely utilitarian concept of the functions of a newspaper: but, besides news, they now began to provide what they called 'Remarks on Trade'. As the *Ipswich Journal* put it,

'the Sale of this Paper encreasing, insomuch that it may be presumed now from the Encouragement received, to be out of all Danger as to

[2] Charles Knight, *The Old Printer and the Modern Press*, p. 220.

its Establishment . . . our Endeavours shall not be wanting for the future to render this more Beneficial . . . to our Trading Customers, by adding a True and Authentick Account from Week to Week of the Imports, Exports, and Prices Current of Goods on Shore'.[3]

So important a feature of the country newspapers did these 'Remarks on Trade' become that, after 1713, that phrase was frequently incorporated in the actual title of many newspapers.[4] The 'Remarks' included lists of the goods imported and exported, either at the London Customs House or, more usually, at the 'Bear Key'—the Bear Quay off Thames Street, London, where most of the grain ships discharged their cargoes, and where the first great corn market had been established. These lists comprised such commodities as wheat, rye, barley, oats, beans, peas, malt, tares and hops. Some papers gave even more impressive and detailed lists. Under the heading 'Goods Imported', for instance, the *Northampton Mercury* included such categories as 'Linnens, Paper, etc.; Liquids, Fruits; Spices; Silks; Foreign-Corn; Drugs, Seeds, Weeds, etc.; Material Commodities for Diers'; while under 'Goods Exported' came 'Woollen; Metals; Corn; Wrought Leather; Iron; Silks; Haberdashery Wares'.[5]

Apart from the 'Bear Key', most papers gave also lists of bankrupts and of the prices of stocks. For good measure, many threw in the weekly 'London Bill of Mortality', with all its weird 'causes' of deaths in the capital. The Bill which appeared in the *Gloucester Journal* on 21 February 1727 may be regarded as typical:

'Aged	49	Fever	67	Plurasie	0
Abortive	2	Fr. Pox	67	Rheumatism	1
Apoplexy	3	Gout	2	Rickets	3
Asthma	8	Griping i' the Guts	1	Rising of the Lights	2
Cancer	2	Hooping Cough	1	Small Pox	24
Canker	0	Horseshoehead	1	Spotted Fever	1
Childbed	3	Horsemouldshot	0	Stillborn	7
Colick	0	Jaundice	2	Stone	0
Consumption	63	Imposthume	0	Stoppage i' the Stone	2
Convulsion	144	Leprosie	0	Suddenly	0
Dropsie	26	Measles	3	Teeth	36
Evil	1	Mortification	6

Thrush 2   Tiffick 15   Vomiting 0   Water in the Head 0   Worms 2
Christened 352   Buried 507   Decreas'd in the Burials 55.'

[3] *Ipswich Journal*, 22 April 1721.
[4] e.g. *York Mercury, Nottingham Weekly Courant, Stamford Mercury, Northampton Mercury, Suffolk Mercury.*
[5] *Northampton Mercury*, 1 May 1721 onwards.

The completeness and accuracy of these lists soon became matters
to boast about. The *Kentish Post* in 1717 evidently regarded its
inclusion of the London Bill of Mortality as one of its major attractions, for its title-page asserted proudly that the paper contained 'a
Historical and Political Account of the most remarkable Occurrences,
Foreign and Domestick, Together with the London Bill of Mortality'.[6] The *Northampton Mercury* made a point of its thoroughness
and accuracy,

'particularly in our Accounts of Goods imported and exported, where
omitting all trivial Matters, we shall make Choice of the most remarkable Commodities, as Wines, Brandies, Tobacco, Gold, Corn, Woollen,
Wrought Iron, etc. The Bill of Mortality, or Account of Christ'nings
and Burials, shall also be inserted with the precicest Exactness.'[7]

So lengthy did many of these lists become, however, that one suspects that they were often included more as a means of filling space
than for their intrinsic interest. Certainly, the printer of the *Derby
Mercury* maintained in 1732 that

'the Accounts of Goods exported and imported, which take up so much
Room in some of our Country Weekly Papers, are so stale and imper-
fect (I might say false), that the Publication of 'em is rather an Imposition on the Public than any real Advantage; also the Diseases so
particularly mention'd in the London Bill of Mortality, with an Account
of the Ages of Persons dead, are what very few read over'.[8]

At first, the emphasis of these trade lists was wholly upon London,
which completely dominated the economic life of the country. No
matter how far removed from the capital the papers might be, they
all included these lists. As the tempo of provincial economic life
began to quicken, however, the London lists were supplemented by
lists of more local interest. The 'Bear Key' list and the prices of
stocks remained firm favourites throughout, and up to the very end
of the period there were few country newspapers which did not
include both. But, from about the second decade of the century,
some newspapers began to give lists of prices at local markets. These
lists were sometimes extremely long and detailed, and, although
seldom completely regular in their appearance, they do provide an
accurate picture of the prices of basic foodstuffs. Until the 1730's,
the *Northampton Mercury* gave fairly regularly a list of the prices
ruling at Oxford, Peterborough, St. Neots and Reading; less regularly, it gave those at Hitchin, Northampton itself, Henley, High

[6] *Kentish Post*, 23 October 1717.
[7] *Northampton Mercury*, 24 April 1721.
[8] *Derby Mercury*, 23 March 1732.

Wycombe and Stony Stratford; and very occasionally those at Witney, Leicester, Salisbury, Gloucester and Mansfield. From 1745 onwards, it usually gave the prices at St. Albans, Hempstead, Hitchin and Aylesbury. Similarly, the *Stamford Mercury* between 1716 and 1724 often devoted a whole page to such lists.

Later, the emphasis began to move away from the purely local market, and away from simple foodstuffs. By 1739, the *York Courant* was giving details of the imports and exports at the port of Hull,[9] and in 1741 it added those at Liverpool. Similar lists appeared also in the *Leeds Mercury* and the various Manchester newspapers.[10] In the south, the Bristol newspapers had always given a good deal of attention to shipping news, although until the 1740's they made only small mention of their own port. From that time onwards, however, they regularly printed long lists of shipping arrivals and departures at Bristol, together with tables of the time of high tide. And in 1744, the printer of the *Bristol Oracle* announced that

'for the Future, an exact Account of every Ship enter'd outwards, the Place where bound, the Master's Name, and as soon as it can be known, the time of its intended Arrival, will be publish'd Weekly for the better Information of all Persons who may have Occasion to correspond with their Friends beyond the Seas . . . And as a further Encouragement to all Pursers and Masters of Ships to give proper Notice to the Public, for the better Carrying on so useful a Project, he likewise promises to insert all such Notices gratis'.[11]

In this way, the earlier abject dependence upon London for the 'Remarks on Trade' was gradually thrown off. By the early 1750's, the newspapers of the two great sea-ports, Bristol and Newcastle, were virtually trade papers, with their main emphasis upon local trade and commerce; but the Manchester newspapers were not far behind, and *Harrop's Manchester Mercury* in particular devoted considerable space to such matters, giving the shipping lists of Hull and Liverpool, the 'Course of Exchange', and Lloyd's List. Clearly, the evolution of the provincial trade paper was only a matter of time—despite an unexpected legal hitch in 1752, when Harrop was forced to announce that,

'being inform'd that we cannot legally extract the Ship News out of Lloyd's Marine List, nor the Imports and Exports at Liverpool, etc. and threaten'd with a Prosecution if we do not desist (which Notice we likewise hear has been given to the Publishers of other Weekly Papers in

[9] *York Courant*, 18 September 1739.
[10] Cf. *Lancashire Journal*, 10 December 1739.
[11] *Bristol Oracle*, 21 July 1744.

this Town), therefore we shall postpone printing any Extracts from them until we are thoroughly inform'd of the Legality or Illegality thereof'.[12]

That Lloyd's should have considered it necessary to issue such a threat is some indication of the growing influence of the provincial newspaper. Earlier in the century, the country printers could extract their items from the London papers with impunity: but towards the middle of the century, the London printers apparently began to fear the effects of this piracy upon their own circulation, and sought to intimidate their country colleagues. In this case, the threatened prosecution did not materialize: and the way was now open for the birth of a provincial trade paper. With the publication in 1756 of *Williamson's Liverpool Advertiser*—to be followed in 1757 by the *Liverpool Chronicle*—that paper may be said to have been born. Both these papers devoted so much space to the extracts from Lloyd's List, the course of exchange, tables of the wind and weather, the winds at Deal, and local shipping notices and advertisements that they had little to spare for ordinary news items. The information thus supplied was obviously both detailed and accurate, for, during the Seven Years War, the printer of the *Liverpool Advertiser* received a most unexpected testimony in the form of a letter signed by some forty of the local magnates. The letter—which he printed in his paper in answer to complaints over his omission of the lists of ships due to sail from Liverpool—read: 'To Mr. Robert Williamson . . . The Publishing a List of the Ships that enter Outwards and sail from this Port every Week, we have too much Reason to apprehend, has been a very bad Consequence this War: We therefore desire that for the Future, you will omit it in your Paper.' [13] Evidently, the accuracy of the reports had been much appreciated by French privateers. The whole incident suggests that the country newspaper had moved far since its early days, when its items were brief, contradictory and unreliable.

The first reaction of the printers to the enlargement of their papers in 1712 and to the simultaneous end of the war news was, therefore, to provide for what they called the 'Trading Part' of their public. 'Remarks on Trade' became an accepted part of every country newspaper throughout the whole period: but significant developments in this direction were largely restricted to the newspapers published in the sea-ports, and in such growing centres of industrial activity as Manchester and Leeds. In most other papers, the trade lists were limited to the 'Bear Key', the price of stocks, bankrupts and per-

---

[12] *Harrop's Manchester Mercury*, 7 April 1752.
[13] *Williamson's Liverpool Advertiser*, 2 March 1759.

haps the London Bill of Mortality. And the printers of these papers had to find some other means of satisfying a reading public which was steadily demanding something more from its newspapers than a bare news-summary.

Early efforts to expand a newspaper's appeal by means of a general section devoted to essays and correspondence had hardly been satisfactory. The attempt of Henry Cross-grove to devote a section of the *Norwich Gazette* to literary miscellanea had suggested that the provincial public was not yet ready for anything in the nature of 'belles-lettres', for the section had degenerated rapidly into a collection of anecdotes and riddles. Typical was a reader's question as to how many days there were in a year—and the printer's answer: 'there are but Seven. . . . I know of no more; if you do, pray name 'em.' [14] The general intellectual level of most of the contributions was summed up by the indignant printer himself, in an editorial statement 'to acquaint such plaguy Enigmatical Wits that the *Norwich Gazette* is not design'd an Entertainment for Children and Fools, but for the judicious and ingenious of this City, and therefore no such childish Whimsies shall be answer'd'.[15] In 1718, a correspondent of the *St. Ives Post-Boy* had urged the printer 'not only to give an Impartial and Historical Account of the most material Foreign Occurrences, but at the same Time to recreate your Readers with Mirth and Pleasantry', and he had enclosed an extremely dubious anecdote as a sample of the sort of mirth and pleasantry he had in mind.[16] He was, perhaps, going rather too far. But by 1719 the newly established *Ludlow Post-Man* was regularly devoting its front-page—and often more—to light-hearted correspondence and humorous advice to its readers. In one issue, 'Silvia Cautious' wrote in to ask whether, if her lover should try to climb into her bedroom in the night and in the attempt fall over and so wake up her family, she should cry 'Rape!' or keep quiet and let her family batter the door down. The editor's answer was that she should lie still, for if she made an outcry she might lose the young man's love. Another reader wanted to know whether he might lawfully marry his grandmother. The editor replied suitably.[17] Later, the paper printed a letter addressed 'To the Younger of the two Ladies in Callicoe (who sat in the 3rd. Seat in the Pit, at the School-boys Play on Thursday last, and had with them a Brother, or some Acquaintance that was

---

[14] *Norwich Gazette*, quoted A.D.E.(uren), *The First Provincial Newspaper*, p. 17.
[15] Ibid.   [16] *St. Ives Post-Boy*, 25 August 1718.
[17] *Ludlow Post-Man*, 20 November 1719.

as careless of that pretty Creature as a Brother, which seeming Brother usher'd them out)'. The writer went on, 'with profound Respect', to propose marriage. And even the printer was forced to admit that 'the Author of the foregoing letter has made a use of me which I did not foresee I should fall into'.[18]

The general idea soon caught on, and nearly every printer was obliged to devote a section of his paper to what was known as 'entertainment'. Thus, in 1720, the *Northampton Mercury* announced that its news would be 'continually interspers'd with some delightful and instructive Entertainment'.[19] But perhaps the editorial announcement which introduced the *Reading Mercury* in 1723 best sums up the aims and content of the provincial newspaper at this stage of its development. The printers of that paper promised to present their readers with

'Historical and Political Observations on the most remarkable Transactions in Europe; Collected from the best and most authentick Accounts, written and printed; with Imports and Exports of Merchandize to and from London, and other Remarks on Trade; also the best Account of Corn in the most noted Markets 20 or 30 Miles circular. And when a Scarcity of News happens, we shall divert you with something Merry.'[20]

The main emphasis was still upon news and trade, and the 'entertainment' was purely a stop-gap measure.

Despite this emphasis upon foreign and political news, however, it is clear that a new reading public was steadily growing up outside London—and that this new public was beginning to demand a more varied and satisfying diet. The provincial printers were soon forced to pay more attention to recently published books. Lists of such books appeared in the *Exeter Mercury* as early as 1716, the *Stamford Mercury* in 1720, the *Derby Post-Man* in 1721 and the *Worcester Post* in 1723. And by 1725 they had become so long that the *Northampton Mercury* announced that they would be printed separately and issued gratis every month.[21] Such lists did not, however, satisfy the needs of many of the readers of a country newspaper—readers who, as the *Northampton Mercury* itself explained, 'would gladly be improv'd . . . but either for Want of Time to read large and voluminous Books, or that they care not (and many not well able), to lay out so much Money at one Time', did not read many actual books.[22] Such readers looked to their weekly newspaper to supply

---

[18] *Ludlow Post-Man*, 25 December 1719.
[19] *Northampton Mercury*, 2 May 1720.   [20] *Reading Mercury*, 8 July 1723.
[21] Ibid. 17 May 1725.   [22] Ibid. 5 April 1736.

their literary and intellectual needs. At the same time, the printers seem to have woken up to the possibilities of a general or miscellaneous section in their newspapers. Such a section could be used for literary extracts; it could be used for private contributions in the way of letters, poems and essays; for political propaganda; or for the discussion of current events, supplementing and reinforcing the brief paragraphs of the actual news items.

In this way, from the 1720's, three broad types of provincial newspapers began to develop. There were the chronicles of news pure and simple, such as the *Derby Mercury* and the *Kentish Post*, which printed essays and letters only rarely. There were papers such as the *Northampton Mercury* and the *Leeds Mercury*, which had a large literary and general content. And, finally, there were the political papers, such as the *York Courant* and the *Stamford Mercury*, which rigidly excluded all lighter fare from their pages, and printed only political essays. Later in the period, a fourth type, the trade paper, began to emerge. But most papers undoubtedly belonged to the second category, and from the 1720's onwards began to provide their readers with what was usually called 'entertainment'.

The printers were always most careful to explain that no material news would ever be omitted in favour of the lighter or more general matter. The printer of the *Stamford Mercury* insisted most emphatically that only 'when contrary Winds or other Accidents prevent the foreign Mails arriving in due Time, in such Vacation we shall entertain our Readers with such Subjects as shall be useful or entertaining'.[23] But the idea of a general section soon caught on, and was greeted with enthusiasm by many readers. In 1720, for example, a correspondent of the *Northampton Mercury* wrote warmly to the printer that

'Your Mercury having of late been something more diverting than usual, has caus'd several of your Readers to wish that it was to be so continu'd, by inserting every Week something of an Entertaining Subject, which would not only add a Pleasure to the Reading, but undoubtedly render it much more acceptable than now it is. . . .'[24]

The variety of this 'entertainment' makes any exact description of it almost impossible. In 1723, the *Worcester Post* regularly gave up its first page to a History of England—while the following year the *Norwich Mercury* gave a whole series of County Histories. The *Northampton Mercury* in 1736 announced a series entitled 'Observations and Directions on Planting and Gardening . . . with plain

---

[23] *Stamford Mercury*, 15 April 1736.
[24] *Northampton Mercury*, 26 December 1720.

Directions, and a Kalendar of the Work necessary to be done in the Field, Wood, Nursery, Apiary, Fruit, Distillery and Kitchen Gardens.'[25] Other papers preferred theological controversy, and not a few included frankly bawdy stories of love and gallantry. As an example of the variety offered, *Brice's Weekly Journal*—which was one of the earliest genuinely literary provincial papers—gave its readers, in fairly rapid succession, a discussion of the perpetual virginity of Jephthah's daughter, a 'History of the Pyrates', an extremely popular humorous dialogue in the local dialect entitled 'An Exmoor Scolding', a critical review of a recent poem, and a summary of Milton's 'Paradise Lost'.[26] It must be admitted that few other papers rose to such sustained heights, however, and it is hardly surprising that, when Brice attempted to confine his paper to news items alone, he was forced to admit that 'Repeated Complaints have been made against me for discontinuing of late the little Essays and Discourses which were wont to fill the first Pages of my Journals; and some have gone so far as to assure me that my Scribbles have generally met with good Acceptance from many of the Best and Judicious Men. . . .'[27] Brice's readers were fortunate in having a local printer of some literary ability—and, apparently, local contributors who were above the general average. Other printers were not so happily situated. Since the demise of the *Tatler* and *Spectator*, there had as yet appeared no London literary periodical of real note upon which the country printers might levy tribute; and most printers were therefore very largely dependent, as the *Northampton Mercury* explained, upon 'whatever curious Letters as may come to their Hands from any of their ingenious Correspondents, also those that are to be found in the London political Papers'.[28] And as few printers were as yet prepared to risk halving the number of their readers by printing partisan political essays, this meant that, to all intents and purposes, they were dependent upon private contributions.

Appeals for private contributions were frequent—and were rarely made in vain. But in most cases, the contributions received, essays, verses and enigmas, were neither inspiring nor original. Most popular of all was the Addisonian essay. But whereas this, in its original form, had provided a vehicle for excellent satire and comment upon dress and manners, in the pages of the provincial newspaper it was

---

[25] *Northampton Mercury*, 5 April 1736. A similar series appeared in the *St. Ives Post-Boy* after 23 June 1718.
[26] *Brice's Weekly Journal*, 30 April 1725; 17 October 1725 to 12 May 1726; 2 June 1727; 25 June 1725; 21.28 June 1728 respectively.
[27] Ibid. 12 April 1728.   [28] *Northampton Mercury*, 28 August 1721.

almost invariably moral and didactic, filled with pompous platitudes upon such uplifting subjects as 'Wisdom and Folly', 'Pride and Emulation' and 'Conjugal Love'. The verses were almost as monotonous, being usually in the form of an imitation of either the classical ode or the pastoral poem. And after a somewhat dreary succession of such effusions, the printer of the *Derby Mercury* felt obliged to explain that 'I would not have my Readers imagine that I shall every Week fill this Paper with Verses, but entertain them with various Subjects as they offer'.[29] Unfortunately, his correspondents apparently had little else to offer.

Thus, after the promising beginning made by such papers as the *Ludlow Post-Man* and *Brice's Weekly Journal*, the 'entertainment' offered by the provincial newspapers flagged rather noticeably. The general aim of the essays and poems which now appeared so regularly in the country papers was hardly that of 'entertainment' in the normal sense of that word. It was clearly summed up by a correspondent to the *Northampton Mercury* who informed the printer that 'with Satisfaction I observe your discreet Method at once to profit and please your Readers, intermixing sometimes a Moral Paper with your News; whereby you endeavour to insinuate Virtue to a Man while he is barely looking for Facts, and render him good while he is inquisitive'.[30] A letter in the *Manchester Magazine* spoke in similar vein of essays 'insensibly leading the Reader to a Love of the Virtues of some, and an Abhorrence of the Vices of others'.[31] One can only assume that these approving letters were written by the very people who contributed the essays and sermons in question. And so long as the printers were dependent upon purely local contributions for their general section, they would be very much at the mercy of the local clergy, who had by now recognized the possibilities of the newspaper as an auxiliary to the pulpit.

Thus, for some few years, the general section tended to be drab and unchanging. By 1728, however, the *Leeds Mercury* was regularly inserting a weekly essay taken from a new London periodical, the *Universal Spectator*: and the essays of that paper were different. They were, in fact, ideally suited to answer the requirements of the reader who, somewhat late in the day, drew the printer's attention to what he called 'the Fashion of your Brother News Writers in London to treat their Customers with a Letter, Essay or Dissertation on some

[29] *Derby Mercury*, 3 August 1732.
[30] *Northampton Mercury*, 26 October 1726.
[31] *Manchester Magazine*, 27 February 1749/50. Similar in the *Newcastle Courant*, 14 December 1728; *Bristol Oracle*, 29 May 1742; *Middlewich Journal*, 7 December 1756.

agreeable Subject. . . . Love and Gallantry even in Low Life, as well as High, would not give an unpleasant Relish even to the plodding industrious Manufacturer.'[32] The tastes of the provincial reading public were beginning to change. More important still, the readers were beginning to assert themselves. They still demanded news before anything else; but, when the foreign mails proved unexciting, they wanted something more than didactic essays and insipid poems. They wanted to be amused or informed. A correspondent to the *Kentish Post* summed up the situation: 'instead of News now a Days about the Turks and People beyond the Sea, we are fobb'd off with something which never tells us anything of the War or even makes us laugh'.[33]

What had particularly aroused the ire of this reader was the attempt of the *Kentish Post* in 1738 and early 1739 to enter the literary field with a section entitled the 'Kentish Spectator'. The whole episode suggests that popular taste was developing rapidly—and that the new reading public had reached the stage where it was determined to make its views known. Certainly, the printer of the newspaper was subjected to continuous criticism during the short lifetime of his 'Kentish Spectator'. Much of the criticism was directed against the title itself. By this time, the original *Spectator* had acquired such a reputation that, as one correspondent put it, imitations were 'displeasing after the masterly Essays usher'd into the World under that Venerable Name';[34] and the printer was forced to admit that the title had been 'perhaps unadvisedly and unguardedly chosen'.[35] Other criticisms were directed against the general lack of humour, and, more significantly, the parade of classical learning and the fact that the section contained 'too little about the Common Concerns of life'. The unfortunate printer sought to placate his critics, promising that the section should not be 'stuff'd with classical Names (however applicable) in order to appear learned', although, with reference to the demand for humour, he insisted that 'we must not be so little Philosophers as to be always upon the Grin'.[36] Nevertheless, the 'Kentish Spectator' quickly expired.

Behind these various criticisms may be traced a significant change in the reading public of the provincial newspaper. When the literary or general section had first appeared, it had been the happy hunting-ground of the local clergy and others of similar education, proud of

---

[32] *Leeds Mercury*, 9 November 1731.
[33] *Kentish Post*, 9 December 1738.
[34] Ibid. 13 January 1738/39.
[35] Ibid. 9 December 1738.
[36] Ibid.

their classical knowledge, and anxious to air it. Typical of their effusions was a letter printed in *Farley's Exeter Journal* in 1726 in which the writer deplored the neglect of Greek studies, and for more than a page of the newspaper held forth on the various excellences of the Greek language.[37] Similarly, Latin epigrams and poems appeared very frequently. But, from the 1720's onwards, a rougher and ruder type of reader was beginning to make his needs known, and the contents of the newspapers underwent a subtle transformation. As early as 1724, a long series of detailed theological dissertations in Brice's *Post-Master* had aroused hostile criticism, and Brice, after observing that ' 'tis Pity Pearl should be cast before Swine', had been forced to agree that, in future, more 'mean and homely Cheer' should be provided.[38] Naturally, the printers could not afford to disoblige their more educated patrons. Latin poems continued to appear, but it is noticeable that the printer would often add some personal comment to the effect that 'for the Sake of some Readers, we could have wished it translated'.[39] And the *Norwich Gazette* on one occasion announced that 'a Latin Epigram, the same, in Effect, as the following, was some Time since published in this Paper; but, as the greater Part of our Readers are unacquainted with that Language, the Author has been prevailed upon to put the same Sentiments into English'.[40]

In the 1730's, the number of private contributions declined sharply. This was caused partly by the change in the tastes of the reading public, and partly by the fact that such literary periodicals as the *Universal Spectator* and the *Grub-Street Journal* had now become available in the capital. These periodicals provided the sort of 'entertainment' that the provincial public wanted. So popular did they become that local contributions were almost crowded out of the pages of the country newspapers. So little room was left, in fact, that the amateur poets and essayists found themselves obliged to plead for consideration. A correspondent in the *Leeds Mercury* remarked to the printer that 'as you have sometimes entertain'd your Readers with Essays cut out of the *Universal Spectator* and other Writers . . . so it is hop'd you will not discourage any of your own Country Manufacturers of this Sort';[41] while a letter in the *Newcastle Courant* in 1733 declared that

---

[37] *Farley's Exeter Journal*, 9 December 1726.
[38] *Post-Master*, 7 August 1724.
[39] *Original York Journal*, 12 November 1728.
[40] *Norwich Gazette*, 20 May 1749. Similarly, the *Manchester Magazine* printed a quack cure in Latin on 7 August 1759 and its translation on 16 October 1759. [41] *Leeds Mercury*, 28 April 1730.

'I hope you may always spare a little Room at the Beginning . . . for short Essays, Letters of Wit, Humour, Speculation or Argument. I believe it will be very acceptable to several of your Readers to find a Piece of your Paper set apart as a Field or Arena, for the Use of such of your Correspondents as have Courage enough to enter the List of Authors.'[42]

For a time, 'entertainment' reigned supreme. But the earlier printers had also expressed a somewhat vague desire to 'instruct' their readers. Until now, the instruction had been limited to the moral essay. But in the late 1730's, the country printers began to recognize the needs of their new readers. They had, of course, always supplied a certain amount of historical and geographical information: but now that incidental information was replaced by a far more ambitious and sustained effort to educate their readers. Perhaps the most ambitious scheme was that launched in 1739 by the *Newcastle Journal*, whose printer announced his intention of printing every week an essay on

'the Geography and Natural History of the World, [and] occasional Essays on useful Subjects, which, tho' they may not be thought worthy of much Notice from those who are absolute compleat Adepts in Science, yet we hope they cannot fail of a general Use amongst the greater Part of our Readers, who have not had Leisure or Opportunity to apply themselves steadily to the Perusal of large Discourses and Regular Systems of Philosophy'.[43]

Henceforward, each issue of the paper contained an essay on such subjects as the solar system, the poles, the Gulf Stream and so on. The intention was to work through such general topics as a preliminary to a series of descriptions of all the different countries of the world; but the outbreak of war with Spain in 1739, and the consequent popular interest in the attacks of the British fleet upon the Spanish colonies in the New World, led the printer to announce that

'as we have now declar'd War with Spain . . . it will probably be no unacceptable Thing to our Readers if we defer the Geography of such Parts of the World as a regular Procedure would lead us into, and which at present have little Concern with our Political Affairs, so that we may more readily fall into a Description of such Places as the present circumstances of this Nation are more nearly related to, particularly the Dominions of the King of Spain'.[44]

[42] *Newcastle Courant*, 3 March 1732/33.
[43] *Newcastle Journal*, 19 January 1740. The series began on 14 April 1739.
[44] Ibid. 24 November 1739.

The printer now proceeded to give a weekly description of the various Spanish colonies, although he still found room for a highly technical essay entitled 'Towards a mechanical Account of Freezing'.[45] Interestingly enough, the same geography course and the same essay appeared in the *Lancashire Journal*, although always a month or so after they had been printed in the Newcastle paper; and that paper also reported in early 1740 that 'several of our Customers are impatient for our coming to a Description of the Spanish Territories in America'.[46] Not to be outdone, the rival *Manchester Magazine* also printed a series of articles on the Spanish colonies.[47]

Many other provincial papers reacted in a similar manner. The *Leeds Mercury* in 1739 adopted the suggestion of a correspondent that a section of the paper be set aside each week for problems to be posed and answered by readers. The rules to be observed were that 'those in Mathematicks be few, because of the Scarcity of Proficients in that Arduous and by most Genius's Impenetrable Science; that those in Arithmetick be more; and that those in Divinity be by far the most'.[48] A classical question was added later.[49] Another country paper to include mathematical problems in its columns was the *Derby Mercury*, also in 1739.[50]

Such competitions were extremely popular. According to the printer of the *Leeds Mercury*, his section was 'admirably calculated for the encreasing of the Credit and further Extensiveness of my Readers',[51] and he even went to the quite considerable expense of purchasing special algebraical types.[52] But it soon became clear that such high-pressure instruction could not be continued indefinitely. Both the *Newcastle Journal* and its shadow, the *Lancashire Journal*, were forced to admit that 'we find every Taste does not so much relish the Natural History of the World',[53] and a correspondent in the *Newcastle Journal* stated with evident truth that 'Lessons too often repeated will blunt your Readers' Appetites'. This reader's solution to the problem was to limit the formal instruction to one dose a fortnight, giving, in between, essays in which, he suggested, 'might be painted in just Lights the Foibles and Excellencies of Mankind . . . to show every one the Deformity of the Vices they indulge,

[45] Ibid. 19 January to 16 February 1739/40.
[46] *Lancashire Journal*, 17 March 1740.
[47] *Manchester Magazine*, 16 June to 11 August 1741.
[48] *Leeds Mercury*, 17 April 1739.   [49] Ibid. 5 July 1739.
[50] *Derby Mercury*, 12 July 1739 to 23 October 1740.
[51] *Leeds Mercury*, 17 April 1739.   [52] Ibid. 5 July 1739.
[53] *Newcastle Journal*, 8 September 1739; *Lancashire Journal*, 1 October 1739.

and the Beauty of the Virtues they neglect'.[54] Such a proposal really meant a return to the moral instruction of earlier days.

Perhaps fortunately for the printers, the difficulty was resolved by the intensification of the war and the excitement of the Forty-Five. As always, as soon as war news became abundant, all extraneous matter tended to disappear, and the papers were filled almost entirely with what Defoe called 'those dear Things call'd Blood and Battle'.[55] After the war, the printers were once again obliged to introduce a general section: but now the whole emphasis had changed. The endeavour to provide a really solid education had died a natural death. It had, in fact, been too severe for human frailty. Instead, nearly all the country printers now printed every week extracts from the society papers which flourished in the capital. Most popular were the *World*, the *Rambler* and the *Covent Garden Journal*. Perhaps the editorial announcement which ushered in the *World* most aptly summed up the aims of these papers. The *World's* intentions were 'to ridicule with Novelty and Good Humour, the Fashions, Follies, Vices and Absurdities of that Part of the Human Species which calls itself the World'.[56]

The general purpose of the essays now printed was still to improve the morals of the readers—and particularly of the female readers. Fashions, extravagance and gallantry among the fair sex were the perennial topics, and were described, analysed and denounced in essay after essay. But despite the ostensible moral aim of these essays, the whole emphasis was upon passion and seduction, and the humorous note was never absent for long. Typical was a letter in the *Covent Garden Journal* which appeared in the *Cambridge Journal* in 1752. The author began by taking the high moral tone, insisting that the windows of inns were intended for epigrams and sonnets, and not for what he called 'bawdy and immorality'. It was, apparently, an eighteenth century custom to write upon the windows of inns. But he then went on to spoil the effect of his little homily by giving an example of the type of effusion he deplored. He quoted at length an extremely lyrical sonnet which he had seen on one such window—a sonnet which ended with the lines:

> 'Give me sweet Nectar in a Kiss,
> That I may be replete with Bliss'.

But, he added, beneath this some 'Brute' had inserted two extra lines:

[54] *Newcastle Journal*, 2 June 1739.
[55] *Applebee's Original Weekly Journal*, 21 August 1725.
[56] Quoted in *Harrop's Manchester Mercury*, 30 January 1752.

'Give me sweet Nectar in a Glass,
And as for kissing, kiss my A - -'[57]

This note of Rabelaisian humour, the continued emphasis upon sex
and seduction, and the lurid descriptions of love and passion certainly tend to make one doubt the sincerity of the announced moral
aims of these papers. Nevertheless, it is clear that the provincial
reading public much preferred to be 'instructed' in this way than by
the former moral essay, and the popularity of these London society
papers was not challenged until 1755, when war with France again
became imminent, and foreign affairs once more predominated.

However, if the strictly moral essay was eventually discarded, the
country newspaper never managed to shake off completely its role
as an auxiliary of the pulpit. The religious note was always liable to
crop up—although often in the most incongruous company. A religious controversy was always welcome. The Norwich papers had
thrown themselves happily into the Methodist controversy in the
1750's;[58] and the *Bristol Weekly Intelligencer* in 1749 deliberately
sought to provoke a similar dispute in its own pages, printing a series
of vicious attacks on the Methodists by one 'Amicus Veritatis', and
inviting 'for the Entertainment of my Readers . . . any Thing by Way
of Vindication from the Persons whom Amicus Veritatis points to'.[59]
From the point of view of the printer of the *Intelligencer*, an added
spice was provided by the fact that his rival printer, Felix Farley,
was a staunch Methodist. In 1731, the *Northampton Mercury's* brief
account of a book entitled *A Preservation against Quakerism* inspired a lengthy series of letters from a gentleman calling himself
'Parrhesius Philalethes', who defended episcopacy in a manner
strikingly reminiscent of the medieval dispute between the Regnum
and the Sacerdotium, resurrecting all the old arguments over the
power of the keys and of the sword.[60]

This religious note was stimulated by the Forty-Five, which most
country newspaper saw in simple terms as a conflict between Popery
on the one side and the Church of England and Protestantism on
the other. The Whig papers in particular engaged in religious propaganda of the most virulent type. A similar flaring-up of all the
religious passions and prejudices occurred during the campaign
against the so-called 'Jew Bill' in 1753. Even without such exceptional episodes, however, the religious note was never silenced for

[57] *Cambridge Journal*, 22 February 1752.   [58] *Supra*, pp. 86, 87.
[59] *Bristol Weekly Intelligencer*, 18 November 1749.
[60] The review appeared in the *Northampton Mercury* on 27 December
1731. The dispute was still raging in July 1732.

long. In 1747, the *York Journal*—which later changed its title, somewhat pointedly, to the *Protestant York Courant*, with the implication that the rival *York Courant* was suspect from the religious point
of view—published a magnificent series of articles entitled 'The
Controversy about the Pope's Supremacy'. In these articles, history
was ransacked for examples of papal iniquity, and all the ancient
disputes over such matters as the Donation of Constantine were
given a new lease of life. In 1750, the same paper embarked with
obvious gusto upon a new series, 'The View of Popery'. And when,
after some considerable time, it seemed at long last to have ex-
hausted that fertile subject, it began to reprint the religious essays
from an old periodical called the *Observator*.[61] Even the rival *York
Courant*, which had nobly resisted all these efforts to draw it into a
religious controversy—and had, indeed, endeavoured to exclude
from its pages everything but news and politics, sharply informing
would-be contributors that 'the Design of the *York Courant* is to
present their Readers with News, not with a Collection of Ballads'[62]
—was forced to bow its head to popular demand, and to announce
that 'we have, occasionally, given our Readers a Political Essay;
we shall, for once, venture to give them a Sermon'.[63]

Of course, lurid accounts of the evils of Popery were always
popular in that age of religious passion and prejudice, when the
surest way to arouse the mob was to raise the anti-Popery cry.
Similarly, attacks on the Dissenters and the Methodists were always
sure of a ready response among the mob element. But the constantly
recurring religious note, manifested in the frequent printing of sermons and moral essays, suggests that, in this age of the flesh, a great
amount of rather fierce and uncomfortable Puritan feeling still
survived among the middle classes throughout the country, however
avidly they might follow the printed accounts of sin and passion in
London society, as revealed in such papers as the *Covent Garden
Journal* and the *World*.

But essays and sermons certainly did not exhaust the 'entertainment and instruction' offered by the provincial newspapers. As early
as 1719, the title-page of the *Nottingham Mercury* had promised a
'Weekly Account of News with Extracts and Abridgments of
Books'[64]—although the newspaper had hardly lived up to its
promise. Little progress was made in this particular field until the
1730's, when once again a new vigour becomes apparent. Then, the

[61] *York Journal*, &c., 31 March 1747 to 14 April 1747; 6 March 1749/50
to 29 January 1750/51; 26 March 1751 to 28 November 1752 respectively.
[62] *York Courant*, 5 February 1740.   [63] Ibid. 2 October 1750.
[64] *Nottingham Mercury*, 12 March 1719.

Lancashire Journal treated its readers to weekly instalments of a recent novel, *The Life of Mr. Cleveland, Natural Son of Oliver Cromwell*. That novel lasted for six months.[65] Not to be outdone, the rival *Manchester Magazine* was soon reprinting '*The Chronicles of the Kings of England*, after the Manner of the Kings of Israel, suppos'd to be wrote by Mr. Dodsley',[66] and when this came to an end, it continued with 'A Collection of Choice Stories, Fables and Allegories' taken from the old *Spectator* and *Guardian*.[67] So popular were these thirty-six stories apparently that they were printed separately, and sold for nine-pence, ten-pence and one shilling.[68] In the 1750's, *Felix Farley's Bristol Journal* filled excess space with extracts from Hervey's *Reflections on the Starry Heavens* and *Reflections on a Flower Garden*,[69] and many other papers introduced similar literary excerpts. The *Union Journal* of 1759, despite the fact that the Seven Years War was providing an abundance of exciting news, still found space every week for instalments from *The Memoirs of Frederick III, King of Prussia*.[70]

No provincial newspaper approached the achievement of the *Cambridge Journal* in the literary field. From 1749 onwards, that paper every week gave its readers an instalment of a novel. These novels included: *The Life of Mme de Beaumont, a French Lady who was forced to leave her Lord and fly that Kingdom on Account of her Religion; Narzanes or, the Injur'd Statesman; Hippolita de Centellas; or, The unexpected Resolution; Mistaken Jealousy; or, the happy Perseverance; Henriques and Elvira; or, The Force of Love; Don Carlos de Godoy, The Fortunate Stranger; The Twins; or, The Disguised Page; Reciprocal Love; or, the History of the Count de Lemos and Victoria de Valasco; The Generous Country Girl; or, Disinterested Love; The History of Polydore and Emilia; Female Revenge; or, the Happy Exchange; Distress'd Beauty; or, Love at a Venture*; and finally, in 1753, *Good out of Evil; or, the Double Deceit*.[71] At intervals during this long series of the popular and

---

[65] *Lancashire Journal*, 1 January 1739 to 23 July 1739.
[66] *Manchester Magazine*, 19 January 1741/42. The series began on 9 February.
[67] Ibid. 5 December 1749.   [68] Ibid. 27 February 1749/50.
[69] *Felix Farley's Bristol Journal*, 9 May 1752 to 23 July 1753, irregularly.
[70] *Union Journal*, 7 August 1759 to 2 September 1760.
[71] *Cambridge Journal*, 21 April to 22 July 1749; 9 September to 9 December 1749; 30 December 1749 to 17 February 1750; 24 February to 21 April 1750; 6 May to 23 June 1750; 30 June to 28 July 1750; 4 August to 8 September 1750; 15 September to 29 December 1750; 27 July 1751; 30 May to 4 July 1752; 4 November to 23 December 1752; 30 December 1752 to 17 March 1753; 24 March to 19 May 1753 respectively.

romantic novels of the day, the *Journal* had also given a version of Chaucer's 'Miller of Trumpington' and what it called 'Heroic Charity', a story about King Alfred, taken 'from our antient Chronicles'.[72]

No other paper approached this record, although, according to a well-known and often quoted story, the printer of the *Leicester Journal* was on one occasion so short of news that he was reduced to reprinting chapters from the Old Testament each week, getting half-way through Exodus before the foreign mails could provide him with anything more topical.[73] There seems to be no evidence for this story, and one must assume that its author had in mind either the 'Histories of the Holy Bible', which appeared in all of the papers printed by Robert Walker—who, however, was not the printer of the *Leicester Journal*—or the parodies upon the Old Testament which were a popular feature of the vicious political campaign against the 'Jew Bill' in 1753.

During this literary phase, even foreign works were occasionally described, and in the 1730's the *Northampton Mercury* actually included a sub-heading entitled 'Foreign Literary Advices', in which books by foreign authors were sometimes discussed.[74] The works of Voltaire received an honourable mention from time to time in the various country newspapers. His essays 'Of China' and 'On Trade' were described in the *Ipswich Journal* and the *Derby Mercury* respectively, while both the *Salisbury Journal* and *Harrop's Manchester Mercury* gave extracts from his 'Siècle de Louis XIV'.[75] Towards the end of the period, certain newspapers began to lay more stress upon this aspect of their contents. In 1757, *Ayscough's Nottingham Courant* announced that 'In order to render this Paper still more extensively Useful, some Account of such Foreign Books as are published, in any Part of Europe, worthy the Observation of the Curious, will be here taken Notice of', and it followed this with a lengthy critical review of M. Mehegan's *Considérations sur les Révolutions des Arts*, pointing out that that author 'does not confine his considerations to the liberal and mechanical arts, but comprehends all that vast circle of knowledge which is emphatically

---

[72] *Cambridge Journal*, 21.28 December 1751; 9.16.23.30 November, 7.14 December 1751 respectively.

[73] The story originated in C. H. Timperley, *Encyclopaedia of Literary and Typographical Anecdotes*, p. 680.

[74] *Northampton Mercury*, 28 May, 4.11 June, 6 August, 3 September 1733.

[75] *Ipswich Journal*, 5 November 1757; *Derby Mercury*, 6 December 1733; *Salisbury Journal*, 8 June 1752; *Harrop's Manchester Mercury*, 23 June 1752 respectively.

included under the general name of Science'.[76] Similarly, the *Coventry Mercury* in 1759 declared its intention to present 'Abstracts of new Books on Knowledge and Science'.[77]

Obviously much of the material included under the general heading of 'Instruction and Entertainment' was unsuitable for a newspaper, especially when the meagre size of the weekly paper of this period is taken into account. Much of it was inserted purely as a temporary expedient to fill up space, and what the public demanded above all else was news. But it is also clear that the general section soon became popular with the more educated readers, and no printer could afford entirely to ignore it. So popular was a competition run by the *Northampton Mercury* in 1721 that the printers attempted to resolve the problem by publishing a separate periodical. They announced that

'we propose for the future to insert every particular Answer with the Author's Name and Place of Abode. Perhaps it may be objected, This cannot be done in a three halfpenny paper. At least the Country must want News in the meanwhile. I Grant it; and therefore for the Entertainment of the Lovers of Ingenuity in all its Branches, the Proprietors of this Paper design and propose to publish a Monthly Pamphlet, at 6*d.* each or 1/- per Quarter.'

This magazine, named the *Northampton Miscellany*, was to contain:

'Firstly, the respective Answers to the several Questions hitherto proposed, together with their Algebraical Processes and Geometrical Construction; as also the Questions proposed for Solution the ensuing Month. Secondly, The material Occurrences foreign and domestick; which by their being too prolix have escap'd our Press. Thirdly, a complete Abstract of the most material Pamphlets that have been publish'd that Month, and likewise a Catalogue of all the Books printed and publish'd in London. . . .
Fourthly, Some diverting Tale, Poetical Performance, Remarkable Accident, or in fine some Subject that may either be instructive or diverting.'[78]

This ambitious venture lasted only for six months. It was, in fact, ahead of its time. As yet there were in London no magazines of the calibre and prestige of the *Gentleman's Magazine* or the *London Magazine* to provide an easy quarry for the provincial printers. And few country readers were apparently prepared to lay out the sum of six-pence each month on a collection of riddles and mathematical

---

[76] *Ayscough's Nottingham Courant,* 26 March 1757.
[77] *Jopson's Coventry Mercury,* 19 March 1759.
[78] *Northampton Mercury,* 30 January 1720/21.

problems, even if supplemented by abstracts of pamphlets and a series of news items which were not only stale but had previously been considered too tedious to be included in the newspaper proper.

The prospect for a provincial periodical seemed brighter after 1730, when the reputable London magazines had made their appearance. However, when Thomas Gent launched his *Miscellanea Curiosa* in 1734, he ignored such London models, and insisted upon going his own wilful independent way. His periodical was to contain only: '1. Enigmas 2. Paradoxes 3. Mathematical Questions suited both to Beginners and also to such as have made higher Advances in those Studies'.[79] With so restricted and intellectual an appeal, the magazine did not last long. Another provincial periodical to suffer in the same way was the Oxford *Student* of 1750. This, too, endeavoured to exclude all topical items from its pages. Its aim was simply 'to promote Learning in General', and no 'political Disputes' were allowed, despite a correspondent's warning that such a plan could not succeed.[80] That warning was apparently justified, for very soon the printer found it necessary to give away each month a supplement called the *Inspector*, which was really a small newspaper containing an abstract of the previous month's news.

All these early attempts to produce a provincial periodical failed abjectly. Any publication excluding news from its pages seemed doomed to failure. Even if a periodical did attempt to include a summary of news, that news was, of course, stale by the time the periodical in question was published. In fact, the only provincial magazine to be successful during this period was the *Newcastle General Magazine*, which first appeared in 1747. This alone seems to have achieved the balanced composition of its illustrious London models, the *Gentleman's Magazine* and the *London Magazine*—upon which it drew heavily. Moreover, it satisfied the news-hungry by publishing the extremely popular Parliamentary Debates. Undoubtedly, the *Magazine* owed a great deal of its popularity and success to such other factors as the distance of Newcastle from London, the slowness of the post and the initiative of the printer in organizing a private postal service of his own. All these advantages were described in the 'Proposals for Printing':

'I. The distance of *Newcastle* from *London* rendering it impracticable for any of the MAGAZINES, or other *Monthly Performances*, to arrive here at the soonest before the 13th., and frequently the 20th. Days of the succeeding Month for which they are publish'd; and the Carriers from the *Northern Counties*,

---

[79] *Miscellanea Curiosa*, January 1734.   [80] *Student*, 31 January 1750.

and *North Britain,* not coming to this Town till the Week after their Arrival here, it frequently happens, that great Numbers of Country Readers never see any of these Pamphlets till near a Month after their Publication: by which Delay some Parts of their Contents are quite stale, and the rest less acceptable. This MAGAZINE is therefore design'd to remove the said Inconveniences as much as possible; for it will be circulated in the *North* a Week or ten Days sooner than any other Pamphlet of the kind.

II. It will consist of about four Sheets, printed on the same Type, and of the same Size as these Proposals, on fine Paper, in the most correct and beautiful Manner, which will much exceed the Quantity of any other Magazine.

III. The *Debates* of the POLITICAL CLUB, (which at this critical Juncture, are greatly increas'd in their Importance) and the most valuable *Essays* in any of the MONTHLY REPOSITORIES of approv'd Literature, will be inserted in it.

IV. As the Number of Sheets in this MAGAZINE will enable us to oblige our Readers with greater Variety than any Book of the Price and Kind, no Pains shall be spared in collecting and inserting the most useful and entertaining WEEKLY ESSAYS, theological, moral, philosophical, or political, publish'd at *London* or *other Places;* for which a Correspondence is settled.

V. EXTRACTS shall also be made from the PHILOSOPHICAL TRANSACTIONS, and from such other NEW BOOKS or PAMPHLETS, *Foreign, British* or *Irish,* as may best deserve the Notice of the Publick.

VI. By means of this Magazine, the *Learned* and *Ingenious* of this Country, whose Studies have been turn'd to Natural, Experimental, or Moral Philosophy, Divinity, History, Mathematicks, Poetry, Painting, Musick, Antiquity, Trade, Navigation, Farming, or any other useful Branch of Art and Science, will have an Opportunity of communicating their *Discoveries* and *Observations* to the Publick; and the Favour of their Letters or Essays will be gratefully acknowledged.

VII. In each MAGAZINE will be inserted a regular and concise History of the most important Transactions of the Times, collected from the most authentick Accounts; to be illustrated by PLANS of such Battles, Sieges, Sea Fights, etc. in which our Arms have had any Share, or in which this Nation is particularly interested. Done by the best Hands.

VIII. A Catalogue of such new Books or Pamphlets as are published within the month, will be inserted at the End of each Magazine, with the Prices of Stocks, Grain, etc., the Course of Exchange, Accounts of *British, French* and *Spanish* Captures, and Lists of Marriages, Births, Deaths, Preferments, etc.

IX. As soon as the Trials of the Rebels are published, and an authentick History of the Rise, Progress and Suppression of the late

Rebellion can be had, so much thereof shall be inserted Monthly as can be conveniently admitted.'[81]

This very nice balance between literary and political interest, and between published works and private contributions cost only sixpence a month. But the *Newcastle General Magazine* was the only successful provincial periodical in this period. So long as the weekly newspapers were able to serve both as chronicles of news and providers of 'Entertainment and Instruction' there was little demand for anything more ambitious.

The importance of this expansion of the simple news-sheet of the earlier years can scarcely be exaggerated. Until libraries became cheaper and more plentiful, the local newspaper catered for a public which had but little access to printed matter. Books were expensive, and their reading required ample leisure. But a newspaper was still cheap, and working hours were never so long as to make it impossible to read a weekly newspaper. By expanding their subject matter, the newspapers stimulated the reading habit and supplemented the meagre education so many of their readers had received at school. In so doing, they were potent forces in the gradual enlightenment which characterizes the eighteenth century. As the *Liverpool Chronicle* explained in 1757, 'the Articles of News seem to be a natural Decoy to draw great Numbers to the Reading these short Dissertations, who, perhaps, scarce read anything else, and who, indeed, were it not for their News-Writers, might happen to forget to read at all'.[82]

[81] *Proposals for Printing . . . the General Magazine.*
[82] *Liverpool Chronicle*, 6 May 1757.

CHAPTER SIX

POLITICS AND THE PROVINCIAL PRESS

T HE evolution of the provincial newspaper from a simple news-sheet into the proud purveyor of 'intelligence, instruction and entertainment' had been accomplished without any great difficulty. All possible objections to the inclusion of such extraneous matter had been silenced by the repeated editorial assurances that no material news would be sacrificed in its favour. The development of a provincial political paper was, however, a very different proposition. So sensitive was Authority to any form of public criticism that political comment was only too likely to lead to prosecution for libel, if not worse. Moreover, the adoption of a firm party line would inevitably estrange potential customers. All too often it would encourage a rival printer to set up a paper printed ostentatiously in the opposite interest: and few country towns could support two local newspapers. Certainly, the average eighteenth century country printer could not afford expensive legal actions, the loss of custom or the appearance of a rival newspaper.

The printer's aim was to print the county paper, read by Whig and Tory alike. Most printers therefore started off with the firm intention of avoiding political controversy at all costs. The *Ludlow Post-Man* of 1719 was resolved 'to be of no Party, and to meddle with no Quarrels, Publick or Private, Civil or Religious',[1] explaining later that 'we would never be concern'd in the publishing any Thing that might seem to be partially set forth in Favour of some one or other Party, lest by so doing we disoblige our Correspondents and plunge unadvisedly into the Malice of the adverse Party'.[2] Other printers realized that party feeling was so strong that they would be unable totally to exclude politics from their pages; but they were determined to be impartial. The printer of the *Derby Mercury* candidly announced in 1734 that, 'as it is undoubtedly my Interest to be equally willing and faithful in serving all Parties, so I hope all who read my News Paper may be convinced that I am so far from being such a Bigot as to act contrary to that Interest'.[3] And

[1] *Ludlow Post-Man*, 9 October 1719. [2] Ibid. 15 January 1719/20.
[3] *Derby Mercury*, 21 February 1733/34.

similar protestations of strict neutrality were regularly made through-out the period.[4]

So high did party feeling run in the reign of Queen Anne, how-ever, that few printers found it possible, despite these protestations, completely to suppress their own personal preferences. But they sought to avoid undue provocation—a decision made easier by the meagre size of the newspapers and the absence of anything in the nature of a political essay—and their political sympathies were re-vealed only in the slant given to the odd news-item. In 1711, for example, the *Newcastle Courant's* account of an election contest at Liverpool was obviously taken from a Tory London newspaper, and informed its readers that the Whig candidate had 'boasted of his prodigious Interest, consisting of Whigs, Dissenters, and the meanest People'.[5] But the same paper had practically nothing to say about the furious battles being waged in Parliament over the Treaty of Utrecht, when a Whig House of Lords defied the Tory majority in the Commons and maintained that the Treaty was dishonourable and a betrayal of the true interests of the country. Eventually, the Queen was obliged to create twelve Tory peers in order to overcome the opposition to the Treaty. But this very significant act was reported only briefly in the *Courant*, without emphasis or explanation.[6] The same paper devoted an entire issue to the Queen's speech to Parlia-ment on the conclusion of the peace—again without editorial com-ment of any kind.[7]

Rather more outspoken was the *Worcester Post-Man*, whose printer's sympathies were strongly Tory, if not Jacobite. In 1712, he remarked on the nation-wide rejoicing at the expiration of the sen-tence on the Tory martyr, Dr. Sacheverell, who had been impeached by the Whigs for his outrageously provocative sermon preached on the anniversary of both the Guy Fawkes' Plot and the landing in England of William of Orange, and forbidden to preach for three years.[8] Later, he informed readers of a dastardly Whig plot against the good doctor:

---

[4] e.g. *Sam Farley's Bristol Post-Man*, 31 December 1715; *Post-Master*, 26 February 1724/25; *Original Mercury, York Journal*, 24 February 1729/30; *Derby Mercury*, 23 March 1732; *Stamford Mercury*, 15 April 1736; *Newcastle Journal*, proposals for printing, 22 January 1739; *Cambridge Journal*, 18 May 1745; *Bristol Weekly Intelligencer*, 27 February 1749; *Manchester Magazine*, 27 February 1750; *Oxford Journal*, 3 May 1753; *Boddely's Bath Journal*, 23 July 1757; *Union Journal*, 27 March 1759.
[5] *Newcastle Courant*, 7 November 1711.
[6] Ibid. 2 and 5 January 1711/12.
[7] Ibid. 11 June 1712.   [8] *Worcester Post-Man*, 24 July 1713.

'a young Woman who is a Prisoner in the Marshalsea for Debt, having before she was arrested (upon Promise of Marriage) granted her Lover the Ultimate Favour: Of which Misfortune the Faction taking Advantage, thought she wou'd be an immediate Instrument for their Purpose; and trying her Pulse, found she was somewhat inclinable; on which Account they made a Collection of about 60 Guineas, which they proffer'd to give her, besides paying her Debt, and discharging the Prison Fees, if she would swear her Great Belly to Dr. S[acheverel]l: But having more Honesty, than to accept of their Gold, to make herself an Instrument of their Hellish Designs, has discover'd the Intrigue'.[9]

In such ways, the *Worcester Post-Man* lost no opportunity to 'smear' the Whigs. In 1713, it told its readers that the Thanksgiving for the Peace had been strictly observed 'by all Persons but the Factious Party, who despises that Blessing, choosing rather to see this Nation and Europe still wading in Blood'.[10] In the elections of 1715, it maintained that 'the Church Party for the most part carry it in the Counties, where the Numbers of Gentlemen were not to be bribed. But in many of the little Burroughs, where Subtilty and Money prevails, there they loose Ground'.[11] And certainly, the frequent references to tumults and riots which appeared in the *Post-Man* during the years 1714 and early 1715 would give the impression that the Protestant Succession had been achieved only against tremendous odds and was likely to be short-lived.

A decisive stage in the political development of both the country newspaper and the public it served was reached in the crisis of the Jacobite Fifteen. That episode naturally aroused tremendous public interest, and so encouraged printers to establish new papers. And it was during the rebellion that the printers discovered the possibilities of the political essay—a device made possible by the enlargement of the newspapers after the Stamp Act of 1712. Thus, in 1715 a lengthy essay in the *Protestant Mercury*, a Whig paper printed in Exeter, warned the 'good People of England' against the related abominations of Popery, wooden shoes, and the Pretender and his 'nominal Dad'.[12] The following year, in answer to Tory murmurings at the severity with which the Whig government had put down the rebellion, the *Nottingham Mercury* gave a detailed description of the atrocities committed by Judge Jeffreys after the Duke of Monmouth's rebellion against James II,[13] the implication being that the Whigs had been considerably more merciful in 1715 and 1716 than the Tories had been when placed in a similar situation. The same

[9] Ibid. 20 May 1715.   [10] Ibid. 27 March, 3 April 1712.
[11] Ibid. 11 February 1715.   [12] *Protestant Mercury*, 11 November 1715.
[13] *Nottingham Mercury*, 1 March 1716.

paper followed this up with a long 'Address to the Tories', urging them to see the light and become 'Turncoats'.[14]

Clearly, the whole vocabulary of politics was changing now. From being a mere vehicle of news, the country newspaper was becoming a weapon in the political strife, an instrument for shaping and leading public opinion. Certainly, Samuel Negus saw the liberty of the press as 'the principal cause of the late rebellion and disturbances',[15] and Addison agreed that the country newspapers had been partly responsible for the intense party passions which were a feature of this period. According to him,

'there is scarce any man in England, of what denomination soever, that is not a freethinker in politics, and hath not some particular notions of his own, by which he distinguishes himself from the rest of the community. Our nation, which was formerly called a nation of saints, may now be called a nation of statesmen. Almost every age, profession and sex among us has its favourite set of ministers and scheme of government. Our children are initiated into factions before they know their right hand from their left. They no sooner begin to speak, but Whig and Tory are the first words they learn. . . . Of all the ways and means by which this political humour hath been propagated among the people of Great Britain, I cannot single out any so prevalent or universal as the late constant application of the press to the publishing of state matters. We hear of several that are newly erected in the country, and set apart for this particular purpose. For it seems that the people of Exeter, Salisbury, and other great towns are resolved to be as great politicians as the inhabitants of London . . . and deal out such news of their own printing as is best suited to the genius of the market-people and the taste of the country. . . . Besides, as their papers are filled out with a different party-spirit, they naturally divide the people into different sentiments, who generally consider rather the principles than the truth of their news-writers.'[16]

Despite its obvious exaggeration and irony, this account affords striking testimony to the growth of political consciousness in the English countryside—and to the part played in that growth by the provincial newspapers.

Of course, the precocious development produced by the Fifteen and its aftermath of great political trials could not be long maintained at the same pitch. It was in part discouraged by a wave of prosecutions of newspaper printers. But it seems doubtful whether

[14] *Nottingham Mercury*, 29 November 1716.
[15] Samuel Negus, *Compleat and Private List of all the Printing Houses. . . .* (1724), reprinted in Timperley, *Encyclopaedia*, pp. 630–3.
[16] Addison, *Freeholder*, no. 53, quoted Fox Bourne, *English Newspapers*, p. 99.

the general public in the countryside was in fact mature enough to take a deep interest in the ordinary give-and-take of politics. To interest the humble reader politics had to be unusually exciting. They had been so during the whole of Anne's reign, with its great continental wars, the threat of a French invasion, and the very genuine doubts as to the future of the Protestant Succession. The Fifteen, of course, stood in a class by itself. But after the Fifteen there was a lull. For many years to come, it was to be difficult to arouse the ordinary public on a purely political issue, and almost the only topics to excite any real expression of popular opinion were food shortages and religious prejudice. A long process of education was necessary before public opinion was likely to play any real part in the ordinary political issues of the day.

For these reasons, there was, after the excitement of the Fifteen, a marked toning-down of political propaganda in the country newspapers. Andrew Brice established his *Post-Master* in Exeter in 1717 with the declared object of answering what he called, with obvious reference to the Tory Farleys, 'the Scandalous Insinuations spread perpetually by Presses in this City, disaffected to our happy Constitution'.[17] But he was soon informed by a correspondent that 'the Essays on Politicks . . . were ungrateful to some of your Readers. . . . The Cause of this Complaint being taken away, your Paper will more generally please.' [18] Other correspondents agreed: according to one, ' 'twere advisable that these Pages were kept as free as possible from Party Cavils'.[19] And very soon the printer was forced to announce that 'we will carefully avoid all personal Censures and Party Cavils as being injurious to our Paper'.[20]

Even the scandal of the South Sea Bubble failed to arouse any great interest. The crisis was reported fairly adequately, but no paper seems to have attempted to make political capital out of the affair. The Opposition cry that Walpole was the 'screen', protecting the guilty from justice, was not taken up by the country newspapers, which displayed far more hostility towards the 'nouveaux riches' and the stock-jobbers than towards the politicians. The *Stamford Mercury* maintained that great profits had been made by 'the meanest of People; some of whom, in a few Months, have gain'd greater Wealth by meer gambling, without Merit, than was ever got by any

---

[17] Andrew Brice, 'The Author's Case' (1730), quoted Brushfield, 'Andrew Brice and the early Exeter Newspaper Press', op. cit. p. 165.
[18] *Post-Master*, 11 October 1723.
[19] Ibid. 12 February 1724/25.   [20] Ibid. 26 February 1724/25.

British Minister'.[21] Other papers included similar comments; and
the *Northampton Mercury*, a paper which was always inclined to
support the Whig ministry, reproduced three political cartoons—
the only ones to appear in the whole period—illustrating with great
vigour the ravages caused by the Bubble, and the unpleasant fate
desired for the stock-jobbers.[22] On the whole the provincial papers
made little of the crisis.

If the political essay had dropped into the background, however,
and the printers sought to avoid controversy, the process of political
education went on in the extracts from the written news-letters. In
these extracts, the country newspapers possessed their one great
advantage over the London newspapers, which were too close to the
Court and Westminster to dare to defy the frequent resolutions of
the House forbidding the publication of its debates; and which, in
the matter of domestic politics generally, tended to prefer the alle-
gorical parallel, the innuendo or the abstract essay to direct political
criticism. But the more exclusive and private news-letters continued
to defy all restrictions, and provided their readers with detailed,
although admittedly very brief, accounts of the cut-and-thrust of
parliamentary debates, and with intimate gossip about the great
political personalities of the day. These comments were often remarkably well-informed and accurate. Thus, an extract from *Wye's
Letter* in the *Nottingham Mercury* in 1717 reported that, during
the course of a debate, 'Mr. Lech[me]re said, he had heard Mr.
Wal[po]le had entred into new Alliances, but intirely disbelieved it
till now'.[23] In fact, Walpole had now entered into opposition. Similarly, the following year, the *St. Ives Post-Boy*, in an item from a
news-letter, related how, in the debate on the King's speech, 'Mr.
Shippen seconded Mr. Walpole in the Debate on the Words Entire
Satisfaction, and call'd him Old Friend, though they formerly were
known to be as much at Variance as ever were Herod and Pontius
Pilate'.[24] This item about the sudden and unnatural alliance between
Walpole and Shippen, the notorious Jacobite, was just the sort of
news that the politically minded squire wanted to read. And undoubtedly a surprising amount of up-to-date and accurate political
information was imparted in these brief extracts from the written
news-letters. This political education slowly bore fruit. The intimate

---

[21] *Stamford Mercury*, 3 November 1720. See also the issues of 8 September, 6 October, 1720, 14.28 April 1721; *York Mercury*, 23 February, 28
March, 4.11 April, 15 August 1721; *Northampton Mercury*, 8 July 1720.
[22] *Northampton Mercury*, 5.12.26 December 1720.
[23] *Nottingham Mercury*, 16 May 1717.
[24] *St. Ives Post-Boy*, 17 November 1718.

4. AN EIGHTEENTH CENTURY POLITICAL CARTOON, 'THE USE OF THE DIAL', IN THE *NORTHAMPTON MERCURY* OF 5 DECEMBER 1720.

The caption reads: 'Take a S.S. Stockjobber and hang him cn a Gibbet (but be sure to tie him fast; for he will slip the Knot by some Equivocation) let him hang (and be d——d till he is at Par) in a Perpendicular Line without Motion: Then turn him gingerly towards the Sun, with his Mouth open, and observe where the shadow of his Nose falls upon the Hour times, and then you will see the true Hour of the Day in any part of Great Britain.'

little details about the Court and Parliament made politics more exciting and personal.

As always, real progress depended upon developments in the capital. There, the general tendency throughout the period was for politicians in opposition to address themselves more and more to the lower strata of society. Indeed, after 1720, as Walpole became ever more firmly entrenched in power, the inflaming of popular opinion was almost the only weapon left to an Opposition facing an administration secure in the royal favour and controlling the vast machine of patronage and 'influence'. This tendency was noticeable in the pages of such papers as the *London Journal, Read's, Applebee's* and, above all, *Mist's Weekly Journal*—of which a government informer complained that it was 'written ad captum of the Common People'.[25] The antics of these papers were followed with keen interest by the country papers, and the names of their printers rapidly became household words throughout the country—even if those words were not always polite ones. Indeed, in 1719 the Nottingham *Weekly Courant* was referring to

'Dull Read, vile Applebie and Mist,
Three as great Rogues as ever Pist
Are these notorious Journalists.' [26]

With the publication in 1726 of the *Craftsman*, the age of the political newspaper may be said to have begun. At the same time, the bold originality of that Opposition paper, its daring attacks upon Walpole and his Whigs, and the particularly bitter newspaper war which it provoked in the capital provided the final impetus to the emergence of the political paper in the country. Politics had again become really exciting—and the country printers found it increasingly difficult to maintain that God-like impartiality they had so often proclaimed, and quite impossible to attempt to exclude politics altogether from their pages. The growing popular interest in politics was manifested in the increasing number of political essays and letters sent in by readers—essays which the printers found it difficult to refuse. Thus, in 1730 a correspondent to the *Original York Mercury* informed the printer firmly that 'tho' I am sensible of your pacifick Inclinations, yet I insist you will insert the following Lines from the *Flying Post* . . . You know Poor Robin has many Enemies';[27] and he enclosed a strong defence of 'Poor Robin'—Sir Robert Walpole.

[25] *SPD* 35, vol. 29 (67).   [26] *Weekly Courant*, 22 October 1719.
[27] *Original Mercury, York Journal*, 24 February 1729/30.

The unfortunate printer found himself in a difficult situation. He could not exclude politics altogether from his paper. The Oxford *Student* started out with that intention—and failed; for, as a reader remarked, 'if you don't take Occasion sometimes (notwithstanding your Advertisement) to treat of Politicks, to vindicate or condemn the Conduct of our Ministers . . . your Readers and your Purchasers will make but a very small Number'.[28] If he endeavoured to maintain an attitude of strict impartiality, he would also find himself in difficulties with the more party-minded among his readers. As the printer of the *Manchester Magazine* explained,

'if, when there is a dearth in the Land of Politicks, an anti-ministerial Paper should be inserted . . . some would cry out, is not this Fellow, meaning me, an ungrateful Wretch, thus to abuse the Government which has done such great Things for him? On the other Hand, should I publish a Paper in favour of the Government, it would be said, I have every Reason to believe by a great Majority of the Readers of this Paper, why are we troubled by this Whiggish Stuff?'[29]

Generally speaking, from about 1726 onwards, the provincial newspapers fell into two broad groups. On the one hand, there were the papers which flung themselves wholeheartedly into the political fray. On the other, there were those which avoided the outspoken political essay and strove to steer a middle course between the two parties. This distinction remained reasonably sharp until 1742; but thereafter the whole situation was radically transformed.

In 1724, Samuel Negus had written a long letter to the Secretary of State, Lord Townshend, in which he gave an 'Account of the Printing-Houses in the several Corporation Towns in England'.[30] In that account, he painted a lurid picture of the disaffection which flourished within the printing-trade:

'Your lordship may not be altogether insensible of the hardships and the temptations a young beginner in printing may meet with from the disaffected; and how hard it is for such a man to subsist, whose natural inclinations are to be truly loyal and truly honest, and at the same time want employ; while the disaffected printers flourish and have more than they can despatch. . . .

When your lordship is pleased to cast an eye on the number of printing houses there are in and about the cities of London and Westminster, your lordship will not be so much surprised at the present ingratitude and dissatisfaction of a rebellious sort of men. They have no way to vend their poison but by the help of the press. Thus printing houses are daily set up and supported by unknown hands. The country printers in

[28] *Student*, 31 January 1750.
[29] *Manchester Magazine*, 20 December 1737.　　[30] Negus, *Compleat List.*

general copy from the rankest papers in London; and thus the poison is transmitted from one hand to another through all his majesty's dominions. How far this may tend to the corrupting the minds of his majesty's subjects, and how detrimental it may prove to the state, your lordship is a competent judge. . . ."

It must be admitted that Negus was largely correct in his assertion that the country printers in general copied from 'the rankest papers in London'. Certainly, the country papers which supported Walpole were always very much in the minority. Of these, the most outspoken and important were the *Northampton Mercury*, *Brice's Weekly Journal* in Exeter, the *Leeds Mercury*, *Norwich Mercury*, and, perhaps, the *Original Mercury, York Journal. However*, the first three were not primarily political papers, but emphasized rather their literary content. And the other ministerial supporters—such papers as the *Gloucester Journal, Ipswich Journal, Kentish Post* and *Derby Mercury*—tended to be even more lukewarm in serving the cause. In some ways, the Walpole ministry was unfortunate in that it was often defended by papers which had no immediate rival, and which therefore always had one eye upon possible Tory readers. In such cases, mercenary considerations tended to triumph over party zeal. There was no doubting, for instance, that such papers as the *Gloucester Journal* and the *Ipswich Journal* were Whiggish in their sympathies. The former was violently attacked in 1727 by the Tory *Farley's Bristol Newspaper* for its reporting of the Tory victory in a local parliamentary election. According to Farley, 'the puny Gloster Printer being one of the Scrutineer Party has not done the Publick that common Justice to insert it in his Journal; where he found Room enough for Things of lesser Moment. . . . Had the Cause issu'd for his own Clan, we should have seen it in distinguishable Characters, no doubt.' [31] Significantly enough, the attack was on the fact that the *Gloucester Journal* had simply suppressed unwelcome news. Similarly, the *Ipswich Journal* often came in for some heavy handling by the Tory *Norwich Gazette* on the grounds that it was 'disguisedly talk[ing] in the Interests of One Party while it is actually and industriously doing the Drudgery of the Other'.[32] These ministerial papers were really non-politically Whig. They tended to avoid the provocative essay, and seldom ventured upon the offensive. They therefore played but a small part in the political battles of the time.

Perhaps the most influential supporter of the Whig ministry was the news-letter writer, William Wye. By the 1730's, *Wye's Letter*

[31] *Farley's Bristol Newspaper*, 23 September 1727.
[32] *Norwich Gazette*, 22 January 1742/43.

had virtually ousted every rival from the field. No country newspaper could afford to be without a regular weekly extract from it,
and Wye's political sympathies were definitely with the Whig
ministry. The efforts of the City of London authorities in 1727 to
cast a slur upon the Walpole administration he condemned roundly
as 'factious Practices'; during the uproar over Walpole's proposed
Excise Scheme in 1733 he constantly urged the people 'to suspend
the Noise and Clamour till they see in what Shape it appears', and
he maintained, with some truth, that the whole panic had been
artificially stirred up by the *Craftsman*, which, he said, 'may be call'd
to Account for Misrepresentation'; and in 1737 he was still pro-
testing at what he termed the Opposition's 'Endeavour to keep up
the Spirit of Faction. . . . How can we expect to be fear'd or respected
by our Neighbours, if his Majesty's Measures are thus expos'd and
revil'd?' [33]

Wye's Letter, the universal source of information about Court and
Parliament, thus gave rise to a curious contradiction in the pages
of the provincial Opposition papers, whose political essays would
be thundering against the Walpole ministry, while the extracts from
Wye's Letter urged exactly opposite sentiments. Even the great *York
Courant*, perhaps the most outspoken and powerful of all the country
newspapers which opposed Walpole, did not succeed in resolving
this problem until 1739, when it went to the extraordinary lengths
of employing a private news-writer of its own. Otherwise, Wye remained all-powerful until about 1745.

Such were the ministry's supporters. They were feeble indeed when
compared with the country papers which took the side of the Opposi-
tion—feeble in numbers and, above all, in fire and enthusiasm.
Against the Walpole ministry stood such papers as the *York
Courant*, *Chester Courant*, *Stamford Mercury*, *Worcester Journal*,
Farley's Exeter Journal, *Farley's Bristol Newspaper*, *Norwich
Gazette* and many others. All were solidly against Walpole—although it is extremely difficult today to make any distinction between
the true Tory papers and those which belonged properly to the
Whig Opposition. Henry Cross-grove, printer of the *Norwich
Gazette*, was undoubtedly a Jacobite in his sympathies, and made
no secret of the fact. The Farleys were clearly regarded as Tory by
their various opponents, as were the printers of the *York Courant*
and the *Chester Courant*. But contemporaries could, of course,
seize upon slight nuances of opinion which the passage of time has

[33] Respectively, *Leeds Mercury*, 25 July 1727; *Derby Mercury*, 15 February, 11 January 1732/33, 2 June 1737.

now obscured. By and large, all the Opposition papers quoted from the same London newspapers, and pushed the same sort of views. And it is probably more satisfactory—and certainly simpler—to regard them all as simply 'Opposition' papers than to try to disentangle the subtle contemporary distinctions between 'Tory', 'Hanoverian Tory' and 'Whig out of office'.

The Opposition papers flung themselves whole-heartedly into the political battles of the day. The outstanding example was the *York Courant*, which regularly gave up two of its four pages to a political essay attacking the ministry. And from 1729 onwards it reprinted each week the essay from the *Craftsman*, the great propaganda weapon forged by Lord Bolingbroke against his arch-enemy, Walpole. Every week it reprinted the *Craftsman's* thundering denunciations of 'corruption', together with the whole of the 'History of England'—in which Walpole was always easily recognizable as the 'evil counsellor' who invariably came to a very unpleasant end—and all of Bolingbroke's 'Dissertation on Parties'. Above all, it reproduced the steady attack upon 'Robinocracy'—the vicious assault upon Walpole personally and the way in which he was perverting the whole system of government to feather his own nest and that of his family. Typical of this last attack was the biting item in an issue of 1731 to the effect that ' 'tis said Peter Leheup Esq., who is Sir Robert Walpole's Brother's Wife's Sister's Husband's Brother, will be made a Master in Chancery'.[34] So politically-conscious was the printer of the *York Courant*—and, apparently, his public—that on one occasion in 1735 the political essay took up virtually the entire paper, leaving only three-quarters of a column for the actual news. The readers were simply informed that the essay would make 'ample Amends' for the omission of the news items.[35] When, after 1736, the *Craftsman* had lost much of its original fire, the *York Courant* proceeded to extend its range, announcing that

'in our Choice of Political Papers we shall always prefer those which appear most deserving the Attention of the Publick, and therefore propose to print sometimes the *Craftsman*, and sometimes *Common Sense*, not doubting but as they are both engag'd in the same Common Cause of Liberty and this Country, they will be equally acceptable to our Readers'.[36]

Later in 1740, the *Champion* was adjudged to have attained to the necessary standard of violence, and was admitted to the select circle.

The *York Courant* was outstanding. But many other country

---

[34] *York Courant*, 1 June 1731. [35] Ibid. 14 January 1734/35.
[36] Ibid. 6 February 1740.

papers indulged in the same sort of weekly outbursts against the Walpole ministry. Both the *Newcastle Courant* and *Farley's Bristol Newspaper* frequently reprinted the *Craftsman's* political essays— although both made the mistake, avoided by their York colleague, of reproducing the notorious Hague Letter in 1731. That letter virtually betrayed the government's foreign policy; and for this act of indiscretion the two printers enjoyed the dubious honour of being prosecuted in the company of their illustrious London model. *Farley's Exeter Journal* apparently preferred the even more reckless political essays from *Mist's Journal*.

In this way, the countryside rang every week with the full-blooded outcries of the Opposition papers. Against the sustained violence of this campaign, the ministry's supporters put up only a feeble and spasmodic defence. All too often their attitude was that of the printer of the *Original Mercury, York Journal* in 1729. He was, he declared, prepared to print anything 'except waving the poor Reflections of discontented Parties since we are now under the happy Government of King GEORGE. And such always shall be the Method of this Paper, not to seek to please those who delight in Faction and Sedition'.[37] His policy was therefore one of suppression only, and rarely did he venture to attack the Opposition. On one occasion, he did have the temerity to print a verse:

> 'Believe me, Lads, the H[i]gh C[hur]ch Zeal
> Is like the noisy Jack-Daws Peal,
> When perch'd up high on Steeple,
> Who to the Ch[ur]ch did ne'er do good,
> But only daub and soil the Wood,
> And sh–te down on the People.'

He added at the bottom that 'the Gentleman who sent me this may see my Readiness to oblige, though I could wish to give as little Offence as possible, hating all Reflections. Those who may take it ill are at liberty to respond'.[38]

Fortunately for the ministry, such papers as the *Northampton Mercury* and *Brice's Weekly Journal* adopted a more positive attitude. Both regularly described ministerial pamphlets at length. In 1727, Brice even reproduced in its entirety the pamphlet 'An Enquiry into the Reasons of the Conduct of Great Britain', while in 1731 the *Northampton Mercury* on one occasion devoted more than four columns to an abstract of 'The Case of his Majesty's German Dominions set in a clear Light, and their *natural Relation* to the

[37] *Original Mercury, York Journal*, 14 January 1728/29.
[38] Ibid. 21 January 1728/29.

Interests of Great Britain impartially considered.' [39] Rarely did the *Northampton Mercury* miss an opportunity to denounce the various Opposition writers and newspapers. It was particularly severe on *Mist's Journal*, which at various times it described as 'scribble scrabble' and as 'a monstrous Mass of foul corrupted Matter'.[40] And on one occasion, having quoted Mist several times, the printer remarked that 'we must avoid being too familiar with that heterodox Paper, lest we be forced to alter our Title, and instead of The Northampton call it the Romantick Mercury. Touch Pitch, and be defiled.' [41] In 1731, it achieved what was probably its most effective piece of political propaganda, in a clever attack upon Lord Bolingbroke in what purported to be a letter written 'on reading the Speech of Satan in "Paradise Lost" ':

'I could not but reflect with myself; that if there be any Person among us who has formerly been promoted to great Honour and Dignity, but is now, through Pride, Envy and Malice fall'n from that happy State; how just and natural it is to suppose him looking round upon the Glories of his Country, reflecting at the same Time upon the happy Condition from whence he fell, and breaking forth into a Speech like this of Satan, softened in the beginning with all the most Tender Touches of Remorse and Self Accusation, but in the End hardening himself in his Impenitence, and in his Design of drawing other weak and innocent Persons into his own State of Guilt and Misery, and into a rash Vow and wicked Resolution to destroy that Man by whose wise and sturdy Administration this Country now flourishes and is restored to the most Glorious State of Peace and Happiness. . . .

> O Walpole, to tell thee, how I hate thy Sight.
> Which Way I fly is Hell, my self is Hell . . .
> The lower still I fall, only Supreme
> In Misery; such Joy Ambition finds . . .
> Evil, be thou my Good! By Thee at least
> Divided Empire with Britannia's King I hold.' [42]

But this letter set a standard only rarely approached. Usually, all the initiative was in the hands of the Opposition papers, and even the sturdy Andrew Brice at Exeter was generally on the defensive. He could only try to answer what he called 'Mist's fallacious vile Account of Whig and Tory reprinted by his second Author Mr. Farley' with a long and rather tedious historical essay on the origin and principles of the two political parties.[43] To make matters worse, this account appeared some considerable time after the article it was

[39] *Brice's Weekly Journal*, 20 January to 3 March 1726/27; *Northampton Mercury*, 8 March 1731.
[40] *Northampton Mercury*, 20 June 1720, 17 August 1730.
[41] Ibid. 3 July 1721.   [42] Ibid. 20 September 1731.
[43] *Brice's Weekly Journal*, 10 November 1727.

supposed to be answering, and so had lost much of its point. Brice had intended to reply earlier, but changed his mind, announcing that 'considering withal the Ticklishness of the Time, and how flippery a Thing Reputation is . . . I am oblig'd to defer this Entertainment'.[44] Obviously, however, his opponents were not so worried about reputation. Later, Brice produced a somewhat feeble imitation of Mist's notorious 'Persian Letter'—a vicious personal attack upon Walpole—in an attempt to forestall Farley and draw his sting.[45] But usually the replies came too late to repair the damage, and certainly could never approach the power and daring of the original attacks.

The overwhelming anti-ministerial emphasis in the country newspapers was undoubtedly due in part to the greater excitement provided by the Opposition papers. No sober defence of Walpole could possibly compete with Mist's savage 'Persian Letter', or the *Craftsman's* biting personal attacks upon him. Much of the popularity of these papers came from the public's craving for sensationalism. The public wanted excitement; and it undoubtedly relished the spectacle of journalists risking their necks for its entertainment. As the editor in Foote's play, *The Bankrupt*, remarked, 'writers in journals, like rope-dancers, to engage the public attention, must venture their necks every step they take. The pleasure people feel arises from the risks that we run'.[46] And the *Freeholder* agreed with this somewhat cynical estimate of the popular sentiment: 'unless you Journalists now and then cut a bold stroke, they give you over; cry, you are grown insipid'.[47]

But the political emphasis was also due to the preponderance of 'Tory' feeling through the country. It seems clear that the vast majority of the readers of the country newspapers were 'Tory' in their political sympathies, in the sense that they were against the government. The country as a whole was prosperous: but, from the point of view of the lower classes, it was an unstable kind of prosperity. Their financial margin of safety was negligible, they were very much at the mercy of forces beyond their control, and they tended to look back to a past when their place in society had been fixed and protected. For this reason, the Walpole ministry had few out-and-out supporters. Printers who personally favoured the Whig cause were clearly deterred from taking up a positive attitude towards politics by the fear of losing readers, and they always displayed a far more tender regard for the political susceptibilities of

---

[44] *Brice's Weekly Journal*, 27 October 1727.   [45] Ibid. 30 August 1728.
[46] *The Bankrupt*, Act III, scene 2, quoted Hunt, *The Fourth Estate*, p. 215.
[47] *Freeholder*, 22 August 1722.

their readers than did the Opposition printers. The 'Tory' printer rarely made any concessions to his Whiggish readers—but the Whig printers were inordinately shy and retiring, painfully anxious to please. Their whole attitude suggests that they were only too conscious of the fact that their own personal views were not shared by the majority of their readers. Occasionally they said as much. Soon after the Fifteen, the printer of the *St. Ives Post-Boy* had refused to print a letter 'From the Pope to the Pretender' on the grounds that 'it being but early Days for me at present, I can't tell whether it might not give Disgust to some of my Readers'.[48] The title of the letter would suggest that it contained anti-Jacobite sentiments: and that the printer should refuse to publish it at a time when, according to the official theory at least, the Jacobite cause was dead and the country was solidly behind the Hanoverian dynasty, would certainly seem to indicate that the political situation was not as stable as the Whigs purported to believe. Later, too, the printer of the *Manchester Magazine* remarked that 'should I publish a Paper in favour of the Government, it would be said, I have every Reason to believe by a great Majority of the Readers of this Paper, why are we troubled by this Whiggish Stuff?'[49] In this respect, it may well be significant that, in any local newspaper war, the Opposition paper was usually the victor. At York, Chester, Nottingham, Bristol and Newcastle, the Opposition paper triumphed over its Whig rival. On the ministerial side, the *Northampton Mercury* successfully survived a very feeble challenge; the *Norwich Mercury* withstood the threat of Cross-grove's *Norwich Gazette* for over twenty years, and eventually emerged triumphant; and in Exeter, Andrew Brice saw the downfall of the Tory Farley—although his victory was due not to his own merits but to the death in gaol of his unfortunate rival. Indeed, Brice had previously threatened to leave Exeter altogether, and set up business elsewhere.[50]

It is very noticeable also that few papers ever launched out into open praise of Sir Robert Walpole. In fact, his name was obviously deliberately avoided—and certainly no one reading these papers would dream that Walpole was 'prime' minister in a way that no one had ever been before, or has been since, wielding immense power. The Whiggish papers might reprint the more vicious attacks of the ministerial organs in London upon the Opposition newspapers. From time to time, they might even attempt to defend the ministry's

---

[48] *St. Ives Post-Boy,* 17 November 1718.
[49] *Manchester Magazine,* 20 December 1737.
[50] Brushfield, 'Andrew Brice, etc.', op. cit. p. 183.

measures. But rarely indeed did they so much as mention the name of Walpole. This policy of suppression was particularly noticeable during the great Excise Crisis of 1733, when the Opposition papers throughout the country were screaming for Walpole's blood. Again, the initiative was completely with the Opposition.

After that crisis, the ministerial papers in the country virtually retired from the fray. Defences of the ministry became fewer and fewer, and most of the printers turned instead to literary essays. In contrast to this apathy on the part of the ministry's erstwhile supporters, the Opposition papers redoubled their efforts. The indifference of the so-called ministerial papers and the unchecked enthusiasm of the Opposition papers became especially marked in the early years of the Spanish War which broke out in 1739. The Opposition printers did not hesitate to bring party politics into their reporting of that war—a war which they had been urging for years, but which Walpole had not wanted, and had done his utmost to avoid. The *York Courant*, indeed, followed its announcement of the declaration of war with a lengthy political manifesto:

'His Majesty's Declaration of War against *Spain* being now proclaim'd and publish'd, it manifestly appears *which Party* hath form'd the best Judgment of all our tedious Negociations with that Court and particularly the late Convention.—It would fill one large Volume in Folio to show how we have been flatter'd by the ministerial Writers from Time to Time for almost 20 Years together with Assurances of Peace, and Panegyricks on the Wisdom of our Ministers.—It would require another Volume to show the Sense of the Country Writers upon all our late Treaties and pacifick Measures . . . at least 3 or 4 more Volumes of the same Size to form a little Compendium of the Abuses, Insults and barbarous Treatment of our Merchants from their own unnatural Countrymen as well as the Spaniards . . .

But as the Ministerial Writers have long had nothing left to say, besides cavilling and prevaricating; in Order that their numberless Absurdities and Contradictions may not be forgot, I will refresh the Reader's Memory with a short Specimen of them from 2 Pamphlets only, printed last Year, being one on each Side, with a few Extracts from his Majesty's Declaration of War: which will be sufficient to convince any Man of common Sense that these Writers have been arguing for several Years, not only against the general Sense of the People, but even against His Majesty's Judgment of these Affairs.'

There followed a slashing indictment of the ministry's whole policy towards Spain. The manifesto concluded:

'The Public are now desir'd to judge impartially . . . . I am ready to agree with them that all Heads and all Hands ought to be united upon this Occasion, in the Common Cause; which can never be effected without such a national Union or Coalition of Parties, as We have constantly recommended, and They have constantly opposed. I am not asham'd to revive this Doctrine at present, however scandalously it hath been ridicul'd already, and may be again; for I am thoroughly convinced that Nothing will so effectively strengthen the Hands of His Majesty and that nothing will promise such a Coalition so much as a PLACE BILL.' [51]

So outspoken and definite a statement of policy—anticipating the leading article of the future—was quite exceptional at this period. But this statement set the tone for all the Opposition reporting of the war. The obvious mismanagement of that war undoubtedly provided the Opposition papers with a splendid opportunity, and one which they did not waste. And the actual military and naval operations were therefore carried out against a background of constant derision and disparagement. Hardly a word was printed on the opposite side, for by now the ministerial papers had virtually abdicated. The *Manchester Magazine* could dismiss all the military preparations of 1740 as 'Much Ado about Nothing';[52] and the *Lancashire Journal* reprinted all the vicious little poems from the *London Evening Post* deriding the war effort in general. Typical was its sarcastic 'Farmer's Address to the Army':

'To you, brave Lads, encamp'd at Home. . . .
The British Flag too well display,
'Twill serve to scare the Crows away.' [53]

At last, in 1742, Walpole fell. This event was an important one in the history of the development of the political newspaper. Naturally, the downfall of the hated 'prime' minister was greeted with yells of triumph from the Opposition press throughout the country. All these papers now proceeded to print at length the various Addresses and petitions to Members of Parliament calling for justice against the fallen minister. Typical was the Address of the Lord Mayor, Aldermen and Common Council of London—always bitterly hostile to Walpole—which appeared in the *Norwich Gazette* in 1742. This urged Parliament to promote 'a Place Bill, a Pension Bill, and the Repeal of the Septennial Act in order to restore the ancient Freedom of our Constitution and to secure it against all future Attempts whether of open or secret Corruption'. It demanded 'the earliest and

---

[51] *York Courant*, 20 November 1739.
[52] *Manchester Magazine*, 24 June 1740.
[53] *Lancashire Journal*, 20 October 1740.

strictest Inquiry into the Causes of all past Mismanagements'. And
it concluded,

'and they congratulate themselves and the whole Kingdom, that from
the Virtue and Spirit of the present Parliament every odious Name or
Distinction will be lost among us; and that from this happy Period they
may date the intire Abolition of Parties . . . and that no Distinction will
remain but of those who are Friends or Enemies to the Constitution;
of those who would maintain the Freedom and Independency of Parliament, and of those who would subject it to Corrupt and Ministerial
Influence'.[54]

Similarly-worded Addresses were printed every week.[55]

With the appointment of a Select Committee to enquire into Walpole's supposed corrupt administration, the joy of the Opposition
papers reached its height. Then, gradually, a note of disillusionment
began to creep in. By 12 June 1742, the *Norwich Gazette* was remarking that 'our Domestick Political Affairs are so enveloped in
Mystery and Secrecy that our wisest Prognosticators cannot tell what
even a Day may bring forth: Miracles and Wonders are expected
by some; but Wonders last only Nine Days, and Miracles are ceas'd'.
An almost treasonable note appeared in some of the papers when it
became clear that Walpole was not to be condemned. The *Stamford
Mercury* commented darkly that 'the Power of the Crown is indeed
formidably great',[56] and emphasized that 'we have seen the P[reroga-
tive] R[oya]l brought into Play to force the only Means out of our
Hands which could have thrown the necessary Light upon these
dark and iniquitous Transactions'.[57] The *York Courant* rumbled
obscurely about 'the Royal Puppet . . . Tool Royal . . . his Reign
no better than an Inter Regnum'.[58]

The failure of the so-called 'Patriots' who had overthrown Walpole
to live up to their much-vaunted ideals caused an outcry. Typical
was the attitude of the *Norwich Gazette*, which reprinted many of
the biting attacks made by the *London Evening Post*, now the most
savage of all the newspapers, upon its one-time heroes. William
Pulteney, the former leader of the Opposition to Walpole, was
singled out for special treatment. Pulteney had not only joined the
ministry—which still contained all of Walpole's old colleagues—but
had accepted a peerage into the bargain, becoming Earl of Bath.
Thus, he joined his former enemy in the House of Lords. This made

[54] *Norwich Gazette*, 20 February 1742.
[55] Ibid. 27 February, 13.20 March, 17 April 1742, etc.
[56] *Stamford Mercury*, 2 September 1742.   [57] Ibid. 10 June 1742.
[58] *York Courant*, 10 May 1743.

him the target of much vicious abuse. The *Norwich Gazette* faithfully reproduced all the stinging satires of the *London Evening Post* on this event, such as the poem, 'The Riddle Explain'd':

'To some, 'tis strange that equal Honours now
Shou'd grace a W[alpole]'s and a P[ulteney]'s Brow:
That *They*, who long with unrelenting Hate
At Heads of disagreeing Parties sate;
Who Wars continual in St. S[tephe]n's wag'd,
Led on the Husts, and with such Hate engag'd;
That *They* so widely different should deserve,
From the same P[rince] (whom but one seem'd to serve)
The same Rewards! But oh! they little know
The Wiles of C[ou]rt[ie]rs who can reason so!
Believe me, Friends, the *Riddle's* soon explain'd;
   On Rival Schemes intent themselves they feign'd,
   Which others really were; and by this Show
   Of Mutual Enmity, they wisely drew
   Both Sides into their Snares, of both the Secrets knew;
   Still seeming Diff'rent, still in Fact the same,
   Into each other's Hands they play'd the Game;
   The self-same Ends pursu'd, by various Means,
   One on the Stage, and *One* behind the Scenes.'[59]

Briefer, and more pungent, was its poem 'Judas for Silver sold his Lord'.[60] So inflamed had political passions now become, that the *Stamford Mercury* could dismiss the whole war as a 'Military Phrenzy . . . to divert the Attention of the Publick from what was done or left undone at Home'.[61]

But the same note was making itself heard in those papers which had previously been sympathetic towards Walpole. It was, of course, only natural that these papers should make the most of the obvious discomfiture of their rivals over the fall from grace of the 'Patriots', and should reprint with evident glee the bitter epigrams and verses of the *London Evening Post*. As the generally anticipated improvements both in the administration and in the conduct of the war failed to materialize, however, this humorous note was replaced by a more serious tone. After 1742, in fact, it is difficult to distinguish between the true Opposition papers and those which had previously supported Walpole. By 1743, even the *Northampton Mercury*, once the most outspoken of the ministry's supporters, could print an essay from the *Craftsman* condemning Walpole for having entrusted the conduct

[59] *Norwich Gazette*, 4 September 1742.
[60] Ibid. 9 October 1742. Similar in issues of 14 August, 13 November, 4 December 1742, 8 January 1743.
[61] *Stamford Mercury*, 11 November 1742.

of the war to 'those who had a visible Interest in rendering it burden-
some and ineffectual'.[62] All the papers were, indeed, becoming increasingly critical of the Whig government: and although the outbreak of the Forty-Five temporarily stilled the clamour, the provincial press henceforward presented an almost united front against
the Whig oligarchy.

It seems clear that, despite themselves, even those papers which
had supported Walpole had been to some extent won over by
Opposition propaganda, and had expected great things when the
'Patriots' took over the conduct of affairs. The failure of the
'Patriots' to live up to their high ideals now produced complete
disillusionment, and gave added weight to all Bolingbroke's attacks
upon corruption. And from this time onwards, the *Craftsman's* old
attacks were to be repeated with ever-growing emphasis in almost
all the provincial newspapers. As early as 1744, the *Stamford Mercury* had insisted that 'a Change of Men avails Nothing. . . . What
we have long wanted is a Change of Measures.' [63] And this demand
was to be taken up time and time again for the rest of the period.
The whole emphasis in the country newspapers was upon the absolute necessity of more frequent parliamentary elections, purity of
elections, the abolition of sinecures and the exclusion of place-men
and pensioners from the House of Commons.[64]

So violent did the tone of some of the country papers become that
occasional efforts were made to set up papers in the opposite interest.
In 1741, the *York Gazetteer* was founded 'to correct the Weekly
Poison of the *York Courant*'.[65] In 1749, the *Bristol Weekly Intelligencer* appeared, introducing itself with an ostentatious declaration
of its political policy:

'as we establish it as a certain Principle, or Maxim, that Party Distinc-
tions, are not only the Bane and Canker of every Nation, but also of all
Civil Societies wherever they exist; so we can by no Means show
Countenance, or give Reception, either to personal Invectives, or
general Hints, or Arguments founded on an Attempt to kindle the
Flames of Division, or Misunderstandings, among any of our Fellow
Countrymen of whatever Rank, Profession or Degree; well-knowing
that the unnatural Maxim, and Practice, of Divide et Impera, is the
Ground Work only of all bigotted Popery and Enthusiasm.
And, as on the one Hand, we shall always avoid prostituting these our

[62] *Northampton Mercury*, 24 January 1742/43. See also 11 October and
15 November 1742.   [63] *Stamford Mercury*, 6 December 1744.
[64] Cf. *Norwich Gazette*, 24 December 1743, 5 August 1749; *Norwich
Mercury*, 21 December 1751, 10 February 1753, 6 September 1755; *Ipswich
Journal*, 16 July 1757; *Oxford Journal*, 23 August 1755, &c.
[65] *York Gazetteer*, 15 December 1741.

Intentions to the Vindication of any publick Measures, or Transactions, whenever they shall appear manifestly wrong in their Tendency for the good of the whole: — So, on the other we declare ourselves true and sincere Friends to the present happy Establishment, the illustrious Royal Family, who now adorn the British Throne, under whom as a free People, we are so mildly and prudently governed and protected on all Occasions in the Enjoyment of our Liberties, Properties, and Religious and Civil Rights.' [66]

Finally, in 1755, the *Manchester Magazine* deliberately adopted as its sub-title the slogan 'an Antidote to the Poisonous Nonsense of the *London Evening Post*'. Its aim henceforward, its printer declared, would be 'to prevent the terrible Effects of the treasonable, enthusiastic Stuff so long circulated in the Sink of Scandal and Nonsense, the *London Evening Post*, and in some Country News Papers',[67] But so popular had that London paper now become that no country paper could afford to ignore its vicious little poems and epigrams; and very soon the *Manchester Magazine* was itself printing extracts from the very paper it had set out to demolish.

The type of 'entertainment' provided by that London scorpion was admirably revealed during the uproar over the so-called 'Jew Bill' in 1753. By that Bill, it became, for the first time, legally possible for individual Jews to be naturalized by Act of Parliament. That simple measure raised such a storm of protest throughout the country that eventually the Pelham ministry was forced to repeal it. At first sight, the uproar might seem to indicate that the English people as a whole were violently anti-Semitic. In actual fact, however, mob passions and prejudices were to a large extent deliberately created and exploited for purely political ends, as a means of bringing down the Pelham administration. In that campaign, the *London Evening Post* played a leading role, attaining heights of virulence and scurrility never before achieved. Sheer superstition, religious prejudice, the menace of racial pollution and the economic threat represented by the Jews were its great themes, and history was ransacked for examples of Jewish cruelty and deceit. The whole mixture was well flavoured with 'fables', very doubtful jokes and the pithy verses so characteristic of this newspaper. And this campaign was reproduced throughout the country in the pages of the provincial papers.

The *Cambridge Journal* may, perhaps, be regarded as a typical country paper of this period. Politically, its sympathies undoubtedly lay with the Opposition, but its general attitude was one of modera-

[66] *Bristol Weekly Intelligencer*, 3 September 1749.
[67] *Manchester Magazine*, 13 May 1755 and 28 October 1755 respectively.

tion. After a preliminary blast at 'goggle-eyed Creatures' in a great city 'which now goes by the Name of the Anti-Christ City',[68] the *Journal* attempted to live up to its announced policy of political impartiality by giving a reasoned explanation of the true scope of the Act taken from the ministerial *General Evening Post*.[69] But it gave no more such explanations, and henceforward drew mainly upon the *London Evening Post* for its material. From now on, few copies of the *Journal* did not contain some attack upon the Jews. According to one number, the Jews 'alone of all Animals, when harbour'd and well treated, grow more venomous and cruel'.[70] Usually, however, a more humorous note prevailed.

'Many well-dispos'd *Christian Jews*' [remarked the *Journal*] 'are intimidated from fulfilling the Law, by an Apprehension of the Pain and Confinement attending the Mosaic Rite of Circumcision, as it is commonly perform'd in England and Berwick upon Tweed; This is to inform the Publick, that there is just arriv'd from Holland Mr Ishmael Levy, who had the Honour of being Circumciser to the Synagogue at Rotterdam upwards of twenty Years. This Gentleman gives as little Pain in the Exercise of his Art as the Italian Tooth-drawer. . . . All such *Venerable Personages*, N—n [noblemen], M—s of P—t [Members of Parliament], Etc. therefore who are already circumcised in their Hearts, may now have an Opportunity of becoming Apostates from Christianity to all Intents and Purposes, without hindrance of Business or the least uneasy Sensation.'[71]

From this point on, the campaign gradually increased in intensity. From the *Gray's-Inn Journal*, the Cambridge printers took the famous 'News from One Hundred Years Hence', purporting to give the news of the year 1853, when, as a result of the Jew Bill, England would be completely under the domination of the Jews. In this article, all the names of the ministers and notables were Jewish; instead of the debates of Parliament, those of the Sanhedrin were described—including a Bill to take 16,000 Philistines into British pay; and the loyal toasts at a banquet included 'our present happy Establishment in Sinagogue and State. The glorious and immortal Memory of Harry the Ninth'.[72] 'Harry the Ninth' was, of course, Henry Pelham, the author of the Bill. The *Journal's* campaign really culminated in its biting paraphrase of the 34th. Chapter of the Book of Genesis:

'21. The Pelh—tes [Pelhamites] and Germ—tes [Germanites] are peaceable with us, therefore we will dwell in their land, and trade

<hr>

[68] *Cambridge Journal*, 2 June 1753.   [69] Ibid. 16 June 1753.
[70] Ibid. 10 November 1753.   [71] Ibid. 4 August 1753.
[72] Ibid. 13 October 1753.

therein; for behold the Land is large enough for us; let us take their Daughters to us for Wives, and their Lands for Portions.

24. Only herein will the Pelh—tes consent unto us, that we clear off their Mort—[Mortgage], and give them a sufficient Number of Bank Notes; then will they order every Male to be circumcised.

25. And it came to pass on the third Day whilst their Private Parts were sore, that the Jews took up their Swords and slew every Male of the Britons. . . .

28. And took their Sheep and their Oxen, and their Asses, and that which was in the City, and that which was in the Fields;

29. Their Lands, and their Houses, their Vineyards, and all their Wealth; and all their Little-ones, and their Wives, took they captive. . . .' [73]

The same sort of campaign was being carried on in nearly every country paper in England. Like the *Cambridge Journal*, the *Norwich Mercury* at first adopted an attitude of moderation. In particular, it quoted from the ministerial *General Evening Post*—which rightly pointed out that

'in 1750 when the Opinions in the House of Commons were divided in relation to the Propriety of passing the general Naturalisation Bill, it was nevertheless the avowed and declared Opinion of Persons of all Sides that the Naturalising rich Jews would be a right and prudent Measure, and what every body was ready to agree to.—If this be true, as it certainly is, it is difficult to account for the Torrent of Abuse and Clamour the passing of the present Act hath produced, on any other Principle but the Hopes of misleading People at the next General Election.' [74]

But very soon, the *Norwich Mercury* was printing all the vicious items in which the *London Evening Post* specialized: a rich Jew was buying up estates; the Sanhedrin had 'unanimously resolved upon a Bill being presented . . . for the more effectively abolishing Christianity out of this Kingdom': a ship was ready to take in 'those Christian Families that may be inclined to transport themselves to any Part of Turkey, as chusing to live under a Mahometan rather than a Jewish G—t [Government]'; a fine statue of Pontius Pilate was to be erected 'by Order of the *Jews* . . . in Memory of the Victory over the Christians'; and, as usual, a famous surgeon would perform the operation of circumcision quite painlessly. [75] No paper, in fact, could afford to ignore such items, with all their savage humour and appeal. And the whole episode may be regarded as the

[73] Ibid. 27 October 1753. [74] *Norwich Mercury*, 30 June 1753.
[75] Ibid. 28 July and 11 August 1753.

first propaganda campaign to be conducted upon almost national lines.

The 'Jew Bill', the General Election of 1754 and the mismanagement of the early stages of the Seven Years War all combined to produce an increasingly critical note in almost all the country newspapers. Regularly, these papers denounced the political corruption of the time, and the moral and national corruption it had supposedly encouraged. Only with the coming to office of the great national hero, the Earl of Chatham, was the clamour partially stilled, with the newspapers rejoicing in the newly found national unity. It was, said the *Norwich Mercury*, a sign that 'the odious Distinction of Party is on a fair Way of being annihilated'.[76] But the critical note was never entirely absent now; and the *Bath Journal* could still assert that 'neither the Petulancy of a disgusted People nor the Influence or Obstinacy of a K[ing] should be able to engage any one to yield to bad Measures'.[77] Such a statement shows only too well how far the country newspaper had moved since its early years when its political utterances had been few and tentative. It was now well on the way to becoming the Fourth Estate, an instrument of publicity and criticism, shaping and leading public opinion. As such it invited—and received—the close attention of the authorities of the time.

[76] *Norwich Mercury*, 26 February 1757. Similar in *Manchester Magazine*, 21 December 1756 and *Union Journal*, 27 March 1759.
[77] *Bath Journal*, 11 July 1757.

CHAPTER SEVEN

PROSECUTION AND THE PRESS

I F modern historians have tended to assume that the political influence of the provincial newspaper was negligible, that view was not shared by Authority in the eighteenth century, and the growing importance of the provincial press was faithfully reflected in the number of prosecutions it suffered as the century progressed. After 1715, when, politically, the country newspaper came of age, and the printers discovered the possibilities of the political essay, there was a sudden spate of prosecutions. Hitherto, it had never been found necessary to prosecute a country printer.

The first to suffer was Henry Cross-grove, the unashamedly Jacobite printer of the *Norwich Gazette*. In a letter to a friend, he wrote that his local enemies had 'drawn up a petition to the R and Council for the silencing my press, and it was I hear sign'd by the Mayor, several Justices of this City, the High Sheriff, and our good Dean'.[1] His offence was the publishing of a pamphlet entitled 'A short Account of the State of England when James II intended to call his second Parliament'—an account which, incidentally, had already run into some ten editions in London.[2] Later in the same year, Cross-grove was again in trouble: 'I am told within this Hour', he wrote, 'that an Indictment for High Treason will be preferr'd against me; the Substance whereof is (as I am told, for a Copy is denied me) for endeavouring to raise Men against his Majesty and for promoting Rebellion, etc.'[3]

In the following year, 1716, the Grand Jury of Lincoln presented the printer of the *Stamford Mercury* for 'false and scandalous Reflections on the Government', and fined the printer of the Nottingham *Weekly Courant* for a similar offence.[4] And at Exeter the provincial press suffered its first martyrdom, when Philip Bishop, printer of the *Exeter Mercury*, died in gaol while awaiting trial for printing a most

[1] Letter to Strype, 21 March 1714/15, quoted J. B. Williams, 'Henry Cross-grove, Jacobite, Journalist and Printer', p. 212.
[2] *Weekly Journal*, 12 March 1714/15, quoted H. R. Plomer, *Dictionary*, 1688–1725, p. 88.
[3] Letter to Strype, 15 August 1715, quoted Williams, 'Henry Cross-grove, etc.'; op. cit. p. 214.   [4] *Nottingham Mercury*, 23 March 1716.

indiscreet ballad entitled 'Nero the Second', in which the parallel to George I was rather too obvious.[5]

This sudden wave of prosecutions was, of course, due to the quite exceptional excitement of the time, when the new dynasty was very far from being secure. With the miserable collapse of the Fifteen, and the obvious consolidation of the Hanoverian Succession, the enthusiasm on both sides died down—although the incorrigible Cross-grove was again in custody in 1718, this time in London, for what he was pleased to call 'inadvertedly Copying from such Papers as I now perceive are obnoxious to the Government'. And having thus, somewhat belatedly, recognized the error of his ways, he assured the Secretary that 'I will for the future so strictly regulate and reform my Conduct in that Affair, that your Honour may see I do not immerit and have a Gratefull Sense of any such Clemency from the Government'.[6]

After this, the government was on the whole content to leave the provincial newspapers to the mercy of the local authorities, and concentrated its attention upon the London press. So long as the country printers copied their political essays and comments from the London newspapers, it was obviously both simpler and more effective to deal with the supply of seditious material at its source. For this reason, the government sought to repress the London political papers, relying upon the zeal of local authorities to curb any excessive enthusiasm on the part of those country printers who supported the Opposition. However, the government continued to keep an eye upon the activities of the country press by means of informers. And in the State Papers are preserved four copies of provincial newspapers which must have been sent in by such agents. The papers in question are two copies of the *Norwich Gazette* dated 22 March 1718 and 19 December 1724; the *Norwich Mercury* of 19 December 1724; and the *Weekly Worcester Journal* of 10 September 1725.[7] The first three seem to be entirely innocuous, and it is difficult to understand why they should have been brought to the attention of the government in this way. In the case of the copy of the *Weekly Worcester Journal*, however, one item has been carefully marked. It is an innocent enough little paragraph, describing a pamphlet recently published in Glasgow, and ending with the following 'fable':

[5] *Protestant Mercury*, 13 July 1716, 26 December 1716.
[6] Letter to Mr. Secretary Delafaye, 2 January 1718/19, *SPD 35*, vol. 15(1).
[7] *Norwich Gazette*, 22 March 1718, *SPD 35*, vol. 11(50b); *Norwich Mercury* and *Norwich Gazette*, both of 19 December 1724, *SP Geo. I*, vol. 54(31); *Weekly Worcester Journal*, 10 September 1725, *SP Geo. I*, vol. 58(16).

'an Ass, being overburdened, hung her Ears, and as she was travelling along some Distance before her Master, a Horse met her, and asks why she was so cast down? oh, says the Ass, my Burden is heavy, and what can I do? Do, says the Horse, Kick! upon that the Ass kick'd, overthrew her Burden, and ran away from her tyrannical Master.'

The item is apparently a somewhat oblique reference to the riots which had recently taken place in Glasgow over the Malt Duty, and which had had to be put down by the military. But to suggest that this paragraph was likely to promote disaffection was absurd, and illustrates the futility of relying upon information of this type.

As the provincial press grew in stature and influence, some more effective method of keeping an eye upon its political activities became desirable. In 1724, Samuel Negus warned the Secretary of State of the danger of 'corrupting the minds of his Majesty's subjects' (see p. 124), and though His Lordship may not have been impressed at the time, by 1726 the Treasury had evidently come to recognize the need for a more direct method of supervision. From now on it intended to watch over the activities of the country papers as closely as it observed those printed in the capital itself. And a Treasury memorandum dated 28 November 1729 referred to the sum of £75 as representing 'Mr. Bell's expenses for procuring and laying before him for perusal all the newspapers printed in England (beyond the extent of the bills of mortality) as well as those published in North Britain and Ireland during three years ended at Michaelmas last'.[8] Henceforward, Mr. Bell, who was the Comptroller of the Post Office, purchased copies of all the country newspapers for the perusal of the Treasury Solicitor, who then reported to the Secretaries of State 'when the King or Government are traduc'd or slander'd'.[9]

The system produced immediate results. It was directly responsible for the prosecution for high treason of Edward Farley in 1728 for reprinting the famous 'Persian Letter' from *Mist's Weekly Journal*— a letter described by the Grand Jury of the county as an 'infamous, scandalous and terrible Libel, calculated to poison the Minds of his Majesty's Subjects with groundless jealousies; to sow Sedition and overturn the Peace of this Kingdom and in favour of a spurious, abandon'd and abjur'd Pretender'. It led also to the prosecution in 1731 of John White, printer of the *Newcastle Courant*, and Samuel Farley of Bristol. In both cases, their offence was that they had reprinted from the *Craftsman* the notorious 'Hague Letter', revealing the secret negotiations taking place between Britain and the

[8] *Cal. Treasury Books and Papers*, 1729–30, entry for 17 April 1730.
[9] Cf. *Cal. Treasury B and P*, 1735–8, entry for 6 July 1737, p. 422.

Empire.[10] And in 1728 the Grand Jury of Nottingham had presented the local printer for what it called 'printing and publishing severall scandalous and indecent expressions . . . tending to bring the King's Ministers of State into contempt'.[11]

Once again, therefore, as in 1715 and 1716, there was a sudden flurry of prosecutions. Again, however, the prosecutions were largely unsuccessful. Legal actions against the press were, in fact, rarely satisfactory from the point of view of the ministry. This was shown only too plainly in the proceedings over Mist's 'Persian Letter'. The government's legal experts went very carefully indeed into the question of affixing the responsibility for the printing and publishing of that libel; and they decided that the two London compositors who had been arrested could be charged only with a misdemeanour. 'If', they stated, 'the Compositors for the Press in London shd. be indicted for High Treason, there seems to us no Probability of convicting them, notwithstanding the Heinousness of their Offence.' Farley's case was different:

'he is the Master of the Press at Exeter, there are two Witnesses of his reprinting the Libel at Exeter, and one of these speaks to his explaining it in the Criminal Sense at the Time it was so reprinted, and he hath added a Paragraph, from whence it is evident that he understood it in a Sense which is criminal. . . . However, as his Case appears at present to us, we together with others of his Majesty's Council with whom we have consulted upon this Occasion think there is Ground to prosecute him for Treason.'

But this recommendation was far from confidently given, for it concluded with the comment that 'this is a Matter of Great Importance, and in Consideration of Prudence as well as Law we did not think it proper to take upon ourselves to Determine it'.[12] Despite this warning, the ministry determined to prosecute. But some eight months later, the Attorney General had to report that the prosecution's case rested absolutely upon two witnesses: one was a 'Person of a loose Character', whose testimony would not have 'sufficient Weight with the Jury to convict'; the other was Farley's own father-in-law, who, said the Attorney General, was 'so far from being a willing Witness, that nothing will come from him but what is forced'. And, he concluded, 'upon this State of the Case, I cannot think it proper to proceed to Tryal upon this Indictment', nor could

[10] *Cal. Treasury B and P*, 1731-4, entry for 4 May 1731; see also *Leeds Mercury*, 2 and 9 February 1731.
[11] *Records of the Borough of Nottingham*, vi., 1702-60, entry for 19 July 1728.
[12] *SPD 36*, vol. 9 (60-1), memo. dated 24 November 1728.

he advise proceeding upon the lesser charge of misdemeanour. He could only console himself with the comforting thought that Farley had 'lain in Prison almost a Year upon this Charge of High Treason, which is some Punishment, tho' by no means adequate'.[13] Actually, the unfortunate Farley had died in gaol during these lengthy discussions.

The case illustrates perfectly the government's difficulties in prosecutions of this type. Witnesses were rarely forthcoming: and the apprentice who had betrayed Philip Bishop in 1716 had thereby drawn upon himself what an official called 'the inveterate enmity and hatred of the disaffected' to such an extent that the Treasury was obliged to find him some other employment.[14] In fact, the ministry could seldom make its charge of treason stick: yet to press any lesser charge was to reveal its weakness. The point was argued at some length by the Attorney General in 1728:

'the principal Consideration and what weighs most with me, is in respect of the Crown. I think it of great Consequence that the Offence with which Farley is charged should be deemed High Treason, and that has been so far established that the Grand Jury have found a Bill of Indictment upon it, and the terror of that will in some measure continue, altho' for prudential reasons the Prisoner should not be brought to Tryal. But if, after all this, the Crown should prosecute for the same fact as a misdemeanour, that would be absolutely giving up the point of High Treason, and owning to the World that it is in Law an Offence of a lower degree.'[15]

And as early as 1718 the Secretary of State had warned his colleagues with regard to Henry Cross-grove of Norwich that 'it will be better to leave these people alone than to meddle with them only to show our impotency'.[16]

Quite apart from the weakness of its legal position, the ministry was well aware of the fact that any attempts to repress hostile criticism could only provide the Opposition with wonderful material for propaganda. As a writer to the Treasury pointed out, 'there was never a Mist or any other Person taken up or tryed, but double the number of papers were sold upon it, besides ye irritating the people from ye false Notion of Persecution'.[17]

All these factors combined to render the government's attempts at physical repression largely fruitless. After 1731, it intervened in no more provincial cases. The last payment to Mr. Bell was made on

[13] Copy of the Attorney General's Report upon Mr. Farley's Case, dated 14 July 1729, *SPD 36*, vol. 13(79–81).
[14] *Cal. Treasury B and P*, 1714–19, p. 375.   [15] *SPD 36*, vol. 13(81).
[16] *SP Geo. I*, vol. 74(40).   [17] *SP 35*, vol. 117(266).

15 December 1736: [18] but long before that the government had retired from the field. Henceforward, it concentrated upon the London
press, and left the country papers to the zeal of the local authorities.
These were sometimes ready to take action against a printer for his
comments on local politics: but only Nottingham seems to have
been ardent enough to proceed against one for his views on national
politics, when in 1753 it cautioned Samuel Creswell for selling the
Leicester Journal, a paper which was violently opposed to the 'Jew
Bill'. According to the very hostile report of the magistrates' actions
which appeared in the *London Evening Post*,

'Mr Creswel, a Bookseller there, was . . . summon'd to appear before
the *worthy* Magistrates of that Corporation, and rebuk'd for selling the
Leicester Journal; in which, they say, are very severe Reflections on
the Ministry for promoting the late Jewish Naturalisation Bill, greatly
tending to create Fears and Jealousies in his Majesty's good Subjects
and promote Sedition and Rebellion by persuading the People they
were in Danger of losing their Liberties: When, offering to defend
himself, he was threatened to be sent to Goal, unless he found Securities
for his Good Behaviour: However he was discharg'd, on Consideration
he sold no more of these Papers reflecting on the Jews, who are now to
be incorporated amongst us . . .' [19]

The ministry now endeavoured to use its control over the Post
Office to prevent the transmission of the more dangerous Opposition
papers out of London. As early as 1728, *Wye's Letter* in the *Gloucester Journal* had reported that 'the Grand Jury of Middlesex have
presented *Mist's Weekly Journal* of August 24 as a treasonable Libel,
and the said Journal is forbid passing thro' the Post Office and
Secretaries' Office into the Country, as is also the Paper called the
Craftsman'.[20] Later, it was the turn of the *London Evening Post*,
which in 1733 bore the defiant announcement:

'This Day the Clerks of the several Roads in the Post-Office, received
Orders not to send away any more of *The London Evening Post* to
their Customers in the Country. This Order, we presume, is occasion'd
by the said Paper having so often inserted such Paragraphs against the
late Excise-Scheme, and of the Reception at the several Cities, Boroughs, etc. of those Worthy Members that voted in Opposition to that
pernicious Project: But as this Paper has received the Universal Approbation of the Publick, for constantly pursuing the TRUE INTEREST
OF OUR COUNTRY, its not doubted but Gentlemen will either have

[18] *Cal. Treasury B and P*, 1735–8, 278.
[19] Quoted *Norwich Mercury*, 22 September 1753.
[20] *Gloucester Journal*, 10 September 1728.

the said Paper sent them by their Friends, or some other Way convey'd to them, and not suffer a *Court Paper* to be forc'd upon them.' [21]

A few weeks later, the same paper remarked that,

'as *some People* have doubted, whether *any Persons* could be so WEAK as to order the *Clerks of the Post Office* to omit sending the LONDON EVENING POST to their Customers, the underwritten is the Copy of a Letter sent by the *Clerks* on that Occasion.

> *General Post-Office, Octob. 13, 1733.*
> SIR.
> . *Being ORDER'D the 11th. Instant to omit sending any LONDON EVENING POSTS, is the Occasion of my sending you others; and shall continue so to do till I receive your Directions therein.*
> *I am, Sir, etc.'* [22]

Later in the period, the papers *Common Sense* and *Champion* were also banned, and in 1754 it was the turn of the *London Evening Post* once again—this time for its attitude over the Jew Bill.[23]

Such measures seem to have been largely ineffectual. They had a certain nuisance value, undoubtedly, and made it more difficult for country people without influential connexions in London to obtain the newspapers affected. But all too often they seem actually to have encouraged the circulation of the papers they were intended to destroy. Something more positive was obviously required than this policy of suppression: and for this reason the ministry subsidized London newspapers in an attempt to counteract the influence of the Opposition press. The *London Evening Post* took some delight in exposing the ministry's activities in this field, and in mocking the efforts of the leading ministerial writers, Walsingham and 'Mother' Osborne. In October 1733 it informed its readers that,

'in Order to let the World see what Methods are taken to disperse the Works of those doting old Gentlewomen, Walsingham and Osborne, the underwritten is a Copy of a printed Letter sent by the Comptroller of the General Post-Office to the Post-Masters in the Country.

> *General Post-Office, London, Octob. 9, 1733.*
> SIR.
> *I shall send you the inclosed Papers Gratis as oft as they come out, and desire you will make them as publick as you can: If there be any Coffee-houses in your Town, or within your Delivery, where Gentlemen resort to read the News, please to send me the Names of such Coffee-*

[21] *London Evening Post*, 9/11 October 1733.
[22] Ibid. 27/30 October 1733.
[23] Reported in the *York Courant*, 15 May 1739; *Ipswich Journal*, 29 November 1754; and *Northampton Mercury*, 2 December 1754 respectively.

houses, or the Persons who keep them, and I will furnish them Gratis
with the same Papers.

Your Humble Servant,
Jos. Bell

P.S. You will have the Free Briton *and* London Journal *once a Week as*
they come out.
Directed thus:

To the Post-Master of ——
Free, J. Bell.' [24]

According to the obviously prejudiced *London Evening Post*, these
efforts to flood the country with ministerial papers were hardly
successful:

'if they were to be supported *only* by the *Common Sale* of the Papers,'
it commented, 'what a starving Condition would they soon be reduced
to? for the *Daily Courant, Free Briton*, and *London Journal* were grown
so contemptible that scarce any body in Town would *buy them*; nay,
very few even of those to whom they were sent down to in the Country
Ministerially (i.e. *gratis*, Papers and Postage paid) wou'd *read* them;
so these *heavy Authors* have now join'd all their Forces together, and
are to cram into *one* Paper what they retailed before in three, and the
stale Repetition of the *Courant, Free Briton* and *London Journal* are to
be told in the *Daily Gazetteer*, which is to be sent down to the *Post-
houses, Excise-Offices*, etc. in the *Country*'.[25]

On another occasion, it announced that

'whole Piles of Pamphlets and Papers, sent *Gratis* by the Post-Office,
lye neglected and unread, and in some Places the Packets are not yet
open'd . . . the Waiters in several Places have been very near having
their Heads broke for carrying *London Journals, Free Britons, Courants*,
etc. to light the *Company's* Pipes, Gentlemen thinking it gives an *ill-
Taste* to their *Tobacco*, and order'd them to the *Necessary-House*, as
the most proper Place'.[26]

The country was thus flooded with ministerial papers. But one
obvious means of influencing public opinion in the provinces seems
to have been overlooked by the ministry. Papers were sent gratis to
local gentlemen and clergy, to coffee-houses and to government
offices in the country—but not, it would seem, to the printers of
country newspapers. Certainly, the ministry during this period does
not appear to have attempted any such positive policy towards the
country press as that adopted later by the Younger Pitt, who, when
he 'began to find a constant instrument for the inoculation of his

[24] *London Evening Post*, 16/18 October 1733.
[25] Ibid. 3/5 July 1735.   [26] Ibid. 1/3 November 1733.

views indispensable to bear along with him the force and currency
of popular sentiment', appointed, according to a provincial printer
of the next century, an officer whose duty it was

'to open a communication with the proprietors of journals of large
communication, and the result was, that to a vast majority of them,
two or three London papers were sent gratuitously, certain articles of
which were marked with red ink, and the return made was the insertion
of as many of these as the space of the paper would allow. Thus was
the whole country agitated and directed by one mind, as it were; and
this fact accounts in no small degree for the origin, propagation and
support of that public opinion which enabled the minister to pursue
his plans with so much certainty of insuring general approbation.' [27]

Nothing along such systematic lines seems to have been attempted
in this earlier period.

The 'terror' thus proved surprisingly ineffective—despite the
savagery of the possible penalties that could be exacted. According
to Jos. Bliss, Philip Bishop's punishment was to have been 'to stand
in the Pillory three several Times, and to have his Ears (if not his
Hands also) cut off and nail'd to the same; To be whipp'd at the
Cart's Tail three several Market Days round this City; And to be
imprison'd during Life'. And this, according to the obviously un-
sympathetic Bliss, was 'a Sentence indeed too mild for his inexorable
Villainy'.[28] Quite apart from the threat of such punishments,
Authority also possessed formidable weapons in the shape of exceedingly heavy fines and the demands for huge securities for future
good behaviour, which no country printer could at that time have
been expected to afford. In a few cases, such considerations did help
to deter a printer from plunging too rashly into political controversy.
Even Henry Cross-grove, the printer of the *Norwich Gazette*, and
an individual not otherwise noted for his prudence, on certain occasions recognized that discretion was called for. In 1730, he refused
to print the details of what he simply referred to as a 'smart
Protest' by the House of Lords;[29] and in 1749 he informed his
readers that 'whoever is desirous to see our N[o]b[i]l[i]ty and Officers
of the Army set in a proper Light, may look into the *Hague Gazette*
of the 5th. of December N.S. under the London News, which for
Reasons too obvious we cannot translate'.[30] Such instances were,
however, comparatively rare, and by and large the country printers
seldom allowed themselves to be unduly influenced by the threat

[27] *New Monthly*, vol. xlviii., 133, quoted Hunt, *Fourth Estate*, pp. 278–9.
[28] *Protestant Mercury*, 26 December 1716.
[29] *Norwich Gazette*, 7 February 1730.   [30] Ibid. 9 December 1749.

of governmental action. Their public demanded political news and comment; and their public was, in the main, opposed to the Whig ministry. Libels on the ministry were clearly extremely popular: and normally they went unpunished. Apart from its two brief spasms of activity in 1715–16 and again from 1728 to 1731, the central government left the problem of the country newspapers to the local authorities: and these authorities, with the exception of those at Exeter, Norwich and Nottingham, were noticeably reluctant to take action.

Local politics were a different matter altogether. Local authorities were apparently quite prepared to proceed against the printers over local issues. Once again, the authorities at Norwich were exceptionally active. As early as 1714, Cross-grove was lamenting that he was 'continually binding over and prosecuting by juries',[31] and that his paper had cost him 'some pounds by way of prosecution'.[32] In 1729, however, it was the turn of his Whig rival, William Chase, printer of the *Norwich Mercury*. Chase was committed to gaol for a sarcastic reference in his paper to what he called the 'fair and honest Way of Proceeding' of the 'Managers of the Tory Poll' in a recent Common Council election in Norwich which the Tories had won.[33] Chase had his revenge in 1735, when Cross-grove was yet again prosecuted for a 'false, scandalous and infamous Libel, highly reflecting on the Conduct of the present Sheriff, at the late Election of Members for that City'. According to the somewhat partisan report in the Whiggish *Northampton Mercury*, 'what was very remarkable, and must be acknowledged a glaring Instance of the notorious Falsity of that Account, the Grand Inquest, though composed of Gentlemen of both Parties, agreed the same to be such, and signed it accordingly'.[34]

It must be admitted that Cross-grove asked for trouble. Many of his news items were deliberately provocative. Regularly each year, he proclaimed the anniversary of the execution of King Charles I with some such paragraph as the following, which appeared on 31 January 1740: 'Yesterday being the Anniversary Fast and Day of Humiliation for the Unparallelled Murder of the Blessed King and Royal Martyr Charles I who was most inhumanly butcher'd by a damnable Crew of Republican Sectaries, Wretches, whose Religion was Hypocrisy, and whose Loyalty was Rebellion . . .' Similarly, May 29th. was always celebrated as the 'Anniversary of the happy

---

[31] Letter to Strype, 2 December 1714, quoted Williams, 'Henry Cross-grove, etc.', op. cit., p. 211.
[32] Ibid. letter of 1715, 213.   [33] *Norwich Mercury*, 19 April 1729.
[34] *Northampton Mercury*, 19 August 1734.

Restauration of the Royal Family after a tyrannical Usurpation of several Years carried on by a damnable Pack of Hypocritical Sectaries'.[35] It is, in fact, scarcely surprising that the obviously unrepentant Cross-grove was continually in trouble. Indeed, he seemed to thrive upon it.

Most country printers were naturally rather more prudent: but nearly all found themselves in trouble sooner or later. Many only avoided prosecution by making the most abject of public apologies. Thus, in 1748, Elizabeth Adams and her son John, printers of *Adams's Weekly Courant* in Chester, publicly announced that 'we are guilty of printing and publishing a base and scandalous Libel in the said *Courant* against the Right Reverend the Lord Bishop of Chester . . . and the Reverend Doctor Powell, Dean of St. Asaph'.[36] Similarly, in 1753, *Jackson's Oxford Journal* apologized for what it called 'several low, false and infamous Paragraphs' reflecting on the Principal of St. Mary Hall.[37] The last printer to suffer actual prosecution during this period seems to have been Felix Farley, the strongly Tory printer of Bristol. Rather rashly, he commented at some length upon the somewhat dubious methods used by the Whigs in winning a disputed parliamentary election, with particular reference to 'the obvious P[a]rt[ia]l[i]ty conspicuous throughout the whole, and open Injustice . . . great Variety of undue Influence . . . dark Contrivances . . . to evade the Majority and not return Mr. Smith'.[38] Such an account of a local election was quite unusually outspoken for this period: and it is hardly to be wondered at that Farley was prosecuted in 1756. He was, however, acquitted. It is interesting to note that the *London Evening Post* gave the episode some considerable publicity, calling it a trial 'in which the *Rights* and *Liberties* of every *British Subject* were intimately concerned . . . an Attempt was made to infringe the Liberty of the PRESS by a virulent Prosecution for inserting a Paragraph (in one of our former Journals) of some Truths concerning the Election of our worthy Representative'.[39]

On the whole, however, this fear of prosecution—combined with the printer's very natural desire to estrange as few potential customers as possible—largely gagged the country newspapers in the matter of local politics. This was particularly the case with papers which had no immediate local rival. No matter how partisan might

---

[35] *Norwich Gazette*, 30 May 1741.
[36] *Adams's Chester Courant*, 29 November 1748.
[37] *Jackson's Oxford Journal*, 19 May 1753. See also 23 March 1754.
[38] *Felix Farley's Bristol Journal*, 20 March 1756.
[39] Quoted *Norwich Mercury*, 3 September 1757.

be their attitude towards national politics, such papers tended always to insist upon their complete impartiality and neutrality in questions of local politics. Even the great *York Courant*, despite the ferocity of its weekly essays from the *Craftsman*, took no part in local politics, accepting election notices and propaganda from both sides quite impartially until 1741, when the *York Gazetteer* was established with the express purpose of fighting the parliamentary election of that year in the ministerial cause. In the same way, the Farleys of Bristol, despite their strong Tory views, barely mentioned local politics at all until the appearance of the Whig *Bristol Weekly Intelligencer* in 1749.

Only when there was really intense local rivalry between newspapers did the printers venture to speak at all boldly. At Norwich, the continued existence side by side of the Tory *Norwich Gazette* and the Whiggish *Norwich Mercury* meant that each paper was far more outspoken in its accounts of local elections than was usual with eighteenth century provincial newspapers. The same was true of Manchester, particularly in the aftermath of the Forty-Five, when the Whiggish *Manchester Magazine* joined battle with the Tory *Chester Courant* over the conduct and principles of Thomas Deacon, the Non-juring Bishop, in particular, and the loyalty or disaffection of Manchester in general.[40] Even here, however, the printer of the *Manchester Magazine*, although supporting the Whigs and government party, showed himself to be a cautious man. On one occasion in 1746 he informed his readers that 'I have received some intelligence relating to Manchester which I am not willing to be the first in publishing'. The following week there appeared a news item to the effect that 'the Duke of Newcastle Monday last committed the two Manchester Constables to the County Goal . . . in order to be tried at the ensuing Assizes for aiding and abetting his Majesty's Enemies in the late Rebellion. This is the News the Printer hereof was, last Week, unwilling to be the first in publishing'.[41]

Usually, the printers were extremely careful in their reporting of local elections, and virtually confined themselves to printing the election notices of both sides without comment of any kind. There was, however, one great exception to this general rule. During the key General Election of 1734, which, following the Excise crisis and the apparent weakening of Walpole's position, was fought with more than usual keenness and bitterness, the *Northampton Mercury*, a

[40] See O. M. Tyndale, 'Manchester Vindicated', *Lancashire and Cheshire Antiquarian Society*, 53, 1938, 119.
[41] *Manchester Magazine*, 15 and 22 July 1746 respectively.

paper with no immediate rival, suddenly cast aside its habitual caution and moderation, and flung itself wholeheartedly into the fray. What particularly outraged the printer was the action of the Tory corporation in creating, at three guineas a head, one hundred and seventy-one Honorary Freemen. Since only Freemen could vote, this stratagem effectively ensured a Tory victory at the poll, swamping the Whig supporters. The *Northampton Mercury* promptly denounced the action of the corporation as 'a Violation of the Liberties of their Fellow Freemen and Householders (for whom they are Guardians in Trust only, to preserve, not to destroy, their Liberties)'.[42] It was, said the *Mercury*, 'a Method of Proceeding . . . extraordinary in its Kind (and the like having never been attempted here, but in the unhappy Reign of King James II)'. And the printer proceeded to give a list of the names and addresses of all the newly created Freemen, together with their occupations.[43] When the inevitable Tory victory was declared, the paper was able to prove, by means of a careful distinction between what it called 'Legal Votes' and those of 'Honorary Freemen', that the Whig candidate had won the moral victory.[44] Not content with this, the printer now went on to widen his range, printing a letter from Warwick condemning 'the Bold Attempt made totally to overthrow the Rights and Liberties of Both [i.e. Northampton and Warwick], by introducing an incredible Number of Occasional Voters'.[45] The letter then gave a long list of the new voters at Warwick whose names, it said, had been 'surreptitiously inserted in the Parish Book of Rates'. Again, the occupations of the new voters were carefully noted, in order to emphasize their lowly station in life. Many were described either as 'servants' or 'paupers'. And a few weeks later, the *Northampton Mercury* exposed similar malpractices at St. Alban's.[46]

No other country printer was ever to venture to criticize his local corporation so boldly. Here was a struggling provincial printer daring to condemn the actions of whole corporations and publicly to expose local abuses. Undoubtedly, the *Mercury's* campaign must have created something of a local sensation, for it was exceedingly rare for a printer to go so far. Normally, a country printer would go to almost any lengths to avoid brushes with Authority, and corrupt practices involving local notables were usually studiously ignored. On one occasion during the General Election of 1727, the *Gloucester Journal* published a statement by a local dignitary to the effect that

[42] *Northampton Mercury*, 18 February 1733/34.
[43] Ibid. 8 April to 27 May 1734.   [44] Ibid. 29 April 1734.
[45] Ibid. 13 May 1734.   [46] Ibid. 10 June 1734.

'One Hundred and 19 Persons having at one Vote been voted to be made Freemen of the City of Gloucester on the 5th. and 20th. days of July without the usual Claim of Birth or Service, and it having been publicly asserted that when I, Thomas Webb, one of the Aldermen, was Mayor of the said City, Freemen were made in the same Manner against the Time of an Election, I do hereby solemnly declare, that to the very best of my Remembrance, no one Person whatsoever was made free during my Mayoralty, unless entitled by Birth or Service'.[47]

And in 1753, Felix Farley ventured to print Lord Gage's protest at the decision of the borough officials of Tewkesbury to vote only for candidates prepared to give £1,500 towards the cost of repairing the local roads.[48] He added that similar decisions by the boroughs of Andover and Calne had brought down upon those towns the righteous wrath of the House of Commons. But most printers clearly regarded details of this kind as being too dangerous to publish. Their references to local elections were sometimes pungent. In the election campaign of 1754, for instance, Felix Farley was pleased to refer to his Whig opponents as 'a Plague of Locusts . . . devouring Insects who have their Origin in Filth and Ordure, and whose very Existence depends on Corruption'.[49] But, by and large, the country newspapers of this period do not provide the intimate and detailed account of eighteenth century electioneering we might have expected. Only when there was a rival newspaper on the spot did printers come out into the open: and then their shafts were directed rather at the morals of the rival and the accuracy or otherwise of his news than at the political principles he supported. In 1747, for example, the printer of the *York Journal or Protestant Courant* flung himself upon the *York Courant*. That paper was, he declared, a 'dirty Vehicle . . . the Property of B[ankru]pts and Ja[cobi]tes',[50] fit only for the service of 'Madam Cloacina';[51] and he published with evident approval a letter sent in by a local school teacher attacking the *York Courant's* 'dull stupid Poison' which, however, 'serves now and then to divert my younger Boys on a Play Day for Translations'.[52] The printers threw themselves with gusto into exchanges of this type: but they tended to avoid the more fundamental issues of local politics and local electioneering. Such issues were, perhaps, too explosive to be tackled by a struggling country printer. And it may well be significant that, after its outburst in 1734, the *Northampton Mercury* virtually retired altogether from the political arena.

[47] *Gloucester Journal*, 1 August 1727. See also 9 September 1727.
[48] *Felix Farley's Bristol Journal*, 20 January 1753.   [49] Ibid. 9 March 1754.
[50] *York Journal or Protestant Courant*, 24 March 1747.
[51] Ibid. 31 March 1747.   [52] Ibid. 7 April 1747.

In the same General Election which had provoked the *Northampton Mercury*, the *Kentish Post* gave an unusually detailed account of the local campaigns. In this particular election, however, the traditional issues of corruption and the frequency and integrity of Parliaments were ignored, and the campaign in Kent was fought on purely economic issues. The Whigs stressed the eminently correct attitude of their candidate upon such all-important local issues as the need to continue the bounty on corn and the future of the distilleries. And a Tory who tried to raise such political questions as the Excise Scheme and the matter of foreign subsidies was promptly squashed by a correspondent who ridiculed the idea that anyone would vote for a candidate who supported a decrease in the price of corn. According to this single-minded correspondent, 'it is a Thing of no Profit to us what Manner Tobacco Merchants were to pay honestly their Duties, which . . . is all that is meant by what they call the Excise Scheme'.[53] In much the same way, the newspaper war in York during the General Election campaign of 1741 was fought mainly over purely local issues. Once again, the Whigs stressed the impeccable record of their candidate, Turner, on the question of preventing the Irish from illegally sending their wool to France.[54] The Tories, evidently embarrassed by the fact that their candidate was himself an Irish landowner, were forced to fall back upon such time-honoured political issues as the highly unpopular Convention with Spain which had been recently signed, Place Bills, the Septennial Act,[55] and personal attacks upon Turner—

'And try to roast him—he's so lean and sallow,
'Tis Ten to One he drops more T—d than Tallow.'[56]

Such detailed accounts were, however, exceptional, and by and large the country newspapers played little part in local politics.

If the printer successfully avoided prosecution either at the hands of the central government or at those of the local authorities, he had still to fear the possibility of action by that other great national authority, Parliament. The debates in Parliament were secret: and there existed a formidable array of privileges to keep them so. Even such matters of public interest as the Speech from the Throne and the text of Acts passed were the monopoly of officially appointed printers, who guarded their monopoly jealously, and the only authorized information was that contained in the *Votes*, in which

[53] *Kentish Post*, 21 May 1733.
[54] *York Courant*, 27 October and 3 November 1741.
[55] Ibid. 15 September and 27 October 1741. See L. Curtis, *The Politicks of Laurence Sterne* for the controversy.   [56] Ibid. 5 January 1741/42.

appeared meagre and formal details of Resolutions, sums of money voted and taxes granted. This was lenten fare indeed to a public hungry for details of the cut-and-thrust of the actual debates. The really serious student of parliamentary affairs might subscribe to Boyer's *Political Register*, which, during the recess, contained belated and cautious accounts of the speeches made in the previous session. The *Register* was, however, expensive; and its accounts were so out of date that they had lost much of their force and interest. The vast majority of country people depended absolutely upon their weekly newspaper for all their information.

The country newspapers catered quite admirably for this demand for details of the debates in Parliament. The writers of the news-letters defied the Resolution of Parliament in 1694—'that no news writers do in their letters or other papers that they may disperse, presume to intermeddle with the debates or other proceedings of this House' [57]—in a way that the more vulnerable London printed newspapers dared not do. In their extracts from the news-letters, country newspapers provided an up-to-date and often surprisingly well-informed account of parliamentary affairs, with brief details of important speeches, the division figures and any points of particular interest. Thus, in 1717, the Nottingham *Weekly Courant* gave its readers a brief account of one of the most daring speeches of the session, when, during the debate on the forces, the Jacobite leader, 'Mr. Shipp[en] reflecting upon his Majesty's Speech, and saying that he neither understood our Language nor Constitution, which differs from a German Province . . . [was] order'd to withdraw to the Tower'.[58] In 1729, the *Newcastle Courant* gave William Pulteney's famous retort to a ministerial speaker who had quoted a passage from the *Craftsman*: that 'tho' he always took a Pleasure to hear that Gentleman talk . . . yet he believed he had improved from that Paper'.[59] And in 1741, in the crisis over the impending fall of Walpole, the *Lancashire Journal* printed an extract from *Wye's Letter* describing how 'The L[or]ds sat till One this Morning when the Question was put upon the Motion made by the L[or]d C[artere]t, seconded by the E[arl] of A[bingdo]n, to address the K[ing] to remove the Right Hon. Sir R[obert] W[alpole] from his Majesty's Presence', together with the division figures and the information that 'the whole B[enc]h of B[ishop]s' had voted against the motion.[60]

---

[57] *House of Commons Journals*, xi. 193.
[58] *Weekly Courant*, 5 December 1717.
[59] *Newcastle Courant*, 1 February 1728/29.
[60] *Lancashire Journal*, 23 February 1740/41.

Undoubtedly, this was the sort of information the public wanted —and it appeared only in the extracts from the written news-letters.

Such reports were, however, dangerous, no matter how carefully the printer sought to disguise the names of the speakers. Fortunately for the printers, official action was spasmodic and uncertain, and it seems clear that Parliament was hampered by its lack of accurate information as to what was being printed in the country newspapers. Unless its attention was specifically drawn to a particular newspaper, no action was taken. Presumably the House's attention was drawn to the Exeter newspapers by the prosecution there of Philip Bishop, for in 1718 and 1719 all three printers in that city—George Bishop of the *Exeter Mercury,* Jos. Bliss of the *Protestant Mercury,* and Andrew Brice of the *Post-Master*—were summoned to the bar of the House and taken into custody for publishing accounts of its debates.[61] In 1728 and 1729, Robert Raikes of the *Gloucester Journal* was punished for a similar offence.[62]

The somewhat arbitrary nature of the House's proceedings is shown by the passage in the *Gloucester Journal* which called down the wrath of the Commons upon the unfortunate printer. The item reads as follows: ·

'From *Wye's Letter,* Westminster, March 5. Yesterday, the House of Commons, after reading the Lord William Pawlet's Bill a second Time, resolving itself into a Grand Committee to consider of the State of the Nation in relation to the National Debt, and after examining divers Officers and Clerks belonging to the Exchequer touching the Sums issued out of the Sinking Fund, towards paying the National Debt. The Question being propos'd, That it appears to this Committee, that the Moneys already issued and applied towards the discharging the National Debt incurr'd before Christmas 1716, (together with the Sum of 220,435 1. 16s. 4d 3q. which will be issued at Lady Day 1728, towards discharging the said Debts) amount to 6,648,762 1. 5s. 1d 1q. And the Question being put to leave the Chair, the Committee divided, Yeas 97, Noes 250; so the main Question was resolved in the Affirmative. The Debates on the said Question, wherein Mr. Pulteney and Sir Robert Walpole were chiefly engag'd, one against the other, lasted till past 9 at Night. . . .'[63]

It is clear from this very innocuous paragraph that the House was not so much concerned with the relative importance of the information that was divulged as with the fact that its proceedings had been published at all.

[61] *House of Commons Journals,* xix. 30, 42, 43, 44, 53, 54.
[62] Ibid. xxi. 85, 104, 108, 117, 119, 227, 238.
[63] *Gloucester Journal,* 12 March 1728.

Like the ministry, the House sought to cut off the supply of information at its source. Thanks to the confession of Robert Raikes, several news-writers were taken into custody: Edward Cave, the redoubtable William Wye, John Stanley, Elias Delpouch and John Willys in 1728, and Gythens and Stanley again in 1729. And the House resolved 'That it is an Indignity to, and a Breach of the Privilege of this House, for any Person to presume to give, in written or printed News Papers, any Account, or Minutes, of the Debates, or other Proceedings of this House, or any Committee thereof.' [64] However, the House's action in 1728 and 1729 did little to restrain the news-writers and the provincial printers. By 1738, the Commons was again resolving, this time with still more emphasis, that the publishing of any account of its activities was 'an high Indignity to, and a notorious Breach of the Privilege of, this House'.[65] And a few years later, in 1745 and 1746, it was the turn of the York printers, both of whom were hauled before the bar of the House.[66]

In all the cases, save that of John Gilfillan of York, the offence was the publishing of accounts of the debates and proceedings of Parliament. All the printers pleaded guilty, naming the various news-writers as their sources of information. They were usually discharged upon paying their fees. This was no light matter, for against the offending item in the *Gloucester Journal* is written in ink, on what was obviously the office copy: 'the Wofull Paragraph . . . this Paragraph cost R.R. 40 1.'.[67] It will be noticed that the House summoned Whigs and Tories alike. But it would seem that the Whig printers received rather more lenient treatment. Jos. Bliss was discharged from attendance on writing a most humble letter of apology; Raikes was excused from a second attendance, possibly for his co-operation in naming the authors of his news-letters—and possibly for his general support of the ministry, for as he himself asserted in his paper, 'since the Printer hereof hath been under the Displeasure of the House, it hath been industriously and maliciously insinuated that it is for Printing against the Government, which is a false and scandalous Aspersion'.[68] Finally, John Gilfillan, the York printer, seems to have escaped the usual consequences of his offence, which was a libel against Admiral Vernon, a Member of Parliament. The libel, made during the Forty-Five, was blatant and obvious; 'Admiral Vernon is said to be recalled; the Escape of the Rebels back into Scotland is imputed to him, by his occasioning an Express to be

[64] *House of Commons Journals*, xxi. 238.
[65] Ibid. xxiii. 148.   [66] Ibid. xxiv. 798, 854; xxv. 27, 36, 69.
[67] J. Pendleton, *The Reporter's Gallery* (1890), p. 115.
[68] *Gloucester Journal*, 2 April 1728.

sent which lost the Duke near Two Days March'.[69] Yet the Journals of the House record nothing after his examination.[70]

The efforts of the House to enforce its privilege were thus spasmodic and haphazard. The fear of such actions naturally hung over the printers' heads, but few allowed it to deter them for very long from publishing the extracts from the news-letters describing the debates.

The main defect of the news-letters lay in their extreme briefness. As early as 1721, the printer of the *Ipswich Journal* tried to remedy this fault. In doing so, he to some extent anticipated the enterprise of the *Gentleman's Magazine* later. He announced that

'we having weekly given an Account of the Proceedings of both Houses of Parliament (as transmitted to us by a discerning Hand) . . . which we find gives Content by the Encrease of this Paper; the following Debates of the Lords and Commons being more full and large, will, (we hope), be an acceptable Amusement to our more curious Readers'.[71]

And he proceeded to give a two-page account of the debates which had taken place two months previously. The account is interesting in that it is practically identical with the one which appeared in Boyer's *Parliamentary Debates*,[72] and the two were clearly taken from the same original. However, the *Ipswich Journal* did not repeat this experiment, probably for the same reasons that forced the printer of the *Manchester Magazine* later to discontinue his series of debates taken from the monthly magazines. As that printer explained,

'many Persons who condescend to encourage this Paper having expressed their Dislike of the Debates in Parliament, I have at present determined to discontinue the Publication thereof. I own the Method of publishing them by Scraps is tedious, and on that Account disagreeable because the Arguments cannot be seen at one View. . . . Some say the Debates are disagreeable in themselvs. . . . Others more polite buy the *Gentleman's* or *London Magazines*.' [73]

Indeed, such accounts would be so out of date by the time they appeared in the newspaper that most readers would find them tedious in the extreme. In general, the requirements of most readers were probably better satisfied by the admittedly brief but up-to-date and stimulating extracts from the news-letters. These could always be supplemented by longer accounts after the close of the parliamentary

[69] *York Journal*, 7 January 1745/46.
[70] *House of Commons Journals*, xxv. 69.
[71] *Ipswich Journal*, 4 March 1721.
[72] Boyer, *Parliamentary Debates*, vii. 393–6, 399–400; viii. 1–3, 5–6.
[73] *Manchester Magazine*, 20 December 1737.

session, when it was generally held that the ban on the publication
of debates no longer applied—this despite the specific resolution of
the House in 1738 that its privilege operated 'as well during the
Recess as the Sitting of Parliament'.[74] Thus, the *Bristol Oracle* in
1743 reprinted all the *Gentleman's Magazine's* accounts of the fiery
debates of the Commons concerning the government's foreign
policy,[75] and in 1754 the *Newcastle Journal* gave a 'Summary of the
Proceedings of the last Session of Parliament'.[76]

Selected speeches were often reprinted for political purposes—as
party propaganda. One of the first country newspapers to make use
of this stratagem was, as might be expected, the *York Courant*, which
in 1739 printed 'the Speech of the Right Hon. the Lord Viscount
G[a]ge against the Convention with Spain'.[77] The same paper gave,
in 1741, Sandys's motion to remove Sir Robert Walpole—a lengthy
address, which the *Courant* printed in full.[78] After the fall from grace
of the self-styled 'Patriots', when they accepted office and proceeded
to make use of the very methods which they had formerly so bitterly
denounced, the *York Courant* used this weapon with telling effect,
reprinting the former speeches of its old heroes urging measures
which they had now so conveniently forgotten, or principles which
they had now betrayed. In this way, the *Courant* in 1742 gave its
readers the great speech of William Pulteney in 1734 demanding the
repeal of the Septennial Act, and in 1743 Sandys's speech on the
motion to remove Walpole in 1741.[79]

Other papers from time to time printed at length parliamentary
speeches of more than usual interest. The *Bristol Oracle* in 1745
gave 'Lord P[erceva]l's Speech upon the Report of the Hanoverian
Troops'; *Harrop's Manchester Mercury* in 1753 included the Earl
of Egmont's speech against the 'Jew Bill'; and during the bitter
election contest at Bristol in 1754, *Felix Farley's Bristol Journal*
accused the Whig candidate, Nugent, of having been the 'principal
Promoter' of that Bill, and, to prove its point, reprinted his speech
on that Bill from the *Gentleman's Magazine*.[80] Many country newspapers gave their readers the Duke of Argyle's thundering denuncia-
tion of the mismanagement of the Spanish War in 1740. Even the
normally cautious and neutral *Newcastle Journal* found room for

---

[74] Resolution of 13 April 1738, *House of Commons Journals*, xxiii. 148.
[75] *Bristol Oracle*, 11 June to 19 November 1743.
[76] *Newcastle Journal*, 25 May and 13 July 1754.
[77] *York Courant*, 7.14 August 1739.
[78] Ibid. 19 May to 16 June 1741.   [79] Ibid. 13 April 1742, 5 April 1743.
[80] *Bristol Oracle*, 4 May to 20 July 1745; *Harrop's Manchester Mercury*,
20 November 1753; *Felix Farley's Bristol Journal*, 20 April 1754 respectively.

this particular item, introducing it somewhat timidly with the comment that

'as the following Speech has not only been printed singly and distributed into a Multitude of Hands, but has also been offer'd to the Publick in several News Papers, it is thought proper by many impartial Persons that our Readers ought not to be depriv'd of satisfying their Curiosity with the Perusal of it. . . . We hope therefore that our inserting it . . . cannot be construed to our Disadvantage, as following any particular Interest or Party. Let the Speech and the Sentiments which it contains recommend or condemn themselves; we do neither.' [81]

Most of the speeches thus reprinted came from the Opposition. But they were inserted not only in the true Opposition newspapers throughout the country, but also in those which professed sympathy for the ministry, or complete political neutrality. Obviously, no printer could afford to omit them. Once again, therefore, the Opposition had the whip-hand.

The same was true of the Protests of the House of Lords. The Opposition in the Upper House was always hopelessly outnumbered. However, as it contained the best speakers in the country, it usually won the debates—although it lost the divisions. And it made the most of its debating talents by exercising its privilege to register Protests. These Protests were invariably described by Wye in his news-letter —and so were published everywhere. Some papers gave great prominence to these declarations. The *Stamford Mercury* in 1723 sometimes devoted three pages at a time to what was called 'A Collection of the several Protests in the House of Lords in the Session . . . 1722 and 1723',[82] while in 1744 the *Reading Mercury* announced that 'there having been very great Debates last Session of Parliament on several important Subjects, we apprehend the inserting the Protests of several Noble Peers on those Occasions will be an agreeable Entertainment to our Readers'.[83]

Finally, some printers ventured upon what was possibly the most dangerous ground of all: the publishing of the division lists. In 1722, the *Stamford Mercury* printed, as part of its private election campaign, 'a List of those Members who voted for Repealing the Triennial Act and for continuing themselves',[84] and from time to time other papers followed its example. Even the staid *Northampton*

---

[81] *Newcastle Journal,* 7 June 1740. The speech also appeared in the *York Courant,* 27 May 1740; *Lancashire Journal,* 9 June 1740; *Newcastle Courant,* 7.14 June 1740; *Leeds Mercury,* 3 June 1740.
[82] *Stamford Mercury,* 29 August to 10 October 1723.
[83] *Reading Mercury,* 21 May 1744.
[84] *Stamford Mercury,* 22.29 March 1722.

Mercury went so far as to print as a supplement in March 1736 a
list of the Members of Parliament 'who voted pro and con about
the Hessian Troops in 1730; for and against the Excise Bill in 1733,
for and against continuing the Septennial Bill in 1734',[85] and
in 1735 it had printed the names of the peers who voted for and
against the Quakers' Tithe Bill.[86] Obviously, the danger increased
as the length of time between the actual division and the publication
of such lists grew shorter. The printers of the *York Courant* accurately summed up the position when, in 1739, they decided to present
a list of the northern M.P.s, showing how they had voted over the
highly unpopular Convention with Spain, although, as they pointed
out, 'the Printers of this Paper are not fond of Political Martyrdom,
or of thrusting their Heads into a Pillory'.[87] In this case, apparently,
the risk paid dividends, for the following week the printers announced that, in view of the 'great Demand for last Week's Paper,
and to gratify the general Enquiry of the Publick after the Behaviour
of ALL the Representatives of the Kingdom on that Memorable
Occasion, we shall begin the whole Alphabetically, and continue the
same weekly, till finished'. To add still more spice to the list, the
'places' held by those voting were carefully noted.[88] No other paper
was quite as bold in this respect as the *York Courant*. The danger
of prosecution was, in fact, too great: and the printers of the *Cambridge Chronicle* ruefully commented in 1763 that

'the Publishers of the *Cambridge Chronicle* have been favoured with a
List of Names entitled, A Minority; which they would gladly have inserted, had it not been probable that if they did, another List might
soon be recommended to their Notice, to wit, a List of the Fees to be
paid by all such as are taken into Custody of the Serjeant at Arms'.[89]

Despite the official ban, a surprising amount of information was
thus made available to the readers of the country newspapers. Had
the news-letters been preserved, they would probably have provided
the modern historian with his most accurate and detailed accounts
of the parliamentary debates of this period. In most cases, however,
our knowledge of these news-letters is limited to the extracts in the
country papers. Brief as these were, they often gave details which
are missing from the recognized sources of information. The *Stamford Mercury's* division list for the repeal of the Triennial Act does
not appear in Chandler's *Parliamentary Debates*—which also omits
the list of the members of the Secret Committee who voted for the

---

[85] *Northampton Mercury*, 1 March 1735/36.   [86] Ibid. 7 July 1735.
[87] *York Courant*, 3 July 1739.   [88] Ibid. 10 July 1739.
[89] *Cambridge Chronicle*, 15 January 1763.

Hanoverian forces in 1743. That list appeared in the *York Courant*, being supplied by 'R.F.', the *Courant's* private correspondent in London.[90] Again, the brief extracts from the news-letters often described the atmosphere of the debates more vividly than do our other sources of information. In the *Ipswich Journal's* account of the debate over the Mutiny Bill in 1721, for example, we are told that Walpole 'spoke several Times above Two Hours', and that he carried the day 'by the Torrent of his masterly Eloquence'.[91] Neither comment appeared in Boyer's description of the same debate.

After a General Election, it was the common practice for the newspapers to print lists of the successful candidates. Even this had its dangers, for these lists were officially the property of the printer appointed by the House. And in 1727 *Farley's Bristol Newspaper* was obliged to announce that 'we promis'd our Readers to print a List of all the Members of Parliament as soon as the same would be compriz'd; but are disappointed by a strict Order That no Person shall presume to reprint the same'.[92] This, however, seems to have been an isolated act of interference, and the papers continued to print these lists throughout the period.[93] Between 1739 and 1742, when Walpole's downfall was imminent, and politics had become exceptionally exciting, many papers added the refinement of distinguishing the party connexions of every candidate elected.[94]

Once again, however, the increasing influence and circulation of the country newspapers forced the London printers to take steps to protect their own interests. So long as the circulation of the provincial newspapers was small, they could afford to ignore the infringements upon their various monopolies. By the late 1730's, the position had become very different, and in 1739 the printer of the *Lancashire Journal* had to inform his readers that 'the Reason why I did not insert the King's Speech, Addresses of the House of Lords and Commons, in this Journal, was, I could not do it, without being liable to a Prosecution from the King's Printer for the Speech, or the Printers appointed by the House of Commons for the Addresses'.[95] By 1747, it is clear that the various London printers were making

[90] Of the other division figures mentioned, the Convention division appeared in Chandler, *Collection of the Parliamentary Debates in England*, xvii. 242–60; Excise, xi. 53–70; Septennial Act, xii. 154; Quakers' Tithe Bill, viii. 525.   [91] *Ipswich Journal*, 4 March 1721.

[92] *Farley's Bristol Newspaper*, 4 November 1727.

[93] e.g. *Stamford Mercury*, 28 June, 5 July 1722; *Northampton Mercury*, 21 August to 2 October 1727; *Stamford Mercury*, 25 March 1736; *Newcastle Journal*, 15 June 1754, etc.

[94] e.g. *Northampton Mercury*, 12 February 1738/39; *York Courant*, 30 June 1741; *Newcastle Journal*, 11 July 1741; *Norwich Gazette*, 11 July 1741; *York Courant*, 9 March 1741/42.   [95] *Lancashire Journal*, 26 November 1739.

a very real effort to protect themselves against what they regarded as the illegal invasion of their privileges. In that year, in a lengthy editorial statement, the printer of the *Ipswich Journal* summed up the very uncertain situation:

'several of my Readers have complain'd, that I was last Week guilty of a great Neglect at least, if not some Degree of Disloyalty, in not giving them the King's Speech . . . I am therefore obliged to trouble them with a short Account of my Reasons for this Omission.

Whether it is legal or not to reprint his Majesty's Speeches in News-Papers is a Point about which the Printers of these Papers seem to be of different Opinions; Some of them never failing to insert the whole, while others never venture to quote the least Part of them, for this Reason only, that they apprehend it might subject them to a trouble-some Prosecution. Which of these are the best Lawyers I know not. . . .' [96]

He admitted that he himself was under prosecution for having ex-tracted passages from a recent publication.

'I have often,' [he said], 'given my Readers Extracts or Quotations from Pamphlets or other Books: But as they have never been very long, I have found that they have been so far from hindering the Sale of the Books that they have promoted it much more than a mere Advertise-ment could have done: And I believe there is not a single Instance of any Person that has suffer'd a Farthing Damage by them . . . I never imagin'd that any such Person would be displeased with them, till I receiv'd the following Letter from Mr S. B.

Mr Creighton, You having in your *Ipswich Journal* in August last Presumed to print and Publish a Piratical and Spurious Copy of the Lord High Steward's Speech on Pronouncing Sentence on the Earls of Kilmarnock, etc . . . and thereby been guilty of a Contempt and Breach of Privilege, I Give you this Notice to Acquaint you, That unless you immediately make me Satisfaction for the Damages I have sustain'd by that Infamous Act of Piracy and Injustice, Com-plaint will be made to the House of Peers, and you will immediately be taken into Custody—The Consequences of which as a Printer you must be very well acquainted with. . . .'

The unfortunate printer had written to Mr. S. B., pointing out that the extract complained about had taken up only two-thirds of a column. Mr. B. had replied that the printing of such an extract justi-fied his action. Moreover, the printer had also been guilty of two further acts of piracy in publishing extracts regarding the trial of the Jacobite Lords from London newspapers. By placing these piratical pieces in the hands of 'several Thousand Persons', he maintained,

[96] *Ipswich Journal*, 27 June 1747.

the printer of the *Ipswich Journal* had deprived him of the sale of as many thousands.

'Whether Mr. B. ever made any Complaint to the House of Peers, I have not heard' [went on the printer], 'But this I certainly know, that last Month he brought his Action against me. And as this Affair is now to be determin'd in the Court of King's Bench, I am inform'd that the Contempt and Breach of Privilege is at Present out of the Question. . . .

But if only a Quotation from a Speech Mr. B. claims a Property in, which in fact promoted the Sale of it, can possibly be deem'd an Injury to him; must it not have been a greater Injury to the King's Printer to have published his Majesty's whole Speech? And as to printing a Part of it; I am well inform'd that if I had only presum'd to go so far, and an Action have been brought against me for it, that Action could have been much more easily supported than this of Mr. B.'s can. This being the Case, I hope I shall be excused for not involving myself in a second expensive Law-Suit while the first is depending . . .'

As a matter of fact, in this same year, 1747, Felix Farley printed the King's Speech to Parliament, and was thereupon compelled to publish a humble apology for this 'Infringement upon the Patent of his Majesty's Printer', with the promise that 'no Speech or Speeches from the Throne shall be inserted or publish'd in this Paper for the future'.[97] And, somewhat naturally after all this excitement, the printer of the *Gloucester Journal* refused to insert the King's Speech at all.[98]

This legal uncertainty, and the increasing readiness of the London printers to defend their privileged position, explain the reticence of the country printers on the subject of Acts of Parliament. Acts of exceptional importance were usually given in abstract form in the official *London Gazette*. They were then regarded as fair game by the country printers, who reproduced them, as the *Northampton Mercury* put it, 'for the Conveniency of many of our Readers who may not have the Opportunity of perusing Acts of Parliament'.[99] In this way, abstracts of such important bills as the Schism Act of 1714, the Succession Act, Calicoes Act, Window Act and Spirituous Liquors Act were printed in the various country newspapers.[1] *Harrop's Manchester Mercury* even printed the highly controversial

[97] *F. Farley's Bristol Journal*, 1.8.15 August 1747.
[98] *Gloucester Journal*, 20 June 1749.
[99] *Northampton Mercury*, 5 August 1723.
[1] Respectively, in the *Worcester Post*, 6 August 1714; the same, 13 August 1714; *Gloucester Journal*, 31 December 1722; *Stamford Mercury*, 26 February 1747 (and also the *York Journal*, 24 March 1747, and *Kentish Post*, 21 March 1747); and *Derby Mercury*, 21 June 1751. *Farley's Exeter Journal* of 19 August 1726 devoted the whole of the front page to abstracts of various Acts of Parliament.

'Jew Bill' of 1753, adding carefully that this 'verbatim Copy' was 'printed by the Express Consent of the King's Printer obtain'd for that Purpose'.[2] Beyond such abstracts, however, the printers dared not go, and minor Acts, however important locally, were never published in the newspapers. The printer of the *Bristol Journal* on one occasion refused point-blank to explain such Acts, because, he said, they were 'the Property of the King's Printer'.[3] Later, he informed his readers that 'any Person may have the Perusal of the whole Act for 3*d*. provided they send for it at their own Homes, and return it again in 2 Hours'.[4]

Certainly, as Mr. Hanson so ably explains, 'the impression left by a review of the privileges of Parliament and of the law of libel in general, is one of a press hemmed in by countless restrictions, and subject to the most arduous restraint'.[5] Had the various restrictions been systematically enforced, the press as a whole could hardly have become the Fourth Estate. But the efforts of Authority to control the press were characterized more by their irregularity and uncertainty than by their efficiency, and were too spasmodic and infrequent to have any serious effect. The government proved quite unable to restrain the growing boldness of the Opposition press throughout this period, and its own efforts at counter-propaganda were insignificant and inept.

Historians have perhaps tended to assume that the country newspaper was only a small and struggling enterprise, extremely limited both in circulation and influence. Moreover, they have also tended to assume that, because it was dependent upon the London newspapers for both its news and its views, its political importance was only slight. That very dependence, however, made the country newspaper a far more effective force in the political development of the eighteenth century than it could ever have been had it acted simply as the organ of local and parochial politics. By means of the country newspapers, the views of the leading London political papers were being disseminated throughout the country, and a new reading public, one wholly dependent upon its local newspaper, was being educated in the major political issues of the day—and educated to the point where it could appreciate essays such as those in the *Craftsman*, which were intended for adult minds. No longer was the influence of the capital upon the provinces slow and uncertain; and no longer was there simply a mass of isolated individual

[2] *Harrop's Manchester Mercury*, 3 July 1753.
[3] Quoted Latimer, *Annals of Bristol*, p. 267.
[4] *F. Farley's Bristol Journal*, 21 March 1746/47.
[5] Hanson, *Government and the Press*, p. 34.

opinions, misinformed and leaderless. Instead, there was now a centralized, almost national opinion. Moreover, that opinion had for years been nourished upon the radical ideas of the *Craftsman* and its later imitators. With the improvements in communications and the growth of a strong provincial newspaper press, a political campaign on a national scale had become a practical possibility. And the culmination of this long period of preparation, instruction and education was to be seen in the awakening of the provinces after 1769.

CHAPTER EIGHT

THE CIRCULATION OF THE
PROVINCIAL NEWSPAPER

T HE circulation figures of the provincial newspapers, were
they available, would throw light upon what was not the least
significant of the many changes which, in the eighteenth century, were beginning to transform English life. Unfortunately, such
figures do not exist. Most of the statistical records of the Stamp
Office were destroyed during the nineteenth century, and those that
survived are concerned either with the London newspapers alone,
or with the gross number of newspapers sold in London, the rest of
England and Scotland, and so are of little value in estimating the
circulation of the provincial newspapers either individually or as a
separate group. Private records are equally scanty. None of the
ledgers and account-books of the country printers seems to have
survived—if, indeed, they were ever kept, for the business organization of an eighteenth century provincial printing-house was rudi-
mentary. In the absence of such public and private records, therefore, we are dependent upon statements made in the newspapers
themselves: and even these will be found to be extremely few in
number and very disappointing in content.

Eighteenth century country printers appear reticent upon a subject which their modern counterparts are inclined to over-emphasize.
Their editorial announcements were largely confined to savage attacks upon rival newspapers, appeals for contributions, and lengthy
descriptions of the areas served by their newsmen and agents. Circulation was clearly regarded as a rather sordid subject, and one to
be avoided if possible: and the *Newcastle Journal* could dismiss the
whole subject with the comment: 'it would be Vanity in us to print
the Number of our Subscribers'.[1] Fortunately, not all the printers
were quite as modest as this, and, under the stress of local competition, printers occasionally gave more precise information. Their
claims, it is true, might be regarded as suspect, and few printers were
inclined to sacrifice a good round figure upon the altar of strict truth.
Nevertheless, their claims show the sort of circulation figures which

[1] *Newcastle Journal*, 7 April 1739.

a newspaper of the time might be expected to have—figures which would be accepted by the readers, and which would not lay the printer open to the derision of his rivals.

The evidence suggests that, during the first two decades of the century, the provincial newspapers had a circulation of only one or two hundred copies a week. There were rather more impressive claims. In 1706, Dr. Tanner stated that Francis Burges, printer of the *Norwish Post*, was selling 'vast numbers' to the country people[2]; and in 1710 the rival *Norwich Gazette* declared that the number of copies it sold every week was 'prodigious great'.[3] It is possible, however, that a more accurate estimate may be read into the *Gazette's* attack upon the *Norwich Post-Man* in 1707, when it warned the public that 'whatever News is cry'd about in less than an Hour after the Post is come in, must be an Imposition'.[4] As the hourly production of two men operating a hand-press was only a 'token' of two hundred and fifty sheets, the *Post-Man* must have printed considerably less than this number, for no matter how superficially the latest London newspapers were treated, the mere selection of items and the actual composition would take up a certain amount of time. Admittedly, the point of the *Gazette's* attack was that the rival paper was cheating the public by omitting the news which had arrived by the last post. But the printer of the *Gazette* seems to have regarded a newspaper published in anything over an hour as a legitimate venture, and so could hardly have printed many more copies than his rival, although in 1708 he did claim that he sold 'at least Nine times as many as any other Person'.[5]

By 1712, the circulation may have risen slightly. Among the papers of Lord Harley some scattered reports have recently come to light of the number of newspaper stamps purchased by various printers from the day on which the Stamp Act came into force until 1714.[6] These figures refer mainly to London newspapers: but they include the purchases of stamps made by one provincial paper, called the 'Bristol Post'—presumably the *Bristol Post-Boy*—between 1 August and 16 September 1712. During that period, the paper purchased 2,016 stamps, which would mean that its average weekly circulation during the seven weeks covered by these records was two hundred and eighty-eight.

---

[2] Dr. Tanner to Browne Willis, 1 August 1706.
[3] *Norwich Gazette*, 4 March 1710.
[4] Ibid. 4 January 1707.   [5] Ibid. 10 January 1708.
[6] J. M. Price, 'A Note on the Circulation of the London Press, 1704–1714,' *Bulletin of the Institute of Historical Research*, xxxi. no. 84, November 1958, 220.

During the year 1715, three country newspapers made some reference to their circulation. *Sam Farley's Bristol Post-Man* informed the public that the paper would be 'publish'd every Saturday Morning Two Hours after the London Post comes in' [7]—a statement which suggests that the number of copies printed was at least considerably in excess of that of the Norwich papers in 1707. Another paper, the Exeter *Protestant Mercury*, asserted that 'this Paper circulates 40 Miles round, and several Hundreds dispers'd every Week' [8] As this paper was then being published twice a week, however, the claim was not a large one. More specific was the printer of *Sam Farley's Salisbury Post-Man*, who, in his opening announcement, promised that his paper would be published three times a week 'provided a sufficient Number will subscribe. If 200 subscribe, it will be deliver'd to any private or public House in Town'.[9] Such a venture was too ambitious, and a small town evidently could not find two hundred people who were prepared to buy three newspapers each week.

The figure had not changed greatly by the 1720's, despite the bold claim of the *Gloucester Journal* in 1723 that it sold 'several Hundreds (Weekly) more . . . than the Papers printed at Worcester'.[10] When Andrew Brice, the Exeter printer, announced the changes necessitated by the Stamp Act of 1725, however, he remarked that 'according to a moderate Computation, I shall pay Duty to his Majesty about 100 1. per Annum more than ordinary'.[11] Hitherto, he would have paid only the pamphlet duty of three shillings each week—a total of £7 16s. 0d. a year. If he continued his paper at its present size of a sheet and a half, he would have to pay a stamp duty of three-halfpence on every copy printed and sold. If the annual difference between the two duties was about one hundred pounds, then the number of copies printed each week must have been about three hundred and thirty. Such a figure agrees well with the estimate of the historian of the Berkshire newspapers that the *Reading Mercury* at this time had a circulation of about four hundred copies a week.[12] We would expect the Reading paper to have a wider circulation than Brice's own paper, for it did not face the same local competition. And with the increase in the price of his newspaper, Brice could not long maintain his circulation even at this lower figure, for he was soon to comment that 'the Clemency and Indulgence of power-

[7] *Sam Farley's Bristol Post-Man*, 31 December 1715.
[8] *Protestant Mercury*, 16 September 1716.
[9] *Sam Farley's Salisbury Post-Man*, 27 September 1715.
[10] *Gloucester Journal*, 8 April 1723.   [11] *Post-Master*, 23 April 1725.
[12] K. G. Burton, *The Early Newspaper Press in Berkshire*, University of Reading M.A. thesis, p. 10.

ful Friends have kindly rid us of above one half the Burthen of former Profit and the Fatigue of serving so many Customers as we were wont to do (for a vast Number will not pay the impos'd whatd'ye-call it)'.[13]

If ordinary newspapers were fortunate to sell more than a couple of hundred copies a week, a literary magazine, with its far more limited appeal, could hardly approach such a figure. In 1734, the York printer, Thomas Gent, launched his *Miscellanea Curiosa*, one of the earliest and most ambitious of all provincial periodicals. He was soon in trouble, and obliged to inform his readers that

'this, 'tis probable, will be the last, except they approve it so far as to subscribe towards the Expence. He desires not to gain any thing by the Undertaking and is willing to give in his own Labour; And if there are 60 Persons to be found, who will each subscribe for Half-a-Dozen . . . every Quarter as they are publish'd (which will about defray the Charges) it will be carried on as formerly.' [14]

His moving appeal apparently fell upon deaf ears, for this issue was, in fact, the last number to be published.

Not until the late 1730's did the circulation of the provincial newspapers increase noticeably. In that year, the printers of the *York Courant* vaguely boasted that 'we print every Week several Hundreds more than our Predecessors in the Printing Office ever did'.[15] But other claims were more specific, and, in the same year, and only a few weeks after the appearance of their first issue, the printers of the *Newcastle Journal* stated flatly that 'we now sell nearly 2000 of these Papers weekly'.[16] And, also in 1739, an indignant reader of the *London Evening Post* maintained that the *Gentleman's Magazine* had falsely ascribed articles filched from the *Sherborne Mercury* and *Salisbury Journal* to the *Gloucester Journal*:

'this you'll say is doubly cruel, to determine not only to rob the Proprietors of these two Papers of the Performance, which at great Expence they oblig'd the Publick with, but likewise at the same Time to deprive them of the Honour of it.—The Bill for a Charitable Lottery, for the Relief of the distress'd Virgins of Great Britain, which he has inserted in his Magazine for March, and there says it is now first publish'd, was printed in the *Sherborne Mercury*, June 7, 1737, and above 2000 sold. . . .' [17]

Less precise was the statement of a London publisher in 1747, when he threatened to take legal action against William Creighton, printer

[13] *Brice's Weekly Journal*, 15 October 1725.
[14] *Miscellanea Curiosa*, July–September 1735.
[15] *York Courant*, 3 July 1739.   [16] *Newcastle Journal*, 14 July 1739.
[17] *London Evening Post*, 7/10 April 1739.

of the *Ipswich Journal*. Creighton's offence was that he had reprinted extracts from the *Trials of the Jacobite Lords*, a work in
which the London publisher claimed a property. It was asserted that
Creighton's action had put the 'piratical Pieces' in the hands of
'several Thousand Persons'.[18] But the mere fact that a London
publisher should threaten a country printer with such an action is
proof of the increasing circulation of the provincial newspapers in
general—and of the *Ipswich Journal* in particular.

In this year, 1747, *F. Farley's Bristol Journal* made a curious announcement which may, or may not, accurately represent its circulation. The issue of 18 April 1747 was numbered 145, and contained the declaration that 'the Number printed and sold is not that
at the Head of the first Page, as some imagine'. And the following
week's issue bore the number, not 146, but 1560. This curiously
precise figure can, of course, be interpreted in two ways. It may have
been intended to indicate the size of the circulation—or the number
which would have appeared on the title-page had the newspaper
maintained a consistent system of numeration from the beginning.
As the printer continued with this new numeration, the latter explanation is probably correct. If so, the printer had erred badly in
his calculations, for he had given his paper an existence of exactly
thirty years, whereas it was several years older, being descended
from *Sam Farley's Bristol Post-Man* of 1713.

Fortunately, no such doubts are attached to the other available
figures. In 1755, the *Manchester Magazine* claimed a sale of eleven
hundred copies, and later stated that 'Twelve Hundred were printed
December 23rd. 1755, and still increases'.[19] And a detailed account
exists of the circulation figures of the *York Chronicle*, a paper begun
in 1772 by Christopher Etherington.[20] Etherington printed no less
than three thousand copies of the first two issues for free distribution; of the third, which was to be sold, he printed sixteen hundred
and fifty. By September 1773 his circulation had reached two thousand five hundred, although it later sank to nineteen hundred. That
a new paper, launched in the face of the formidable *York Courant*,
could sell such numbers is proof of the growing power and influence
of the provincial newspaper; and that this particular venture should
fail, despite the effort, money, and organization put into its establishment, is a tribute to the popularity of the *York Courant*.

Evidently there was a considerable reading public for the country

[18] *Ipswich Journal*, 27 July 1747.
[19] *Manchester Magazine*, 3 June 1755 and 30 December 1755 respectively.
[20] Davies, *Memoir of the York Press*, pp. 332-5. The ledgers from which
these figures were taken have since disappeared.

newspapers. In 1739, the *Newcastle Journal* could claim a weekly sale of nearly two thousand copies despite competition from the long-established *Newcastle Courant*—which eventually out-lived it. *F. Farley's Bristol Journal* had two local rivals in 1747; in 1755, when the *Manchester Magazine* claimed a weekly circulation of twelve hundred, it was clearly losing ground before the rising *Manchester Mercury*; and the *York Chronicle* could achieve a weekly sale of between nineteen hundred and two thousand five hundred despite the popularity of the *York Courant*. When this competition is taken into account, the claims made by the newspapers become even more significant. It is true that such figures were claimed only by the larger provincial papers. *F. Farley's Bristol Journal* was at pains to explain that its circulation 'equals, if not exceeds, BOTH the Numbers of the *Oracle* and t'other, put together'.[21] And the printers of the *Newcastle Journal* insisted similarly that 'we vend at least 3 or 2 of any other Paper in the North'[22]—although even this statement implies that other northern papers might have a circulation of about one thousand. By 1764, however, the *Cambridge Journal* thought it necessary to issue a formal denial of rumours that it had a sale of only three hundred copies, and stated that 'upward of 600' were sent to one town in Lincolnshire alone.[23]

The claims of the larger papers are to some extent borne out by the fact that some printers were obliged to print more than one edition to satisfy the demand. Two distinct editions of the *York Courant* have been preserved side by side for the period between 1 September and 30 December 1741.[24] The outside pages—pages one and four—are in every case identical, obviously printed off in one operation; but the two inner pages contain marked differences between the editions, and evidently the two sets of inner pages were printed off separately; between the two operations there was time for another post to arrive from London. Thus, the later edition frequently contains news items not in the earlier version. In the issue of 27 September, for instance, the first edition mentioned that the embargo on shipping in Russian ports was still in force; but the later edition reported the lifting of the embargo. Again, the final section, which, in the early edition of 10 November, had been called, prematurely perhaps, 'Monday's Post' had become 'Saturday's Post' in the later edition, which had an entirely different section of late news

---

[21] *F. Farley's Bristol Journal*, 18 April 1747.
[22] *Newcastle Journal*, 8 September 1739.
[23] *Cambridge Journal*, 1 September 1764.
[24] In the office of the *Yorkshire Herald*, York.

devoted to the voyage and hardships of Lord Anson's squadron in the Pacific. This account was deemed so important that it was reprinted in full in the early edition of the following week. It seems clear that the early edition was for country readers. The *York Courant* had an exceptionally large sphere of influence, covering the whole of the north of England, and if its more distant readers were to receive their newspaper punctually it was essential to send the newsmen off on their stages as early as possible. The early edition would therefore be printed off on Monday, and the newsmen dispatched. The second edition, intended for more local distribution, could be held back until early Tuesday morning, the official day of publication. For this reason, the early edition always contained far fewer local items. It was obviously considered that such items would be of little or no interest to distant readers.

No similar runs of other newspapers have been preserved, although they undoubtedly existed. Two distinct versions of the *Newcastle Courant* of 8-11 August 1711 have survived, however.[25] The two are identical until the last page, when only one has a 'Postscript' reporting a Russian victory over the Turks. Probably this item had arrived after the printing had begun, and had been inserted only in the later copies. In other words, it represents an early example of 'stop-press news'. But on several occasions during the 1740's, *Farley's Bristol Journal* and *Farley's Bristol Advertiser*—which were really one and the same paper, although numbered separately and published on alternate Saturdays—announced that the demand for copies had been such as to require several editions. On 18 May 1745, for example, the *Bristol Advertiser* stated that 'the Demand for our Paper is so great, that last Saturday there were no less than Three Impressions of the Day's Paper'. In 1746, the same paper announced —without undue modesty—that

'our Paper requir'd no less than Three Impressions last Saturday, owing to its choice Intelligence and the great Variety of amusing and entertaining Articles generally to be found therein—One advertising in this old establish'd Paper is of more real Service than Six Times in either of the others, This being read TEN to their ONE, as is impartially judged from the SUPERIOR NUMBER we print, and the Manner in which they are dispersed'.[26]

And at various times between 1745 and 1747 the printer claimed 'three Extraordinary Editions', 'three Extraordinary', 'three', 'two', 'several', and 'two extra'.[27]

These few facts, figures and statements comprise virtually all the information available about the circulation of provincial newspapers in the early eighteenth century. It would appear that, until the late 1730's, few country papers had a circulation of more than two or three hundred copies a week. From that time onwards, however, all the signs point to a steadily increasing circulation—until by the 1750's the figure was often surprisingly large. This is apparent in the official figures which have survived of the gross number of newspaper stamps sold each year from 1750 to 1756:

1750	7,313,766 stamps
1751	7,271,658
1752	7,844,326
1753	7,675,286
1754	8,179,072
1755	8,639,864
1756	10,746,146 [28]

These figures do not distinguish between the stamps sold to London newspapers and those sold to provincial and Scottish printers; but they do provide evidence of a striking increase in the popularity and sale of newspapers generally—an increase in which the provincial newspapers would obviously have shared.

It is noticeable that the total began to grow in 1754, the year of the great General Election and of steadily rising tension between England and France in North America and India; and it jumped very sharply indeed in 1756, when the sporadic skirmishes finally became the official Seven Years War. Indeed, according to the Mr. Yeates who analysed the stamp duties at the end of that War, the total for 1756 was the highest recorded until after 1764.[29] The same authority also maintained, with regard to the Stamp Act of 1757, that 'the Additional Duty did not affect the Consumption any great Degree: the Vent of them depending much less upon the Price than upon the Circumstances of the Time exciting more or less Curiosity'. That statement was almost certainly incorrect: for he himself declared that the annual income from the stamps on newspapers during the Seven Years War was 'never less than £21,824. 16s. 0d.'—and that

[27] Ibid. 9 October 1745, 29 September 1746, 18 April, 29 August, 14 November and 19 December 1747.
[28] *House of Commons Journals*, xxvii. 769.
[29] Liverpool MSS., Add. MSS. 38, 338, fo. 125, p. 8.

very precise figure would indicate that the number of stamps sold had fallen off considerably. The income from the stamp duty may not have diminished: but the duty itself had been doubled, from one half-penny to one penny—so that the gross income represented a sale of only some five and a quarter million newspapers. The press itself was unanimous in condemning the new duty; and the *London Evening Post* went so far as to state that 'it is certain that many of the News Papers in Town, and most, if not all, in the Country, would be dropt'.[30] Although this gloomy forecast was not altogether accurate, very few new country papers were started after 1757, and many of the existing ones were seriously affected by the increase in the duty. The *Ipswich Journal* had difficulty in obtaining a supply of the new stamps, and succeeded in purchasing only a quantity 'very much short of the Number printed last Week'; but, said the printer, 'if we had received a sufficient Quantity . . . we should still have made a large Abatement in the Number of our News Papers, on Account of the advanced Price'.[31] Even the wonderful military and naval triumphs of the year 1759 failed to encourage country printers to start new papers, although popular interest probably did revive the falling circulation figures. The *Gentleman's Magazine* stated later that the number of newspaper stamps sold in 1760 was 9,464,750.[32]

These are the only official figures available. They show that, towards the end of the period, there were some ten million newspapers sold annually in England and Scotland. How many of these were provincial newspapers is, of course, never stated. But it has been shown that some of the larger provincial papers might well have a circulation of two thousand copies a week, while a circulation of one thousand was possible for papers which had to fight strong local competition. Admittedly, some country newspapers still had a circulation well below such figures. But it does not seem unreasonable to suppose that the average weekly circulation of the forty-odd country newspapers in existence towards the end of the period would be in the region of one thousand copies. In that case, the total weekly sale of the provincial press would be about forty thousand copies, and the annual sale some two million copies—about one-fifth of the grand total of all London, English and Scottish newspapers. Such a total is quite reasonable: if anything, it falls beneath the

[30] *London Evening Post*, quoted in the *Ipswich Journal*, 9 July 1757.
[31] *Ipswich Journal*, 9 July 1757.
[32] *Gentleman's Magazine*, 1794, pt. I, 21–22.

true figure, for at this time the Scottish press was still relatively undeveloped.

Certainly, the provincial newspaper had a far wider circulation and influence than used to be thought. Moreover, it was always accepted that an eighteenth century newspaper had far more readers than actual purchasers. Addison thought twenty readers for each paper sold 'a modest Computation'.[33] Coffee-houses and taverns, of course, provided the main means whereby a man could read the newspapers without actually buying them: but there were others. Group purchase was common. The *Cambridge Journal* once printed a letter from a member of a 'Friendly Society of Neighbours', which met weekly to read and discuss the news;[34] and *Brice's Weekly Journal* included a letter written from what the writer, evidently a shoemaker by profession and a wit by nature, was pleased to call 'our Aerial Citadel, by the Vulgar call'd a Garret. . . . Here are four of us, as true fiddling Blades as ever united dissenting Soles, who weekly join our Half-pence a-Piece to buy your Paper . . . So that we are above those your narrow-sol'd Half-penny Friends that hire your Works of the Rascally Hawker.'[35] This hiring-out of news-papers was apparently another common practice of the time—and one very unpopular with the printers. In Derby, the printer of the *British Spy* protested vigorously in 1728 at what he called

'an Association against me, a Combination betwixt some of my gentle Readers and my ungentle Distributors, to take from me this poor Requisite; what I mean is, an ungrateful Practice which now prevails of borrowing a Paper to read for a Penny, and too often the Lent of it Gratis; which ill Custom, if once laid aside, would be instrumental in multiplying the Numbers of my Subscribers'.[36]

The appeal apparently went unheard, for a few years later the *British Spy's* successor was also condemning the practice, mentioning in passing that the price charged by the hawkers was now usually only one half-penny.[37] And by 1757 the abuse had become so prevalent in Bristol that the three newspaper printers there went to the most unusual lengths of shelving their customary hostility in order to issue a joint letter of protest.[38]

A far greater threat to the success of the country newspapers lay, however, in the competition of the London papers, and it is clear that there was an extensive public for London newspapers in the

[33] Addison, *Spectator,* 12 March 1711.
[34] *Cambridge Journal,* 30 November 1746.
[35] *Brice's Weekly Journal,* 23 September 1726.
[36] *British Spy or Derby Post-Man,* 5 December 1728.
[37] *Derby Mercury,* 28 September 1732.
[38] Printed in *Felix Farley's Bristol Journal,* 2 July 1757.

country. London newspapers could be obtained in various ways. Those countrymen of some local political standing and 'influence' could put pressure upon their friends at the political centre to send them newspapers. In 1711, for instance, Viscount Cheyne wrote to Lord Fermanagh as follows:

'I have been severall times at Westminster since the Parlt. met, with designe to speak to your Lordsp. that you would be favourable and kind to send the *Votes*, the *Post Boy* and *Post Man* to Sherrington, at the Crown in Chesham, Postmaster, as your Lordsp. did last Session of Parliament. He has a Club of your friends meet every Friday at his House, who will desiert for want of hearing from their friends.' [39]

It was part of a politician's duties to see that his 'friends' in the country were kept supplied with newspapers—and, of course, newspapers of the right political complexion. The Duke of Newcastle was the greatest of the borough-mongers: and the sending of 'news' to his connexions cost him a considerable sum of money. Various statements of newspapers sent on behalf of the Duke are in the *State Papers Domestic*. They show that, between 30 April 1723 and 30 April 1724, the 'news' cost the Duke £47. 11s. 8d.[40] That sum had been spent in two ways. Twenty-four pounds of it went on what was simply described as 'one Years News sent to His Grace the Duke of Newcastle, and to Captain Harrison, Mr. Darby and Mr. Lulham'. This expensive item referred, presumably, to a written news-letter. The rest of the money was spent in sending the *London Journal*, then a ministerial organ, to various Sussex gentlemen—Sussex being the Duke's own county. They included Captain Harrison and Mr. Darby; Dr. White and Dr. Benbrigg; the Reverend Mr. Smith and the Reverend Mr. Williamson; Captain Markwick; and several others. The following year, the 'Account of Newspapers sent by Order of His Grace' came to £39. 8s. 2d.[41]

The only disadvantage of this method of obtaining newspapers cheaply was, of course, the fact that the choice was restricted to those papers supporting the ministry. And in 1725 a certain Mr. Jackson wrote to Mr. Payzant at the office of the other Secretary of State, Lord Townshend, complaining that

'I gave you the trouble of a few lines some time ago to let you know that Mr. Poyntz constantly communicates to me what newspapers he receives as I also do to him such as I get from any place, and therefore we were both desirous to have different papers, so I requested you

[39] Viscount Cheyne to Lord Fermanagh, letter dated 18 December 1711, *Verney Letters of the Eighteenth Century*, p. 308.
[40] *SPD Geo. I*, 49(38).   [41] *SPD Geo. I*, 62(23).

Instead of the *London Gazette* to send me *Mists Journall*; but you have for some Weeks past sent me always the *London Journall* which Mr Poyntz also gets. I must desire again to have the other Journall call'd *Mists*; and as the advertisements usually fill half the paper and are of no use, I pray cut them off, that half sheet costing me each time at the very least 3 shillings; and you will oblige. . . .'[42]

Mr. Jackson was either remarkably innocent or a supreme optimist; for it was inconceivable that a Secretary of State would send him so notorious a paper as *Mist's Journal*.

The reason for this constant pressure upon politicians was financial. To order a newspaper through the ordinary post would have been very costly. But Members of Parliament could send newspapers through the post under frank, quite free. The recipient would, in most cases, have to pay the flat cost of the subscription: but he would not have to pay the exorbitant postal charges. So high were these charges, in fact, that no one even considered paying them. If a would-be country subscriber did not have such powerful connexions as a Member of Parliament or a friend in one of the offices of State, then he applied to the Clerks of the Roads at the Post Office in London. These Clerks also had the privilege of franking, and they acted as newsagents on the grand scale.

Between them, Members of Parliament and Clerks of the Roads sent out a large number of London newspapers into the country. A Select Committee of the House of Commons was appointed in 1764 to enquire into the several frauds and abuses in relation to franking. Its report showed that the revenue lost in the one week 6 March to 13 March 1764 by the franking of newspapers by M.P.s amounted to £465. 5s. 8d. For the same week, the franking of newspapers by the 'Public Offices' cost £310. 15s. 4d.; and the six Clerks of the Roads were responsible for another £1,055. 10s. 8d.[43] In this one week, therefore, the revenue lost by franking amounted to £1,831. 11s. 8d. It would be impossible to estimate how many newspapers such a sum represented, for, according to the rates laid down in 1711, the postal charges varied from twelve-pence per ounce up to eighty miles, to sixteen-pence over eighty, and twenty-pence to Edinburgh. However, a Post Office memorandum of 1791 states that between 5 April 1764 and 5 April 1765 the number of newspapers which passed through the General Post Office in London was 1,090,289 [44]

---

[42] *SPD Geo. I*, 58(52). See also *SPD 35*, vol. 44(141); *SPD 36*, vols. 6(220) and 18(234).

[43] *House of Commons Journals*, xxix. 997–1000.

[44] *Proposal by the Clerks of the Roads for increasing the circulation of Newspapers and in consequence the Revenue*, 1791, Post Office Archives, 'Newspapers', bundle 52.

—or roughly 20,000 a week. If the sum of £1,055 which, according to the Select Committee, was the cost of the franking privilege of the Clerks of the Roads for one week, be taken to represent some 20,000 newspapers, then the total cost of franking in that week—£1,831—would represent nearly thirty-five thousand papers. Some of these would go to Scotland and Ireland, and some even farther afield; but it seems probable that the great majority would go into the provinces.

That a considerable reading public existed in the country was a fact well recognized by the London printers. The evening papers were, indeed, aimed primarily at the country reader, and for that reason were published on the three main post nights. In a document which purports to give the circulation of the London papers in the year 1704, it is noticeable that the totals for the three post-days—Tuesday, Thursday and Saturday—are markedly higher than those for the other days of the week.[45] Similarly, the accounts of the newspaper stamps purchased by the various papers in 1712 and 1713 in the Harley records show that, on the average, the numbers bought by the tri-weekly papers were larger than those of the daily and weekly papers. The only exceptions were the *London Gazette*, a bi-weekly paper which always stood in a class by itself as the official mouth-piece, and the weekly *Spectator*, which could hardly be classed as a true newspaper.[46] The dependence of the evening papers upon the country market is further suggested by the failure of the attempts to produce an evening paper outside the three main post-nights. In 1716, for example, *Jones's Evening News-Letter* made the attempt, its printer remarking in the first issue on the fact that it had been

'a long Time a matter of surprise to the Publick that amidst the great Crowd and Hurry of News-Papers which start out almost every Week, not one, worthy of Notice, hath yet been offer'd for the Evenings of Mondays, Wednesdays and Fridays, which would undoubtedly have been acceptable to the Town, when so many Events as well Foreign as Domestick, happen on those Days'.[47]

However acceptable such a newspaper might be to the Town, it had little appeal to country readers, and the venture quickly expired. In

---

[45] J. R. Sutherland, 'Circulation of Newspapers and Literary Periodicals in the Eighteenth Century', *Library*, 4th series, xv., 1935, 111.

[46] Price, 'Note on the Circulation of the London Press', op. cit.

[47] See S. Morison, *Ichabod Dawks and his News Letter* (Cambridge, 1931), pp. 38–39.

1727, yet another paper, the *Evening Journal*, attempted to 'supply the Chasm', only to suffer the same fate.[48]

All the London printers, however, sought to appeal to the reading public which existed in the country and Robert Walker even brought out a special country edition of his weekly paper, the *London and Country Journal*. And although the *London Gazette* and the various evening papers enjoyed a special popularity in the country, there was always a ready market for London newspapers which had acquired a reputation. This was particularly true of the Opposition papers. One gentleman complained to the government of the popularity of the notorious *Mist's Journal*, insisting that 'it is scarcely credible what Numbers of these Papers are distributed both in Town and Country'.[49] In 1721, 'A.B.' warned Lord Carteret, Secretary of State, of the evil influence of the *London Journal*, which at that time was an Opposition paper. According to 'A.B.', copies had been sent to Birmingham hawkers by 'one Pasham, a Bookseller of Northampton', and were being distributed for thirty or forty miles around; and he pleaded that 'some Method may be taken, whereby the Country may be preserved agt. the Poison that insinuating Libel begins to spread around us, not only here but in other great Towns'.[50] After 1726 the *Craftsman* became the great Opposition paper; and by 1728 Dr. Stratford, a strong Tory, could write that 'the *Craftsman* is the chief supporter of our spirits in the country'.[51]

It would seem that the people who subscribed to these London papers were the very people who are usually assumed to have been the main supporters of the country papers—the local gentry, the clergymen and the town magnates. The few diaries which have survived from this period were usually kept by people of this type: and those diaries reveal that, in nearly every case, the writer read the London newspapers. Parson Woodforde occasionally mentioned local papers—but he spent literally hours studying the London newspapers in local taverns.[52] William Stukeley, another churchman, rarely mentioned newspapers at all, but when he did included both

---

[48] See S. Morison, *The English Newspaper* (Cambridge, 1932), p. 131.
[49] *SPD 35*, vol. 29(67).
[50] Letter dated 16 August 1721, *SPD Geo. I*, 28(15).
[51] Dr. Stratford to the Duke of Portland, 29 May 1728, Portland MSS., vol. vii., *HMC*, 1901, 464.
[52] *Diary of James Woodforde, 1758–81*, ed. J. Beresford (Oxford, 1924). Local papers referred to on pp. 116, 133, 271, 282, 321; London papers, pp. 18, 21, 254, 332.

London and local ones [53]—as also did farmer Prior, of Berkshire.[54] In most cases, however, the diarists were actually subscribing to London papers. Timothy Burrell of Sussex shared a subscription to both the *London Gazette* and the *Flying Post*;[55] John Hobson of Yorkshire took in the *Evening Post*;[56] and the Reverend Dr. Weston of Berkshire had the *St. James's Evening Post*.[57] In the case of Timothy Burrell and Dr. Weston, it is true, there was as yet no local paper available: but there is nothing in the other evidence to suggest that the publication of such a paper would have made them relinquish their subscriptions to London papers. In fact, of all the diarists studied, only one, Benjamin Rogers, a rector of Northampton, made no mention of London papers, but was faithful throughout to his local paper, the great *Northampton Mercury*, from which he regularly copied out lengthy extracts.[58]

The wealthy or influential townsfolk were similarly subscribing to London newspapers. In 1742, the Bristol Corporation decided to take in three such papers in addition to the *London Gazette*, for use in the Council House, instead of members having to go to the coffee-houses to read them;[59] the following year, the Liverpool Council ordered the *St. James's Evening Post* to be purchased at the expense of the Corporation,[60] while the Trustees of Sheffield subscribed to the *Evening Post, Votes* and the *Gazette*.[61] Quite apart from such subscriptions, the taverns and coffee-houses in the country towns provided a large selection of London newspapers for the entertainment of their customers. According to an advertisement in the *Reading Mercury*, for instance, a coffee-house at Winchester took in 'the *Votes*, King's Speech and Addresses, the *Gazette, Daily Advertiser, General Evening Post, Evening Advertiser*, and *London Chronicle*, Weekly Journals, Monthly Magazines, the Sessions

[53] *Commentaries, Autobiography, Diary and Common-place Book of William Stukeley* (Surtees Society I, 1880), p. 293.
[54] *A Berkshire Bachelor's Diary*, ed. F. Turner (Newbury, 1932), entries for 2 January 1784 and 3 October 1773.
[55] Extracts form the Journal and Account-Book of Timothy Burrell, ed. R. W. Blencowe, *Sussex Archaeological Collections*, iii., 1850, entries for 12 November 1698, 3 May 1702, 3 December 1711, 26 March 1709, &c.
[56] Journal of John Hobson, entries for 27 January 1725/26, 18 June 1727.
[57] K. G. Burton, 'Early Newspaper Press in Berkshire', p. 2.
[58] Diary of Benjamin Rogers, pp. 10, 17, 22, 38, 45, 62, 71.
[59] Information kindly supplied by Mr. D. F. Gallop.
[60] A. C. Wardle, 'Some Glimpses of Liverpool during the first half of the eighteenth century', *Historical Society of Lancashire and Cheshire*, 97, 1945, 148.
[61] R. E. Leader, *Sheffield in the Eighteenth Century* (Sheffield, 1901), p. 131.

Papers, and Dying Speeches'.[62] The patrons of that establishment certainly had no cause to complain of any lack of variety in the entertainment provided. The connexion between newspapers and coffee-houses was, of course, particularly close: but taverns also began to take in London newspapers for the further delectation of their customers—and in the next century it was said that the landlord did so because 'it attracts people to his house, and in many cases its attractions are much stronger than those of the liquor there drunk, thousands upon thousands of men having become sots through the attractions of these vehicles of novelty and falsehood'.[63]

The London newspapers were thus a major threat to the success of the country newspaper. A large area surrounding London, and including Surrey, Middlesex and a great part of Kent, was regarded as being within the direct sphere of influence of the London papers, and no country printer dared to attempt to set up a local newspaper there. But the threat of the London papers was by no means confined to the immediate neighbourhood of the capital. There was the obvious advantage of reading the news at first hand and early in the week, instead of having to wait for what, at best, would be a second-hand version printed in the local weekly paper. And even at this early stage, a subscription to a London paper would probably confer a certain local prestige. For the country gentleman who was keenly interested in politics, a subscription to one of the London political papers was almost a necessity, for such papers as the *Craftsman, Mist's Journal* and the *London Evening Post* were in a class by themselves, and few country printers had either the space or the courage to reproduce their bolder essays.

But London newspapers were expensive. Most country subscribers had to order their copies through the six Clerks of the Roads, and the Select Committee of 1764 estimated that the profit the Clerks made by franking newspapers amounted to £3,000 or £4,000 a year.[64] Their charges were still far lower than the costs of ordinary postage: but they were high enough. An investigation in 1764 revealed that the Clerks in the Post Office and other government offices were charging £2. 12s. 6d. per annum for newspapers which actually cost them only about £1. 6s. 0d.[65] And the investigator, Mr. Yeates, suggested that, if the circulation of London papers in the provinces was to be increased so that the government might reap a greater revenue

[62] *Reading Mercury,* 21 March 1757. See also *York Journal,* 10 December 1745.
[63] A. Aspinall, *Politics and the Press c. 1780–1850* (1949), p. 11.
[64] *House of Commons Journals,* xxix. 998.
[65] *Liverpool MSS.,* vol. cxlix, op. cit., fo. 139.

from the stamp duty, the Clerks should be forbidden to charge more than forty shillings. Even so, such charges covered only the cost of delivery to the nearest post-master to the subscriber, who must either go to the post-office to collect his newspaper himself, or pay the post-master an extra fee for delivering it. According to a Post Office memorandum of 1791, this arrangement meant that 'people who live at a distance from a post Town must pay an additional half-penny a paper, some a penny, and some two-pence on the receipt of each paper'.[66]

Such heavy expenses, together with the delays involved, presented the country printer with his great opportunity. His paper was cheap —or, at least, no dearer than any single London paper—although, as was constantly emphasized, it contained the main items of a dozen or more London papers; and it could be delivered regularly and punctually to the subscriber without extra postage. As the printers of the *Northampton Mercury* explained to the readers, their news-paper was 'brought Home Weekly to their own Doors, without Postage or any other Charge or Trouble . . . at the same Rate which is paid in London or in the Country for any single Paper of the same Size'.[67]

From the very first, therefore, the country newspaper set itself up in conscious rivalry with the London papers, but evidently the com-petition was considerable. The gentry, clergy and town merchants might find the local weekly 'collection' useful; they might read it for its advertisements; and for those with any literary ambitions it pro-vided a most welcome outlet. But it was not their only, nor their most favoured, source of news. If the country printer were to flourish, he had to address himself to a humbler type of reader—to the reader who could not afford a subscription to a London newspaper, and who was not a regular patron of the coffee-house. And through-out the period, we find that the country printers were careful to emphasize their popular appeal. They addressed themselves 'to the worthy Body of Merchants and Citizens', to the 'Clergy, Gentry, Farmers, etc.', or to 'the Gentlemen, Tradesmen and Others';[68] their papers, they insisted, were suitable for 'all Persons of all Orders and either Sex', and for 'all Degrees and Capacities'.[69] Their aim, in

[66] *Proposal by the Clerks of the Roads*, 1791.
[67] *Northampton Mercury*, 5 April 1736.
[68] *Bristol Weekly Intelligencer*, 3 September 1749; *Sherborne Mercury* pre-liminary announcement, 19 February 1737; and *Derby Mercury*, 23 March 1732 respectively.
[69] *Stamford Mercury* announcement in the *Northampton Mercury*, 26 June 1732; *Gloucester Journal* hand-bill, 10 March 1721/22 respectively.

the words of the *Worcester Journal*, was 'to do Justice to all Persons of all Conditions and of either Sex'.[70]

This appeal to the humbler members of rural society raises the difficult question of the number of these people who could read and write at this time. According to one authority, 'the state of eighteenth century education was hardly sufficient in itself to create a reading public'.[71] It would seem that this view must be qualified. Higher education may have declined sadly during the eighteenth century; but primary education undoubtedly made significant advances. The great expansion of trade and the steady development of manufactures created an insistent demand for literate clerks and skilled artisans. To meet this demand there appeared the Society for Promoting Christian Knowledge, and the far more important Charity Schools Movement. And when the Charity Schools Movement began to decline, other schools were ready: for the very success of these schools had forced the middle classes to set up schools of their own in sheer self-defence.[72]

The Charity Schools Movement, although centred upon London, had schools all over the country. In 1735, according to the *Northampton Mercury*, there were one hundred and thirty-two Charity Schools in and about London and Westminster. These were now attended by 3,158 boys and 1,965 girls, and, from their beginning in 1697 to 1734, had educated a total of 21,399 children. In the rest of England, the report went on, there were 1,329 Charity Schools, attended by 19,506 boys and 3,915 girls.[73] In Norwich alone there were, according to the *Norwich Mercury*, seven such schools for boys and five for girls, attended respectively by 210 boys and 150 girls.[74] It would seem, therefore, that there were far more of these schools in the country areas than is generally realized, and that perhaps their part in the formation of a provincial reading public has not received sufficient attention.

Quite apart from the Charity Schools the countryside certainly did not lack its educational facilities. The advertisement columns of the provincial newspapers show that there were very many schools in existence during this period. To take only one example, between 1723 and 1760 the *Northampton Mercury* contained over one hun-

[70] *Worcester Journal*, 15 September 1748.
[71] M. Plant, *The English Book Trade* (1939), p. 34.
[72] M. G. Jones, *Charity School Movement in the Eighteenth Century* (Cambridge, 1938), p. 86.
[73] *Northampton Mercury*, 21 April 1735. See also *Derby Mercury*, 3 July 1735.
[74] *Norwich Mercury*, 6 July 1751, 22 September 1753, 24 August 1754, 2 August 1755, 23 October 1756.

dred and twenty educational advertisements, relating to more than one hundred different schools in its area. At Rugby, for instance, there was 'a good Free Latin School and two other Schools'; at Guisborough, 'two noted flourishing Free Schools, the one a Grammar School, and the other on Arithmetick';[75] and few towns, it would seem, did not possess at least one school. The most popular subjects advertised were writing, reading and arithmetic, followed by Latin and Greek, and, significantly, book-keeping and accounts. The fees ranged from ten pounds per annum to fourteen pounds,[76] for these schools were usually boarding-schools.

Such schools were, of course, expensive, and catered only for the well-to-do; but it is clear that there were many smaller and far cheaper schools available. As early as 1701, Francis Brokesby declared that 'there are few country villages where some or other do not get a livelihood by teaching school, so that there are now not many but can read and write'.[77] This estimate of the general standard of literacy was undoubtedly over-generous. But there were very many of these little village schools, and Shenstone's statement in 1742 that one could assume the presence of a dame school in every village marked with a little spire [78] seems to be supported by the advertisements in the country newspapers. These schools conducted by the parish clerk or the village dame may well have been considerably more efficient than is usually thought. At least, it is quite clear that there existed ample facilities for the children of the poor to acquire some sort of education, even if it were limited to the rudiments of reading and writing. The hero of *Joseph Andrews* learned to read 'very early' at such a local school, his father paying sixpence a week for that purpose;[79] and in the *History of Tom Jones* the village schoolmaster had nine pupils, of whom seven were 'parish-boys' learning to read and write at the ratepayers' expense.[80]

Of particular interest, in view of the general estimate of the extremely low standard of female education in the eighteenth century, are the regular appeals made by the country printers to women readers. As early as 1719, the *Ludlow Post-Man* declared its inten-

[75] *Northampton Mercury*, 4 November 1723, 9 August 1731.
[76] See *Northampton Mercury*, 4 February 1722/23, 6 January 1734/35, 6 December 1742, 18 April 1743, 6 January 1745/46 for examples.
[77] Francis Brokesby, 'Of Education', 1701, quoted *Cambridge History of English Literature*, ix. 405.
[78] Shenstone, 'The School Mistress', 1742, quoted ibid. p. 405.
[79] Henry Fielding, *The Adventures of Joseph Andrews* (O.U.P. World's Classics, 1945), p. 15.
[80] H. Fielding, *The History of Tom Jones* (Everyman's, 1942), p. 41.

tion of seeking 'to please the Fair Sex';[81] and this policy was to be echoed by many other papers during this period.[82] It must be admitted, however, that the country newspaper was essentially a man's paper, and most printers adopted a most condescending attitude towards the opposite sex. Had women been encouraged to contribute to the *Northampton Mercury*, wrote one 'Vega Violet', the public would have been 'oblig'd with many a curious Receipt in Cookery, Medicines for Agues and sore Eyes, Remedies . . . some plain and easy Instructions for the Tea-Table . . . besides all this, I would not have been wanting, now and then, for a Dish of Scandal'.[83] Many of the moral essays were obviously aimed at the female part of the population. This applied especially to the essays taken from the *Universal Spectator*. In the space of a few weeks in 1728–9, the *Leeds Mercury* reprinted from that paper, with evident approval, a letter describing how a marriage had been wrecked by the wife's passion for quadrille; a violent criticism of the antics of what the writer called 'our gingling Girls . . . giddy Creatures'; an attack upon old women who dressed themselves up like young girls; and a lengthy homily on the well-worn theme of the 'good old days', when women were frugal and concentrated upon 'house-wifery'.[84] Essays of this type appeared very frequently indeed in the pages of the country newspapers throughout the period.

The rise of this new reading public may be reflected in the printed books of the period, where it is noticeable that the ornate style of the seventeenth century gives way to a simpler style and vocabulary.[85] But the whole story of the expansion of the newspaper press bears witness to it, above all in the numerous contemporary references to the enthusiasm with which the poorer classes were exercising their newly acquired ability to read. According to Chief Justice Scroggs, 'so fond are men in these days that when they will deny their children a penny for bread, they will lay it out for a pamphlet; and the temptations are so great that no man can keep two-pence in his pocket because of the news'.[86] That very astute foreign observer, César de Saussure, remarked on the fact that 'all Englishmen are great newsmongers. Workmen habitually begin the day by going to coffee-rooms in order to read the daily news. Nothing is more enter-

[81] *Ludlow Post-Man*, 9 October 1719.
[82] e.g. *Howgrave's Stamford Mercury* announcement in the *Northampton Mercury*, 26 June 1732; *Bristol Weekly Intelligencer*, 3 September 1749.
[83] *Northampton Mercury*, 17 July 1732.
[84] *Leeds Mercury*, 12 November 1728, 11 March 1728/29, 20 May 1729 and 27 May 1729 respectively.
[85] J. H. Plumb, *England in the Eighteenth Century* (1950), p. 32.
[86] C. J. Scroggs, *State Trials*, vii. 1120.

taining than hearing men of this class discussing politics and topics of interest concerning royalty'.[87] Hogarth's 'Beer Street' depicted a butcher and a blacksmith absorbed in the latest newspaper, while pretty fish-wives studied a printed ballad. In fact, contemporaries were convinced that the poor were reading—and that they were reading newspapers above everything else. Working-hours might be long, but the reading of a weekly newspaper would not take up a great amount of time. Wages might not be high, but the price of a weekly newspaper was still low enough in this period to be within the reach of most pockets. Lord Ernle has referred to the eighteenth century as 'probably the nearest approach to the Golden Age for the labouring classes',[88] and recent researches into eighteenth century wages have revealed a steady increase in the earnings of nearly all trades.[89] In view of regional variations in wage rates, any generalization is dangerous, but probably the average unskilled labourer would receive about one shilling a day, while the skilled worker would take between one and two shillings.[90] To these wages must be added the earnings of the family in agricultural work or cottage industry. Yet even after the Stamp Act of 1757, a country newspaper still cost only twopence-halfpenny a week—which was considerably less than it was to cost later under the 'Taxes on Knowledge'. In any case, a newspaper in those days was not an object of purely ephemeral interest, to be hastily scanned and thrown away. All too often, it was the only printed matter that was available to its readers, and was something to be read and re-read, discussed and argued over, passed from hand to hand, and finally carefully preserved and bound into annual volumes. In the process, many people who could not afford a paper, and who perhaps could not read, would become acquainted with its contents. Family readings would be common: and Charles Knight has described how, in the early years of the following century, 'my learned friend would make the stirring events of the week known to his household, in reading aloud the *Reading Mercury*'.[91] And there were also public readings of newspapers. Charles Leslie remarked that 'the greatest part of the people do not read books; most of them cannot read at all; but they will gather together about one that can read, and listen to an *Observator*

[87] César de Saussure, *A Foreign View of England in the Reigns of George I and George II*, tr. Mme van Muyden (1902), p. 162.
[88] Lord Ernle, *English Farming Past and Present* (5th ed., 1936), p. 262.
[89] S. Gilboy, *Wages in Eighteenth Century England* (Harvard, 1934), p. 220.
[90] L. W. Moffit, *England on the Eve of the Industrial Revolution* (1925), p. 251.
[91] C. Knight, *Passages of a Working Life* (1872), i. 22.

or *Review*, as I have seen them, in the streets'.[92] An interesting example of this type of public reading appeared in a more recent work on Switzerland, where, in the village of Champéry in the late nineteenth century, there were 'on three of the houses . . . curious balconies, which are in reality old pulpits. . . . They now serve the place of the country newspapers, for on Sundays after Mass, a man calls out from them the news of the week, what there is for sale, what cattle have been stolen or have strayed, and other items of interest.'[93] It is not difficult to visualize such scenes occurring in the local taverns or market places of England in the eighteenth century.

That the newspaper was essentially the poor man's diversion was recognized as early as 1701, when a proposal to tax newspapers aroused the protest that

'the said newspapers have been always a whole sheet and a half, and sold for one half-penny to the poorer sort of people, who are purchasers of it by reason of its cheapness, to divert themselves, and also to allure herewith their young children, and entice them to reading; and should a duty of three-halfpence be laid upon these newspapers (which by reason of the coarseness of the paper the generality of gentlemen are above conversing with) it would utterly extinguish and suppress the same'.[94]

It was for this reason that the printers were to lay such stress upon their dual function of providing both news and what they called 'entertainment and instruction'. In fact, they showed a keen awareness of their social responsibilities, and endeavoured, so far as lay in their power, to supplement the somewhat meagre instruction so many of their readers had received at school, and so to educate their public.

[92] C. Leslie, Preface to *The Rehearsal* (1750), quoted C. Knight, *The Old Printer and the Modern Press* (1854), p. 219.
[93] E. Fanny Jones, 'Swiss Life and Scenery', in the *Canadian Magazine*, August 1898, p. 287, quoted K. Buecher, *Industrial Evolution*, tr. S. M. Wickett (1901), p. 232n.
[94] Quoted C. H. Timperley, *Encyclopaedia*, p. 584.

CHAPTER NINE

NEWSMEN AND AGENTS:
THE DISTRIBUTION SYSTEM
OF THE PROVINCIAL NEWSPAPER

U NTIL the very end of the period, there was little to choose between the various provincial newspapers as regards the actual news they contained. The fact that, despite this general similarity, some papers flourished, while others little different in style and content languished and died, suggests that success depended to a very considerable extent upon the ability of the printer to organize a regular and reliable delivery service to his potential customers.

This problem of distribution was one which grew as the provincial press itself developed. In the early years of the country newspaper it hardly existed: circulation was small and largely confined to the immediate neighbourhood. The newspapers were published on market-day, and sold over the counter of the printing-office to the visiting country-folk. In 1715, for example, the printer of the *Worcester Post-Man* announced that copies were obtainable from 'the Printing Office . . . and a Woman every Saturday from Ten in the Morning till Four in the Afternoon, near St. Martin's Church in the Corn Market, where all Country People may be furnish'd'.[1] Such a system of direct sales was, however, suited only to a small country town. In a highly populated city like Norwich—where the situation was further complicated by the early development of intense local competition—some more efficient means of reaching the public was required: and by 1707 the Norwich printers were employing hawkers to cry their papers about the streets.[2]

For some years, the whole emphasis was upon the purely local market. Very soon, a system of local delivery was evolved, and in 1719 the printer of the *York Mercury* was requesting 'any that are willing to take this Book Quarterly . . . to send in their Names . . .

---

[1] *Worcester Post-Man*, 24 June 1715.
[2] *Gazette or the Loyal Packet*, 4 January 1707.

and shall have 'em delivered every Monday Morning, before they are cry'd about this City by the Hawkers, they omitting many Families which should have 'em left at their Houses'.[3] Customers in town thus had their newspapers delivered to their door. But country customers picked up their own copies when they came in to visit the market. If they wished, they could have them delivered —but they would have to pay extra for the service. In 1715, the *Salisbury Post-Man* announced that it would be delivered to any private or public house 'in Town' for three-halfpence a copy, while 'any Persons in the Country may order it by the Post, Coach, Carriers, Market-People, to whom they shall be carefully deliver'd'.[4] The *Exeter Mercury* was similarly delivered to subscribers in the city for thirteen shillings a year, or 'seal'd and deliver'd to Country Subscribers at 15/- a Year, they paying Carriage'.[5] In Bristol, the local newspaper cost three-halfpence when delivered in town, and two-pence in the country.[6] And even as late as 1726, *Farley's Exeter Journal* could still inform prospective customers who lived outside the city that they might be 'constantly supply'd, either by the Post or Carriers'.[7]

But to have any hope of real financial success, the printers had to address themselves more and more to the potential readers outside the towns, who were scattered thinly through the surrounding countryside far off the beaten track. They formed the natural public for the provincial newspaper—provided that the local printer could devise some means of supplying them cheaply and punctually. But to charge extra for delivery was to nullify the country newspaper's greatest asset—its cheapness.

In response to this challenge, a new profession came into being —that of the newsman, whose job it was to travel the countryside delivering the local newspaper and the various other wares sold by an eighteenth century country printer. As early as 1714, the Stamford Corporation made it a condition of the admission to the freedom of that borough of the two printers, William Thompson and Thomas Baily, that they should 'make use of and employ such poor people in their service to disperse Newspapers etc. as shall be recommended to them by the Mayor for the time being and noe

[3] *York Mercury*, 30 March 1719.
[4] *Salisbury Post-Man*, 29 September 1715.
[5] *Exeter Mercury*, 28 October 1715.
[6] *Sam Farley's Bristol Post-Man*, 31 December 1715.
[7] *Farley's Exeter Journal*, 18 November 1726.

other'.[8] By 1719, the printer of the *Ludlow Post-Man* was announcing that his paper was 'dispers'd 30 or 40 Miles round, by Men imploy'd for that Purpose';[9] and in 1723 the *Reading Mercury* claimed to be distributed forty or fifty miles around.[10]

At first, the newsmen apparently delivered all the papers personally. But as the various newspapers' spheres of influence began to grow, and the newsmen had to travel longer and longer distances, their routes naturally tended to become fixed; and subscribers who lived at some distance from the route travelled by the newsmen were expected to make some private arrangement to pick up their copies at some agreed point. Thus, in 1745, the *Cambridge Journal* announced that 'Persons living at a Distance from such Places as our Messengers go thro', may have them left in Market Towns or other Places, where they shall appoint'.[11] At the same time, most printers rapidly realized the necessity of setting up agencies in the more important towns and villages in their area.[12] These agents had the responsibility of organizing intensive local distribution, for which purpose they often employed newsmen of their own.

In this way was evolved the distribution system which was to remain in operation until the coming of the railways in the next century. It was a system based essentially upon the newsmen and the agents. The routes followed by the newsmen radiated out from the printing-office like some great spider's web; and each agent was, in turn, the centre of a smaller web of intensive distribution. In summer and winter alike the newsman was expected to deliver his stocks of newspapers, often over surprisingly great distances. At various times, the *Northampton Mercury* mentioned the routes followed by its newsmen, and these invariably averaged between thirty-five and forty miles.[13] Two of the newsmen employed by the *Kentish Post* went from Canterbury to Barham, Elham, Folkestone, Hythe, Dymchurch, Romney and Lydd in the one case, and from Canterbury to Faversham, Sittingbourne, Milton, Chatham and Rochester in the other.[14] These distances were admittedly shorter: but these particular newsmen would probably have to make more personal

---

[8] Stamford Corporation, minute dated 15 January 1714, quoted F. H. Evans, *Brief Sketch of the Career of the Lincoln, Rutland and Stamford Mercury* (Stamford 1938), (4).   [9] *Ludlow Post-Man*, 9 October 1719.
[10] *Reading Mercury*, 22 July 1723.
[11] *Cambridge Journal*, 16 March 1745.
[12] The newspapers of Liverpool and Norwich made little reference to distribution, and were apparently satisfied with a circulation restricted to the town and the immediate neighbourhood.
[13] *Northampton Mercury*, 15 December 1746, 13 July 1730, 13 November 1752.   [14] *Kentish Post*, 3 December 1726, 29 July 1738.

deliveries than most, for their newspaper had very few agents. Also, they would not have so much time at their disposal, for the *Kentish Post* was published twice a week. In the more rugged north, the newsmen were obviously expected to cover even greater distances. One of the men employed by the *York Courant* went from York to Selby, Snaith, Thorne, Hatfield and Doncaster on the day of publication— a distance of some thirty-five miles—and continued on to Bawtry on the following day.[15] A newsman of the *Manchester Magazine* visited Chapel-en-le-Frith, Buxton, Bakewell, Chesterfield and Sheffield in one day, returning via Eginton, Middleton and Castleton the next— a round trip of about one hundred miles. It is hardly surprising that on one occasion the printer of the newspaper in question had to apologize because its previous newsman on this route had 'neglected to deliver the said Papers in due Time'.[16] But other newsmen travelled stages nearly as extensive. One man, Peter Pass, was employed by both the *Manchester Mercury* and the *Liverpool Advertiser*, carrying the Manchester paper to Bolton, Wigan, Preston and Kendal, a distance of about eighty miles, and then returning within two days in order to begin his travels for the *Liverpool Advertiser*.[17]

The average stage would seem to have been about forty miles— and this was sometimes covered on foot. In 1719, for instance, the *Ludlow Post-Man* advertised for 'any honest Man that will walk well, and be constant two or three Days a Week'.[18] For some of the longer stages, of course, horses would be a necessity, although they are rarely mentioned. Certainly, Peter Pass had a horse, although he was always referred to as 'the famous running Footman'; for, in 1759, the *Liverpool Advertiser* reported the theft of his horse and bags while he was delivering a paper, and offered a reward of five guineas.[19] And, early in the next century, Charles Knight mentions the delivery of the *Reading Mercury* by 'an old Newsman on a shambling pony'.[20] But, whether on horse-back or not, the newsman was expected to cover his stage regularly and punctually, delivering his papers to the agents and to individual subscribers on his route, collecting advertisements and the money to pay for them, and at the same time carrying stocks of the books, patent medicines and

[15] *York Courant*, 26 June 1750.
[16] *Manchester Magazine*, 16 June 1747.
[17] *Harrop's Manchester Mercury*, 12 November 1754 and 27 May 1755; *Williamson's Liverpool Advertiser*, 26 January 1759.
[18] *Ludlow Post-Man*, 16 October 1719.
[19] *Williamson's Liverpool Advertiser*, 17 August 1759.
[20] C. Knight, *Passages of a Working Life*, i. 22.

other goods sold by the printers. The printers of the *Stamford
Mercury*, when explaining the benefits which could be expected from
the publication of a local newspaper, laid particular stress upon 'the
large Quantity of Goods which will be Weekly carried out by the
Persons which distribute this Mercury'.[21] He must often have been
a sorely over-loaded man. But for the most part he performed his
duties to the general satisfaction and quickly became a well-estab-
lished feature of local life. Some care was naturally taken in the
selection of the newsmen, and *Farley's Bristol Journal* on one occasion assured its readers that a newly employed man was 'of sober,
honest Character, no way given to Drinking or Idleness'.[22] The same
paper had previously had trouble with one of its newsmen, who had
simply 'run away'.[23]

Winter-time naturally caused the greatest difficulties. During the
exceptionally severe winter of 1725-6, the printers of the *Northampton Mercury* were forced to produce one issue dated for a fortnight—'From Monday, December 27, to Monday, January 10
1725-6'. In an editorial announcement they explained that

'the great and deep Snow which fell on the 1st. Instant having kept
back the Post, which should have been here on Sunday, till Tuesday
the 4th. in the Evening, together with the great Floods, etc. making the
Ways in some Parts across the Country almost, if not altogether Im-
passable, will we hope excuse us if some of our Men have not gone
thro' the Extent of their Stages the last Week; but for the Conveniency
of such of our Customers who may thereby have miss'd of these Occurrences, we have compil'd the most material Paragraphs from both the
Weeks past. . . .'

And the following winter, *Farley's Bristol Newspaper* made the
cautious announcement that 'this Paper will continue to be dispos'd
of about the Country by the Running Footmen all the Winter, as far
as they can reach for Road and Weather'.[24] The care taken by the
printers to explain and justify any delays in the production or
delivery of their papers suggests that serious delays were exceptional. On one occasion in 1757, the printer of the *Middlewich
Journal* explained to his readers that 'the Winter approached, and
the Post coming in late, hinder'd the News-Carriers from travelling,
I was oblig'd to defer the Publication till Tuesday Morning, as did
all the other Printers hereabouts'.[25] And in 1735 the *Gloucester*

[21] *Stamford Mercury* advertisement, in the *Northampton Mercury*, 26 June
1732.
[22] *Farley's Bristol Journal*, 21 November 1747.
[23] *Farley's Bristol Newspaper*, 20 August 1726.
[24] Ibid. 24 December 1726.   [25] *Middlewich Journal*, 19 April 1757.

Journal remarked that 'it is hop'd that those of our Readers who may not receive this Journal at the usual Time, will excuse it, on account of the late heavy Rains, which have render'd Travelling dangerous'.[26] Such statements do not suggest that readers were accustomed to any delays in the delivery of their newspapers.

Quite apart from the weather, however, the newsmen had to face all the hazards common to eighteenth century travelling. In 1735, a newsman of the *Worcester Journal* was robbed near Coventry by 'a Fellow who, presenting a cock'd Pistol to his Breast, swore he would kill him if he did not immediately dismount and deliver'.[27] In 1743, the *London Evening Post* contained an announcement to the effect that 'whereas Jacob Newton, a Hawker of the *Leeds Mercury*, was attack'd about a Mile from Namptwich in the County of Chester, and robb'd of his Papers, Money and a Horn, and almost kill'd, by three Persons unknown, for selling and distributing the said News-Paper, *as they themselves declar'd*, This is to give Notice, that if any one will discover the said Persons concern'd in the said Robbery, etc. (so as the Offenders may be convicted thereof) they shall have Ten Guineas Reward, to be paid by James Lister, Printer, in Leeds aforesaid'.[28] And at various times other newsmen suffered a similar fate,[29] any delays in the delivery of their newspapers being attributed by the printers to some such contretemps.

Even at the best of times, the distribution of the newspapers was a slow business. The newsmen of the *Bristol Journal* were posting advertisements up in near-by Bath and Wells two days after publication;[30] *Farley's Bristol Newspaper*, published on Saturday, did not reach Bradford and Devizes until Monday;[31] and the *Gloucester Journal* apparently took four days to reach Bristol and Taunton.[32] Such delays obviously presented a wonderful opportunity for a more local printer to set up in opposition. Nevertheless, despite all the difficulties involved in distribution, the efforts of the printers were almost invariably directed towards enlarging even further their spheres of influence. Only the printers at Norwich and, towards the very end of the period, those at Liverpool made little mention of newsmen and agents, and seem to have remained content with purely local distribution. Elsewhere the tendency was to expand,

---

[26] *Gloucester Journal*, 2 December 1735.
[27] *London Evening Post*, 20/23 December 1735.
[28] Ibid. 2/5 April 1743.
[29] e.g. *Northampton Mercury*, 13 July 1730; *Williamson's Liverpool Advertiser*, 17 August 1759.
[30] J. Latimer, *Annals of Bristol*, p. 293.
[31] *Farley's Bristol Newspaper*, 26 February 1725/26.
[32] *Gloucester Journal*, 13 May 1735.

and the *Bristol Journal* in 1748 advertised that 'several honest Men, well recommended, will be shortly wanted to carry the News yet further, even to the remotest Parts of the Country'.[33]

Quite apart from encouraging prospective rivals, the length of time necessary to deliver the newspapers had an important effect upon the frequency of publication. Of course, the Stamp Acts helped to discourage printers from producing their papers too frequently. But it would seem that the difficulties involved in distribution proved an equally powerful deterrent. As the spheres of influence of the newspapers continued to expand, so even those champions of speed and endurance, the newsmen, required two or even three days in which to complete their stages before starting back to the printing-office. And when, during the Seven Years War, the printer of *Williamson's Liverpool Advertiser* published special editions to commemorate great victories, he often found it necessary to reprint the contents of these supplements in the ordinary edition of the following week, explaining that 'it was impossible for the Publisher to serve all his Subscribers in the Country with the extraordinary Newspapers dispers'd here gratis last Monday (the Hawkers not being return'd Home)'.[34] This necessity of awaiting the return of the newsmen meant, in effect, that the provincial newspaper had to be a weekly paper. It was becoming a physical impossibility to publish more than once a week. And after 1725 only two provincial newspapers did appear more frequently, the *Kentish Post* and the short-lived *Eton Journal*. The first-named was the great exception to the general rule. First published in 1717, it soon became a bi-weekly paper, and remained one throughout the whole period. A study of its lists of agents and of its advertisements reveals, however, that the paper had only a very restricted sphere of influence. Its expansion westward was blocked by London, while in every other direction the sea was not far distant. The problem of distribution was not therefore a difficult one, and the newsmen would not have the lengthy stages to travel which belonged to other and less constricted papers. The *Eton Journal* was born in the excitement of the Forty-Five. As a new paper, its sphere of influence would not be large; and consequently it was able to exploit the quite exceptional news-interest of the time by appearing twice a week. Once the rebellion was over, however, the newspaper rapidly reverted to type, and became a weekly paper.

[33] *Bristol Journal*, 26 March 1748.
[34] *Williamson's Liverpool Advertiser*, 27 May 1756.

So familiar and accepted a part of the local scene did the newsmen become that the printers rarely thought it necessary to describe their routes, and it is therefore difficult to estimate just how many newsmen were employed by the different papers. When the system of newsmen was first introduced, and the country circulation was still very small, there were not many of them. Even in 1726, *Farley's Bristol Newspaper* could inform its readers that 'for the Conveniency of People in the Country, the same will be constantly sent abroad by Two or Three Running Footmen'.[35] The number soon increased, however, particularly in the case of the larger newspapers, although printers were still reluctant to give any exact details themselves. In an advertisement in the *London Evening Post* in 1743, the printer of the *Reading Mercury* claimed that his paper was 'distributed throughout Berkshire, Buckinghamshire, Oxfordshire, Wiltshire, Hampshire, Surrey, Sussex and part of Kent and Middlesex, by fifteen Men, who are constantly employ'd for that End'; [36] and in 1764, the *Cambridge Journal* declared that 'there are 7 Men, at a great Expence, who convey this Paper through the Counties of Cambridge, Huntingdon, Bedford, Hertford, Northampton, Leicester, Rutland, Nottingham, Derby, and part of Norfolk, Suffolk and Essex'.[37] Otherwise, the papers themselves are silent. But it is often possible to estimate the number of newsmen from the lists of agents which appear so regularly in the country newspapers. Often these agents were set out in the order in which they were visited by the newsmen, and if they are plotted on a map the familiar spider's-web pattern emerges. Of course, such estimates can never be completely accurate. They omit the hawkers employed to cry the paper about the streets, and these were often numerous. In the case of Andrew Hooke, the Bristol printer, for example, five women were employed to carry his paper about the city. All were arrested in 1743 for selling unstamped papers.[38] Also, such estimates ignore such arrangements as that mentioned casually in the *York Courant* of 1750, whereby one of its newsmen was intercepted at Thorn by 'Edward Wilson of Crowle, who distributes the *York Courant* in Lincolnshire'.[39] These estimates, therefore, are on the conservative side. They suggest that, between 1745 and 1757, the *Manchester Maga-*

[35] *Farley's Bristol Newspaper*, 27 August 1726.
[36] *London Evening Post*, 31 March/2 April 1743.
[37] *Cambridge Journal*, 1 September 1764.
[38] *Bristol Oracle*, 16 July 1743; see also *London Evening Post*, 14/16 July 1743.
[39] *York Courant*, 26 June 1750.

zine had seven newsmen proper; and the *Bristol Journal* about five
in 1756. The larger papers employed more. In the late 1740's, the
York Courant had at least twelve, and the *Newcastle Journal* fourteen, while the historian of the Berkshire press has discovered the
names of thirteen newsmen written against the advertisements they
brought in to the *Reading Mercury*.[40] The smaller papers, therefore,
and those which addressed themselves mainly to a purely local
public, employed about half a dozen newsmen, while the larger
papers had a dozen or more.

Besides the newsmen, the printers soon realized the need to appoint agents in the surrounding towns and villages. The first issue in
1723 of the *Reading Mercury* made no mention of agents; but by
1743 the paper boasted thirty-six.[41] Similarly, the *Worcester Post-
Man* had no agents until 1717, when a list of seventeen was printed.[42]
The agent's job was primarily to organize intensive local distribution, and for this purpose he sometimes employed newsmen of his
own.[43] Often, the printers themselves acted as agents for other newspapers. Robert Raikes of the *Gloucester Journal* and Thomas Aris
of the *Birmingham Gazette* were agents for the *Worcester Journal*[44];
Raikes was also an agent for *Boddely's Bath Journal*, together with
Benjamin Collins of Salisbury, Hervey Berrow of Worcester, and
Robert Goadby of Sherborne.[45] One can only assume that their willingness to act in this capacity stemmed less from a disinterested
generosity than from a desire to keep an eye upon one another's
activities. Most of the agents were booksellers by trade, although
men of very different occupations were often appointed. Post-masters
were naturally a very popular choice, and the *Newcastle Journal's*
list of agents in 1746 included no less than seven.[46] The *Worcester
Journal* preferred innkeepers—another natural choice—and named
five among its agents in 1753.[47] But often the printers engaged men
who had no such obvious connexion with either the printing trade
or with communications. The *Birmingham Gazette* had four 'Writing Masters and Teachers of the Mathematicks' among its agents in
1760; and amongst other trades mentioned in different newspapers
were a livery-lace weaver, a snuff-maker, tobacconist, peruke-maker,

[40] K. G. Burton, 'Early Newspaper Press in Berkshire', p. 258.
[41] *Reading Mercury*, 13 February 1743.
[42] *Worcester Post-Man*, 17 May 1717.
[43] Cf. advertisement in the *Reading Mercury*, 19 March 1749/50.
[44] *Berrow's Worcester Journal*, 20 December 1753.
[45] *Boddely's Bath Journal*, 24 January 1757.
[46] *Newcastle Journal*, 28 June 1746.
[47] *Berrow's Worcester Journal*, 20 December 1753.

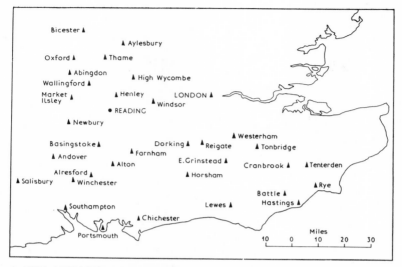

5. THE AGENCIES OF THE *READING MERCURY* OF 13 FEBRUARY 1743.

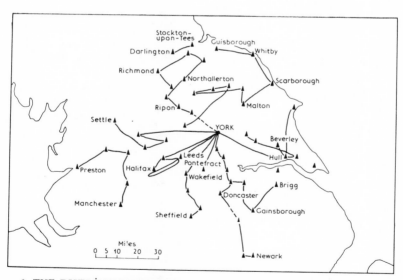

6. THE DISTRIBUTION SYSTEM OF THE *YORK COURANT*, BASED ON INFORMATION IN THE ISSUES OF 2 SEPTEMBER 1740, 13 APRIL 1742, 28 JUNE 1743, 26 JUNE AND 31 JULY 1750.

salter, engraver, bell-founder, attorney, surgeon and a 'Governor of the Work House'.[48]

Undoubtedly, the newsmen and the agents were the back-bone of the distribution system. But no means of reaching a potential customer was ignored. The system of direct sales continued throughout the period, for naturally many people preferred to collect their own copies rather than wait for their delivery by the hawkers or newsmen. The *Cambridge Journal* therefore announced in 1745 that copies were on sale at the printing-office, where 'all Persons living in this Town, or coming to the Market, may be supply'd . . . after Seven O'Clock'.[49] The system of casual sales also continued. The protests of the various printers at the hiring-out of newspapers by the hawkers show that the papers were still being cried about the streets, and as late as 1754 the *Manchester Magazine* advertised for a man 'to cry this Paper for this Town'.[50] But with the exception of a few large towns, this practice can never have been widespread. The provincial newspaper was essentially run upon a subscription basis, and its finances were rarely strong enough to allow of the printing of more copies than there was a guaranteed sale for—particularly when every copy had to be stamped.

The post office was little used for the distribution of country newspapers, although of course the printers depended upon it for their supplies of London newspapers. The traffic was not all one-way, however. The increasing stature of the country newspaper, and its obvious value as an advertising medium meant that it could not be ignored by the businessmen of the capital. London coffee-houses began to take in provincial papers for the information of their customers, and at the same time the country printers appointed agents in the capital.[51] They advertised from time to time in the London newspapers, aiming their appeal particularly at potential advertisers. For instance, in the *London Evening Post* in 1743 appeared the following announcement:

'This is to give *Notice*, to all Persons who may have Occasion to advertise in the South and West Parts of England, that the READING MER-

---

[48] Respectively, *Leeds Mercury*, 21 November 1721; *Boddely's Bath Journal*, 24 January 1757; *Sherborne Mercury*, 24 January 1744; *Creswell's Nottingham Journal*, 11 December 1756; *Nottingham Mercury*, 3 September 1719; *Exeter Chronicle*, 10 April 1761; *Bath Advertiser*, 1 March 1760; *Middlewich Journal*, 10 August 1756; *Reading Mercury*, 13 February 1743; *Derby Mercury*, 2 July 1741.

[49] *Cambridge Journal*, 16 March 1745.

[50] *Manchester Magazine*, 5 February 1754.

[51] e.g. *Salisbury Journal*, 10 July 1739; *Reading Mercury*, 13 February 1743; *York Courant*, 1 January 1760, etc.

CURY, OR WEEKLY POST, is the most convenient Paper for that Purpose, it being distributed throughout Berkshire, Buckinghamshire, Oxfordshire, Wiltshire, Hampshire, Surrey, Sussex, and part of Kent and Middlesex. . . . N.B. Gentlemen who live in London may see that their Advertisements are properly inserted, if they apply to Mr. John Kemp at Sam's Coffee-house in Ludgate-street, or to Mr. John Winder at the Horseshoe-Inn in Goswell-street, London, to whom Papers are sent Weekly for that Purpose.' [52]

This two-way traffic between the newspapers of the capital and those in the provinces was vastly increased during the Forty-Five, when such papers as the *Newcastle Journal* and the *Derby Mercury*, with their first-hand accounts of the rebels, enjoyed a very considerable sale in London, and were widely quoted by all the various newspapers there. The Newcastle paper became the principal source of information regarding the progress of the rebellion in the north, while the *Derby Mercury* was in great demand for its descriptions of the appearance and behaviour of the Prince and his highlanders during their occupation of Derby. Later, the two Liverpool papers, with their emphasis upon shipping news, achieved something like a nation-wide reputation, and were clearly making considerable use of the post-office for distribution purposes. In its first issue in 1756, *Williamson's Liverpool Advertiser* declared that

'this Paper is circulated through London, Bristol, Edinburgh, Glasgow, Dublin, Cork, Hull, Scarborough, Whitehaven, Chester, Lancaster, Manchester, Warrington, Preston, Blackburn, Bolton, Kendal, Shrewsbury, Wrexham, Flint, Denbigh, Northwich, Namptwich, and many other Capital Places in Great Britain, Ireland and the Isle of Man'.[53]

The *Liverpool Chronicle* contained a very similar announcement, announcing that copies were sent 'Gratis to the principal Coffee-Houses and Taverns' in all the principal towns.[54]

Only one provincial newspaper attempted to use the post-office for systematic distribution. Many printers, of course, made occasional use of it for the sending of odd copies to London and other towns, and still more attempted to avail themselves of some of the facilities of the post-office by appointing post-masters as agents, and post-boys as newsmen. But Andrew Hooke, of the *Bristol Oracle*, went one step farther, and sought to make the post-office the basis of his whole distribution system. To do so, he seems to have taken

[52] *London Evening Post*, 31 March/2 April 1743. See also its issues of 6/8 September 1744 (*Bath Journal*); 9/12 June 1744 (*Manchester Magazine*).
[53] *Williamson's Liverpool Advertiser*, 28 May 1756.
[54] *Liverpool Chronicle*, 6 May 1757.

the local post-master into partnership. And in 1743 he informed his readers that 'Advertisements for this Paper, which has the singular Privilege of being freely circulated throughout all the Cross-Roads in England, may be sent by Post, without any Expense, to the Author (under Cover to Mr. Thomas Pyne, Post-Master in Bristol)'.[55] The paper enjoyed a 'singular Privilege' indeed, for Mr. Pyne, as post-master, possessed the right of sending and receiving letters and parcels post-free. And his post-office was most strategically situated. Bristol and Exeter had been connected by a cross-road post in 1696 —so that letters beween the two went direct instead of, as before, by way of London; in 1698 this post had been extended to Wotton-under-Edge; in 1700 to Chester and in 1703 to Truro.[56] Finally, in 1741, a new branch, 'erected under the Care of Mr. Allen of Bath', connected Bristol, Bath, Bradford, Devizes, Frome, Warminster and Salisbury.[57] The Bristol post-office therefore lay at the centre of a great network of cross-road posts: and there was possibly some truth in the Oracle's claim that it was 'circulated by Post to all the considerable Towns, North and South, from Liverpool to Plymouth, through Wiltshire, Dorsetshire, and all South Wales'.[58] The printer added that advertisements would be taken in 'by all the Deputy Post-Masters on all the Cross Posts throughout England'.

Ingenious and enterprising as this close connexion with the post-office undoubtedly was, it was imitated by no other country printer. In fact, the post-office was quite unsuitable for the distribution of newspapers. It was useful for sending odd copies to distant agents and readers—although it is highly unlikely that there would be much demand for the Bristol Oracle in Chester or Liverpool. And certainly the privilege of receiving advertisements post-free must have been a boon to both printer and public. But as a medium of intensive local distribution, the post-office was far less efficient than the orthodox combination of newsmen and agents: and by 1744 even the Oracle had apparently recognized this, and had reverted to type, employing the usual methods of distribution.[59]

Apart from the occasional use of the facilities of the post-office, every possible means of distribution was tried at one time or another. Among its distributors, the Bristol Journal mentioned 'the Country-Butchers, Butter-Men, and other Carriers who serve the

[55] Bristol Oracle, 25 June 1743.
[56] H. Robinson, The British Post Office (Princeton, 1948), p. 101.
[57] The Traveller's Pocket Companion (1741), p. ix.
[58] Bristol Oracle, 24 September 1743.
[59] Ibid. 15 September 1744.

neighbouring Gentlemen' [60], and post-boys and common carriers were regularly enrolled among the ranks of the newsmen. The resulting combination of every conceivable means of transport and communication was well illustrated in the distribution system of the *Cambridge Chronicle* in 1762. That newspaper was

'dispatch'd Northwards every Friday Evening, by the Caxton Post, as far as York, Newcastle and Carlisle; into the Counties of Cambridge, Bedford, Hertford, Essex, Huntingdon, Lincoln, Nottingham, Leicester, Rutland, Northampton, and the Isle of Ely by the Newsmen; to London the next Morning by the Coach and Fly; Eastwards by the Yarmouth Carrier to Suffolk, and to several Parts of Norfolk, etc. by other Conveyances'.[61]

By such means, the provincial newspapers of the eighteenth century were able to control surprisingly large areas. Even the new *Bath Chronicle*, launched in 1760 in the face of formidable local competition, could soon claim to be distributed through an area 'One Hundred and Twenty Miles in Length'.[62] Yet such a claim, when compared with those of other papers, was almost insignificant. In 1743, the *York Courant* had agents in forty-three towns throughout a wide area ranging between Scarborough and Manchester;[63] and the first issue of the *Newcastle Journal* in 1739 stated simply that 'the Extensiveness of our Paper is left to our Readers to judge of, from the following', and went on to give a detailed and most impressive list of its various agents and distributors, which is worth reproducing in full. The paper was distributed by:

'Mr. Snarey and Mr. Bunting in Hexam; by Mr. Pattinson, Postmaster in Carlisle; who also distributes to Brampton, Wigton, Annan and Dumfries; by Mr. Fisher, Postmaster in Cockermouth; by Mr. Birkett, Postmaster in Whitehaven, who also distributes to Workington; by Mr. Richardson, Postmaster in Penrith, who also distributes to Hasket and Keswick; by Mr. Parkin, Postmaster in Appleby; by Mr. Robert Wharton, in Kendal, who also distributes to Ambleside, Hawshead, Ulverstone, Cartmell, Milthorp and Burton; by Mr. Isaac Rawlinson, in Lancaster, who also distributes to Hornby, Garstang, and Preston; by Mr. Richard Bayliff in Kirby-Lonsdale; by Mr. John Inman in Sedbergh; by Mr. Dalton, Postmaster, in Kirby Steven; by Mr. Lamb, Postmaster in Brough; by the News Carriers to Bishopauckland, Raby, Staindrop, and Barnardcastle; by Mr. Andrew Spottiswood, Bookbinder in Durham; by the News Carriers to Darlington, Richmond, Rippon, Thirsk, Northallerton, Stoxley, Gisbrough, Yarm, Stockton, Norton and Sedgefield;

[60] *Bristol Journal*, 20 November 1756.
[61] *Cambridge Chronicle*, 27 November 1762.
[62] *Bath Chronicle*, 7 May 1761.
[63] *York Courant*, 28 June 1743.

by Mr. Holmes, Postmaster, in Bedale, who also distributes to Midlam, Askrigg, and Masham; by the News Carrier to Sunderland and Shields; by Mr. Luke Gaire in Morpeth; by Mr. John Thompson in Felton; by Mr. George Shepherd, in Alnwick; Mr. Emmleton, Carrier to Warkworth; Mr. Joseph Blair, in Belford; Mr. George Handaside, in Wooler; Mr. Grieve, Postmaster in Berwick; who distributes to Eymouth; Mr. James Hunter, in Duns; by Mr. Maban, Postmaster in Kelsoe; by Mr. Robert Winterop, in Jedburgh, who distributes to Hawick; by the Booksellers in Newcastle'.[64]

Of course, both the *York Courant* and the *Newcastle Journal* might be regarded as exceptional. But in the south, papers were claiming spheres of influence almost as extensive. In 1743, the *Reading Mercury* had agents in London, Oxford, Henley, Thame, Bicester, Sarum, High Wycombe, Aylesbury, Windsor, Abingdon, Wallingford, Newbury, Market Ilsey, Andover, Basingstoke, Alton, Arlesford, Winchester, Southampton, Portsmouth, Denmead, Chichester, Horsham, Lewes, Battle, East Grinstead, Hastings, Rye, Tenterden, Cranbrook, Tonbridge, Westerham, Reigate, Dorking and Farnham—a total of thirty-five.[65] And in 1752 *Felix Farley's Bristol Journal* had agents in thirty-seven towns, stretching from London to Haverfordwest, and from Penzance to Liverpool.[66]

An agency did not necessarily mean that the newspaper sold many copies in a particular town. It did mean, however, that that town was within the paper's sphere of influence. A study of the places of origin of the advertisements suggests that the agencies were not set up purely for the sake of appearances. Most of the advertisements came either from the immediate neighbourhood of the printing-office, or from places near the various agents. Not a few came from even farther afield—from London, or from remote little hamlets and farms far off the beaten track. The advertisements, indeed, provide some guide to the newspaper's sphere of influence, by indicating the area through which the newspaper was known. However, such advertisements do not provide a reliable guide to the newspaper's actual circulation—a fact which was recognized in the eighteenth century itself. The *Stamford Mercury* apparently made much of the fact that it often received advertisements from very distant places, and held this up as a proof of its wide circulation. The printers of the rival *Northampton Mercury* promptly scorned this claim: the author of *Stamford Mercury*, they said, had

[64] *Newcastle Journal*, 7 April 1739.
[65] *Reading Mercury*, 13 February 1743.
[66] *Felix Farley's Bristol Journal*, 16 September 1752.

'lately given himself an Air of notifying the Publick how far his Paper circulates, by the remote Places from which he sometimes (by Chance) receives an Advertisement; But he might with as much Truth have exemplify'd this, by the different Places from which his Foreign Advices come. For his News as often goes to Constantinople, as to many Places from whence he receives Advertisements. And this may easily be proved, we ourselves have had Advertisements from within a Mile of London, and Towns equally distant either Way. But we are not so much Masters of the Faculty as to assert that our Mercury goes thither.' [67]

There was clearly a great deal of truth in this comment. In the advertisement columns of the provincial newspaper of this time, property notices far outnumbered all other types of advertisements, and were often aimed at a far wider public than the purely local one in the vicinity of the actual property itself. Such notices were inserted in as many newspapers, both London and provincial, as possible, on what was almost a national scale. Nevertheless, their insertion in a particular country paper does at least show that that paper was known in the neighbourhood of the property being advertised.

The distribution system of the early provincial newspaper appears to have been so effective that it reached even those readers in the most remote and isolated hamlets and farm-houses—the sort of reader who write to the editor of the Derby Mercury 'from a Corner of the High Peak in Derbyshire' to the effect that 'though recluse and at a great Distance from you I live, yet your Paper reaches me Weekly, by the Packhorse Track'.[68] In this way, the provincial newspapers played an extremely significant part in the eighteenth century process of opening up the country and breaking down the old isolation and parochialism. As the printer of the Sherborne Mercury explained in 1737, his newspaper would 'open up easy Communications with the adjacent Towns and villages, by means of the News Carriers'.[69] Often, indeed, such regular communication, particularly with the more remote villages, must have been established for the first time.

Towards the end of the period, however, the spheres of influence of many of the country newspapers began to contract. Success brought competition, and competition prevented expansion. Although immediate competition within the same town usually resulted in the collapse of one or other of the rival papers, the establishment of another paper within an existing paper's sphere of influence was not usually so disastrous. But inevitably it meant a

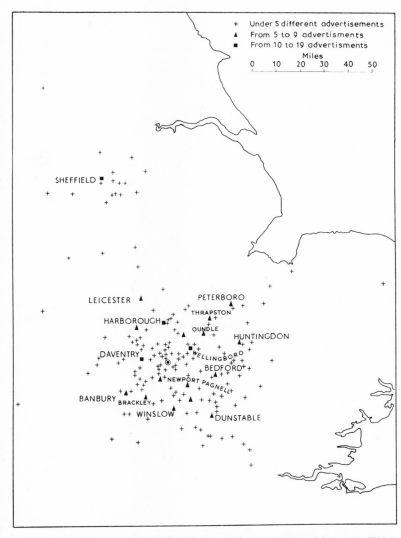

7. THE SPHERE OF INFLUENCE OF THE *NORTHAMPTON MERCURY* IN 1759, ARRIVED AT BY PLOTTING THE PLACE OF ORIGIN OF ALL THE 'INDEPENDENT' ADVERTISEMENTS IN THAT YEAR.

very definite contraction of the latter's circulation—and so was greeted with shrieks of abuse. The foundation in 1722 of the *North-ampton Journal* was hailed by the already established *Northampton Mercury* as 'the Apparition of a frightful Daemon, making a damn-able Harrangue of *Mist's Journal* and the *London Mercury*, etc. . . . gaping Spectre . . . vended for a certain Face-plainer . . . who under-stands Typography just as much as the Lord Mayor of London's Coach-Horses do fortune-telling'.[70] Later, the same paper was to be dismissed as the 'first Parcel of Bum-Fodder',[71] and was highly recommended to 'all true Lovers of broken English, bad Irish, worse Welsh, no Sense'.[72] According to the printers of the *Northampton Mercury*, the rival *Stamford Mercury* was a mixture of 'Bombast . . . Tautology and Ridicule'.[73] In his turn, the printer of the Stamford paper advised the public 'instead of the *Cambridge* WEEKLY FLYING *Post*, to read *The* LYING POST'.[74]

The effect of local competition is clearly revealed in the story of the *Reading Mercury*. In 1743, when that paper was at the height of its power, it had agents in thirty-six towns. Thereafter, its range gradually diminished. Throughout most of its career, it had had to face the steady competition of the newspapers at Gloucester and Bris-tol; but now it had also to meet the challenge of such papers as the *Salisbury Journal, Jackson's Oxford Journal*, the *Sussex Advertiser*, and the various Bath papers. By 1763, the number of its agents had been reduced to nine. The *Northampton Mercury* suffered a similar experience. It reached its peak about 1740, but then was challenged by the *Cambridge Journal*, the *Coventry Mercury*, the *Oxford Journal* and the *Leicester Journal*. Indeed, its sphere of influence diminished so noticeably that, in desperation, the printer sought to break through the circle of hostile papers by establishing an agency in far-off Sheffield.

A few papers, such as the *York Courant* and the *Newcastle Journal*, defied all attempts to cut them down, and they continued to grow as the industrial north they served developed. Elsewhere, however, although circulation increased steadily, the area of dis-tribution contracted. Such a development was quite essential to the future of the provincial newspaper. For years, each paper had en-deavoured to be not merely the county paper but the paper of several counties, and this effort to control vast areas had strained the resources of the printers to the utmost. Moreover, in such news-

---

[70] *Northampton Mercury*, 7 May 1722.   [71] Ibid. 9 July 1722.
[72] Ibid. 23 July 1722.   [73] Ibid. 21 May 1722.
[74] *Stamford Mercury*, 21 November 1745.

papers, local news could play no vital part: for what was local news to the immediate neighbourhood was of little or no interest to readers at the limits of the paper's range. But when the printer was at last forced to abandon such grandiose ambitions to pursue the more practical aim of publishing the local newspaper, local items became an essential feature, more frequent publication became possible, and distribution could be more intensive. The way was opening for the true provincial newspaper, which would voice local views and local news.

CHAPTER TEN

THE ADVERTISEMENTS

T HE steady growth and development both of the provincial
newspaper and of the society it served are nowhere more
clearly displayed than in the advertisement columns of the
country papers. In the early years of the eighteenth century, advertisements were little more than incidental items in these papers,
appearing only at very irregular intervals. Indeed, for many years,
according to the printer of the *Liverpool Chronicle*, 'it was thought
mean and disreputable among tradesmen of wealth and credit to
advertise the sales of their commodities in a publick Newspaper'.[1]
Quite apart from this, however, there was little to be gained by inserting an advertisement when few papers had a circulation which
extended far beyond the immediate neighbourhood of the printing-
office, and when every man knew his neighbour's business and stood
in no need of publicity. Even as late as 1742, the printer of the
Manchester Magazine noticed that

'as it is a Happiness peculiar to this Trading Part of the Kingdom, that
such Articles as are to be sold or lett at a reasonable Rate hereabouts
seldom want Advertising, the Printer . . . is oblig'd to have more News
than others in his Paper, which must certainly be more entertaining to
almost all Persons than Advertisements of such a House, Farm, etc. to
be lett at 30, 40, or more Miles Distance'.[2]

But as economic life developed, and competition became more
intensive, the advertisements began to grow both in number and
length. In the first two decades of the century, the trade announcements were usually limited to one or two brief paragraphs tucked
away at the end of the paper. By 1740, the *Newcastle Journal* was
regularly devoting at least one and a half of its four pages to advertisements; by 1750, two pages were required; and by 1753, not only
did the advertisements take up pages 3 and 4, but they frequently
occupied page 2 as well, and at times even encroached upon the
front page.[3] In the 1750's the *York Courant* regularly gave up more

[1] *Liverpool Chronicle*, 6 May 1757.
[2] *Manchester Magazine*, 19 January 1741/42.
[3] *Newcastle Journal*, 24.31 March, 14 April 1753; 18.25 March, 13 April
1754.

than three-quarters of its space to advertisements.[4] These papers
were admittedly exceptional, but their obvious difficulties over space
show clearly the problems which the development of advertising as
a dominant economic force was producing in the newspapers. All
the papers were feeling this pressure. As early as 1727, the *Norwich
Gazette* was complaining of the difficulties caused by what it called
'the Confinement to Half a Sheet of Paper by the Stamp Act'.[5] And
as the number of advertisements grew steadily, these difficulties increased. In 1736, the printer of the *Stamford Mercury* was forced to
increase the size of his half-sheet because, as he announced, 'it has
become a Matter of Objection by some Persons, to the buying our
Mercury, that near one Half of it is fill'd with Advertisements'.[6]
Such complaints were to become more and more frequent. Even the
Derby Mercury, a paper which rarely contained more than a handful
of advertisements, felt obliged to try to reassure those of its readers
who apparently felt 'a little Uneasiness . . . that we only insert such
Things to fill up the Paper',[7] by stressing that no material news
would ever be omitted in favour of such notices. The same cry was
to be taken up by many other country printers. Clearly, however,
the pressure upon space was becoming intense. By 1751, the printer
of the *Salisbury Journal* was reduced to printing advertisements
in a very small type up the right-hand margin of the front and
back pages; [8] the *Newcastle Journal* was forced, in March, 1739, to
discontinue its series of articles on geography and natural history
because 'Advertisements at this Season fill so large a Part of our
Paper';[9] and in the same year the *York Courant* made much of the
fact that

'the Printer of this Paper having receiv'd great Complaints from his
Correspondents, for delaying their Advertisements, which he has been
oblig'd to do in order to make Room for News; and being very desirous,
as far as in him lies, to give universal Satisfaction, designs next Month
to print the *Courant* in a much larger Size, by which Measure it will
contain more than any Newspaper extant'.[10]

A few months later, the printer was proudly announcing the purchase at an 'extraordinary Charge' of a 'new Set of small Types

---

[4] e.g. *York Courant*, 4 March 1760.
[5] *Norwich Gazette*, 25 November 1727.
[6] *Stamford Mercury*, 19 April 1736.
[7] *Derby Mercury*, 1 November 1739. Cf. *Newcastle Journal*, 7 July 1739;
Williamson's Liverpool Advertiser, 25 August 1758; *Bristol Advertiser*, 9
August 1746.
[8] *Salisbury Journal*, 2 September, 21.28 October 1751.
[9] *Newcastle Journal*, 21 March 1739.
[10] *York Courant*, 13 March 1739.

purposely for Advertisements, that we might make more Room for News'.[11] But even this generous gesture did not pacify all the readers, and the printer had to administer a stern rebuke to those who,

'in this Respect Enemies to the North of England, have expressed a Dislike of there being so many Stallions advertised in this Paper; not considering that the Number of fine Horses bred in this County have enabled the Farmers to pay their Rents and support their Families under the calamitous Effects of the Distemper among the Horned Cattle'.[12]

We may sympathize with these unpatriotic readers when we discover that, in one issue of 1760 alone, there were no less than twenty-nine advertisements of stallions at stud,[13] and that during the spring months there were nearly always twenty such notices.

Before 1712, extant files of the country newspapers are too incomplete to provide any accurate information about the average number of advertisements carried by the various papers. Thereafter, as the files become more extensive, it is possible to estimate this figure. For the present purpose, only the 'independent' advertisements have been taken into account—that is to say, genuine trade announcements emanating from sources outside the printing-office. Publishing notices and the very numerous advertisements of patent medicines have been ignored, for in both the printers had a definite financial interest.

In the 165 issues of the *Newcastle Courant* for the years 1711 and 1712, there were 954 'independent' advertisements—an average of about 5.7 per issue. Such a total was quite exceptional at this time, and for many years to come most papers had far fewer. The *York Mercury* between 1719 and 1721 contained only 42 advertisements; the *Nottingham Weekly Courant* had 143 in 76 issues between 1716 and 1724; the *Leeds Mercury* only 67 in 42 issues of 1723. Most papers rarely contained more than two or three advertisements. But already papers were appearing which had far more. In 1723, the *Stamford Mercury* had a total of 569—an average of over ten each week; and in 1725 the *Norwich Gazette* achieved the remarkable total of 989. By 1740, the *Stamford Mercury* had 1,040 advertisements—and such a figure was to be the peak for most country newspapers in the period under study. But it was eclipsed by a new group of papers which was now beginning to emerge. In its first 52 issues, the *Newcastle Journal* of 1739 contained 1,408 advertisements; and its total was to increase steadily. By the 1750's, the figure of 2,000

---

[11] Ibid. 3 July 1739.   [12] Ibid. 29 April 1755.
[13] Ibid. 18 March 1760.

advertisements per annum was regularly to be attained by such papers as the *Newcastle Journal*, the *York Courant* and the *Ipswich Journal*. The record for the period was the 3,058 'independent' advertisements, reached by the *Newcastle Journal* in 1753.

In fact, from about 1740 onwards, three distinct groups of country newspapers may be distinguished. At the top came the papers like the *Newcastle Journal*, *York Courant* and *Ipswich Journal*. These were advertisers as much as newspapers, and regularly contained more than 2,000 advertisements in a year. Next came the great mass of country newspapers, among which may be mentioned the *Northampton Mercury*, *Bristol Journal* and *Worcester Journal*. These papers averaged about 1,000 advertisements a year. And below these came a small group, which nevertheless included such long-established papers as the *Derby Mercury* and the *Manchester Magazine*, in which a total of 500 was seldom exceeded.

If the number of 'independent' advertisements increased steadily, however, the character of the advertisements themselves changed very little. In 1723, the *Reading Mercury* appealed specifically for advertisements from 'Persons who have Houses or Estates to be Lett or Sold, or have lost Horses, Cattle, etc. or would have any Business made publick';[14] in 1738, the *Mancheter Magazine* reduced its charges for advertisements, 'if very short, and concerning any Thing lost, or Houses, etc. to Lett';[15] and lastly, in 1755, the printers of the *Leicester and Nottingham Journal* addressed themselves particularly to the

'Stocking Manufactury in the opulent Towns of Nottingham and Leicester; as the Masters of that Business are frequently troubled with Apprentices that make Elopement from their Service and generally take their Flight from one of these Trading Towns to the other; so that by advertising such runaway Apprentices in this Journal, they are most likely to bring them back to their Legal Service.'[16]

The types of advertisements thus enumerated—property to be let or sold, lost cattle and runaway apprentices—did, in fact, constitute a large proportion of the advertisements which appeared in the country newspapers. The common feature of all these advertisements was, of course, their appeal to a wider public than the merely local one. Property might attract buyers anywhere, and was therefore advertised as widely as possible, often in papers published in towns far distant. Similarly, runaway apprentices or stolen or straying cattle and horses—not to mention absconding wives—might roam far afield. Such runaways were always described in great detail, with the emphasis upon their defects. Thus, a mare advertised in the *Stamford Mercury* as either stolen or strayed away was described as both 'full aged' and 'broken winded';[17] and the *Cambridge Journal* on one occasion contained a notice concerning the flight of an apprentice named John Hays, who, said the paper, was 'broad set, low of Stature, between 19 and 20 Years of Age, with brown short Hair, very thick Lips and wide Mouth, and speaks thick, full-fac'd, and sour Countenance, short Arms, large hands BUT OF LITTLE WORTH'.[18] Occasionally, a more exotic note was sounded, and in 1730 the *Kentish Post* reported the disappearance of a 'Black Boy born in the East Indies'.[19]

The main emphasis was always upon property, however: and only the printers of the *Reading Mercury* thought it worth their while to address themselves to tradesmen who might wish to publicize their business. Generally speaking, the small trade announcements which today throng the pages of the local newspaper were at this time conspicuous by their absence. Until the later growth of vast conglomerations of population, and the consequent development of intensive and cut-throat competition, there was little to be gained by advertising anything save items, such as property, which might attract distant purchasers, or articles of quite exceptional novelty or appeal. Thus, the ordinary necessities of life were rarely advertised in these newspapers, which throw very little light indeed upon the cost of living of the time. The only goods advertised with any frequency were luxury goods, such as millinery from London, tea, coffee and chocolate, and wines and spirits. Otherwise, trade announcements were usually limited to notices of the opening of new shops or the closing-down of old ones, to the sale of stock, and situations wanted or vacant. Only rarely were prices and wages mentioned. Typical was the announcement in the *Stamford Mercury*, 'This is to give Notice, That Mrs. Blake in the High Street, Stamford, hath to sell some very good Coffee fresh roasted, some extraordinary fine Tea, Green and Bohea, Sweet-meats and Chocolate, to be sold by her for a small Profit'.[20]

Few direct indications of anything in the nature of an 'industrial revolution' appear in these advertisement columns until the very end

---

[17] *Stamford Mercury*, 11 January 1727/28.
[18] *Cambridge Journal*, 3 February 1753.
[19] *Kentish Post*, 26 September 1730. Similar in *Newcastle Journal*, 18 June 1748.
[20] *Stamford Mercury*, 1 February 1727/28.

of the period. In 1759, the *Derby Mercury* contained an advertisement of the sale of fifty stocking frames;[21] and the *Manchester Magazine* in 1756 advertised '10 Dutch Engine Looms'.[22] In this same year, the *Liverpool Advertiser* also announced the opening of a 'silk Manufactury', adding that 'either Women or Children may meet with suitable Encouragement'.[23] This type of advertisement was now becoming increasingly frequent. In 1760, for instance, the *York Courant* at various times advertised the sale of shares in a lead mine, 'very promising Lead Mines', oil mills, and wire-works, while a farm was noted as being 'very conveniently situated near the Rivers Ouse and Air for shipping Corn', and an added inducement to buy a certain estate was the fact that 'there is Coal to be got in Part of these Premises'.[24] But, in general, the impression left by the advertisement pages of these newspapers is one of an overwhelmingly agricultural economy as yet hardly touched by the forces of industrialization and urbanization.

Rare as these indications of expanding industrial life undoubtedly are, however, they do show most strikingly that much of the expansion was due to the arrival locally of craftsmen from London. The picture that emerges from the trade notices in the advertisement pages is one of a steady migration of skilled craftsmen from the capital into the provinces. Between 1720 and 1760, the *Northampton Mercury* gave the names of seventy-two such men as having recently settled within its area; the *Newcastle Courant*, despite the incompleteness of its extant files, yet named sixty-eight between 1711 and 1758; the various Bristol papers named forty; and, in fact, almost all the country newspapers have the same story to tell.

The occupations of these skilled craftsmen varied considerably. Among the most numerous were schoolteachers and surgeons, many of the latter claiming to have been trained under the famous Dr. Smellie: and the presence of such men in the provinces goes far to explain two of the most noticeable features of eighteenth century English life—the increasing literacy of the country, and the fall in the death-rate. Many others were connected with fashions and clothing, with stay-makers, peruke-makers and tailors being especially prominent. Quite obviously, the provinces were rapidly becoming more fashion-conscious. But others had more practical trades: they were braziers, watch-makers, tin-workers, glass-grinders and

[21] *Derby Mercury*, 9 March 1759.
[22] *Manchester Magazine*, 22 October 1756.
[23] *Williamson's Liverpool Advertiser*, 28 May 1756.
[24] *York Courant*, 22 April, 18 January, 25 January, 19 February, 11 January, 30 December 1760 respectively.

so on. The list in the *Northampton Mercury* comprised fifteen teachers and fifteen apothecaries and surgeons, eight stay-makers, five inn-keepers, five upholsterers, three coach-makers, three watch-makers, two limners, two wig-makers, and two dancing-masters; and a distiller, bookbinder, brazier, pot-maker, gunsmith, painter, vintner, bookseller, hat-maker, dyer, tin-worker and saddler. The *Newcastle Courant's* list included seven stay-makers and seven upholsterers, six peruke-makers, only two teachers, two braziers, carvers, silk dyers, booksellers and gardeners; and one oculist, a shoemaker, glass-grinder, glover, mercer, milliner, farrier, druggist, saddler, paper-hanger, accountant, seedsman and tailor. *The Norwich Mercury* between 1750 and 1757 recorded no less than thirty arrivals from the capital: five teachers, five peruke-makers, three tailors, two watch-makers, stay-makers and hatters; and one hosier, clock-maker, leather-seller, inn-keeper, upholsterer, chair-maker, plasterer, druggist, painter, jeweller and a gentleman who called himself a 'Rasper and Tripe-dresser'. The *Kentish Post* gave five such names in 1740, and another five in 1750; between 1735 and 1755, the *Derby Mercury* mentioned thirteen London craftsmen; and in 1760 the *York Courant* gave twelve. At the same time, as certain provincial towns became noted for their pre-eminence in various trades and industries, a similar migration began between these towns and other country centres. In 1760, for example, the *York Courant* reported the arrival in York of a shipwright from Hull and a china manufacturer from Liverpool.[25] But a London training remained something to boast of, particularly in the world of fashion. Within the short space of four months in 1755, no less than six tradesmen emphasized this fact in the advertisement pages of the *Newcastle Journal*: one Joseph Slater, a hair-cutter, 'late apprenticed to Mr John Hay deceased', informed readers that he was 'just returned from London'; John Elder, a tailor, stated that he had served 'seven Years at London and Newmarkett'; a wig-maker, Michael Kelly, had come to Newcastle from London 'for the Season'; Batholomew Kent, upholsterer, had 'served Time with the late Mr. Smith, deceas'd, but since then has been in Business at London and Bath 7 Years'; another hair-cutter and dresser, William Brown, had recently arrived from London; and finally, J. Webster, a peruke-maker, had 'procur'd an excellent Workman from London'.[26]

It is not always easy to ascertain, from the very brief announce-

---

[25] Ibid. 1 and 15 January 1760 respectively.
[26] *Newcastle Journal*, 19 April, 26 April, 17 May, 7 June, 15 March, 14 June 1755 respectively.

ments which these gentlemen put into the local newspapers, whether they were permanently resident in the provinces, or merely temporary visitors. But it is clear that, despite the allegedly deplorable state of the roads in England in the eighteenth century, there was a considerable amount of commercial travelling taking place. London tradesmen regularly visited the country fairs, taking with them stocks of their goods. Thus, the Stamford, Gloucester and Bristol newspapers annually reported in their advertisement pages the arrival of these traders from London.[27] Similarly, the *York Courant* announced the presence 'for the Season', of a London jeweller,[28] and the *Newcastle Journal* the visit of a London milliner, Alice Crowe, and of a wigmaker.[29] Another woman, Elizabeth Chancellor, a lace dealer, was at Norwich every year, and she also visited Bristol.[30] Both cities were also attended each year by a lace firm by the name of Pritchard and Company.[31] Apart from these visits, the Norwich shopkeepers regularly went to London each year to lay in a stock of the latest fashions. In 1756, for instance, in the *Norwich Mercury* advertisements, two tailors, a stay-maker, a glover and a mercer all announced that they had 'lately return'd from London'.[32] But the larger country markets and fairs also attracted traders from other provincial towns. John Steward of Norwich arrived in Bristol to sell Norwich goods, while John Shirtcliffe brought there a stock of 'Sheffield and Birmingham Goods'.[33]

It would seem, therefore, that communications were steadily improving throughout the period, and there were frequent references in the advertisement columns to travelling. A notice in the *Northampton Mercury* in 1722 informed readers that 'the Northampton Stage Coach begins to fly on the 8th. instant', and would reach London in one day.[34] By 1726, according to the same paper, the 'Stamford Flying Waggon' left Stamford at 3 a.m. on Monday each week, arriving in London on Tuesday night or Wednesday morning.[35]

---

[27] e.g. *Stamford Mercury*, 8 March, 14 June 1716, 19 March 1721, 22 February 1721/22, 13 March 1739/40; *Gloucester Journal*, 29 January, 23 July 1751; *Farley's Bristol Newspaper*, 16 July 1726, 21.28 January 1726/27; *Felix Farley's Bristol Journal*, 20.27 July 1754, 21 January 1758.

[28] *York Courant*, 3 June 1760.

[29] *Newcastle Journal*, 17 May 1755, 16 June 1753 respectively.

[30] *Norwich Mercury*, 18 January 1756; *Felix Farley's Bristol Journal*, 19 August 1758.

[31] *Norwich Mercury*, 9 October 1756; *Felix Farley's Bristol Journal*, 21 May 1757.

[32] *Norwich Mercury*, 24 April, 8.15.22 May, 24 July 1756.

[33] *Farley's Bristol Newspaper*, 9 April 1726, 21 February 1726/27.

[34] *Northampton Mercury*, 22 April 1722.

[35] Ibid. 5 December 1726.

By 1752, the stage coach from London was reaching Northampton in twelve hours.[36] Rather less confident was the notice in the *Derby Mercury* to the effect that the stage coach from Derby would reach the capital in three days 'if God permits'.[37] Quite apart from the frequent references to stage coaches, there were also many notices referring to turn-pike meetings. In 1757, the *Newcastle Journal* contained no less than one hundred and thirty-eight such notices, while the *York Courant* in 1760 had seventy-five, and the *Gloucester Journal* of 1751 forty-six.

In this way, great developments may often be traced behind the brief items in the advertisement pages of the country newspapers. In particular, the growth of literacy may be seen in the numerous educational advertisements. The *Northampton Mercury* between 1720 and 1760 contained such notices from more than one hundred schools of various types, many of them newly established; between 1749 and 1756, the *Norwich Mercury* had sixty-three educational advertisements. Typical was the advertisement in the latter paper from one John Holmes, master of the Public Grammar School at Holt. He was prepared to teach the following subjects:

'For Trade or Business   :   Reading, Writing, Arithmetick and Bookkeeping
For Merchandise or Factorage :   Merchants' Accompts, The Balancing and Computation of Exchange, Foreign Bills, Coins
For the University   :   Latin and Greek and all the Classicks, Arithmetick in all its Parts, French, and the Use of both the Globes
For the Law
For Gentlemen's Stewards or Gentlemen that chuse to be their own.'[38]

Many of these educational advertisements were obviously designed to appeal to the rising commercial and industrial interests. Thus, a boarding-school at Norwich taught boys not only such subjects as Latin, Greek, geography, history, dancing, writing and mathematics, but also foreign languages, navigation and accounts.[39] Many schools now included in their curricula such practical subjects as 'Mensuration and Merchants' Accounts', surveying and book-keeping,[40] and

---

[36] Ibid. 22 June 1752.
[37] *Derby Mercury*, 27 March 1735.
[38] *Norwich Mercury*, 16 September 1749.
[39] Ibid. 11 January 1752.   [40] Ibid. 31 March 1753, 14 February 1756.

one Norwich school offered translations of French and Dutch specifically for merchants.[41]

Another feature of these advertisements is their frequent appeal to an adult public. As early as 1712, the *Newcastle Courant* had given two-and-a-half pages of publicity to the proposals of Dr. Jurin, Master of the Royal Free Grammar School, 'for carrying on by subscription a compleat Course of Mechanicks, by which Gentlemen unacquainted with any part of the Mathematicks in the Space of 12 or 18 Months by meeting 3 Times a Week for an Hour at a Time may be enabled to compute the Effect of any Machine whatsoever'.[42] Advertisements of this type were to become steadily more frequent. One teacher in Norwich, with the somewhat exotic name of Del Simon de Lagarde, offered to teach 'The French Tongue in all its Purity', Portuguese, writing, arithmetic and geometry, and, more unusually, navigation, 'fortification' and architecture, adding that he was willing to teach 'Gentlemen and Ladies any of the above at their Houses'.[43] Other teachers announced schools 'for the Instruction of Youth and those of more advanced Years', and for 'youths and grown-up Persons'.[44] Equally characteristic of the developing life of the provinces was the emphasis upon the social graces, and on one occasion the *Norwich Mercury* contained an advertisement to the effect that

'a Norwich la Langue Francoise est enseignee dans toutes les Formes et avec toute la Regularite et Exactitude possible . . . par G. R. Hue. Et comme il ne doute pas, qu'il n'y ait des Messieurs et des Dames qui seront ravis d'une Occasion si favourable sur tout le Francois etant et devenant en Pratique comme il faut Aujourd'hui parmi les Personnes de Qualite. . . .'[45]

At the same time, the number of publishing notices began to rise steeply, and mention was made of provincial lending libraries. At Northampton, a bookseller had a lending library of three hundred volumes, and charged ten shillings per annum, three shillings a quarter, or three-pence a week.[46] Later, a trust for a public library was proposed, the fees to be five shillings entrance and a subscription of five shillings a year.[47] The *Derby Mercury* in 1753 announced that Richard Smith, a Sheffield bookseller, also lent books;[48] and in the

---

[41] *Norwich Mercury*, 23 September 1749.
[42] *Newcastle Courant*, 26 November 1712.
[43] *Norwich Mercury*, 15 December 1753.
[44] Ibid. 7 March 1752, 12 October 1751 respectively.
[45] Ibid. 11 August 1750.
[46] *Northampton Mercury*, 21 January 1760.
[47] Ibid. 1 September 1760.   [48] *Derby Mercury*, 2 March 1753.

same paper a few years later a Derby bookseller, John Sanders, proposed to set up a circulating library, charging two shillings a volume for what he called 'single Plays', while 'small Histories such as the Life of the King of Prussia, Duke of Marlborough, Count Saxe' and so on would be lent out at one penny each, 'leaving the Value in Hand'.[49] In 1742, the *Reading Mercury* also announced the establishment of a lending library locally.[50]

The developing urban life of the provinces may also be seen in the frequent advertisements of local 'Assemblies' and in the notices of the local theatres. Typical was the following announcement, which appeared in the *Norwich Gazette* in 1727:

'This is to give Notice to all Persons of Quality, Gentlemen, and Ladies, That an ASSEMBLY will be held at Mr. Catherall's in Chapel-Field-House in Norwich, on Wednesday the 11th. of January next, being the Sessions Week; where will be the City-Musick, and all other Attendance ready by Six a Clock; particular Care shall be taken to oblige the Gentlemen with a Glass of good Wine, and every Thing as usual at the Norwich Assemblies: Tickets to be had at the said House, and at Brathwaite's Coffee-House, Price 2*s*. 6*d*. N.B. At the aforesaid Mr. Catherall's Gentlemen and Ladies may be accomodated with very good Lodgings for what Time they please, and the House is seated in the best of Air; and they may have their Provisions dress'd at Reasonable Prices, or may be boarded as they please'.[51]

The papers of Norwich and Exeter gave great prominence to performances at the local theatre. At Exeter, the printer, Andrew Brice, was himself actively interested in the drama, often composing the prologues to the plays, and giving those plays publicity in his paper.[52] The theatre in Norwich was particularly flourishing, and its patrons could not complain of any lack of variety in the entertainment they were offered. A typical announcement, from the *Norwich Gazette* of 1727, reads:

'By His Majesty's Permission. This is to give Notice to all Gentlemen, Ladies, and others. That at the White-Swan in St. Peter's, on Monday next, will be Acted an Excellent PLAY call'd, DIDO and AENEAS: Or, The Wandring Prince of Troy. And likewise an excellent Entertainment call'd, The Pye Dancer; or, Harlequin cut out of a Pye: With several Entertainments, too tedious to mention here. There is likewise to be seen the Famous and Original Posture-Master of the World, who turns his Body into all Manner of deform'd Shapes and Postures. And the moving Wax-Work, representing the Court of King Edward IV, with

[49] Ibid. 2 December 1757, 13 October 1758.
[50] *Reading Mercury*, 20 December 1742.
[51] *Norwich Gazette*, 7 January 1727.
[52] e.g. *Brice's Weekly Journal*, 3.31 March 1727.

his Concubine Jane Shore. and the 2 young Princes that were murder'd at the Tower, by the cruel Order of Crook-back'd Richard, to gain the Crown. Perform'd by JOHN KARBY.   Vivat REX.'[53]

The plays advertised in the *Norwich Gazette* in the year 1741 included 'Hamlet', 'Henry IV', 'As You Like It', 'Tamerlain', 'The Double Dealer', 'Love's Last Shift', 'History and Fall of Caius Marius', 'Cato', 'The Beggar's Opera' and 'Twelfth Night'.[54] Undoubtedly, however, outdoor sports were more popular in that robust age, and few issues of a newspaper did not include some announcement of horse-racing or cock-fighting.

Official notices were also frequent. Indeed, the printers of the *Sherborne Mercury* in their preliminary announcement held out as one of the main attractions of their newspaper the fact that it would 'give a Commodious Opportunity of conveying to a Multiplicity of Readers all Publick Notices that shall be advertised therein'.[55] One such notice, which appeared in 1751 in the *Birmingham Gazette*, reveals clearly the problems involved in the sudden growth of the population of the new industrial towns:

'as all the Parish Officers in the Town of Birmingham are become very troublesome, from the Largeness of the Place and particularly Surveyor of the Highways is excessively so, for want of its being in general better understood, many People fancying Statute Duty a Matter of Courtesy, which they may be excus'd from if they please : I beg therefore to explain the Nature of it in brief in order to save future Trouble, both to the Inhabitants and Officers'.

The notice went on to explain that the Surveyor was obliged to write to all the housekeepers to 'send Teams and Labourers to do 2, 3 or more Days Work in the Highways as shall be thought necessary; from which no Person or Profession is exempted, as the Law says every Householder, Cottager and Day Labourer'.[56] In this lengthy statement may be read the breakdown of the older system of relying upon unpaid and compulsory services from local residents in all the work of local government. That system had worked reasonably well in the past: but it collapsed as the population of the industrial towns grew and the work of local government became ever heavier and more complex. Of frequent appearance, too, were such notices as the following, which appeared in the *Norwich Gazette* in 1727 :

[53] *Norwich Gazette*, 7 January 1727.
[54] Ibid. 24.31 January, 7.21.28 February, 14.21.28 March, 4 April, 2 May 1741.
[55] *Sherborne Mercury* announcement, 19 February 1737.
[56] *Aris's Birmingham Gazette*, 25 November 1751.

'whereas there was a Male Infant found in the Parish of Horningtoft in the County of Norfolk, on Monday the 9th. of May last in the Morning, We whose Hands are hereunto written, (Church Wardens and Overseers of the said Parish) do hereby promise to any Person or Persons, that shall discover the Mother of the said Child, and the Person that left the said Child, so that they be brought to Justice, a Reward of Ten Guineas. . . .'[57]

The rest of the 'independent' advertisements can only be classed as 'miscellaneous'; and in these highly assorted notices occur not only the most amusing but also some of the most intimate glimpses of the provincial life of the time. There were, for instance, the defiant verses printed by the *Norwich Mercury* on behalf of one Sarah Peckover. That lady declared that

'whereas I Sarah Peckover was publicly whipp'd for a Crime of which I am innocent of, therefore publish the following Lines in order to justify myself . . .

> Now on my back the Stripes I bear,
> I am not guilty I declare,
> But as innocent as the Child in my Womb
> (I think I am just three Months gone).
> Fourteen Days in Prison I have been,
> Scorn'd and derided by sinful Men.
> A Sinner I am myself 'tis true,
> Though of this Fact I do not know.
> Remember our blessed Saviour dear,
> The Wounds and Stripes that he did bear,
> Not for himself but for sinful Men,
> Whilst Scribes and Priests did him blaspheme.
> Relations I have, though Friends but few
> The Crime laid open to their View,
> I am as innocent as the Child unborn,
> Though some of them do me scorn.
> Remember there comes a Judgment Day,
> When for our Sins we all must pay;
> Before the righteous Judge, the Lord of all,
> He will right the case of Great and Small.'[58]

Among the more amusing advertisements were those concerned with local quarrels, both public and private. Of course, the printers usually avoided any active participation in such controversies, especially those which affected powerful local interests and personalities: but they were willing enough to print the different points of view in

[57] *Norwich Gazette,* 7 January 1727. Similar in *Northampton Mercury,* 28 September 1730.
[58] *Norwich Mercury,* 21 October 1752.

the advertisement columns, charging them as advertisements. In this way, the printer of the *Norwich Mercury* printed a letter discussing the effects of the continuation of the corn bounty—a dispute which had already occupied a great deal of space in its columns—with the comment: 'the Author of the above is desir'd to take Notice, That the Friends of the several Letters have paid for them like Gentlemen. Verbum Sapienti.' [59] The same printer informed another correspondent during the heated controversy over the Methodists in Norwich that 'I will insert no Controversial Papers unless they are paid for'.[60] Similarly, the *Original York Journal* in 1728 invited readers to send in letters to be printed, but added that 'the Printer hopes that along with every Thought will come Three and Sixpence or Half a Crown at least'.[61]

The advertisement columns were also extensively used for private quarrels. In the *Stamford Mercury* in 1722, R. Swann denied the reports that he had 'violently, rashly, and unadvisedly destroyed himself'. Such reports were, he declared, 'false, ill-grounded, scandalous and malicious'.[62] They were, in fact, exaggerated. In the *Derby Mercury*, another indignant citizen informed the public that

'whereas a scandalous Report has been lately propagated that Joseph Russell of Kedleston Inn near Derby, hath two Wives, and that he hath absconded on the same Account, This is therefore to acquaint the Public, that the said Report is false and groundless; and that the Author of so base an Insinuation, was raised by a Nest of Villains, and one T.P. will have the Severity of the Law against him immediately, by me   Joseph Russell'.[63]

These private quarrels usually ended in a public apology; and these ranged from the curious little statement in the *Gloucester Journal* that 'John Hayward Abuesse me John Irband and Enowledg his falt for it to be aduatised if your Pleas',[64] to the distinctly unusual public confession that 'I did say in the presence of several People, That Antony Coller, living at the Sign of the Ship and Dove in the Pithay, in Bristol, was sent to Newgate for putting LIVE TOADS into his Beer, in order to fine it'.[65]

Occasionally, a still more ribald note was sounded. In the *Cambridge Journal*, a 'Bachelor not above 60 with a clear Estate of 5000 1. per Annum', who wanted an heir, advertised for a wife. The

[59] *Norwich Gazette*, 24 February 1753.
[60] Ibid. 11 July 1752.   [61] *Original York Journal*, 23 January 1728.
[62] *Stamford Mercury*, 28 June 1722.
[63] *Derby Mercury*, 4 March 1757.
[64] *Gloucester Journal*, 16 April 1751.
[65] *Farley's Bristol Newspaper*, 7 August 1736.

opportunity was seized upon by the local wits, and the bachelor received many replies, ranging in tone from the merely suggestive to the frankly coarse. One lady stated that, if he were so eager for an heir, she could promise him one within four months.[66]

Quack doctors advertised very regularly indeed in these newspapers. In the *Northampton Mercury*, one Greenbank Dingley, 'the Seventh Son of Francis Dingley . . . (his Father being a Seventh Son) undertakes to cure (with the Blessing of God) by a Touch, the Evil, Wens, Cancers in the Breast, and other Diseases'.[67] An extraordinary amount of space was always taken up, also, with the patent medicines stocked by the printers themselves in this Golden Age of the Quack. The variety and scope of the preparations thus sold is suggested by the list of medicines and other items advertised by the *Reading Mercury* in 1746, when the printer announced that he sold:

'Dr. Hooper's Female Pills, Anderson's Scotch Pills, Aurea Medicine : or Boerhaave's Scots Pills improv'd, the True British Oil, Frier's Balsam, Daffey's Elixir, and Squire's Grand Elixir, Greenough's Two Tinctures, the one for preserving the Teeth, the other for curing the Tooth-Ache, A Tincture to cure the Itch by smelling to, Golden and Plain Spirit of Scurvey Grass, Godfrey's Cordial, Hypo Drops, Golden Cephalick Drops, Lady Moor's, Bateman's, Stoughton's and Chymical Drops, Pile Ointment, The Liquid Shell for the Stone and Gravel, The best Sort of Issue Plaisters, Hungary and Lavender Water. . . .'[68]

One of the most famous of all these preparations, and one stocked by practically every country printer, was 'Daffey's Elixir'. This was advertised as being

'a certain Cure (under God) in most Distempers, viz. The Gout and Rheumatism, with all those torturing Pains attending them; it takes away the Scurvy, Root and Branch, and gives immediate Ease in the most Racking Pains of the Cholick. It's a Sovereign and never failing Remedy against Fluxes, spitting of Blood, Consumption, Agues, Small-Pox, and Meazles; it carries off the most violent Fevers; it eases After-Pains, and prevents Miscarriages; cures the Rickets in Children; Is wonderful in the Stone, and Gravel in the Kidneys, Bladder or Ureter, and brings away Slime, Gravel, and oftentimes Stones of a great Bigness. For Stoppage or Pains in the Stomach, Shortness of Breath, Pains in the Head and Heart, a better Remedy in the World cannot be. It perfectly destroy Worms, tho' you are almost overgrown with them; cureth the black or yellow Jaundice, King's Evil, and those who are stopp'd with

[66] *Cambridge Journal*, 15 March 1746.
[67] *Northampton Mercury*, 16 August 1742.
[68] *Reading Mercury*, 14 July 1746. Similar lists appeared in the *Bath Advertiser*, 1 March 1760; *York Courant*, 24 June 1760; *Lancashire Journal*, 16 October 1739; *Reading Journal*, 31 March 1746, etc.

Flegm, restoring a languishing Body to perfect Health, strengthening the Vessels of both Sexes, and changeth the whole Mass of Blood, being a noble Cordial after hard Drinking.'[69]

Often, the details given of the efficacy of these preparations were so intimate as to be positively revolting. A typical, though mild example, is the following testimonial, which appeared in the *Stamford Mercury*:

'whereas I Thomas Palmer, living in Kenelworth, 4 Miles from Warwick, having a Daughter under a very great Disorder, viz. Feverish towards Night, and the 3 Days Ague 13 Months, a dry Cough, Sleepiness, Doting, Pain in the Stomach, shortness of Breath, a swell'd Belly, frothy Urine, sometimes white, thick and muddy, unequal Pulse, cold Sweats, Loathing, Vomiting, unquenchable Thirst, and Cheeks Red and bluish by Turns; I try'd several Medicines but all to no Purpose; till at last hearing what great Cures the Plaister for the Worms, Ague and Fever had done to several of my Neighbours, gave me Encouragement to send for one to Mr. Bryan's Printing-Office in Worcester. I apply'd the Plaister to the Pit of my Child's Stomach over Night, and the next Morning it brought up the Ague Cake by Vomit, with Abundance of Worm-like Matter as green as grass. Now, thank GOD, the Child is in good Health. . . . This I certify to be true.'[70]

So excessively numerous and lengthy did these advertisements become that when, in 1758, the printer of the *Liverpool Advertiser* chose to cast doubts upon the accuracy of certain news-items which had appeared in the rival *Liverpool Chronicle*, the latter countered with the simple comment that, 'supposing the Paragraph alluded to had been a Fiction, we are sanguine enough to hope that it would be more entertaining to our Readers than the whole Column stuffed up with Notices of Quack Medicines, Corn-Salve, Weal Registers, Nun's Drops, etc. etc. etc.' [71] But almost as numerous and lengthy were the publishing notices. Often, indeed, the advertisements of quack medicines and the publishing notices would together take up the whole back page of the weekly newspapers.

One of the first books to be advertised at all extensively in the country newspapers was, typically enough, a somewhat lurid work by the title of 'Onania: Or, The Heinous Sin of Self-Pollution, and all its frightful Consequences in both Sexes considered, with Spiritual and Physical Advice to those who have already injur'd themselves by this abominable Practice'.[72] By 1727, this book had run into its

[69] *Newcastle Courant*, 29 August 1724.
[70] *Stamford Mercury*, 28 November 1728.
[71] *Liverpool Chronicle*, 17 March 1758.
[72] *Brice's Weekly Journal*, 10 February 1726/27, 2 June, 27 October 1727; *Gloucester Journal*, 10 September 1728, &c.

twelfth edition, and had proved so popular that there was published separately

'a Supplement to the Onania Etc. printed on the same Letter and Paper, to be bound with it: containing many remarkable and indeed surprising Instances of the Health being injur'd and Genitals spoil'd by that filthy Commerce with oneself, which is daily practis'd as well by Adult as Youth Women as Men Married as Single . . .'[73]

Other books advertised were, however, more respectable. In 1739, the *Kentish Post* devoted a whole page to the publishing notice of 'A Dissertation upon the Surface of the Earth';[74] in 1743, the *Derby Mercury* gave more than a page to an advertisement of the 'Biblioteca Harleiana';[75] and, in the same year, a notice of the publication, by instalments, of a 'History of the Holy Bible' occupied the whole of the back page of the *York Courant*.[76]

However disappointing these advertisement columns may seem to be as sources for the economic history of the period, they undoubtedly shed a most revealing light upon the manners, morals and outlook of the time. Their pages are thronged with highwaymen, runaway apprentices and absconding wives; temptingly worded invitations to horse-races or cock-fights appear side by side with the sternest admonitions of Authority, 'puffs' for quack medicines with descriptions of the heaviest religious tomes. Eighteenth century life, particularly in its seemier aspects, is here depicted perhaps even more vividly than in the news-columns proper.

[73] *Brice's Weekly Journal*, 1 December 1727.
[74] *Kentish Post*, 14 May 1739.
[75] *Derby Mercury*, 24 January 1742/43.
[76] *York Courant*, 25 October 1743.

CHAPTER ELEVEN

THE FINANCES OF THE PROVINCIAL NEWSPAPER

'THE profits of a newspaper,' declared the *Reading Mercury* in 1797, 'arise only from Advertisements.' [1] Probably no modern newspaper proprietor would disagree with that statement. It may even have been true of 1797. But in the earlier period, the income from this source, despite the enormous increase in the number of advertisements, remained relatively small, and the printers were forced to look elsewhere for their profits.

Only before the passing of the Stamp Act of 1712 did the advertisements represent solid profit. And in this early period, there were so few advertisements that only the *Norwich Gazette* seems to have thought it necessary to make any statement of policy regarding them. That statement, made in 1707, reveals clearly the small value then placed upon this section of the newspaper:

'the whole Sheet of News,' it read, 'will be sold for a Half-penny, and Advertisements taken into the *Norwich Gazette* for nothing after this present Date, provided they observe the following Conditions:

(1) That they put them in no other Norwich News
(2) That each Advertisement exceeds not 70 Words
(3) That they are not trifling impertinent Ones'.[2]

It was not long, however, before the printers began to wake up to the fact that the advertisements represented an important, if subsidiary, source of profit. And it is noticeable that when next a similar offer was made—by the *Reading Mercury* in 1723—the whole emphasis had changed. The duration of the concession was now strictly limited 'till Michaelmas next',[3] and the whole thing was quite obviously a 'stunt' to boost the circulation of a new paper. No further offers of this type were to be made.

Unfortunately, just as the printers were becoming aware of the possibilities of advertising, so too did a hungry government seize upon advertisements in newspapers as a convenient source of re-

---

[1] *Reading Mercury*, 10 July 1797, quoted K. G. Burton, op. cit., p. 79.
[2] *Norwich Gazette*, 20 December 1707.
[3] *Reading Mercury*, 22 July 1723.

venue; and in 1712 a duty of one shilling was laid upon every advertisement, irrespective of its length, each time it was inserted in a newspaper. But the Act made no mention of advertisements in pamphlets: and it is possible that the provincial printers, besides evading the actual newspaper duty itself, managed also to avoid paying the advertisement duty. There is, it is true, evidence to the contrary. An extant copy of the *Ipswich Journal* of 24 December 1720 bears upon it the written note:

'by virtue of an Order from the Stamp Office, rec'd. for duty upon this Paper 3s. and for one Advertisement one Shilling by me   John May'.[4]

John May was the local distributor of stamps. And when, in 1723, the *Reading Mercury* announced that it would not charge for advertisements, its printer continued to demand one shilling, which, he said, 'by Act of Parliament' we are oblig'd to pay the Government'.[5] In both cases, however, the papers concerned were in their infancy, and possibly their printers lacked the cunning of their more experienced fellows. Certainly, the total sums collected by the distributors of stamps in the country do not suggest that the provincial papers were in fact paying the advertisement duty. In 1722, the amount collected was only £151. 3s. 0d.; but when, in 1725, the Stamp Act was tightened up, the revenue from this source went up suddenly and sharply, for in 1729—the first year after 1725 for which figures are available—it was £318. 2s. 0d.[6] And it is unlikely that the growth of advertising could have accounted for so considerable a difference. Again, in 1725, nearly all the country printers raised their charges for advertisements, although the Stamp Act of that year had not increased the advertisement duty. Admittedly, in most cases the increase was only six-pence; but this was probably because the printers had begun to realize the financial possibilities of advertising, and the desirability of actively encouraging this source of income.

The Stamp Act of 1725 had little serious effect upon the number of advertisements in the provincial papers. No case has been discovered in which the number decreased; and in most cases it increased steadily, despite the additional charge levied by most papers. It is noticeable, too, that the Act aroused remarkably little criticism. For one thing, the increasing circulation and the growing

[4] In the British Museum Newspaper Library, Colindale.
[5] *Reading Mercury*, 22 July 1723.
[6] A. Aspinall, 'Statistical Accounts of the London Newspapers', op. cit., p. 208.

popularity of advertising to some extent compensated the printers
for the duties which they now had to pay; and for another, they
must also have realized that a stricter enforcement of the provisions
of the old Stamp Act had been only a matter of time, and that on
the whole they had escaped very lightly. The main burden of the
Act was undoubtedly the tax upon the actual newspapers themselves,
for advertising was still in its infancy. But the case was to be very
different in 1757, when another Stamp Act doubled the duty upon
advertisements, raising it to two shillings. That Act was roundly
denounced by many of the country papers, for it struck a heavy
blow at an increasingly important source of income. In 1730, the
distributors of stamps in the country had collected £486. 17s. 0d.
That total had grown steadily—to £668. 1s. 1d. in 1734, £805. 14s. 0d.
in 1739, £956. 12s. 0d. in 1741, £1,248. 18s. 4d. in 1750, and £2,351.
1s. 0d. in 1756.[7] The Act meant that the charge for inserting an
advertisement had to be increased, and, not surprisingly, the number
of advertisements dropped sharply. In 1758, the government distributors of stamps collected £2,787. 8s. 0d.—so that the actual
number of advertisements had been almost halved. Before 5th. July
1757, when the Act came into operation, the *Newcastle Journal* had
been averaging sixty-four 'independent' advertisements in each
issue; after that date, the figure fell to thirty-nine. Other papers
suffered similarly. In no case was the drop fatal, however: and much
of it may well have been due to seasonal causes, advertisements in
the spring months always being more numerous than those in later
months. Certainly, in 1759 the distributors of stamps collected
£5,122. 1s. 0d.—so that the actual number of advertisements was
again increasing.

Until the Stamp Act of 1725, most papers charged two shillings
for small advertisements [8]—although the *Worcester Post-Man*
charged two shillings and sixpence, the *Plymouth Weekly Journal*
three shillings and *Sam Farley's Bristol Post-Man* as much as three
shillings and sixpence.[9] After 1725, two shillings and sixpence became the general rule, and, as competition increased, most printers
were forced to fall into line. Thus, the *Bristol Post-Man*, which in
1725 had raised its price to the very high rate of four shillings, was

[7] Aspinall, op. cit., p. 208.
[8] e.g. *Weekly Courant*, 22 December 1715; *Kentish Post*, 13 November
1717; *Nottingham Mercury*, 27 September 1720; *York Mercury*, 23 February
1718/19; *Leeds Mercury*, 21 November 1721; *Derby Post-Man*, 18 May 1721.
[9] *Farley's Bristol Newspaper*, 15 January 1725/26; *Plymouth Weekly
Journal*, 5 September 1718.

forced to reduce this to three and sixpence by 1743, and to the usual two and sixpence by 1752.[10]

By the late 1730's, the printers had certainly begun to appreciate the possibilities of advertising, and were making a serious bid for the custom of potential advertisers. In 1738, the *Manchester Magazine* announced that 'Advertisements will be inserted at 2*s*. 6*d*. each but if very short, and concerning any Thing lost, or Houses, etc. to Lett, at 2*s*., tho' one Shilling Duty is paid to the King each Time it is inserted'.[11] Not to be outdone, the rival *Lancashire Journal* countered with the offer to take in advertisements at '2*s*. 6*d*. each; if short ones, at 2*s*.; and if continued at Eighteen-pence for each Time'.[12] Henceforward, nearly all the papers charged reduced rates for continued advertisements. The reason was the increasing competition: for in 1740 the printer of the *Ipswich Journal* stated that, 'having been lately inform'd, that at some Places, and particularly at Norwich, an Abatement is made in those Advertisements that are put in more than once', he would in future charge two and sixpence entrance, four and six for two insertions, and two shillings for every further insertion.[13]

The growing importance of advertising was indicated by the increasing popularity of the word 'Advertiser', either as a sub-title in already established papers, or as the main title of newspapers begun after the later 1730's. In 1736, for instance, the old *Salisbury Journal* was revived after an interruption of some six years: and it took as its sub-title the heading '*or Weekly Advertiser*'. The following year, the *Sherborne Mercury or Weekly Advertiser* began publication, and in 1743 *Farley's Bristol Advertiser*. Before the close of the year 1760, ten provincial newspapers made use of this sub-title, while four adopted the word 'Advertiser' as their main title.[14]

From the point of view of the printer, however, advertisements were by no means all profit, for to an uncomfortably large degree the

[10] e.g. *F. Farley's Bristol Journal*, 24 March 1743; *Felix Farley's Bristol Journal*, 2 May 1752.
[11] *Manchester Magazine*, 17 October 1738.
[12] *Lancashire Journal*, 12 January 1740.
[13] *Ipswich Journal*, 10 May 1740.
[14] *Salisbury Journal or Weekly Advertiser*, 1736; *Sherborne Mercury or Weekly Advertiser*, 1737; *Bristol Oracle and Country Advertiser*, 1743; *Farley's Bristol Advertiser*, 1743; *Sussex Advertiser*, 1745; *Harrop's Manchester Mercury and General Advertiser*, 1752; *Orion Adams's Weekly Journal, or the Manchester Advertiser*, 1752; *Whitworth's Manchester Magazine or Universal Advertiser*, 1752; *Old Exeter Journal and Weekly Advertiser*, 1755; *Bath Advertiser*, 1756; *Eyres's Weekly Journal or Warrington Advertiser*, 1756; *Schofield's Middlewich Journal or General Advertiser*, 1756; *Williamson's Liverpool Advertiser*, 1756; *Union Journal or Halifax Advertiser*, 1759; *Public Advertiser* [Sheffield], 1760.

advertising section of a country newspaper had to be run on a credit basis. And although the printers were continually issuing notices demanding cash payments in advance, it is clear that these were statements of an ideal rather than of actual practice. In 1746, the printer of the *Newcastle Journal* explained at some length that

'whereas great Losses and Inconveniences have been experienced and many Losses sustain'd, by allowing Credit to Persons for Advertisements; and as this Grievance is the more hard upon the Printer, by his being oblig'd to pay the King's Duty, which is 1s. upon every Advertisement each Time it is inserted: This is therefore to give Notice, that for the Future no Advertisement will be inserted in this Journal but what is paid for upon its being deliver'd into the Printing Office. Accordingly, all Persons having Occasion to advertise, are desir'd to send Money along with their Orders, or, if they live at remote Places, to pay to any of our Agents . . . or order some Friend or Acquaintance to do it in Newcastle.'[15]

The same point was to be made time and again by the various country printers: that, since they had to pay the advertisement duty immediately, they could not be expected to wait indefinitely for payment themselves.[16]

Unfortunately, it was inevitable that the advertisements should be run on a credit basis. For one thing, it was often quite impossible for the advertiser, however well intentioned he might be, to know in advance how much his advertisement would cost. The charges varied considerably according to the length of the advertisement and the number of times it was to be repeated; and not all the papers explained their scale of charges as carefully as the *Newcastle Journal* in 1746:

'that no Scruple or Question may be made about the Price, the Public is desir'd to observe, that for every Advertisement that does not exceed 140 Words, the Price is 2s. 6d. the first Time, and 1s. 6d. each Time afterwards; and for any Number of Words not exceeding 100 more, the Charge is augmented 6d. and so in Proportion. Also the Price of every Addition to, or Alteration in a running Advertisement of under 100 Words is 6d. and all exceeding that Number is charged according to the Method above said.'[17]

The *Northampton Mercury* followed a different method: 'for each Advertisement of 20 Lines or under, allowing 12 Words to each Line upon an Average, the Price will be 3s. 6d. for the first Time

[15] *Newcastle Journal*, 28 June 1746.
[16] e.g. *York Courant*, 16 January 1739; *Norwich Mercury*, 17 February 1753; *Cambridge Journal*, 28 November 1747.
[17] *Newcastle Journal*, 28 June 1746.

of inserting it, and 2*s*. 6*d*. for every Succeeding Time; and for every four Lines or under above the Number of 20 Lines, 6*d*. for every Time'.[18] Even with such specific instructions, there was clearly still plenty of room for uncertainty; and most printers were far less explicit.

Despite their frequent pronouncements to the contrary, therefore, the printers were literally forced to extend credit to advertisers, particularly to those who lived at some distance from the printing-office. The advertisements sent in by such people had to be accepted and printed, and the newsmen instructed to collect—or try to collect— the money owing. Thus, on the office copy of an issue of the *Reading Mercury* appears, written in ink against an advertisement, the note: 'Twice. Mr. Eatwell at Andover. Ilsley to call.'[19] Ilsley was one of the newsmen. But the customers were not always able or willing to pay promptly: and the office files of these old newspapers, when they have been preserved, frequently bear vivid witness to the difficulties experienced by the printers and their unfortunate newsmen in trying to extract money from reluctant debtors. There was obviously quite a story behind the written comments in the *Reading Mercury* regarding an advertisement in that paper in 1755. On its first insertion, the advertisement had written against it the memorandum: 'to be in 8 weeks running and then every other week 8 times more. Mr. Scott and Co. could get no more than 2/6 for this Advertisement so that 8 in the Bill was bated'.[20] Six months later, the bill had still not been paid: and the advertisement now carried the terse comment: '(16) done Pd. only 2/6 Remember Messrs. Scott and Co.' So difficult was it to collect such debts that a copy of the office file of the *Newcastle Journal* bears a written exhortation to the newsmen: 'mind that you take in no Advts. without Money unless you know them to be good Hands but *never never* trust any of the missing ones'.[21] Not surprisingly, the printers protested frequently at this reluctance of their customers to pay up. The *Reading Mercury* explained at some length how 'the Printers have sustain'd so many Losses by giving Credit for Advertisements and find such Difficulty in collecting a Number of small debts, widely dispers'd',[22] while the printers of the *Ipswich Journal* also complained bitterly that they had been obliged to give credit 'to . . . Customers who have not had

---

[18] *Northampton Mercury*, 26 January 1756.
[19] *Reading Mercury*, 9 June 1755, quoted K. G. Burton, op. cit., p. 95.
[20] Ibid. 28 October 1755. The episode is described in K. G. Burton, op. cit., pp. 83–84.
[21] *Newcastle Journal*, 17 October 1749.
[22] *Reading Mercury*, 4 September 1786.

an Opportunity of sending the Money with their Advertisements, or to too many who could have done it but would not. We know to our Sorrow that many Hundreds of Pounds have been paid by us to the Government on these Accounts, which we have lost'.[23]

Perhaps fortunately for the printers, the rule laid down in the Stamp Act that the advertisement duty was to be paid within thirty days was not always strictly enforced. In some few cases, the office files of country newspapers have been preserved, and these occasionally throw some light upon the book-keeping methods in use at the time. In particular, they show that the local distributor of stamps would periodically visit the printing-office, count the number of advertisements printed since his last visit, charge accordingly, and write his receipt in the margin of the last issue of the paper included in his total. Thus, the *Gloucester Journal* of 30 December 1729 bears in ink the entry:

'rec'd Feby. 4 1729 of Mr. Robt. Raikes Eight Pounds on shllg. for One Hundred Sixty one Advertisements from Sept. 30 1729 Excls. to Decr. 30 1729 Incls.

Saml. Worral.'

Of these very rare office files, only those of the *Newcastle Journal* and *Felix Farley's Bristol Journal* are sufficiently detailed and complete to provide any significant information. They show that the methods of the distributors of stamps varied considerably. In the case of the *Newcastle Journal*, the local distributor was clearly an extremely efficient man, for he paid no fewer than eleven visits to the printing-office between 17 May 1740 and 9 November 1742. Normally, he called every month, although on one occasion there was a gap of five months in his visits.[24] The amount of money he collected, of course, varied: on 2 June 1740, he took only £7. 3s. 0d. for one hundred and forty-three advertisements, whereas on 15 February 1742, after the gap in his visits, he collected £32. 19s. 0d. for six hundred and fifty-nine advertisements. There is no record of the amounts he collected from 3 July 1740 to 21 February 1741, inclusive. Nevertheless, during these two and a half years, he still managed to extract from the printer the impressive sum of £171. 1s. 0d. The distributor of stamps at Bristol was far less regular. On 21 September 1752 he collected £21. 1s. 0d. for four hundred and twenty-one advertisements up to 1 August; but his next visit did not take place until 10 October 1753, when he received £42. 1s. 0d. for

---

[23] *Ipswich Journal*, 9 July 1757.
[24] From 7 September 1741 to 15 February 1742.

the duty on all advertisements printed from 8 August 1752 to 28 July 1753. More than a year later, on 25 October 1754, he called again, and this time collected £34. 10s. 0d.—the duty on one thousand and nine advertisements. In all, he received £95. 12s. 0d. during this period of just over two years. It would seem, therefore, that the advertisement duty was sometimes allowed to mount up until it reached a very respectable sum, and the anxiety of the printers for prompt payment becomes more easily understandable.

Although the bare details of the prices charged for advertisements by the various printers are known, it is quite impossible to estimate with any accuracy the actual income derived from this source. In no case have any printing-office ledgers or account-books survived—if, indeed, any were ever kept. The fact that the distributors of stamps entered their receipts in ink upon the margin of the office copies of the newspapers suggests that the eighteenth century country printing-office was a somewhat primitive establishment, in which such luxuries as ledgers and account-books were unknown. What have occasionally survived are the newspaper files which were kept by the printing-office. In these the printer would enter against each advertisement its price, whether or not that had been paid, the number of times it was to be inserted, and the name of the person responsible for it. In the case of the larger, or more efficiently-run, newspapers, it is possible that these entries may later have been transferred to a ledger,[25] but in most offices it seems unlikely that any other record was kept.

A small number of these marked papers have been preserved. Of these, the annotations in such papers as the *Liverpool Advertiser, Newcastle Journal* and *Jackson's Oxford Journal* are unfortunately too brief and irregular to provide any reliable information as to the income received by the printer. In most cases, their written notes are confined to such terse instructions as 'out', '3 times', 'but once', or 'pd'. In the case of two papers, however, the office files are sufficiently detailed and complete to afford the required information. These are the *Liverpool Chronicle* between 6 May and 28 October 1757, and the *Reading Mercury* between 25 January 1762 and 7 March 1763.[26] In both, the final income received by the printer was surprisingly small. In the twenty-six weeks of the *Liverpool Chronicle*

[25] Cf. *Liverpool Advertiser*, 16 July 1756, which bears the written entry: 'Mem. Book Folio 76'.
[26] In the Liverpool Reference Library and the Reading Reference Library respectively. For the *Reading Mercury* file, see K. G. Burton, op. cit., pp. 259–60.

for which the details are complete, there were seven hundred and ninety-five advertisements of varying lengths, of which seven hundred and sixty-one were paid for in cash. But the final income, after deducting the advertisement duty, amounted to only £49. 2s. 0d. In the fifty-eight issues of the *Reading Mercury*, there were one thousand, four hundred and eighty-one advertisements, and the final income was £125. 6s. 0d.

Such marked copies, although seldom sufficiently detailed or consistent for our purpose, do at least show very clearly the impossibility of even estimating the income of a newspaper without such aids. The *Liverpool Advertiser*, for instance, seems to have varied its charges for advertisements quite arbitrarily. Again, extremely long advertisements were sometimes inserted. In 1718, the Nottingham *Weekly Courant* gave more than two and a half pages to an advertisement—the furious denial by a Mrs. Stanhope that she was in debt to one Charles Clay.[27] Without the office file, it would be quite impossible even to guess how much this tirade would have cost. In 1759, the *Reading Mercury* devoted the whole of its second page to one single advertisement—at a cost of two guineas.[28] And in the *Liverpool Advertiser* in 1756 a lengthy advertisement has written against it the note '80 Lines 10/6'.[29] It is clear that the prices of long advertisements varied very considerably.

Again, advertisements were often concealed in the text of the news. In 1731 and 1732, the *Northampton Mercury* on three occasions included among its news items a lengthy account of a book entitled *A Preservation against Quakers*, taken from the *London Journal*.[30] This item was actually an advertisement, and was inserted at the request of the local Society of Friends, whose records show that, on 23 October 1731,

'Jos Summerfield Brought and Read a Letter which was a copy taken out of ye London Journall and sent to this meeting by a Friend with Desire that it might be put into ye Newspaper in order to Lett People know that an Answer would be printed to Mr. Smith's Book etc. Thomas Binyon and Jos. Summerfield are order'd to Barging with ye Printer to put it in ye Northampton Mercury.'

At the next meeting, 'agreeable to ye Desire of oure last Quarter Meeting Jos. Summerfield Reports he agreed with the Printer

[27] *Weekly Courant* (Nottingham), 13 February 1718.
[28] *Reading Mercury*, 19 November 1759, quoted K. G. Burton, op. cit., p. 88.
[29] *Liverpool Advertiser*, 2 July 1756.
[30] *Northampton Mercury*, 27 December 1731, 3.10 January 1731/32.

£1. 2s. 6d. to advertise that a Book was in ye Press to answer W. Smith's prezarvative'.[31]

The greatest problem, however, is presented by the publishing notices and the advertisements of quack medicines. These were extremely numerous, and often very long, frequently occupying a whole page of the newspaper. And it is quite uncertain whether such advertisements were paid for in actual cash. In the marked office copies of the newspapers, the names of such well-known London publishers as Baldwin, Cave, Henry and Owen were always carefully underlined in ink in their publishing notices, while the names of Dicey and Okell were written in against the advertisements of 'Daffey's Elixir', or those of Warren and Co. against the 'Eau de Luce'. But although the source of each advertisement was always thus indicated, the sordid subject of price was never mentioned, although the price would be written against all the other advertisements. It seems probable that the London publishers and the proprietors of the patent medicines paid for their advertisements in kind. Certainly, John Dunton mentions in his autobiography that, when he published his first book, 'this book fully answered my end; for, exchanging it through the whole Trade, it furnished my Shop with all sorts of Books saleable at that time'.[32] And according to one authority, John Newbery, proprietor of the famous 'Dr. James's Fever Powders', paid for his advertisements in the *Northampton Mercury* by means of consignments of the product in question.[33]

Local publishers were, however, treated differently, and seem to have been charged for their advertisements at the usual rates. In the *Liverpool Advertiser* in 1756, against an advertisement of the 'Newcastle Memorandum Book', the printer has written 'Mem. Book Rec'd. 5/- from T. Anderton', while against proposals for printing the 'Views of Coalbrookside' appears the note 'pd. once more'.[34] In the *Liverpool Chronicle*, three local publishing notices were all charged.[35] And the printer of the *Oxford Journal* charged two shillings and sixpence for an advertisement of a 'Pocket Companion for Oxford', a book which was sold by his own newsmen.[36] Equally, in

---

[31] Undated newspaper cutting in the Local Room of the Northampton Library.

[32] J. Dunton, *Life and Errors*, op. cit. i. 62.

[33] W. Hadley, *History of the Northampton Mercury*, p. 33.

[34] *Liverpool Advertiser*, 24 December 1756 and 16 July 1756 respectively.

[35] *Liverpool Chronicle*, 6 May to 1 July; 27 May to 10 June; 7 October to 28 October 1757 respectively.

[36] *Jackson's Oxford Journal*, 18 August 1758.

the same paper, another local publishing notice is marked 'duty only'.[37]

There is, thus, considerable uncertainty as to the income a printer would derive from his advertisements. Advertisements of products in which the printer had an interest were often paid for in kind. At most, they paid only the official duty. And without the marked office files of newspapers, it is quite impossible to attempt to estimate how much the printer would actually receive in hard cash. Even apparently 'independent' advertisements were not always charged. A study of the first nine issues of the *Liverpool Advertiser*—all of which are marked—shows that, of the three hundred and eighteen advertisements which were ostensibly independent, only two hundred and sixty-three were actually paid for in cash. It is, therefore, impossible to estimate a printer's income by simply counting up the advertisements. All that can be said is that the profits from the advertisements were on the whole quite small. Between 1725 and 1757, when the usual charge for an advertisement was two shillings and sixpence, the printer actually received only one and six; after 1757, he still received only one and six, although the charge had now risen to three shillings and sixpence. And often, he would not take even this, for he had to make concessions for repeated advertisements. Also, it would seem that the newsmen received some sort of a commission on every advertisement they brought in. The office files of the *Reading Mercury* indicate that that paper's newsmen received two-pence for every such advertisement.[38]

The smallness of the profits was due mainly, of course, to the heavy hand which the government had laid upon advertisements in newspapers. And it is hardly surprising that some printers sought ways and means of avoiding the onerous duties. The original Stamp Act had imposed the duty upon newspapers published weekly or more often and about 1740, John Newbery, the London and Reading printer, hit upon an ingenious scheme. In his memorandum book, he proposed that his partners at Reading should produce what would officially be two distinct newspapers: 'let Mr. Micklewright print a *Reading Mercury and Advertiser* once a fortnight, and J. Carnan print a *Reading Mercury and Weekly Post* once a fortnight, and by that means save duty of Advertisements'.[39] It does not appear that this plan was ever put into operation at Reading: but it was certainly tried by the printers at Bristol. There, the eccentric Andrew Hooke

---

[37] 30 June 1753.   [38] K. G. Burton, op. cit., pp. 95–96.
[39] Quoted from John Newbery's memorandum book, dated about 1740, by C. Welsh, *A Bookseller of the last Century* (1885), pp. 30–31.

printed a newspaper entitled the *Oracle: or Bristol Weekly Mercury* from April to December 1742. In 1743, however, two papers appeared, bearing the titles of the *Bristol Oracle and Country Intelligencer* and the *Bristol Oracle and Country Advertiser* respectively. Each was numbered separately, and the two were published on alternate weeks. In 1745, these titles were exchanged for two others, the *Bristol Oracle* and the *Oracle Country Advertiser*. A similar scheme was put into operation by Felix Farley, who from 1743 to 1746 produced *F. Farley's Bristol Journal* and *F. Farley's Bristol Advertiser*, again numbered separately and published alternately.

How successful these efforts to avoid paying the advertisement duty were is unknown. It seems hardly likely that so transparent a device should have succeeded in its purpose, for it would appear that the local distributors of stamps were extremely strict on occasion, and very quick to recognize disguised advertisements. On one occasion, the printers of the *Cambridge Journal* stated that 'a Letter from Horncastle sign'd T.P. has been receiv'd, but we must be excus'd from inserting it, not only from its Tendency to Abuse, but from some Expressions in it as 'twould be liable to pay Duty as an Advertisement'.[40] On another, the *Bath Advertiser* informed a would-be contributor that 'the inserting a Piece of Poetry has no Duty to be paid to the Government for it; but an Advertisement, serious or not, has a Duty of 2/- charged upon it. If the Author will give it another Form, instead of an Advertisement (which must be paid for) we shall with Pleasure comply with his Request'.[41] The same problem was still cropping up much later in the century, for in 1784 the printer of the *Stamford Mercury* wrote to one of his agents:

'I have put in what you order'd under Mr. Lumbley's Address.—It is an Advertisement to all intents and purposes, and would have been charged, if set as a Paragraph.—You'll therefore charge it to the Gentleman as such.—The Paragraph respecting Dr. Petrie will also be charged, and you must at least secure the Duty.' [42]

If the local distributors of stamps were as strict as these announcements suggest, it seems extremely unlikely that the various attempts to evade the duty were successful. Certainly, Andrew Hooke was prosecuted on one occasion for that offence.[43]

[40] *Cambridge Journal*, 20 July 1765.
[41] *Bath Advertiser*, 8 March 1760.
[42] G. H. Burton, 'Notes on Newspapers', *Lincoln, Rutland and Stamford Mercury*, 20 March 1914.
[43] Latimer, *Annals of Bristol*, p. 52.

Whatever might be the case in the future, the advertisements in this period did not provide the major source of a printer's profits. Even the giant *Newcastle Journal's* record total of three thousand 'independent' advertisements in a year would have produced at most only about four pounds a week, and probably a good deal less. And, for this reason, the advertisers, although they were exerting an ever-growing pressure upon the space at the printers' command, were certainly not yet calling the tune. It was still common for printers deliberately to omit advertisements in favour of news items. In 1758, *Williamson's Liverpool Advertiser* announced that advertisements had been left out in order to provide a full account of the capture of Louisburg in the Seven Years' War;[44] and the *Bristol Advertiser* in 1746 omitted what it called its 'long Advertisements' to make room for the speech of the Lord High Chancellor on passing sentence upon the Jacobite earls after the Forty-Five.[45] It is clear that the battle for space between the advertisements and the news items was often acute. But it is equally clear that the advertisers had not yet won the day. The problem was most nicely set forth by the printer of the *Ipswich Journal* in 1756:

'for several Years past, there has not been one Week in which I had not many more [advertisements] than I cou'd find Room for; and consequently every Week several Persons, who wanted to advertise, have been disappointed. Of late, the Advertisements that I have receiv'd have been more than usual; and at the same Time (by Reason of the War) I have had less Room to spare for them; so that, of course, I have been under a Necessity of leaving out a still greater Number . . . I do not mean that it has been absolutely impossible to insert them; But I must beg these Gentlemen to consider that a considerable Part of a Newspaper ought to be allowed for News, and also for other Things which are equally agreeable to the Readers of it; that they, with great Reason, expect these Things; and that the Sale of the Paper must decline, if they are disappointed. I might indeed make great Profit of this Paper for a single Week, if I should fill it with Advertisements from Beginning to End, without any Line of News; and this I could easily do, by taking in those that are offer'd me, relating to Books and Medicines, for which I should be as well paid as I am for any other. But then, who wou'd buy the Paper the next Week? And the third Week, who wou'd think it worth their while to advertise in it?'[46]

The printers were thus obliged to look also to their circulation for their profits. In the early days of the provincial press, there had been

---

[44] *Williamson's Liverpool Advertiser*, 25 August 1758.
[45] *Bristol Advertiser*, 9 August 1746. Cf. also *Derby Mercury*, 1 November 1739.
[46] *Ipswich Journal*, 7 August 1756.

few expenses involved apart from the cost of the actual newsprint itself. No stamp duty had to be paid, and the problem of distribution had scarcely arisen. This halcyon state of affairs was not to last, however. Not only did the government seek to impose a stamp duty, but at the same time the costs of distribution were steadily rising.

In 1716, the distribution costs of the printer of the *Protestant Mercury*, the Exeter newspaper, had been virtually limited to the payment of a small discount to 'Carriers, and all Others that take 3, 4 or more Papers, buying them at my House'.[47] As circulation grew, however, this early simplicity gave way to a far more complex organization, and the great delivery networks were developed. No longer could the cost of delivery in country areas be simply passed on to the subscriber, and the printer was now compelled to employ an ever-increasing number of newsmen, who had to be paid. In most cases, these newsmen received a proportion of the price of every paper which they delivered. Thus, in 1743, the newsmen of the *Birmingham Gazette* were paid one half-penny for each copy they sold.[48] The *Gloucester Journal* also charged its quarterly subscribers slightly more than the actual cost of the papers they received, explaining that what it called the 'overplus Penny' was 'allow'd to the industrious Traveller for his Care to oblige his Customers'.[49] After the passing of the Stamp Act of 1757, the printer of the *Ipswich Journal* referred to these allowances, with the gloomy observation that 'we know that if the Sale of the Paper should be much diminish'd, there will be many of our Hawkers who must either drop their Rounds, or have more than usual Allowance from us. But how can we afford to make this Allowance?'[50]

In this way, the costs of distribution were rising steadily throughout the period. At the same time, the other costs were also climbing. Until 1725, it is true, the printers had managed to avoid paying the full stamp duty levied in 1712. After 1725, however, a stamp duty of one half-penny had to be paid upon every copy of a newspaper which was printed and sold. Naturally, the printers raised the price of their papers to cover this extra levy: but it is unlikely that this increase in price fully compensated them for the additional expenses now involved. Paper could be stamped only at the Stamp Office in London. It could be purchased ready stamped from the local dis-

[47] *Protestant Mercury* (Exeter), 4 May 1716.
[48] *Aris's Birmingham Gazette*, 4 July 1743.
[49] *Gloucester Journal*, 30 April 1734.
[50] *Ipswich Journal*, 9 July 1757.

tributors of stamps who, since they received their stocks of the paper at prime cost and were paid according to the amount they sold, were not supposed to sell the paper at a personal profit. According to an enquiry in 1764 into the revenue arising out of the stamp duties, however, this requirement

'is in most Cases impossible for them to comply with, and they transgress much further than there is any Occasion for, the Unprinted Paper commonly used being issued to them at 4 Pence 7 Pence and 9 Pence the Quire, and They selling it by the Sheet. They cannot fix any Alliquot Part of the Price of the Quire for the Price of the Sheet, and therefore sell every Sheet for one Halfpenny at the least'.[51]

Such a price was far too high for the country newspaper printer, who was driven to purchase his stamped paper in bulk from the London stationers.

The actual paper upon which a newspaper was printed seems now to have cost about one farthing per copy. This estimate was first made by the *Birmingham Gazette* in 1743;[52] and the printer of *Berrow's Worcester Journal* agreed, pointing out that the additional stamp duty of one half-penny levied in 1757 would mean that the cost of the actual paper and of the stamp duty together would account for 'near Three Fifths' of the retail price of each copy—now two-pence half-penny.[53] This same printer later quoted with approval the verdict of the *London Evening Post* that the new duty bore 'no reasonable Proportion to the Value of the Thing tax'd, since a Sheet of Paper [is] worth little more than a Farthing'.[54]

Purchasing stamped paper in bulk from the London stationers was a cumbersome practice, and it was also highly unreliable. Almost as soon as the Stamp Act of 1725 had come into operation, the Exeter printer, Andrew Brice, was apologizing because, 'through the unfortunate Miscarriage of a Letter, I was unfurnish'd with Stamp'd Paper for a Week or two past, having taken all the Care for a Supply (as I reasonably imagin'd) that Human Prudence could admit of'.[55] Apparently the cautious Brice had not published his paper for the past fortnight. Such accidents were very frequent. The printers of the *Newcastle Journal* went to enormous lengths to ensure the arrival in time of their supplies of stamped paper: yet in 1740 they had to announce that

[51] Liverpool Papers, vol. cxlix, Add. MS. 38,338, fol. 134, p. 19.
[52] *Aris's Birmingham Gazette*, 4 July 1743.
[53] *Berrow's Worcester Journal*, 20 June 1757.
[54] Ibid. 15 September 1757.   [55] *Brice's Weekly Journal*, 11 June 1725.

'tho' our Stationer at London . . . had design'd for us a timely Supply, yet, in the first Place, the Stamp Officers detain'd the Paper longer in their Hands than he expected, and after that, having shipp'd Quantities on Board several Ships (in one of them about a Month before we had absolute Occasion) the Winds coming contrary and continuing long so, they were all hinder'd'.[56]

The Liverpool printers arranged to have their stamped paper sent to them by the London waggons: but they, too, had frequently to apologize for their non-arrival.[57] And most printers at some time or other suffered similarly. In such emergencies, most of them simply went ahead and printed their news upon unstamped paper, taking great care to stress the fact that they would pay the amount owing to the government upon oath. Rival printers were apparently only too ready to take advantage of such accidents, and Thomas Gent once went so far as to accuse John White of having bribed one of his servants to print a copy of his newspaper on unstamped paper, substitute it for one of the stamped ones, and lay information against Gent, 'with a view to drawing upon me the displeasure of the government, and subject me thereby to the penalty of £50'.[58] In view of all these difficulties, most printers endeavoured to lay in a considerable stock of stamped paper. When the stamp duty was doubled in 1757, the printer of the *Ipswich Journal* complained that he had ten thousand of the old stamps on his hands.[59] And when, in 1772, Etherington started his *York Chronicle*, he laid in a stock of no less than seventy thousand stamps.[60] These stamps had to be paid for in ready money.

The real weakness of the whole system lay in its dependence upon credit. Subscriptions—and the country newspaper was based essentially upon subscriptions—were usually paid quarterly. The agents, steadily becoming more and more numerous, received their stocks of the newspaper on credit. But the stamped paper had to be paid for before delivery, and purchased in bulk. In this way, much of the printers' liquid capital was expended before any returns could be expected. In some ways, in fact, the country printers were in a far worse position than their London counterparts, who, as the *Ipswich Journal* pointed out,

[56] *Newcastle Journal*, 18 October 1740.
[57] *Liverpool Advertiser*, 8.22 July, 23 December 1757; 27 January, 24 February, 1.8.29 September, 6 October 1758; 16 February 1759; *Liverpool Chronicle*, 11 November 1757; 10.17 February, 12 May 1758. See also *Farley's Bristol Newspaper*, 13.27 August, 3 September 1726; *Reading Mercury*, 26 November 1744; 28 January, 18 March 1745.
[58] Gent, *Life*, pp. 166–8.   [59] *Ipswich Journal*, 2 July 1757.
[60] Davies, *Memoir*, p. 331.

'send out no Hawkers to distant Places; and therefore have no extra-ordinary Allowances to make; they, as we are inform'd, give no Credit except for a short Time, to their Publishers . . . [but] we have always been oblig'd to pay a large Sum beforehand for Stamps, and no inconsiderable one, soon after Publication, for the Duty on Advertisements, of which two Sums all but a very small Part (in Proportion) has to be trusted, either to our Agents who circulate our Paper at distant Places, or to other Customers who have not had an Opportunity of sending the Money with their Advertisements'.[61]

This was serious enough in itself; but, as the printer went on to explain, the additional duties imposed by the Stamp Act of 1757—another half-penny stamp duty upon every copy of a newspaper, and an advertisement duty of two shillings—meant that 'now, upon the most favourable Supposition, that is, that the Sale of the Paper, and the Number of Advertisements should continue the same, a double Sum of Money must be employed in paying the Duties, and all the Hazards with respect to that Money must be doubled'.[62]

In fact, the Stamp Act of 1757 was a crushing blow to the country printers. The printers of the *Cambridge Journal* declared that, as a consequence of the Act, they would be 'oblig'd annually to employ several Hundreds Pounds more to carry on Trade'.[63] Many of the previous concessions made to regular subscribers now had to be dropped, and the *Worcester Journal* informed its readers that

'the great Loss and Inconveniences consequent from this additional Duty will not admit of any Allowance being made to such Persons who might be desirous of taking it in by the Quarter. And it may be necessary to observe as a material Argument for its being paid for Weekly, that the Stamp'd Paper (which will come to near Three Fifths of the Money the Newspaper is to be sold for) must be purchased in a Quantity Sufficient for several Weeks' Sale, and the Whole of it paid before any Part of it will be deliver'd from the Stamp Office.' [64]

The financial position of the country newspaper was perhaps most accurately summed up by the printer of the *Birmingham Gazette* in 1743. He had been one of the few who had endeavoured to charge only three-halfpence a copy after the Stamp Act of 1725. But in 1743 he was forced to announce an increase in price, stating that

'I have already lost a considerable Sum by selling it at three halfpence.—I flatter myself that no Gentleman will take it amiss if I can't continue it at a Price which instead of serving can only injure me. That a great

[61] *Ipswich Journal*, 9 July 1757.   [62] Ibid.
[63] *Cambridge Journal*, 9 July 1757.
[64] *Berrow's Worcester Journal*, 30 June 1757.

Deal of Money can be sunk in a very little Time by a Publication of this Nature cannot seem strange to anyone who knows that out of every Paper, one Halfpenny goes to the Stamp Office, and another to the Person who sells it; that the Paper it is printed on costs a Farthing; and consequently no more than a Farthing remains to defray the Charges of Composing, Printing, London Newspapers, and meet as far as Daventry the Post, which last Article is very expensive, not to mention the Expense of our London Correspondence.'[65]

In view of the crippling effect of the stamp duties, it is hardly surprising that printers endeavoured to avoid paying them. In 1755, indeed, Robert Whitworth, printer of the *Manchester Magazine*, was indicted on a charge of 'uttering counterfeit stamped paper'.[66] This was, perhaps, going too far, and a more subtle device was needed. Andrew Hooke, the Bristol printer, tried the experiment in 1743 of printing, on unstamped paper, two 'Letters from London'. According to Hooke, these had already been printed and published, also without stamps, in London; but, before repeating the performance in Bristol, he had, he declared, 'being well acquainted with the busy, malicious Disposition of a renowned Journalist in this City, whose righteous Spirit, I foresaw, would be exceedingly grieved to see his Labours to propagate Sedition and Disaffection . . . overturn'd', taken particular pains to study the Stamp Act to ascertain whether the publishing of 'single Occurrences' (as opposed to regular newspapers) was covered by its provisions. Deciding that it was not, he had proceeded to print and publish the two letters. His suspicions as to the probable reactions of his arch-enemy, Felix Farley, were as accurate as his decision to go ahead and print was mistaken, for his hawkers were immediately taken up and committed to the local Bridewell on the information of 'Mr. Farley's Servants or Agents'.[67] Later, in 1755, Andrew Brice of Exeter denounced his nephew, Thomas Brice, for having, for the third time, presumed to sell what Andrew called 'the choicest Pieces of Intelligence on unstamped Paper, Price a Half-penny'.[68]

Robert Walker hit upon a rather more ingenious method when he conceived the idea of publishing his 'History of the Holy Bible' in weekly instalments, the outside wrappers of which formed a newspaper. In the case of the single surviving copy of his *Derbyshire Journal*, for example, the news was confined to the outside sheets alone, while the remaining fourteen pages were devoted to the 'His-

[65] *Aris's Birmingham Gazette*, 4 July 1743.
[66] Leary, 'History of the Manchester Newspaper Press', unpubl. MS. in the Manchester Reference Library, p. 18.
[67] *Bristol Oracle*, 16 July 1743.   [68] Brushfield, op. cit., p. 200.

tory'.[69] Significantly enough, this copy bears no newspaper stamp. And it is possible that, after 1757, a still more ingenious system was evolved. According to an indignant official observer,

'the Printers of Magazines do not pay the News Paper Duty because that is laid upon Papers of Intelligence, etc. printed Weekly or oftener, under Cover of which Description they are now beginning in the Country to print News once a Fortnight calling their Papers Magazines, and will probably in a Short Time come to printing them at the end of every Nine Days, which would be a great Detriment to the Duty upon weekly Newspapers'.[70]

And it is certainly true that, towards the end of the period, there appeared in the country a type of publication which is difficult to classify. According to its title, it is a magazine: but its contents belong properly to a newspaper. Thus, the *Plymouth Magazine* of 1758 announced that it would be 'continued Once a Fortnight, containing the Freshest Advices, both Foreign and Domestic, Price of Corn, etc., at Mark Lane, London: Lloyd's List of Ships taken by English and French; Stocks, Lottery Tickets, Bankrupts, and Weekly Mortality'.[71] These attempts to evade the stamp duty were spasmodic and do not appear to have been very successful, however, and by and large the printers submitted to the heavy duties with as good grace as they could affect.

Apart from stamp duties, advertisement duties, and the cost of the paper, the printer had few other expenses, at least in the early years of the period. Many printers must have been encouraged to start a newspaper by the comparative smallness of the initial financial outlay. The printing trade had seen but few advances for some considerable time, and this stagnation had its advantages. It meant that old equipment was still serviceable, and that the cost of setting up a printing-house was not beyond the means of a man of fairly humble birth and circumstances. The modest requirements of a country printing-house in the early eighteenth century are revealed in the inventory of the goods and stock possessed by the York printer, John White. His actual printing equipment consisted of the following items:

'3 Printing presses wth. iron cases and other
        materialls belonging to ye same   £15. 0s. 0d.

[69] *Derbyshire Journal with the History of the Holy Bible*, 31 May 1738, in the Derby Reference Library.
[70] Liverpool Papers, fol. 141.
[71] Quoted J. Ingle Dredge, *Western Antiquary*, vi. 153.

2 iron vices and iron steddy, with other odd things in ye printing room	£1.	10s.	0d.
Cases for letters with frames for bearers, a grinding stone in frame, with 3 composing stones and other small matters	1.	10s.	0d.
21 founts of printing letters of severall sorts besides capitals, at 5 1. per fount	105.	0s.	0d.
18 cases of wooden cuts, small and larger	5.	0s.	0d.'

The value of the printing equipment was thus placed at only £128., of which the type alone was the only really expensive item, accounting for £105. His stock of books, pamphlets and ballads was worth £117. 4s. 6d., and his unprinted paper £69. In all, White was worth £381. 18s. 4d. at his death, and this total included not only all the above items but also the entire contents of his house.[72]

An inventory of the stock of an early American paper, the *Hartford Courant*, in 1777 reveals striking similarities. This inventory went into considerably greater detail over the equipment required by a small printing-house, for which reason it is here reproduced. The *Hartford Courant's* total equipment consisted of the following items:

'1 Printing Press	£20.	0s.	0d.
11 Pair Printing Cases 15/	8.	5s.	0d.
2 large frames for do. 20/ 7 small Do. 25/	2.	15s.	0d.
Lye Trough 24/ Iron for Sign 10/	1.	14s.	0d.
Large Iron Kittle 7/ Iron pot 7/6		14s.	6d.
Iron Pounder 8/ Small iron Kittle 2/		10s.	0d.
Blanks 3/10 Accompt Book 30/	5.	0s.	0d.
Old Wrighting Desk 8/ Iron Skiller 1/6		9s.	6d.
37 Ream Printing Paper 10/	18.	10s.	0d.
Saw 2/ 6 small Gallies 9/ 2 Folio Do. 6/		17s.	0d.
1 Long Do. 2/ Salmon's Gazetteer 4/		6s.	0d.
3 Chairs 7/ 4 Composing Sticks 48/	2.	15s.	0d.
Twine 4/ Bank 4/ old Slice and handiron 2/6		10s.	6d.
All the old Printing Types	50.	0s.	0d.
New Types lately imported from Philadelphia	161.	0s.	0d.' [73]

If the equipment required to set up a printing-house was not unduly elaborate or expensive, the other office expenses were equally modest. An eighteenth century country printer did not have to employ a large staff. In 1707, when Sam Hasbart, the proprietor of the *Norwich Gazette*, proposed a merger between his paper and the *Nor-*

---

[72] Reproduced in Davies, *Memoir*, pp. 376–80.
[73] J. E. Smith, *One Hundred Years of the Hartford's Courant* (New Haven, 1949), p. 13.

wich Post, he declared his willingness to retire from the scene on condition that Mrs. Burges paid him for his types—always the most
expensive item in a printer's equipment—and that she provided employment for his man.[74] Thomas Gent, in his *Life*, mentions the
names of at least eight journeymen and apprentices employed by
him at various times, but seldom simultaneously.[75] In 1763, Andrew
Brice of Exeter had a staff of at least two men, for in that year
W. Andrews, journeyman, and T. Trewman, an apprentice, staged a
minor revolution against their erstwhile employer, and started up a
rival newspaper. Later, in the 1770's, Etherington, printer of the
York Chronicle, employed three assistants.[76] The largest staff actually mentioned in this period was that of Gent in the 1730's: for
when he was accused of printing news on unstamped paper, he had
testimonials to his innocence signed by his four employees—William
Bradely, apprentice, John Macferson and William Nost, printers and
journeymen, and Mary Pybus, servant.[77] It would seem, however,
that printer, journeyman and apprentice formed the usual working
team—although the printer's wife must always have been a quite
essential member of the establishment. Many printers undoubtedly
dispensed with the services of a journeyman, and certainly it was to
the printer's advantage to limit the number of journeymen in his
employ, for journeymen printers fell into the class of better-paid
tradesmen. In London at least they could earn £1 a week, although
country wages were naturally lower. In 1714, Gent himself received
£18 a year from John White, plus board and washing.[78] Even these
wages must have been higher than many country printers could
afford to pay.

Apart from wages, production costs, at least in the early days,
were virtually limited to the cost of the actual paper itself and of the
various London papers and news-letters—though even here, some
still endeavoured to cut their losses, and in 1746 Felix Farley was
trying to sell his old London papers, announcing that 'any Merchant
who may want to oblige a foreign Correspondent with the *L. Gazette*,
L. and *Gen. Evening Posts*, as also the *Daily* and *General Advertiser*
that come in on Friday may be supply'd therewith at an easy Rate
by applying to the Printer hereof.—Loose London Papers for several
Months back may now be had'.[79] Undoubtedly, however, production
costs were rising, particularly after the late 1730's.

[74] Quoted A.D.E.(uren), op. cit. p. 11.
[75] Gent, *Life*, pp. 160, 166, 173, 174, 181, 183, 184.
[76] Davies, *Memoir*, p. 332.   [77] Gent, *Life*, p. 166.   [78] Ibid. p. 18.
[79] *F. Farley's Bristol Journal*, 12 April 1746.

The motive which inspired printers to publish a country news-paper was primarily mercenary, and such aims as the propagation of knowledge or the inculcation of political propaganda were second-ary. As the printers of the *Northampton Miscellany* explained with almost brutal frankness, their paper was 'calculated for the Diver-sion of the Country and the Profit of the Printers'.[80] Yet, in view of the weight of the government taxation, the steadily-growing cost of distribution, and the increasing cost of production, it seems doubtful whether this ambition was often realized. Although circulation was growing steadily throughout the period, the profit made by the printers remained disappointingly small. The largest circulation actually claimed was the two thousand copies a week of the *New-castle Journal* in 1739. As the retail price of the paper was then two-pence, this represented a gross return of £16. 13*s*. 4*d*. Out of this, of course, the printer had to pay the cost of the government stamp, that of the paper on which the news was printed, the newsmen's com-missions and various other charges. According to the *Birmingham Gazette* in 1743, 'out of every Paper, one Halfpenny goes to the Stamp Office, and another to the Person who sells it . . . the Paper it is printed on costs a Farthing'.[81] Applying this scale of charges to the *Newcastle Journal*, the printer would have to pay £4. 3*s*. 4*d*. to the Stamp Office, and another £4. 3*s*. 4*d*. to the newsmen, while the cost of the paper would amount to £2. 1*s*. 8*d*. This would leave him only about £6 a week, out of which sum he would still have to find the rent of his house, wages for his journeymen, the keep of his ap-prentices, the cost of the London newspapers and news-letters and of his various special correspondents, the cost of employing a man to go to meet the London post, and any renewals of his printing equipment. And the *Newcastle Journal* was perhaps the greatest pro-vincial paper of the time. Most papers had a circulation only half as big.

Unfortunately, in only one case, that of the *York Chronicle* of 1772–6, are any exact details available—and that paper was hardly typical. Its circulation, to begin with, was 1,650 copies a week; that figure rose to 2,500, but sank below 1,900 in May, 1775. The number of its advertisements was seldom below forty a week, and sometimes reached seventy. Thus, by contemporary standards, the paper was a very successful and flourishing one indeed, ranking with the *New-castle Journal*. Yet, by May, 1775, the printer's outlay over his receipts had reached the astonishing figure of almost £2,500. The

[80] *Northampton Miscellany*, 31 January 1721.
[81] *Aris's Birmingham Gazette*, 4 July 1743.

preliminary expenses alone had amounted to £500; and the annual costs of distribution, of the London newspapers, and of the printer's private express service to Grantham to intercept the London post came to £240. In January, 1777, the printer went bankrupt.[82] Of course, this was an exceptional case, for the cost of setting up in opposition to so powerful and long-established a paper as the *York Courant* would clearly be far greater than that involved in establishing a new paper elsewhere. Nevertheless, the episode is significant as an indication of the increasing costs a country printer had to contend with.

The average newspaper in the later years of the period had a circulation of about one thousand copies a week, and would contain a thousand or so advertisements in a year. The profits from the advertisements would amount to about £2 a week. From the sale of his newspaper, the printer would receive a gross income of about £8, of which some £5 would go on stamp duties, payments to the newsmen, and the cost of the actual paper. The printer's final return would be about £5 a week, out of which he had to meet his various other expenses. It was perhaps with good reason that, in 1714, when the Stamford Corporation admitted two printers to the freedom of the borough, it was careful to stipulate that they should provide 'good Security to save the Towne harmless from their respective Charges'.[83] Certainly, the unfortunate printer of the *York Chronicle* was not the first country printer to go bankrupt. Robert Whitworth, the Manchester printer, had done so in 1759,[84] while Andrew Brice very nearly did in 1730. Most printers did not wait to undergo this final indignity, however: they preferred to follow the example of Willoughby Smith, printer of the ill-fated *Hereford Journal* of 1739, who vanished into the night with all his possessions, leaving affixed to the door of his house the pathetic little note:

> 'Pray, Landlord, Landlord, be content
> With the Key, instead of the Rent'.[85]

It was, in fact, almost impossible for a printer to live by his newspaper alone. And the newspaper, so far from being the most important part of his business, was often only a subsidiary interest, a

---

[82] Davies, *Memoir*, pp. 332–4.
[83] Minute in the Corporation records, dated 15 January 1714, quoted F. H. Evans, *A Brief Sketch of the Career of the Lincoln, Rutland and Stamford Mercury* (Stamford, 1938), p. 4.
[84] *Union Journal*, 13 February 1759.
[85] Quoted Mrs. R. Berkeley, 'A Sketch of Early Provincial Journalism', *Associated Architectural Societies' Reports*, xxiv. (1896), 556.

useful supplement to his various other enterprises. First and foremost, the country printer was always a general printer. William Bonny of Bristol regularly performed printing work for the local city authorities, his commissions including 'pages for the discovery of the persons who made the Bonfire on Brandon Hill', 'an abstract of the Act for punishing such Persons as seduce Soldiers to desert', 'letters to the tenants in this City to pay their Rents', and 'A Ream of Paper and printing it into Tickets for Summoning the Council'.[86] The Nottingham printers also printed for the local Council.[87] Apart from such commissions, all the printers regularly advertised their stocks of the official forms of the period. Thus, in 1725, *Farley's Bristol Newspaper* announced that

'as the Time for pricking new Sheriffs for the Year ensuing is near at Hand, I think it proper to acquaint such as may be assign'd Under-Sheriffs, that I have Warrants, Executions, Outlawries, Chancery and Exchequer Attachments, Hundred Court Warrants, Assize and Sessions Warrants, and Attachments, and Bayliff's Bonds, all by me ready printed'.[88]

Perhaps the most impressive list of these official forms was that advertised in the *Oxford Gazette and Reading Mercury* in 1745, when the printer informed the public that he could supply

'the following Blanks, viz. Parish Certificates, Warrants for Removal of poor People, Warrants for Overseers of the Poor, Warrants for Collectors of the Land Tax, Warrants for Assessors of the Land Tax, Receipts for the Land-tax, Warrants to appoint Surveyors of the Highways, Warrants for Collectors of the Window Tax, Affidavits for burying in Woollen, Copies of Writs for the King's Bench, Ditto for the Common-Pleas, Subpoena's for the Assizes, Warrants to search for stolen Goods. Tickets and Biscuit-Papers for Funerals.[89]

In this way, local officialdom and red-tape provided the printers with a steady source of income, supplementing the multitude of official notices which appeared in the advertisement columns of all the country newspapers.

Apart from such bread-and-butter work, practically every country printer sought to exploit the popular interest in crimes of more-than-

[86] *Mayor's Audit Books*, 1704–1710 and 1716. Information kindly supplied by Mr. D. F. Gallop.
[87] W. J. Clarke, *Early Nottingham Printers and Printing* (Nottingham, 1942), pp. 14, 18.
[88] *Farley's Bristol Newspaper*, 2 October 1725.
[89] *Oxford Gazette and Reading Mercury*, 10 February 1745. Similar lists appeared in the *Weekly Worcester Journal*, 11 March 1725/26; *Stamford Mercury*, 29 December 1720; *British Spy or Derby Post-Man*, 6 April 1727; *Derby Mercury*, 17 April 1747, etc.

ordinary enormity and horror by publishing special pamphlets or broadsheets. On one occasion, *Farley's Bristol Newspaper* announced that 'Mrs. Jones's Tryal being so very remarkable in all its Circumstances, it is intended to be Frinted single, and sold for Three Halfpence'.[90] Typical was the statement in the *Norwich Mercury* that 'this Day Thomas Clark will be executed for the Murder of John Bonney; and at Noon will be publish'd (by the Printer of this Paper) his Confession, sign'd by himself'.[91] A great deal of the printing work of the country printers was of this nature: but some printers were considerably more ambitious. Thomas Gent wrote and published many serious works, of which his histories of York, Ripon and Hull were the best known;[92] and he and William Dicey of Northampton became famous for their chap-books. Collyer, the Nottingham printer, also published many reputable works,[93] while such country printers as Newbery, Collins and Goadby were among the greatest publishers of the period, having managed to break into the exclusive ring which then controlled the London book trade.

It was almost inevitable that the country printers should become stationers and booksellers. That transition was not achieved without some difficulty, however. The admission of William Bonny to the freedom of Bristol in 1695 contained the reservation that he should not, 'after he hath obteyned his Freedom, become a Retayler of Books or use any other Trade or occupaceon in this City than that of Printer only'.[94] And in 1726 the Company of Painters, Glaziers, Embroiderers and Stationers of Chester brought an action against William Cooke, printer of the *Chester Weekly Courant*, on the ground that his selling books was a breach of the custom of the Company and an offence against an ancient Act of Parliament. Cooke's reply was that, since the art of printing was 'a modern invention within the time of the memory of man', no particular trade or corporation ought to have the right to the sole use and exercise of it.[95] The upholders of the 'one man, one trade' principle were fighting a losing battle, for, in fact, every country printer sold stationery and books. The *Eton Journal*, for example, declared that its printer sold 'all books in general, either new or old, at the lowest price,

[90] *Farley's Bristol Newspaper*, 17 December 1726. See also *Derby Mercury*, 18 January 1732/33; *Kentish Post*, 6 June 1752.
[91] *Norwich Mercury*, 1 September 1750.
[92] A list of Gent's works appears in Davies, *Memoir*, pp. 162–98.
[93] See Clarke, *Nottingham Printers*, pp. 46–52.
[94] *Common Council Proceedings*, 1687–1702, p. 120.
[95] R. Steward Brown, 'Stationers, Booksellers and Printers of Chester to about 1800', *Transactions of the Historic Society of Lancashire and Cheshire*, lxxxiii. (1932), 109.

without any advance, as is customary in the country. Also books neatly bound and letter'd. Likewise fine writing paper of all sorts, shop-books and books of accompts, copybooks, slates, pens, wax, ink, and all other stationery ware'.[96]

Publishing notices often occupied more space in the advertisement columns of the country newspapers than did the 'independent' advertisements, and these notices almost invariably mentioned that the books described were obtainable from the printing-office. The country papers controlled by Robert Walker contained so many notices of his London publications, indeed, that one suspects that his interest in the provincial press was inspired primarily by a shrewd appreciation of its possibilities as an advertising medium for his London enterprises. But other publishers were also beginning to realize the importance of the country newspapers, and in 1766 Collins wrote to Mr. Nourse, the great London publisher, that 'as Mr. Harris's Books don't seem to move here, I would advise you to advertise 'em in the *Salisbury Journal*, otherwise it will be known to but a few in these Parts that they are publish'd'.[97]

The country printers constantly endeavoured to encourage the sale of books by offering reduced prices to regular subscribers to their newspapers.[98] Obviously, for such small-sized books and pamphlets as made up the greater part of a country printer's stock, the distribution system of the newspapers was admirably suited. Books could be ordered from the newsmen, and would be delivered by them the following week. And the newsmen in their travels would carry not only the newspapers but also a selection of the books, pamphlets and chap-books sold by the printers.

The newsmen also carried supplies of the various quack medicines so frequently advertised in the country newspapers. The country printer very quickly realized that he had at his disposal a ready-made network of agents and newsmen ideally suited to the distribution of such small articles as bottles of medicine and packets of powder—articles which were immensely popular, and commanded a ready sale. At the same time, the proprietors of such medicines were only too pleased to appoint as their agents men who controlled such excellent facilities for the sale and distribution of their

[96] Quoted R. A. Austen Leigh, 'Joseph Pote of Eton', *Library*, xvii. (1936), 137.

[97] Letter dated 2 January 1766, quoted H. Richardson, 'Wiltshire Newspapers', *Wiltshire Archaeological and Natural History Magazine*, xli. (1922), 60.

[98] e.g. *Northampton Mercury*, 5 March 1744; *Bristol Oracle*, 28 May 1748; *Manchester Magazine*, 20 April 1756.

products. Some printers, indeed, were to achieve national fame
through their connexion with these preparations. In 1730, the *Northampton Mercury* contained the proud announcement that its printer,
William Dicey, had joined in partnership with Mr. Benjamin Okell,
Thomas Cobb and Robert Raikes, printer of the *Gloucester Journal*,
to market one of the most famous of all the eighteenth century
patent medicines, 'Dr. Bateman's Pectoral Drops'.[99] For many years,
Dicey and Raikes were to own the rights of this celebrated brand,
in partnership with Okell, and in 1761 Robert Raikes II and John
Newbery of Reading and London drew up an agreement to 'share
and share alike' in this undertaking.[1] Newbery also possessed a
quarter-share in the popular 'Dr. Hooper's Female Pills',[2] and in
1746 he purchased a half-share, with sole right of sale, in 'Dr.
James's Fever Powders'.[3] So lucrative was the trade in these preparations, that Robert Walker actually patented a medicine of his
own, the well-known 'Jesuit's Drops'.[4]

In this way, the distribution system of the country newspapers
was used to distribute many articles other than the newspapers themselves. One of the most frequently advertised side-lines of the newsmen was the carrying of what were called 'small Parcels'. Thus, in
1764, the *Exeter Mercury or West Country Advertiser* announced
that

'the Person engaged to ride between Exeter and Plymouth sets out from
Mr. Lazarus Parker's House, being the Topsham Inn in Plymouth, on
his return to Exeter, every Friday afternoon, where he arrives that
Night, or early the next Morning, and will bring with him small Parcels,
etc. etc. at reasonable Rates. Small Parcels for Plymouth are also taken
in at the Printing Office, on reasonable Terms, which will arrive in
Plymouth some Hours before the Post.'[5]

In that last sentence, and in the mysterious term 'etc., etc.' lay the
real significance of this announcement. In fact, the newsmen carried
letters, and the country printers were setting themselves up as unofficial rivals of the Post Office. The postal services had admittedly
improved steadily throughout the period, and by 1761 there were
daily posts from London to most of the larger towns in the kingdom.

[99] *Northampton Mercury*, 8 June 1730.
[1] A facsimile of the agreement is reproduced in Welsh, *Bookseller of the
last Century*, p. 65.
[2] Ibid., p. 18.   [3] Ibid., pp. 21–22.
[4] See the advertisement in the *Kentish Post*, 24 November 1756.
[5] *Exeter Mercury or West Country Advertiser*, 6 January 1764. Similar in
Kentish Post, 3 December 1726; *Orion Adams's Manchester Weekly Journal*,
25 January 1752; *Felix Farley's Bristol Journal*, 25 May 1752; *Harrop's Manchester Mercury*, 27 May 1755.

But, despite all the efforts of that father of the modern Post Office, Ralph Allen, much remained to be done. In particular, the cross-posts between towns which did not lie upon the same post-road from London were still pitifully few and far between, and in many cases communication between such towns could be made officially only by way of London. Such a system was quite inadequate for the growing centres of social and economic life in the provinces, and not surprisingly there was a widespread use of alternative though illegal methods of communication. Among these, the organized, extensive and reliable delivery net-works of the country newspapers stood pre-eminent: and as the Post Office clerks reported later in the century, 'these Runners not only disperse a considerable Quantity of News Papers but carry also Letters, which most materially injure the Revenue'.[6] That report appeared in 1791: but long before this the Post Office had woken up to the threat represented by the newsmen, and from about 1747 onwards notices were regularly published in the various country newspapers 'by Command of the Postmaster General' to the effect that

'whereas great Number of Letters have hitherto been privately collected and delivered, as well in these as in other Parts of the Kingdom, contrary to Law, to the great Prejudice of the Revenue of the Post Office; Notice is likewise hereby given, That all Carriers, Coachmen, Watermen, Wherrymen, Dispersers of Country News Papers, and all other Persons whatsover, hereafter detected in the illegal collecting, conveying and delivering of Letters will be prosecuted with the utmost Severity.

N.B. The Penalty is 5 Pounds for every Letter collected or delivered contrary to Law, and 100 Pounds for every Week this Practice is concontinued.'[7]

Ralph Allen was even more explicit in his instructions to his agents, and deliberately singled out the newsmen for special mention. 'A Printer at Northampton', he declared, 'was employing a large Number of Persons ostensibly to disperse Newspapers, but in reality to collect Letters'; and he warned his officers to 'cause to be fixed to the most public places some of the printed Advertisements . . . and always have a particular regard of the followers employed in the dispersing of news from the country presses'.[8]

[6] Proposal by the Clerks of the Post Office, 20 December 1791.
[7] *Ipswich Journal*, 11 October 1755. Similar in the *York Journal*, 9 June 1747; *Manchester Magazine*, 2 June 1747, 14 October 1755; *Aris's Birmingham Gazette*, 9 December 1748; *Berrow's Worcester Journal*, 29 December 1757.
[8] Quoted J. C. Hammeon, *History of the British Post Office* (Cambridge, U.S.A., 1912), p. 165.

What influence the country press had upon the development of the postal services in the eighteenth century is, of course, a matter for conjecture. It must at least have acted as an incentive, for the country newspapers proved the practicability of organizing a regular and punctual delivery service even to the more remote parts of the countryside, and their success in poaching upon the Post Office's preserves may well have provoked that august body into defending its interests by expanding its own services. In many cases, the new cross-posts set up by Ralph Allen were simply the belated recognition of long-felt economic needs. In 1735, a new branch was set up between York and Hull; in 1736, between Norwich and Yarmouth; in 1740, between Bristol, Bath and Salisbury; and in 1754 between Nottingham and Loughborough. In 1761, no less than four new branches were established, connecting Newcastle, Durham, Darlington, Penrith, Workington and Carlisle; York, Leeds, Bradford, Halifax, Rochdale, Sheffield and Doncaster; Sheffield, Barnsley and Rochdale; and Derby and Chesterfield. And there were now also many small cross-road stages connecting such places as Ferrybridge, Leeds and Wakefield; Wakefield and Leeds; Cambridge and Caxton; Newark and Nottingham; Appleby and Kendal; and Salisbury and Portsmouth.[9] Other posts were announced in the country papers from time to time: one connecting Derby and Nottingham in the *Derby Mercury* in 1737; one from Leeds to Bradford in the *York Journal* in 1747; one between Shipton, Stratford, Henley and Alcester in the *Worcester Journal* in 1757, and, in the same paper and the same year, one connecting Alcester, Droitwich and Worcester.[10] In every case, there were over-riding economic reasons for these posts: but it may well be significant that the new branch posts set up in this period were almost invariably stages in the distribution systems of local newspapers, stages which for years had been covered by the newsmen.

Such profitable side-lines did not exhaust the country printers' business enterprises, and it is clear that many of these early journalists were men of very considerable resource and initiative. Rarely did they let slip an opportunity of making money. The printer of the *Ipswich Journal* established at his printing-house 'for the Convenience of all Gentlemen, Householders, Farmers, Tradesmen and others . . . a General Office of Intelligence, where any Masters or

    [9] A. M. Ogilvie, *Ralph Allen's Bye, Way and Cross-Road Posts* (1898), pp. 30–35.
    [10] *Derby Mercury*, 7 July 1737; *York Journal*, 9 June 1747; *Berrow's Worcester Journal*, 29 December 1757, respectively.

Mistresses that want Servants for any Office, Apprentices, Journeymen, etc. may be inform'd of such Servants'.[11] His example was followed by Andrew Hooke of Bristol, who also kept a coffee-house and, as a further side-line, taught geography.[12] There were, in fact, few trades which the printers did not follow, and few goods which they did not sell. William Chase, printer of the *Norwich Mercury*, and Robert Williamson of Liverpool were auctioneers, and Williamson was also a broker; Robert Moon of Preston informed his readers that, apart from selling books and newspapers, he was also a 'Haberdasher of Hats and Hosier'.[13] Charles Pocock, one-time printer of the *Reading Mercury*, had served two years in a 'Paper-hanging Manufactory', and continued to sell wall-paper and 'Papier Mache Ceilings';[14] and Isaac Thompson of Newcastle lectured on such advanced topics as 'Mechanical, Hydrostatical, Pneumatical and Optical Experiments' and 'surprising Experiments of Electricity'.[15] The variety of goods sold by the various printers was quite surprising. William Bonny, the Bristol printer, sold old rope, charcoal and Bridgwater peas;[16] Isaac Thompson advertised the sale of 'Stout Old Jamaica Rum, of a Fine Flavour, and neat as imported';[17] and the printers of the *Kentish Post* and the *Derby Mercury* sold, respectively, rhubarb and 'right Herefordshire Cyder'.[18] So popular were lotteries in the eighteenth century that many printers set up offices to register lottery tickets, advising the holders of such tickets of their success or failure in the draw.[19] The printers of the *Northampton Mercury* in 1720 even attempted to run a lottery of their own, offering a prize of goods to the value of £20, and burning their fingers badly in the enterprise.[20]

It is quite obvious that the newspaper was often of secondary interest to these printers. The announcement of John Berry, printer of the *Lancashire Journal*, in 1740 suggests that his newspaper was by no means the most important or the most lucrative of his various enterprises. His trade notice stated that

[11] *Ipswich Journal*, 31 August 1728.
[12] *Bristol Oracle*, 20 April 1745, 5 March 1748, 16 October 1742.
[13] J. H. Spencer, *Preston Herald*, 30 December 1949.
[14] *Reading Mercury*, 29 March 1756.
[15] *Newcastle Journal*, 14 July 1739, 2 May 1747, 2 July 1748.
[16] Latimer, *Annals*, p. 50.
[17] *Newcastle General Magazine*, September 1751.
[18] *Kentish Post*, 9 April 1729; *Derby Mercury*, 21 June 1733.
[19] e.g. *Northampton Mercury*, 29 August 1726; *Weekly Worcester Journal*, 2 September 1726; *Newcastle Courant*, 3 September 1726; *Kentish Post*, 10 September 1726.
[20] *Northampton Mercury*, 1 September, 3.25 October 1720.

'John Berry, Watchmaker and Printer . . . makes and mends all Sorts of Pocket Watches, also makes and mends all Sorts of Weather-Glasses, makes all Sorts of Wedding, Mourning, and other Gold Rings, and Earrings, etc. and sells all Sorts of new Fashion'd Mettal Buttons for Coats and Waistcoats, and hath great Choice of New Fashion'd Mettal Buckles, for Men, Women and Children, all Sorts of Knives, fine Scissors, Razors, Lancits, Variety of Japan'd Snuff Boxes, Violins, Fluts, Flagelets, and Musick Books, Box, Ivory and Horn, Combs, Silk, Purses, Spectacles, Coffee and Chocolate Mills, Wash Balls, Sealing Wax, and Wax Balls for Pips, Corrals, Tea Spoons, Fiddle Strings, Spinner Wire, Naked and Dress Babys, Cards, Can for Hooping, Bird Cages, etc.'[21]

The eighteenth century printer, in fact, must often have conducted something on the lines of a general store; and for many years his newspaper was only one, and that not the most profitable, of his many activities. In 1760, Robert Whitworth informed his readers that 'the Printer of this Paper, finding the Profits not an equivalent for the Trouble, intends to print no more News'; he would, however, keep on his book-selling and printing business.[22] And three years before, the printer of the *Liverpool Chronicle* had given up that paper, 'being engag'd in the Enamelling Tiles, etc.' [23]

Despite such occasional lapses, it would seem that the printers were doing reasonably well. The fact that many of them were both able and willing to purchase new types suggests that their financial position was by no means as weak as it at first sight appears. Types were far the most expensive item of equipment then in use, yet, during this period, newspapers frequently announced the purchase of new sets.[24] And even the printer of the *Ipswich Journal*, for all his shrieks of protest at the Stamp Act in 1757, was forced to admit that 'though our Profits have been very much lessened . . . yet such has been the kind Encouragement we have met with, that we have hitherto, upon the Whole, been very well rewarded for the Pains we have taken'.[25]

What few figures have survived suggest that the profits made by the country printers rose steadily throughout the period. The value placed upon a printing business naturally varied very considerably. In the year 1724, or thereabouts, John White of Newcastle offered his niece, the wife of Thomas Gent and owner of the York news-

[21] *Lancashire Journal*, 25 August 1740.
[22] *Whitworth's Manchester Advertiser and Weekly Magazine*, 25 March 1760.
[23] *Liverpool Chronicle*, 18 November 1757.
[24] e.g. *York Courant*, 9 July 1739; *Newcastle Courant*, 22 December 1739; *Norwich Gazette*, 3 January 1740/41; *Harrop's Manchester Mercury*, 18 May 1756.
[25] *Ipswich Journal*, 9 July 1757.

paper, £50 a year 'to resign the materials and all she was worth in stock to his management'.[26] In 1761, the newspaper and book-selling business of William Creighton, printer of the *Ipswich Journal*, passed on his death to his sister and a nephew; and in 1769 the nephew bought out his partner, agreeing to pay her an annuity of £20 for her half-share—a surprisingly low figure, for the *Ipswich Journal* had previously been one of the most powerful of the country newspapers.[27] When Andrew Brice resigned his newspaper and book-shop to Barnaby Thorne in 1765, he received two guineas weekly.[28] Felix Farley, the Bristol printer, was not so successful; for when his widow, Elizabeth, died in 1771, she stated in her will that her late husband's legacy of £50 to his daughter could not be paid, 'he having no assets to pay the same'. But she then proceeded to show that her own financial position was far more secure, by leaving £50 in trust for her daughter, £100 for her grandson, £150 to her son, 10 guineas to a sister, and her real property, goods and effects to another daughter.[29]

Even more impressive figures were to be quoted in the case of Joseph Pote, one-time printer of the *Eton Journal*, and a very well-known bookseller and publisher of the period. In 1769, Pote assigned to his son his businesses of bookselling, stationery and bookbinding on payment of £600, in addition to £450 for the stock, a payment of £200 a year, and £50 per annum for rent, board and lodging.[30] The stock in question consisted of a vast assortment of knives and forks, buttons, combs, keys, rings and similar oddments. The sums of money involved were, for the period, enormous, and the case was exceptional: but it does show how profitable a country business of this type could become. And the various financial transactions of Benjamin Collins, the Salisbury printer, do not suggest that he was a poor man. He sold his one-twelfth share in the *Gentleman's Magazine* to Francis Newbery for £333. 6s. 8d., and in 1761 bought a quarter-share in the *Monthly Review* for £755. 12s. 6d.[31] Francis Newbery himself sold his share in the *Sherborne and Yeovil Mercury* in 1774 for £200[32]—a sum which indicates very clearly that that paper was a financial success.

[26] Gent, *Life*, p. 154.
[27] S. F. Watson, 'History of Printing and Publishing in Ipswich', *Proceedings of the Suffolk Institute of Archaeology and Natural History*, xxiv. pt. 3 (1949), 206.
[28] Brushfield, op. cit., p. 205.
[29] Will of Elizabeth Farley, dated 26 July 1777, lodged in the District Probate Registry, Bristol.
[30] Austen Leigh, 'Joseph Pote of Eton', op. cit., p. 138.
[31] Welsh, *Bookseller of the last Century*, p. 356.   [32] Ibid., p. 336.

All the other available figures belong, unfortunately, to the later years of the century. They are useful in that they show the growing stature of a general printing business in the country towns. Between 1771 and 1789, a series of letters in a local solicitor's instruction book reveal that, in the various transactions by which the different partners in the *Salisbury Journal* endeavoured to buy one another out, a quarter-share in that newspaper and bookselling business was valued at the remarkably high figure of £1,300.[33] And when, in 1802, Robert Raikes II retired from the management of the *Gloucester Journal*, he received an annuity on the joint lives of his wife and himself of £500, the value of the whole business being estimated at £1,500 a year.[34]

No doubt there were many country newspapers which could hardly have survived without the protective screen afforded by the other business activities pursued by the country printers—activities which were far more lucrative than a newspaper in this period could ever be. Within this protective screen, however, the newspaper had been able to develop and expand, and, from the few figures available, it would seem that the paper was gradually assuming greater and greater importance among the varied enterprises followed by the printers. It had developed to the point where it was ready to take advantage of the changed conditions of later years, when the tremendous growth of the population and the massing of that population in great cities were to enable the country newspaper to become, for the first time, a source of real wealth and power.

[33] M. Richardson, *Supplement to the Salisbury and Winchester Journal*, 7 June 1929.
[34] R. Austin, 'The Gloucester Journal', *N & Q* 12s–x–284; R. Gregory, *Robert Raikes: Journalist and Philanthropist* (1877), p. 18. Both authorities mention that the annuity may have been only £300.

CHAPTER TWELVE

MATURITY

T OWARDS the end of the eighteenth century, according to the oft-quoted editor of the *New Monthly* magazine,

'there was scarcely a single provincial journalist who would have hazarded an original article on public affairs. Their comments were confined to the events of their own town or district so sparingly administered, with such obvious distrust of their own ability, and with such cautious timidity, that they were absolutely of no account. The London papers, a pot of paste and a pair of scissors supplied all the materials for the miscellaneous articles, and the local intelligence was detailed in the most meagre formularies. The provincial journalist of that day was in fact not much above a mechanic—a mere printer—and intellect had as little as possible to do with it.'[1]

This view has gained wide acceptance, and historians have perhaps too readily assumed that the London press alone in the eighteenth century is worthy of serious consideration, and that the provincial press may be safely ignored. Yet the criticism voiced by the *New Monthly* is both exaggerated and unhistorical, and ignores not only the avowed aims of the country printers but also the social and economic background against which they had to work.

Provincial printers in the eighteenth century made few claims to originality, because originality was not demanded of them. They had no local policies to propound or local reforms to urge because as yet there had arisen none of those social and economic issues which were to assume such alarming proportions towards the end of the century. On the whole, provincial life was still both peaceful and contented—although there were sporadic riots at times of food shortages, and the mob was as ready as ever to respond to the anti-Popery cry. Naturally, local affairs were not ignored completely in the pages of the country newspapers; for, as the *Union Journal* remarked in 1759, 'as every One is desirous to know the Occurrences of his own Neighbourhood, Care will be taken to publish every remarkable Event in this and other adjoining Parishes'.[2] But they

---

[1] *New Monthly*, xlviii, 137.
[2] *Union Journal or Halifax Advertiser*, 6 February, 1759.

received only as much attention as their nature warranted. Until the growth of population which, to some extent, counter-balanced the overwhelming preponderance of the capital, London and England were virtually synonymous terms, and it was news of London and of the outside world as revealed in the London newspapers which was in demand. And this demand the provincial newspapers set out to satisfy.

However short the country newspaper of the early eighteenth century may fall when judged by modern standards, it undoubtedly answered the needs of its time, and so fulfilled the purpose for which it was intended. By 1760, despite the most gloomy prognostications to the contrary, it had successfully endured the latest and most savage of all the various attempts on the part of an unswervingly hostile Authority to cripple its growth, and was now firmly established. Circulation had risen steadily, until the more powerful country newspapers could claim a weekly sale of two thousand or more copies: and a newspaper's influence was out of all proportion to its actual sales, since it was generally agreed that every copy was read by anything up to twenty people. The problem of distribution had been overcome by the development of elaborate delivery systems; and, despite an inherent financial weakness, the newspapers had been able to grow steadily in stature and significance. Further advances were largely dependent upon such external factors as the growth and concentration of the population, the expansion of industry, with all its attendant social and economic problems, and the appearance of the railways.

To a countryside which had hitherto been literally starved of news, the arrival of a weekly newspaper was an important event in the lives of its readers, to whom it was often the only available source of information. 'How eagerly', recollects Charles Knight, 'we looked for this messenger, whose budget would provide occupation for many a dull evening'.[3] A newspaper was not something to be hurriedly glanced through and discarded. The printers of the *Northampton Mercury* informed their readers in 1721 that

'as for the Foreign and Domestick Occurrences, they shall be continued in such regular Consequence and Order, that the Second Week's News shall illustrate the First, the Third the Second, and so on. It will be in short a Kind of Political Chronicle, the Newsman's Diary, and, at a Twelve-Month's Growth, merit a Place in any Gentleman's Library.'[4]

Even as late as 1759, the printer of the *Union Journal* could express

[3] C. Knight, *Passages of a Working Life*, i. 22.
[4] *Northampton Mercury*, 24 April 1721.

the hope that 'every One will preserve their Papers, as it is not doubted but they will now, and hereafter, be consider'd as a valuable History of the Present Time'.[5] He could scarcely have foreseen how true his remark was to prove.

At the same time the demand for up-to-the-minute news steadily increased. Printers employed special messengers to intercept the London post at some distance from the printing-office and bring the London papers post-haste. In 1743, the *Birmingham Gazette* was meeting the London post at Daventry;[6] by 1772, the *York Chronicle's* man was awaiting it at Grantham.[7] The most effective achievements were undoubtedly those of the *Northampton Mercury* and the *Sherborne Mercury*. By 1759, the former paper was beginning to feel the pinch of local competition: and it sought to break through the hostile circle of rivals in neighbouring towns by setting up an agency in Sheffield. Nor was this all: for not only was the *Northampton Mercury* now distributed through Yorkshire, but it contained later news than any of its rivals. And, not surprisingly, this caused considerable comment. As the proud printer himself remarked,

'the Introduction of this News-Paper into the Town of Sheffield, and the other great Towns, and Places of Trade in the West Riding of Yorkshire in so expeditious a Manner as to bring to Sheffield very early Monday Morning, Articles of News, which were publish'd in London the preceding Saturday, (and many Hours before they could be had by the London Post) we find, is to some Persons Matter of equal Amazement and Envy'.

And very kindly he went on to explain how this triumph had been achieved:

'We are not driven to the Necessity of using the little Arts of Equivocating, or misrepresenting Facts. We do not say that ALL the Articles of Saturday's London Evening Papers are printed on a Saturday Night at Northampton; but this we say, and can easily prove, that the News in the London Daily Papers of every Saturday will be found in our Mercury at Sheffield on Monday Morning.

If it is to be asked, How it comes to pass that Dicey is so much more expeditious than any others of his Brethren? The plain and true Answer is this, That the extensive Circulation and great Demand for his Paper (not to mention his being within 6 Hours Reach of the Metropolis) has made it worth his while to be at very extraordinary Expences (one of

---

[5] *Union Journal*, 6 February 1759.
[6] *Aris's Birmingham Gazette*, 4 July 1743.
[7] R. Davies, *Memoir of the York Press*, p. 332.

which is his having no less than 4 Horses stationed on the Road every
Saturday) for the quick Reception of News; for the extraordinary Dispatch in Printing it; and for the speedy Conveyance of it through so
many different Counties.'[8]

A similar feat was achieved by the *Sherborne Mercury*, which in
1765 announced that

'the Proprietor uses such Expedition in circulating the Paper that the
Sherborne Mercury, with all the material News of the Saturday Evening
Papers in London, and that Night's *Gazette*, is circulated in all the
populous Towns leading to and in the City of Exeter above 12 Hours
before they can have the same News by Mail from London; and beyond
Exeter and in the Towns leading to and in Plymouth near 18 Hours
before the London Mail arrives; and in most of the principal Towns
and Villages of Dorset, Devon, Cornwall, and Parts of Wiltshire, before
the Post arrives'.[9]

These two papers were outstanding: but all the various country
printers were now endeavouring not merely to print the latest news,
but to publish it before the arrival of the ordinary post.[10]

Again, the developing taste of the public, reflected in the demand
not only for the latest news but also for 'entertainment and instruction', together with the growing pressure upon space exerted by the
advertisements, was forcing the printers to adopt a much more
critical approach towards the news items selected for printing, and
gradually the primitive simplicity of the earlier years gave way to a
more mature technique. No longer was it simply the aim to present
the greatest possible number of items taken from the greatest possible number of London newspapers. Instead, quality rather than
quantity was becoming the ideal, and the printers now began to
select, sift and collate. The change was apparently welcomed by
most readers, for in 1745 the printers of the *Northampton Mercury*
were boasting of the fact that they had been 'assur'd that those
Weekly Improvements of the Daily Posts have been acceptable as
conveying more Information than could be given by such a Number
of unconnected Paragraphs as our Mercury could admit',[11] while
a correspondent of the *Bristol Weekly Intelligencer* in 1750 com-
plimented its printer on 'the Pains and Care you have taken in planning and methodising your several Articles'.[12] To achieve this result,

[8] *Northampton Mercury*, 19 March 1759.
[9] *Sherborne Mercury*, 23 September 1765.
[10] e.g. *Worcester Journal*, 26 January 1748/49; *Manchester Magazine*, 24
June 1746.
[11] *Northampton Mercury*, 14 January 1744/45.
[12] *Bristol Weekly Intelligencer*, 12 May 1750.

the printers ceased to quote the source of each separate news item—
a practice which tended to emphasize their utter dependence upon
their London newspapers—and instead tried to present their news as
a coherent whole. The limitations of the hand-press restricted this
endeavour to each 'Post', and it was not until the next century that
the printer could wait for the whole week's news before going to
press. But from about 1740 the country newspapers were moving
steadily towards that stage in their development described, somewhat prematurely perhaps, by the *Oxford Gazette and Reading
Mercury* as early as 1762:

'it is well known to all whose curiosity hastens them to the earliest intelligence, that the same event is every week affirmed and denied; that the
papers of the same day contradict each other, and that the mind is confused by opposite relations, or tortured with narratives of the same
transactions transmitted or pretended to be transmitted from different
places. Whoever has felt these inconveniences will naturally wish for a
writer who shall once a week collect the evidence, decide upon its
probability, reject those reports which, being raised only to serve the
day, are necessarily refuted before the end of the week, and enable the
reader to judge of the true state of foreign and domestic affairs.'[13]

This ideal of the weekly newspaper was approached, during the
period under discussion, only by the *Ipswich Journal*, a paper which
had apparently managed to effect a radical change in its printing
methods. It seems to have gone a long way towards abandoning the
traditional practice of printing each 'Post' as a separate entity—
almost a separate newspaper. After about 1739, it became common
for items in the earlier 'Posts' of the *Ipswich Journal* to refer to
others in later 'Posts'. Thus, in one issue of 1739, an article in
'Wednesday's Post' ended with the comment that 'there is no further
Confirmation of this News by Friday's Post'.[14] At the same time, the
printer made a genuine effort to arrive at the truth among all the
conflicting reports in the various London newspapers. On one occasion in 1739, he remarked that, although a report of a sea-battle had
been supposedly confirmed by the *St. James's Evening Post*, 'the
London and *General Evening Posts* observe that this is the present
Report . . . [but] little Credit is given to it'; and he then went on to
kill the whole story with the note: 'see the News of our next Post,
by which this Story is intirely contradicted'.[15] Of another news item,
he remarked: 'this is confirmed by a Letter from Bristol in the *St.*

[13] *Oxford Gazette and Reading Mercury*, 25 January 1762.
[14] *Ipswich Journal*, 18 August 1739.
[15] Ibid. 8 December 1739.

James's Evening Post; but no Account of it has yet been published by Authority in the *Gazette*'.[16] It might well be thought that this approach merely added to the general confusion, and represented little advance upon the contradictory 'collections' of the earlier days. Unfortunately, the communication of news, particularly in time of war, was still so uncertain and unreliable that no newspaper printer could afford to ignore such rumours entirely. At least, the printer of the *Ipswich Journal* was making an honest attempt to balance the various reports against each other, and to draw attention to those he considered to be of doubtful accuracy. He was, in fact, accepting some responsibility for what he printed.

In this way, the country printers were beginning to assert their individuality, and were using the London papers with far greater freedom and boldness. No longer was a London paper meekly accepted as the final authority. Nor were the country printers so utterly dependent upon the London papers and news-letters as they had been. In 1739, wearying of the ministerial sympathies so apparent in the famous *Wye's Letter*, the *York Courant* substituted for that hitherto indispensable authority the reports sent in by a certain Peter Tompkin, a private correspondent in London. These reports, the printer insisted, were 'not to be met with in the London Prints'.[17] The experiment paid dividends almost immediately, for in 1740 the printer was able to congratulate Tompkin on his exclusive communication of the news of the British rejection of a French offer to mediate between Britain and Spain.[18] Later in the same year, Tompkin was joined by another special correspondent in London, John Smith;[19] and in 1742 there appeared the first of what was to be a long series of letters from 'our Correspondent at London', a gentleman who signed himself 'R. F.'[20] Similarly, during the excitement of the Jacobite trials after the Forty-Five, the *Manchester Magazine* appointed ' a Person at London to attend the said Tryals',[21] and from July to September 1746 the paper regularly contained one, and often two, letters from this correspondent describing the trials, particularly where they concerned events and personalities likely to interest Manchester readers. And as the advantages to be gained by obtaining exclusive information in this way began to be more widely appreciated, other country printers employed special correspondents, until even so small and newly established a paper as the *Union Journal* could announce in 1759 that 'a Correspondent in London,

[16] *Ipswich Journal*, 18 August 1739.
[18] Ibid. 18 December 1739.
[20] Ibid. 9 February 1741/42.
[17] *York Courant*, 3 July 1739.
[19] Ibid. 20 May 1740.
[21] *Manchester Magazine*, 24 June 1746.

who has great Opportunities for knowing Things of this Kind, will supply him with the earliest Intelligence, after the Evening Papers come from the Press'.[22]

Quite apart from these London correspondents, local correspondents of a more permanent kind than the casual writers upon whom the country printers had previously relied began to make their appearance. In 1739, the *York Courant* had a special correspondent at Hull;[23] in 1745, the *Bristol Oracle* mentioned its 'particular Correspondent at Liverpool';[24] the following year, the *York Journal* had a 'private Correspondent in Edinburgh'.[25] Other printers went still farther afield. Obviously, newspapers which were published in seaports possessed certain advantages in this respect—and their printers made the most of their opportunities. As early as 1725, *Farley's Bristol Newspaper* had a correspondent in Philadelphia;[26] by 1726 it had another in New York;[27] and in 1747 it announced that 'the Boston Correspondent (as also the Printer at Philadelphia) has engag'd to supply us with the most early Intelligences from their Parts of the World by all Opportunities'.[28] The *Bristol Oracle* was also making use of 'particular Correspondents in the American Colonies',[29] while the Liverpool papers quoted extensively from American papers.[30]

Naturally, as the provincial printers improved their techniques, many of the trivialities which had hitherto tended to swamp the more important news items were pruned down. The printer of the *Newcastle Journal* pointed out in 1739 that 'all Intelligence of Importance lies in a little Compass, and Flying Reports, political Conjectures, and Accounts of trivial and common Occurrences fill up the largest Part of the Publick Papers'; and he went on to criticize the rival *Newcastle Courant* for its obsession with what he called 'false Stories of Amours between Men and Favorite Mares, or suffocating Inoffensive Persons with Brandy Bottles, who drop down in Apoplexies, and the like'.[31] Similarly, the printer of the *Man-*

---

[22] *Union Journal*, 6 February 1759. Other papers to use such correspondents included the *Reading Mercury*, 30 September 1745; *Schofield's Middlewich Journal*, 19 April 1757; and the *York Journal*, 15 April 1746.

[23] *York Courant*, 2 November 1739.

[24] *Bristol Oracle*, 1 June 1745.   [25] *York Journal*, 15 April 1746.

[26] *Farley's Bristol Newspaper*, 7 November 1725.

[27] Ibid. 13 August 1726.

[28] *F. Farley's Bristol Journal*, 14 November 1747.

[29] *Bristol Oracle*, 1 June 1745.

[30] e.g. *Liverpool Chronicle*, 17 June 1757, 2 July 1758, 24 March 1758; *Williamson's Liverpool Advertiser*, 16.23 February 1759, 11.25 May 1759.

[31] *Newcastle Journal*, 8 September 1739. An identical announcement appeared in the *Lancashire Journal*, 1 October 1739.

chester Magazine, when under fire from local critics, counter-attacked vigorously with the accusation that the sort of 'news' such critics evidently wanted consisted of 'tedious minute Narratives of every barbarous Murder, Rape, House-breaking, Robbery on the Highway, Commitment to Newgate, etc.'.[32] Yet such items had formerly provided the very life's blood of the country newspapers; and the fact that they could now be rejected so summarily indicates a very significant advance in the printers' sense of relative values. As early as 1733 the *Newcastle Courant* had stated emphatically that its general section would only 'supply the Place which useless Paragraphs would take up';[33] and in 1741 the printer of the *Lancashire Journal* published a list of the ships in the British fleet rather than 'fill up' his pages with what he called 'a Multitude of useless Paragraphs'.[34] Naturally, the increasing pressure upon space exerted by the advertisements encouraged the printers to exercise a greater selectivity in their choice of news items, cutting out repetition and irrelevance. In this way, the *York Courant* evolved a technique whereby it reprinted in detail only the most important paragraphs from the London papers, the rest being dismissed in a few short phrases. On one occasion, for instance, it declared that 'the London Papers vary greatly in regard to the so much talk'd of Change in the Ministry . . . but the general Opinion now seems to be', followed by a considered summing-up of the evidence.[35] A similar technique was developed by the *Cambridge Chronicle* with regard to the London political papers. The more important political essays it would describe at some length; but the others would be dismissed with such admirably brief and pungent comments as the following: 'the *True Briton's* Essay is an illiberal and abusive Libel on the Lord Mayor, Sheriffs and Aldermen; the *Auditor* is fill'd with personal Invectives against some great Personages whose late Resignations do not please the Writer of that Paper'.[36]

In fact, the provincial newspapers were becoming increasingly mature in their techniques. At the same time, their physical appearance was developing rapidly. Their size was gradually enlarged, and the extravagantly large type of the early days was being replaced by a smaller and more economical letter. Thus, the *Newcastle Journal* in 1739 announced that its printers intended 'in the Future to print our Journal on a large Paper; for some People out of a Desire to

---

[32] *Manchester Magazine*, 27 December 1737.
[33] *Newcastle Courant*, 30 June 1733.
[34] *Lancashire Journal*, 10 December 1739.
[35] *York Courant*, 16 November 1756.
[36] *Cambridge Chronicle*, 20 November 1762.

have a Multitude of Intelligence, are pleas'd with a very small Print;
whilst others complain of the Injury thereby done to the Sight, and
of the Difficulty they find in reading so minute a Character'.[37] The
modern reader of, for example, the *York Courant* of 1760 may well
sympathize with such complaints, for the type used by that paper
was so small that it must have ruined the eyesight of many of its
eighteenth century readers. But at least its printers were trying to
give their customers as much news as was humanly possible. After
the Battle of Culloden in 1746, the printers of the *Newcastle Journal*
even went to the lengths of producing a special eight-page edition,
with the announcement that

'the present Conjunction of Affairs both at Home and Abroad, but more
especially the first, having occasion'd a very uncommon Demand for
News Papers, and particularly for this Journal, we are extremely desirous to return this Obligation in the best Manner we can, by presenting
our Customers with the most full Account of Things'.[38]

And during the Seven Years War, the two Liverpool papers regularly published extraordinary editions on the occasion of great victories, presenting them gratis to their subscribers. The *Liverpool
Chronicle Extraordinary* of 17 June 1757, describing the terms of
the capitulation of Guadeloupe, was evidently printed off in such a
hurry that the whole text, apart from the title, was printed upside
down.

In these ways, the printers were coming to recognize their responsibilities to their readers. And with this growing maturity went a
gradual abandonment of the earlier, and somewhat naïve, attempts
to imitate the intimate and personal style and approach of the written
news-letters. In 1715, for instance, *Sam Farley's Bristol Post-Man*
had introduced its news section with a direct address to the reader:
'Sir . . . since our last we have receiv'd the following Advices';[39] and
in the early 1720's, the printers of the *Northampton Mercury* had
regularly begun their local section with such chatty and informal
remarks as: 'let us now see what News this County and the several
Shires around us afford'.[40] Often, these same printers would close a
section with the comment: 'and thus we have gone thro' all the
News in the Printed Papers worth Observation, and will now proceed
to the Occurrences in the Written Letters'.[41] Even more personal was
the pathetic note written in ink on an extant copy of the *York*

---

[37] *Newcastle Journal*, 1 September 1739.   [38] Ibid. 3 May 1746.
[39] *Sam Farley's Bristol Post-Man*, 24 December 1715.
[40] *Northampton Mercury*, 10 July 1721.   [41] Ibid. 22 January 1721/22.

Courant in 1729—presumably by the printer: 'pray good Reader do not Scoff for want of News, I most learn if its trew indeed, I may Lye to deceive your Ears and blind you but I shall show you no luck by selling lyes to be in fashion Tho I believe it would be better both for me, and for my Letter'.[42] It would be interesting to know whether or not this personal appeal appeared on every copy of this paper published in that week, or whether this message was directed to a particularly critical customer. But so obsessed were the early printers of the country newspapers with the written news-letters that in 1730 the *Original Mercury, York Journal* actually printed its extracts from those news-letters in a special manuscript type, imitating ordinary hand-writing.[43]

These personal touches became progressively fewer as the period advanced—although as late as 1742, Henry Cross-grove changed the whole title-page of his *Norwich Gazette* on the death of his wife, substituting for the usual view of the city a somewhat gruesome wood-block in heavy black, depicting skeletons, hour-glasses and other macabre subjects.[44] Otherwise, a more formal and impersonal note was becoming apparent. This was particularly obvious in the system of classifying the different types of news which began to come into general use after 1720. This system was best described in 1755 by the newly established *Leicester and Nottingham Journal*, whose printer explained that his paper would contain

'the earliest and most authentick Advices from all the different States of Europe, and their Colonies in Asia, Africa and America. These will be followed by a faithful Account of Events more immediately relative to this Kingdom, which will be distinguished under the Heads of Ship News, Plantation News, Country News and Domestick Occurrences. Among the Articles under the Head of Domestick Occurrences will be inserted a faithful and minute Account of all the Amusements and Business of our great Metropolis, the Entertainments of the Theatres and publick Gardens, and the Variations in the Price of Stocks and Course of Exchange, Price of Grain, Account of Horse-Races, Cock-Matches, Bankrupts, etc.'[45]

Out of this welter of separate headings there gradually began to emerge an approach to the modern headline. In the 1740's, the *Ipswich Journal* introduced an elaborate system of sub-headings which were altered to suit the circumstances. Thus, at various times during the Forty-Five, such headings as the following appeared:

[42] *York Courant*, 14 October 1729, in the office of the *Yorkshire Herald*.
[43] *Original Mercury, York Journal*, 20 January to 17 March 1730.
[44] *Norwich Gazette*, 13 February 1742.
[45] *Leicester and Nottingham Journal*, 8 November 1755.

'Measures for securing London—French Preparations and Measures for opposing them—Battle in Scotland—Consequences of the Battle —Pursuit, Prisoners, etc.—Prospect of Peace with Spain'.[46] In this particular case, the headline was approached through the system of attempting to classify the different news items. On two isolated occasions, however, the *Worcester Journal* for some reason introduced even its most minor news items with a descriptive heading. A report of an accident was called 'The unfortunate Hunting Match'; the birth of twins appeared under the title, 'The Fruitful Dame'; and a typical eighteenth century newspaper item concerning the finding of a watch by a lavatory cleaner was entitled 'The Bog House Regulator'.[47] Perhaps the nearest approach to the true modern headline—and certainly to the modern newsboy's placard—was achieved by the *Sheffield Weekly Journal*. The four copies of this paper preserved in the York Minster, all addressed to a 'Mr. Andrew Hodgson, Little Horton', bear announcements written in ink across the top of the front page informing the subscriber of the most interesting news items contained in each issue. One announced the paper's main attractions as: 'the Bey of algers killed and strong press for sea men on a war with france sharp press all over England'; the others boasted an even more heterogeneous assortment of items: 'french war ful of Earthquakes at Lisborn How to cure the Bite of a mad Dog'; 'token of a french invasion to England on very hot war Earthquakes at Lisborn a letter on Cruelty on throwing at Cocks in England Guines found in a pair of old Britches'; and, finally, 'War breakin out with france and a teaberl paress in England year's news from france Indin War in america'.[48] Obviously, the popular taste in news has changed but little since these attractions were dangled before the eyes of the eighteenth century reading public.

At the same time, the idea of illustrating their news stories had never been completely absent from the minds of the country printers. The technical problems involved were formidable. The general plan of a wood-block could be copied easily enough from those London newspapers which from time to time made tentative experiments in this field, but the actual carving of the block demanded considerable technical skill and artistic ability. And the appearance of pictures in the country newspapers therefore depended upon the availability

[46] *Ipswich Journal,* 14 December 1746, ditto, 26 April 1747, 10 May 1746, and 4 October 1746 respectively.

[47] *Berrow's Worcester Journal,* 22 February 1756, ditto, and 14 November 1754 respectively.

[48] *Sheffield Weekly Journal,* 18 February 1755, 20 January, 17 February and 16 March 1756 respectively.

of a craftsman able to execute such work. The *Reading Mercury* must have possessed such a man in 1723, when it announced that 'Gentlemen may have their Coats of Arms or other Fansies curiously cut in Wood or engrav'd in Metal'.[49] Nevertheless, this paper still continued to confine its artistic efforts to an elaborately illustrated title-page—as did most other papers of this time. The wood-block for the title-page, of course, once cut, could be used over and over again, as could the illuminated capitals and the small cuts of horses, gallows and running figures with which most papers illustrated their advertisements for lost and straying cattle and horses, wanted criminals and runaway apprentices. In the 1720's, however, one paper, the *Northampton Mercury*, made a genuine effort to illustrate its news items. The paper reproduced three cartoons in 1720 depicting, with great vigour, the ravages caused by the great South Sea Bubble crisis and the fate desired for the stock jobbers responsible.[50] These were the first political cartoons to appear in a provincial newspaper. The following year, the same paper became the first to attempt to illustrate an actual news item, with a picture of a weird sea-monster alleged to have been sighted by a French ship off the coast of South America.[51] And in 1722, the paper followed this up with a picture of a 'monstrous Birth' described in its news columns.[52] No other paper was to be so ambitious in this period. The *Ipswich Journal* in 1720 reproduced one of the same political cartoons, obviously copied from the same London paper,[53] and it promised another, a picture of the 'anatomization' of the South Sea monster showing the different trades which had been 'swallowed up'. That cartoon had already appeared in the *Northampton Mercury*: but either the technical problems proved too difficult for the Ipswich printer, or he considered the task was not worth the trouble, for he failed to keep his promise, pleading rather ingeniously that 'our Agent informs us that it was begun, but the Monster at the first Opening stank so horridly that the Dissector could not proceed with the Operation'.[54] Another paper to include illustrations in this early period was the *Suffolk Mercury*, which in 1721 printed a portrait of 'The Norwich Quaker'.[55] But this sudden burst of enthusiasm for illustrations then died as suddenly as it had been born, and for many

[49] *Reading Mercury*, 8 July 1723.
[50] *Northampton Mercury*, 5.12.26 December 1720.
[51] Ibid. 17 April 1721.   [52] Ibid. 10 December 1722.
[53] *Ipswich Journal*, 10 December 1720. The cartoon was identical with that in the *Northampton Mercury* of 5 December 1720.
[54] Ibid. 24 December 1720.   [55] *Suffolk Mercury*, 30 January 1720/21.

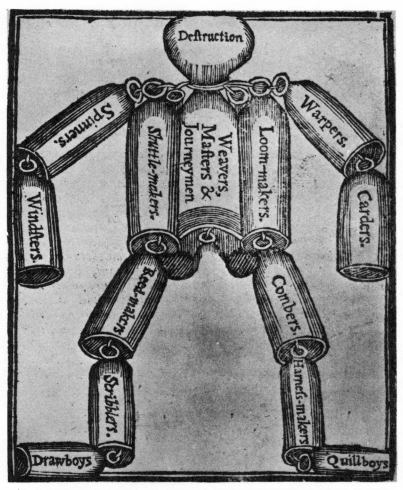

8. ANOTHER POLITICAL CARTOON, 'THE DISSECTION OF OUR STOCK-JOBBER', ALSO IN THE *NORTHAMPTON MERCURY* (26 DECEMBER 1721).

The caption reads: 'To come up to our Promise in our last the Dissection of our South Sea Stockjobber (who upon his anatomizing appeared to be a Trader to India, and a mortal Foe to the Weavers) hang'd up at full length upon a Gibbet erected for that purpose . . . being now perfected, the Reader will be appriz'd of the Danger arising from such Cormorants, to the Consumption of the Manufactures and staple Commodities of this Kingdom, by their putting so many thousands of useful Hands out of Business, as will be found from a due Survey of the Several Handicraft Trades which appear to be entirely swallow'd up and devoured by this Grand Destroyer.'

years to come there were to be no further attempts to illustrate news items.

The provincial newspapers were never without illustrations of a kind, however. Maps, diagrams of the order of battle and simple sketches of a like nature were obviously easier to execute than actual pictures, and from about 1739 onwards were to become fairly common. In 1739, the *York Courant* printed a 'Plan of the City of Belgrade as it stood when besieged by the Turks in 1739', and the following year it gave a map of Chagre, while the *Newcastle Journal* reproduced a plan of Porto Bello, then very much in the news.[56] After this, these illustrations followed thick and fast, with maps of Havana, Dettingen, Porto Bello again, Culloden twice, Carthagena and Port Royal.[57] Occasionally, rather more unusual pictures appeared. Several country papers produced views of the great public fireworks display in 1748 which commemorated the peace with France and Spain;[58] the *Lancashire Journal* printed a splendid portrait of Admiral Vernon, a national hero;[59] and in 1745 the *Northampton Mercury* really excelled itself, devoting the whole front page of one issue to the words of the patriotic song, 'Britons, Strike Home', with a background depicting the Battle of Agincourt.[60] All these pictures were probably copied directly from London newspapers: but very occasionally purely local illustrations made their appearance. Among these might be mentioned the *Newcastle Journal's* diagram in 1749 of the 'Fireworks design'd to be play'd off at Newcastle', and the *Salisbury Journal's* 'Representation of the Triangular Monument Stone of William Rufus . . . in the New Forest'.[61]

The story of the rise of the provincial newspaper in the eighteenth century is no mere academic issue. The newspaper press has a close and vital connexion with almost every phase of human endeavour, and there are few aspects indeed of life in eighteenth century England upon which these newspapers do not throw a revealing, and often

[56] *York Courant*, 2 October 1739, 23 September 1740; *Newcastle Journal*, 22 March 1740.

[57] Respectively, *Northampton Mercury*, 19 May 1740 and 25 July 1743; *Reading Mercury*, 9 September 1745; *Ipswich Journal*, 10 May 1746; *Manchester Magazine*, 6 May 1746; *Northampton Mercury*, 19 May 1746; *Liverpool Advertiser*, 9 March 1759.

[58] *Cambridge Journal*, 28 April 1748; *Reading Mercury*, 30 January 1748/49; *Salisbury Journal*, 30 January 1748/49.

[59] *Lancashire Journal*, 10 November 1740.

[60] *Northampton Mercury*, 16 September 1745. The *Norwich Gazette*, 31 February 1740/41 gave a portraint of Cardinal Alberoni; the *Northampton Mercury*, 16 February 1746/47, a picture of a 'Cruel Machine found at Lord B—e's House in Scotland'.

[61] *Newcastle Journal*, 22 April 1749; *Salisbury Journal*, 7 January 1750/51.

novel, light. Indeed, the social, economic and political life of the time might almost be written from them—and a very unusual and stimulating history it would be. But the interest and importance of these papers lie far deeper than their simple value as historical sources. Small and badly printed though many of them undoubtedly were, they were the forerunners of a power which was later to overturn governments. And already they not only reflected contemporary movements of great moment, but were themselves active forces in promoting those same developments. Furthermore, they helped to stimulate the reading habit, particularly among the poorer classes, by satisfying the natural craving for a somewhat lighter fare than was provided by so many of the published books of this time. Some of the country printers, under the stress of growing competition, began to issue supplements free of charge to their regular readers, many of whom would be too poor to have any other opportunities of reading substantial works. In the next century Timperley was to remark that publications of this type 'must be confessed to have greatly contributed to lay the foundation of that literary taste and thirst for knowledge which now pervades all classes'.[62]

Even without such supplements, the provincial newspapers were steadily educating their public, for their contents were in many ways far more varied than those of the newspaper of today. The meagre education provided by the Charity Schools and dame schools was supplemented to a surprising extent by the informative articles which appeared regularly in the newspapers on such subjects as geography, history, science, mathematical problems and descriptions of the manners and customs of foreign countries. Charles Knight was later to assert that this periodical literature 'has had a more powerful influence than that of all other literature upon the intelligence of the great body of the people'.[63] In fact, the newspapers were the true pioneers in the field of disseminating knowledge in a form which was both cheap in price and easy and pleasant to read. The booksellers were later to claim the credit for the obvious growth of the reading habit in the eighteenth century: and Lackington remarked that

'when I reflect what prodigious numbers in inferior or reduced situations of life have been effectually benefitted, on easy terms, I could almost be vain enough to assert, that I have thereby been highly instrumental in

[62] C. H. Timperley, *A Dictionary of Printers and Printing* (1839), p. 838n.
[63] C. Knight, *The Old Printer and the Modern Press*, p. 217.

diffusing that general desire for reading, now so prevalent among the inferior orders of society'.[64]

But it seems doubtful whether the booksellers' efforts in selling books in numbers would have been so successful had not their market been largely created for them by the newspapers. Dr. Johnson described how 'all foreigners remark that the knowledge of the common people of England is greater than that of any other vulgar'—and he gave the credit to the newspapers: 'this superiority we undoubtedly owe to the rivulets of intelligence which are continually trickling among us, which every one may catch, and of which every one partakes'.[65]

The effect of this growing literacy and thirst for knowledge rapidly made itself felt in the political sphere, for the newspapers were also educating their readers in the major political issues of the day. Thanks to the efforts of the country printers, the provincial reading public was probably far more politically-conscious and politically-informed than many historians have been prepared to admit, and had been educated to the point where it could understand and appreciate political essays which were intended for adult and informed minds, such as those which appeared in the *Craftsman*. It is an interesting fact that the great majority of the country papers adopted an 'opposition' line —which suggests that the country as a whole was predominantly 'Tory', in the sense that it was opposed to the Whig regime. And whenever local newspaper wars broke out, it was usually the Opposition paper which triumphed over the one which supported the Whig ministry. After about 1742, in fact, the country newspapers presented what was virtually a united front against the Whig ministry, and increasingly took on a radical note. They catered, as Professor Butterfield has explained, for the men who were associated with industry and the rising towns, and who made short work of the complexities and anomalies of the eighteenth century constitution.[66] Week in and week out, the campaign initiated by the *Craftsman* against 'influence', placemen, sinecures and corruption was continued by the provincial newspapers, and the *ancien régime* type of government was ceaselessly and mercilessly exposed. The Radical Movement of the 1770's had its roots in Bolingbroke's *Craftsman*: but it owed its widespread popularity to the country newspapers, which for years past had been

[64] J. Lackington, *Memoirs*. p. 234. For an elaboration of the part played by the booksellers, see A. S. Collins, *Authorship in the Days of Johnson* (1927), p. 254.
[65] Dr. Johnson, *The Idler*, 27 May 1758.
[66] H. Butterfield, *George III, Lord North and the People* (1949), p. 183.

steadily inculcating its principles into the receptive minds of their readers.

In this way, the political influence of these newspapers was all the more important in that they did tend to ignore purely local issues. Among the most significant factors in eighteenth century history was the growth of those centralizing forces—whether political, social or economic—which made for national unity. Among these forces the provincial newspapers must certainly be included. By ignoring merely local issues, and concentrating upon national politics, they were teaching the people to think alike. For perhaps the first time, something like the modern national opinion existed; and for the first time, a political agitation on almost a national scale had become possible. In the midst of the uproar over John Wilkes and the Middlesex Election, a politician was to ask: 'How is it possible that the farmers and weavers in Yorkshire and Cumberland should know, or take an interest in the Middlesex Election?' [67] And the answer is clear. This new political awareness and knowledge was in great measure due to the provincial newspapers. Thanks to them, the old barriers and isolation were being whittled down; news could now travel quickly, and the events and opinions of the capital could be rapidly communicated to the countryside.

The country newspapers were themselves becoming aware of their growing importance. The earlier Stamp Acts had aroused little comment and less criticism; but the Stamp Act of 1757 caused widespread protest. Significantly, the protests were not based simply upon such mercenary and material considerations as the effect of the new taxes upon the papers' income and circulation, but in many cases revealed a heightened conception of the duties and responsibilities of the newspaper press. *Berrow's Worcester Journal* quoted with obvious approval the opinions of 'Britannicus' on the new duties:

'First. This is not a general but a partial Tax, a heavy Duty laid on a particular Set of useful and industrious Men.

2. As it in some Measure prevents People from making known to the Publick the Wares, Goods, and Commodities they have to dispose of, and which are wanted by others, it cramps and is a Detriment to Trade and Commerce.

3. It has a direct Tendency to depress Literature and hurt the Morals of the People.

4. It bears no reasonable Proportion to the Value of the Thing tax'd, since a Sheet of Paper worth little more than a Farthing pays a Penny . . .

[67] H. Butterfied, *George III, Lord North and the People* (1949), p. 216.

5. It oppresses the industrious Poor, and hath taken the only Means of Subsistence from many honest People.
6. It will not assure the proposed End; for some Papers have been dropp'd on that Account, and all of them have so decreased in their Advertisements that I am apt to think his Majesty's Revenue will, at the Year's End, be little or nothing increased thereby.' [68]

Other papers were still more outspoken. The *Bath Journal* commented that 'the Liberty of the Press has long been odious to some';[69] the printer of the *Gloucester Journal* remarked darkly that

'I will not presume to say that this Proceeding of the Legislature has its Rise in a Design to subvert the LIBERTY of the PRESS, on which every other Liberty of an Englishman in some Measure depends; or to suppress that Kind of Intelligence which all my Countrymen have a Right, and an Interest, to know. However this be, it is at Present in the Power of my Readers to defeat any Attempt of this Kind, by continuing to take the *Gloucester Journal.* . . .' [70]

And the *Reading Mercury* insisted that 'every Englishman must be sensible that by encouraging a News Paper, he contributes to the support of the LIBERTY OF THE PRESS, to the Promotion of Trade and Business, and to the circulation of useful Knowledge, particularly the Knowledge of Publick Affairs, in which every Individual is deeply concern'd'.[71] In fact, from being a mere collection of second-hand news, the provincial newspaper had become a conscious instrument for forming and shaping public opinion, identifying itself with the Radical principle that every individual had a right to a knowledge of affairs of state. Imbued with this sense of mission, the provincial newspaper press was rapidly approaching the stature and dignity of a Fourth Estate—a remarkable development in the short space of some sixty years.

[68] *Berrow's Worcester Journal*, 15 September 1757.
[69] *Boddely's Bath Journal*, 11 July 1757.
[70] *Gloucester Journal*, 4 July 1757.
[71] *Reading Mercury*, 11 July 1757.

BIBLIOGRAPHY

PRIMARY SOURCES

(a) *Newspapers*

Newspaper files held at the following Libraries and Institutions:

(1) *General collections*
    British Museum
    British Museum Newspaper Library, Colindale
    Bodleian Library,
    University Library, Cambridge
    Press Club, London

(2) *Local collections*
    Central Library, Bristol
    Derby Reference Library
    Reference Library, Liverpool
    Reference Library, Manchester
    Chetham's Library, Manchester
    Reference Library, Newcastle-upon-Tyne
    Central Public Library, Northampton
    Central Library, Nottingham
    University Press Record Room, Oxford, Ephemeral Collection
    Lincoln, Rutland and Stamford Mercury office, Stamford
    Public Library, Worcester
    Public Library, York
    Yorkshire Herald office, York
    York Minster Library

(b) *Other Primary Sources*

State Papers Domestic
Calendar of Treasury Books and Papers
Browne Willis MSS., Bodleian Library, vol. xcv
Liverpool Papers, Add. MSS. 38338, vol. cxlix
House of Commons Journals
Post Office Archives, Bundle 52, 'Newspapers'
Register of Apprentices, Muniment Room, Stationers' Hall, London

SECONDARY SOURCES

This list contains only those books and articles which have been found to be most immediately useful in the writing of this book. For a complete bibliography of the English press, the reader is referred to the exhaustive work of K. K. Weed and R. P. Bond mentioned below.

(a) *Bibliographical Works*

The Cambridge Bibliography of English Literature, ed. F. W. Bateson, 4 vols. (Cambridge, 1941), especially 'Periodical Publications', by H. G. Pollard and W. Graham, ii, 656–739.

R. C. CRANE and F. B. KAYE, 'A Census of British Newspapers and Periodicals, 1620–1800' (*Studies in Philology*, xxiv, 1927).

G. A. CRANFIELD, *A Handlist of English Provincial Newspapers and Periodicals, 1700-1760* (Cambridge Bibliographical Society monographs no. 2, Cambridge, 1952).

——, 'A Handlist of English Provincial Newspapers and Periodicals, 1700–1760. Additions and Corrections', *Transactions of the Cambridge Bibliographical Society*, vol. ii, 3, 1956.

The Times, London, *Tercentenary Handlist of English and Welsh Newspapers, Magazines and Reviews* (1920).

K. K. WEED and R. P. BOND, *Studies of British Newspapers and Periodicals from their Beginning to 1800* (Studies in Philology, Extra Series, no. 2, December 1946).

R. M. WILES, 'Further Additions and Corrections to G. A. Cranfield's Handlist', *Transactions of the Cambridge Bibliographical Society*, vol. ii, 5, 1958.

(b) *Secondary Works on Newspapers, Printers and Allied Subjects*

A. ASPINALL, 'Statistical Accounts of the London Newspapers during the Eighteenth Century', *English Historical Review*, vol. 63, April 1948.

W. E. A. AXON, *Annals of Manchester* (Manchester, 1886).

R. BERKELEY, 'A Sketch of early Provincial Journalism', *Associated Architectural Societies' Report*, xxiv, 1898.

W. G. BLEYER, *Main Currents in the History of American Journalism* (Boston, 1927).

H. R. FOX BOURNE, *English Newspapers*, 2 vols. (1887).

R. STEWART BROWN, 'Stationers, Booksellers and Printers of Chester to about 1800', *Transactions of the Historic Society of Lancashire and Cheshire*, lxxxiii, 1932.

T. N. BRUSHFIELD, 'Andrew Brice and the Early Exeter Newspaper Press', *Transactions of the Devonshire Association*, xx, 1888.

G. H. BURTON, 'Notes on Newspapers', *Lincoln, Rutland and Stamford Mercury*, 20 March 1914.

K. G. BURTON, 'The Early Newspaper Press in Berkshire', unpublished University of Reading M.A. thesis, 1949.

W. J. CLARKE, *Early Nottingham Printers and Printing* (Nottingham, 1942).

A. S. COLLINS, 'Growth of the Reading Public during the Eighteenth Century', *Review of English Studies*, ii, 1926.

——, *Authorship in the Days of Johnson* (1927).

L. P. CURTIS, *The Politicks of Lawrence Sterne* (Oxford, 1929).

R. DAVIES, *A Memoir of the York Press* (1868).

JOHN DUNTON, *Life and Errors* (2nd ed., 1818).

A. D. E(UREN), *The First Provincial Newspaper* (Norwich, 1924).

F. H. EVANS, *Brief Sketch of the Career of the Lincoln, Rutland and Stamford* Mercury (Stamford, 1938).

W. B. EWALD, *The Newsmen of Queen Anne* (Oxford, 1956).

T. GENT, *Life of Mr. Thomas Gent, Printer of York* (1832).

W. GEORGE, 'The Oldest Bristol Newspaper', *Bristol Times and Mirror*, 4 August 1884.

I. GRIFFITHS, *Berrow's Worcester Journal* (Worcester, 1942).

W. W. HADLEY, *1720–1920. The bi-centenary Record of the Northampton Mercury* (Northampton, 1920).

L. HANSON, *The Government and the Press, 1695–1763* (Oxford, 1936).

J. HARLAND, *Manchester Collecteana* (Chetham Society, 1867).

J. T. HILLHOUSE, *The Grub-street Journal* (Duke U.P., 1928).

F. KNIGHT HUNT, *The Fourth Estate*, 2 vols. (1850).

C. KNIGHT, *The Old Printer and the Modern Press* (1854).

——, *Passages of a Working Life* (1872).

J. LACKINGTON, *Memoirs* (10th ed., 1795).

J. LATIMER, *Annals of Bristol in the Eighteenth Century* (1893).

LEARY, 'History of the Manchester Newspaper Press', unpublished MS. in the Manchester Reference Library.

R. A. AUSTEN LEIGH, 'Joseph Pote of Eton', *Library*, xvii, 1936.

L. C. LLOYD, 'The Book Trade in Shropshire', *Trans. of the Shropshire Archaeological Society*, 1935 and 1936.

S. MORISON, *Ichabod Dawks and his News-Letter* (Cambridge, 1931).

——, *The English Newspaper* (Cambridge, 1932).

F. L. MOTT, *American Journalism* (New York, 1949).

Northampton Mercury, History of the Northampton Mercury, Mercury Extras no. 10, Northampton, 1901.

The Norwich Post; its Contemporaries and Successors (Norwich, 1951).

J. PENDLETON, *The Reporters' Gallery* (1890).

M. PLANT, *The English Book Trade* (1939).

H. R. PLOMER and others, *A Dictionary of the Booksellers and Printers who were at Work in England, Scotland and Ireland from 1668 to 1725* (Oxford, 1922).

——, *A Dictionary of the Booksellers and Printers who were at Work in England, Scotland and Ireland from 1726 to 1775* (Oxford, 1932).

J. M. PRICE, 'A Note on the Circulation of the London Press, 1704–1714', *Bulletin of the Institute of Historical Research*, xxxi, no. 84, November 1958.

H. RICHARDSON, 'Wiltshire Newspapers', *Wiltshire Archaeological and Natural History Magazine*, xli, 1922.

M. RICHARDSON, *Supplement to the Salisbury and Winchester Journal*, 7 June 1929.

J. E. SMITH, *One Hundred Years of the Hartford's Courant* (New Haven, 1949).

J. H. SPENCER, 'Preston's early Newspapers', *Preston Herald*, 30 December 1949, 18 August 1950.

H. WICKHAM STEED, *The Press* (1938).

J. R. SUTHERLAND, 'Circulation of Newspapers and Literary Periodicals in the Eighteenth Century', *Library*, 4th series, xv, 1935.

C. H. TIMPERLEY, *A Dictionary of Printers and Printing* (1839).

——, *Encyclopaedia of Literary and Typographical Anecdote* (1842).

O. M. TYNDALE, 'Manchester Vindicated', *Lancashire and Cheshire Antiquarian Society*, vol. 53, 1938.

A. WALLIS, 'A Sketch of the early History of the Printing Press in Derbyshire', *Journal of the Derbyshire Archaeological and Natural History Society*, iii, 1881.

S. F. WATSON, 'History of Printing and Publishing in Ipswich', *Proceedings of the Suffolk Institute of Archaeology and Natural History*, xxiv, pt. 3, 1949.

C. WELSH, *A Bookseller of the last Century* (1885).

R. M. WILES, *Serial Publication in England before 1750* (Cambridge, 1957).

J. B. WILLIAMS, 'Henry Cross-grove, Jacobite, Journalist and Printer', *Library*, 3rd series, v, 1914.

(c) *General and Background Sources*

J. BERESFORD, ed. *Diary of James Woodforde, 1758–81* (Oxford, 1924).

R. W. BLENCOWE, ed. 'Extracts from the Journal and Account-book of Timothy Burrell', *Sussex Archaeological Collections*, iii, 1850.

BOYER, *Parliamentary Debates*, vii and viii.

Bristol Burgess Book, 1689–1705.

Bristol Common Council Proceedings.

Records of the Bristol Society of Merchant Venturers.

K. BUECHER, *Industrial Evolution*, trans. S. M. Wickett (New York, 1901).

H. BUTTERFIELD, *George III, Lord North and the People* (1949).

Cambridge History of English Literature, vol. ix (1911).

Carlisle Papers, H.M.C. 11th Report, App., pt. vi.

CHANDLER, *Collection of the Parliamentary Debates in England*, vols. vii, xi, xii, xvii.

C. H. COOPER, *Annals of Cambridge*, 4 vols. (Cambridge, 1848).

L. DICKINS and M. STANTON, *An Eighteenth Century Correspondence to Sanderson Miller of Radway* (1910).

LORD ERNLE, *English Farming Past and Present* (5th ed., 1936).

HENRY FIELDING, *Adventures of Joseph Andrews* (O.U.P., World's Classics, 1945).

——, *History of Tom Jones* (Everyman's edition, 1942).

S. GILBOY, *Wages in Eighteenth Century England* (Harvard, 1934).

R. GREGORY, *Robert Raikes: Journalist and Philanthropist* (New York, 1877).

J. C. HAMMEON, *History of the British Post Office* (Cambridge, U.S.A., 1912).

'Journal of Mr John Hobson', *Yorkshire Diaries* (Surtees Society Publications, lxv, 1875).

A. Jenkins, *History of Exeter* (1866).

M. G. Jones, *Charity School Movement in the Eighteenth Century* (Cambridge, 1938).

R. E. Leader, *Sheffield in the Eighteenth Century* (Sheffield, 1901).

C. D. Linnell, ed. *Diary of Benjamin Rogers, Rector of Carlton, 1720–71* (Publications of the Bedfordshire Historical Society, xxx, 1950).

Thomas Babington Macaulay, *The History of England* (1864).

L. W. Moffit, *England on the Eve of the Industrial Revolution* (1925).

Roger North, *Life of the Norths* (1741).

Records of the Borough of Nottingham, vi, 1702–60.

A. M. Ogilvie, *Ralph Allen's Bye, Way and Cross-Road Posts* (1898).

Samuel Pepys, *Diary*.

J. H. Plumb, *England in the Eighteenth Century* (1950).

H. Robinson, *The British Post Office* (Princeton, 1948).

Lord Russell of Liverpool, *Though the Heavens Fall* (1956).

César de Saussure, *A Foreign View of England in the Reigns of George I and George II*, trans. Mme van Muyden (1902).

State Trials, vol. vii.

Commentaries, Autobiography, Diary and Common-place Book of William Stukeley (Surtees Society, i, 1880).

The Traveller's Pocket Companion (1741).

A. S. Turberville, ed. *Johnson's England* (Oxford, 1933).

F. Turner, *ed. A Berkshire Bachelor's Diary* (Newbury, 1932).

F. M. Turner, *The Diary of Thomas Turner of East Hoathley, 1754–65* (1925).

Lady M. Verney, ed. *Verney Letters of the Eighteenth Century* (1930).

A. C. Wardle, 'Some Glimpses of Liverpool during the first half of the Eighteenth Century,' *Historical Society of Lancashire and Cheshire*, 97, 1945.

D. Winstanley, *The University of Cambridge in the Eighteenth Century* (Cambridge, 1922).

M. J. Wise, 'Birmingham and its Trade Relations in the early Eighteenth Century', *University of Birmingham History Journal*, vol. ii, no. 1, 1949.

INDEX